BROTHER OF JESUS, FRIEND OF GOD

Brother of Jesus, Friend of God

Studies in the Letter of James

LUKE TIMOTHY JOHNSON

WILLIAM B. EERDMANS PUBLISHING COMPANY
GRAND RAPIDS, MICHIGAN / CAMBRIDGE, U.K.

Wm. B. Eerdmans Publishing Co.
2140 Oak Industrial Drive N.E., Grand Rapids, Michigan 49505 /
P.O. Box 163, Cambridge CB3 9PU U.K.

Printed in the United States of America

08 07 06 05 04   7 6 5 4 3 2 1

Library of Congress Cataloging-in-Publication Data

Johnson, Luke Timothy.
Brother of Jesus, friend of God: studies in the letter of James /
Luke Timothy Johnson.
p.   cm.
Includes bibliographical references and index.
ISBN 978-0-8028-0986-5 (pbk.: alk. paper)
1. Bible. N.T. James — Criticism, interpretation, etc. I. Title.
BS2785.52.J64 2004
227'.9106 — dc22

2004040904

www.eerdmans.com

Contents

CONTENTS

Preface

This book contains a collection of essays on the Letter of James that were written over a period of two decades. Although published at a time when the historical figure of James is the subject of much interest because of the claim that his name, linked to that of his brother Jesus, is inscribed on a first-century ossuary, these studies are directed entirely to the letter attributed to James, in the conviction that, unlike any fragile reconstruction of the past, its words still speak directly and powerfully to contemporary readers, and deserve the same careful and disciplined attention as the other canonical writings.

Some readers will be aware that I am also the author of the Anchor Bible Commentary on James and may wonder at the relationship between the two efforts. The commentary made substantial use of the essays written before 1994. But the format of a commentary does not match that of an essay. In the commentary, some of the arguments and some of the data found in individual studies can be used, but much must also be left aside. This collection also contains a number of essays that have been written since the publication of the commentary. And in them, I sometimes refer to places in the commentary that provide background for the point I am trying to make in the essay. The relationship between the two forms of literary production, therefore, is reciprocal. In my view, the essays provide a richer and fuller examination of specific issues than is possible within a commentary. Previously published essays stand as first written, with no revisions. I must apologize for the mixed style of citation from ancient sources. Because the essays were written at different times and for different formats, there is considerable variation in the case of some authors in particular (e.g., Philo and Plutarch). In the Index of Ancient Sources, I standardize somewhat by using the language and style that occurs most often in the text.

In addition to making more available some essays that are not otherwise easily accessible, and others that have not previously been published, I have written two studies especially for this collection. The first deals with the significance of James for early Christian history, and the second with the theological importance of James. Although written at the end of a decades-long study of this remarkable composition, these two essays are less a summation than a stepping-stone, an invitation to others to go further than I have been able to in engaging a writing that has the potential of revising our understanding of Christian origins, and reinvigorating contemporary Christian theology.

I am grateful to the many students and colleagues who have studied James with me and helped me see more clearly. I owe special thanks to my editor Allen Myers and Eerdmans Press for making possible a publication that is (I hope) sober and solid, but scarcely sensational. And as always, I give thanks to my dear wife Joy, who has been for me one of the "good and perfect gifts" (James 1:17) and to the God who "gives to all simply and without grudging" (James 1:5).

LUKE TIMOTHY JOHNSON
Emory University
March 11, 2003

Acknowledgments

The author and publisher gratefully acknowledge permission to reprint material from the following sources:

"The Use of Leviticus 19 in the Letter of James," *Journal of Biblical Literature* 101 (1982) 391-401.

"James 3:13-4:10 and the *Topos περὶ φθόνου*," *Novum Testamentum* 25 (1983) 327-347.

"Friendship with the World and Friendship with God: A Study of Discipleship in James," in *Discipleship in the New Testament*, ed. F. Segovia (Philadelphia: Fortress Press, 1985), 166-183.

"The Mirror of Remembrance (James 1:22-25)," *Catholic Biblical Quarterly* 50 (1988) 632-645.

"Taciturnity and True Religion (James 1:26-27)," in *Greeks, Romans, and Christians: Essays in Honor of Abraham J. Malherbe*, ed. D. Balch et al. (Minneapolis: Fortress Press, 1990), 329-339.

"The Social World of James: Literary Analysis and Historical Reconstruction," in *The Social World of the First Christians: Essays in Honor of Wayne A. Meeks*, ed. L. M. White and O. L. Yarbrough (Minneapolis: Fortress Press, 1995), 178-197.

"The Sayings of Jesus in the Letter of James" (with Wesley Wachob), in *Authenticating the Words of Jesus*, ed. B. Chilton and C. A. Evans (New Testament Tools and Studies 28:1; Leiden: Brill, 1999), 431-450.

"An Introduction to the Letter of James," *Review and Expositor* 97 (2000) 155-167.

The chapters entitled "Journeying East with James" and "How James Won the West" began as the Carmichael-Walling Lectures at Abilene Christian University, November 1995.

PROLOGUE

James's Significance for Early Christian History

Even before the recent commotion over the discovery that an ossuary dated to the first century CE bears the Aramaic inscription, "James son of Joseph brother of Jesus,"[1] the figure of James had, in one of those odd convergences that seem to characterize scholarly progress, focused attention on James of Jerusalem and his place in early Christianity.[2] The quest for the historical James, however, suffers from the same inherent limitations, and therefore the same inevitable tendency toward distortion, as the search for his brother.[3] Not all efforts have been equally worthwhile.[4]

---

1. For the basic story line of the discovery and the discussion, see H. Shanks and B. Witherington III, *The Brother of Jesus: The Dramatic Story and Significance of the First Archaeological Link to Jesus and His Family* (San Francisco: HarperSanFrancisco, 2003).

2. Among others, B. Chilton and J. Neusner, eds., *The Brother of Jesus: James the Just and His Mission* (Louisville: Westminster/John Knox, 2001); R. Eisenman, *James the Brother of Jesus: The Key to Unlocking the Secrets of Early Christianity and the Dead Sea Scrolls* (New York: Penguin Books, 1998); P.-A. Bernheim, *James, Brother of Jesus* (London: SCM Press, 1997); R. Bauckham, *James* (London: Routledge, 1999); J. Painter, *Just James: The Brother of Jesus in History and Tradition* (Columbia, SC: University of South Carolina Press, 1997); B. Chilton and C. A. Evans, *James the Just and Christian Origins* (Leiden: Brill, 1999).

3. For the historiographical malfeasances carried out in the name of the quest for the historical Jesus, see L. T. Johnson, *The Real Jesus: The Misguided Quest for the Historical Jesus and the Truth of the Traditional Gospels* (San Francisco: HarperSanFrancisco, 1996), and "A Historiographical Response to Wright's Jesus," in *Jesus and the Restoration of Israel: A Critical Assessment of N. T. Wright's* Jesus and the Victory of God, ed. C. C. Newman (Downers Grove, IL: InterVarsity Press, 1999), 206-224.

4. Just as B. Thiering's *Jesus and the Riddle of the Dead Sea Scrolls* (San Francisco: HarperSanFrancisco, 1992) showed how badly the Dead Sea Scrolls could be misread to yield a historical Jesus, so R. Eisenman has provided the same service in his *James the Brother of Jesus*. The positive review of this book by R. Price, "Eisenman's Gospel of James the Just," pp. 186-197 in Chilton and Neusner, eds., *The Brother of Jesus,* can best be termed mischie-

I

Generally, the more critical researchers have been in their treatment of the sources and the more modest they have been in their claims, the more persuasive they have been in their respective portraits.[5] If the ossuary inscription proves to be authentic, it will simply strengthen the already well-supported conviction that James the brother of Jesus was a notable figure in Jerusalem because he was a leader in the nascent Christian movement.[6]

A puzzling feature of all these reconstructions of the historical James is the minor role played by the letter ascribed to him. Either the letter is interpreted within a framework that has been established on the basis of sources much later than any serious scholar would date this composition,[7] or doubts about its authenticity make it something of an afterthought.[8] Only rarely does the "message" serve as the main evidence concerning "the man."[9] But this is a mistake. With the exception of the evidence in Paul, Acts, and Josephus, the letter is the historically most certain evidence we have concerning James.[10] Even if it is supposed that a composition by James

---

vous. For a more balanced review, see J. Painter, "Excursus: Robert Eisenman's *James the Brother of Jesus*," in his *Just James*, pp. 277-288.

5. In this respect, the portraits drawn by Painter, Witherington, and Bauckham are far more convincing than the highly speculative ventures by B. Chilton. See "James in Relation to Peter, Paul, and the Remembrance of Jesus," in Chilton and Neusner, eds., *The Brother of Jesus*, pp. 138-160, and "Conclusions and Questions," in *James the Just and Christian Origins*, 251-267, as well as his *A Feast of Meanings: Eucharistic Theologies from Jesus to Johannine Circles* (Leiden: Brill, 1994), 98-108.

6. The wording on the ossuary resembles that of Josephus, who in *Antiquities of the Jews* 20:200 reports the death in the year 62 at the instigation of the High Priest Ananus. Josephus refers to "the man named James, the brother of Jesus who was called the Christ." For the probable authenticity of the passage, see J. P. Meier, *A Marginal Jew* (New York: Doubleday, 1991), 1:58-59, 72-73.

7. Note how Eisenman follows the lead of F. C. Baur in using the fourth-century Pseudo-Clementine literature as leverage to detect the "real history" that is camouflaged by the canonical writings; see *James the Brother of Jesus*, pp. 70-79.

8. See Bernheim, pp. 243-245; Painter, pp. 227-276.

9. Notably, J. B. Adamson, *James: The Man and His Message* (Grand Rapids: Eerdmans, 1989).

10. I have mentioned already the account in Josephus's *Antiquities* 20:200; for Paul, see 1 Cor 9:5; 15:7; Gal 1:19; 2:9-14; for Acts, see 1:14; 12:17; 15:12-29; 21:18-25. Later evidence is hagiographical. It focuses largely on James's martyrdom (see Eusebius, *Historia Ecclesiastica* II, 1, 5; III, 23; *Pseudo-Clementine Recognitions* I, 70-71; *Manichaean Psalm-Book*, *Psalms of Heracleidea* 192:8-9; *Second Apocalypse of James* 61-62). With respect to James's character or authority, the later sources follow one of three streams: the broadly ecclesiastical (*Gospel of the Hebrews;* Clement, *Hypotyposes* 6 [see *HE* II, 1, 3] and *Hypotyposes* 7 [*HE* II, 1, 4]; Hegesippus [*HE* II, 23, 4], and Eusebius, *HE* II, 1, 2-7), revelational (*Apocryphon of James* 1-2, 16; *Second Apocalypse of James* 61-62; *First Apocalypse of James* 25, 42; *Gospel of Thomas* 12), and polemical (*Letter of Peter to James, Letter of Clement to James, The Ascents of James, Homilies*).

of Jerusalem was later redacted by someone else, the present letter is almost certainly appropriated by early-second-century Christian writings.[11] In fact, however, there are strong reasons for arguing that the extant letter was composed by James of Jerusalem, whom Paul designates as "brother of the Lord."[12] What is more, the evidence provided by the letter fits comfortably within that provided by our other earliest and best sources (Paul, Acts, Josephus), whereas it fits only awkwardly if at all within the framework of the later and legendary sources that are used for most reconstructions.[13]

In this essay, I will not try to do the impossible and demonstrate beyond the possibility of cavil that James of Jerusalem was indeed the author of James, even though I share the view that the preponderance of evidence makes that position one that can be held with a high degree of confidence.[14] Instead, I propose that we begin from the opposite end of things, take as our premise that the letter is indeed early and authentic, and see where that leads. What difference does it make if the Letter of James was written by the brother of Jesus from Jerusalem before the year 62? How does the evidence offered by this letter affect our understanding of history in the first generation of the Christian movement? It is obvious that if the letter is late and pseudonymous, it offers no primary, much less first-hand, information about earliest Christianity or pre–Roman War Judaism. But if it is authentic, what can we learn?

11. See my essay "The Reception of James in the Early Church," pp. 45-60 in this volume.

12. In addition to the authors listed in L.T. Johnson, *The Letter of James: A New Translation with Introduction and Commentary* (Anchor Bible 37A; New York: Doubleday, 1995), 153-156, see R. Bauckham, *James* (New Testament Readings; London: Routledge, 1999), and his "James and Jesus," in Chilton and Neusner, eds., *The Brother of Jesus*, pp. 100-135.

13. See B. Witherington III in *The Brother of Jesus: The Dramatic Story*, pp. 109-143.

14. In light of recent scholarship on Hellenism in Palestine (see below), there is no a priori reason for excluding an early Palestinian provenance on the basis of language. Other factors: a) James lacks any sign of late pseudonymous authorship according to the criteria usually employed (fictional elaboration of author's identity, rationalization for delay of the parousia, doctrinal development, accommodation to society, emphasis on tradition as a deposit, polemics against false teaching, developed institutional structure); b) James reflects the social realities and outlook appropriate to a sect in the early stages of its life: it reflects a face-to-face, intentional *ekklēsia* with intense bonds of social solidarity rather than a highly evolved organization; c) James makes use of Jesus traditions at a stage that is earlier than is found in the late-first-century Synoptic Gospels (see below); d) across a broad range of language and issues, James most resembles our earliest datable Christian author, the Apostle Paul; e) James is used by at least two late-first- or early-second-century writings, *1 Clement* and *Shepherd of Hermas;* f) James's language (especially his use of "Gehenna" in 3:6) suggests local knowledge even more than literary influence.

James as Early Christian Leader

The first and most obvious thing the letter confirms is James's place as a leader of the church. The letter provides literary confirmation of the portrayal of James's influence extending beyond Jerusalem to those "in the dispersion" (James 1:1). Paul speaks of James as one of the three pillars of the church in Jerusalem, whose authority he recognized (Gal 1:19; 2:9), but also speaks of "men from James" visiting the Christian community in Antioch (Gal 2:12). Acts does not connect "those who had come down from Judea" to Antioch (Acts 15:1) with James, but does portray James in its account of the Jerusalem Council as having a pastoral concern and an assumed authority extending well beyond Jerusalem. It is James who declares that Moses is read in the synagogues "in every city" *(kata polin)* on "every Sabbath" *(pan sabbaton,* Acts 15:21), and it is James who makes the judgment (15:19) that is subsequently communicated to churches in Antioch and Syria and Cilicia (15:23-29). In the simplest and most straightforward fashion, the letter presents itself as addressed to the "twelve tribes in the dispersion" from "James, slave of God and of the Lord Jesus Christ" (James 1:1). If Paul's authority even in his own communities was never to be taken for granted, even by him, James's authority, even outside Jerusalem, is never in doubt.

The letter also tends to support the portrayal of James in Acts — as well as a precise reading of the evidence in Paul's letters — that James was a leader in full fellowship with Paul, rather than the basis of a sustained opposition to Paul's Gentile mission in behalf of "the circumcision party."

Luke does not mention James in his Gospel (compare Mark 6:3 and Matt 13:55), but may have James in mind as one among "the mother of Jesus and his brothers" who meet in prayer before Pentecost (Acts 1:14). After Peter's escape from prison, he tells the assembly to "inform James and the brothers of these things" (12:17). After this, James stands as spokesperson for the Jerusalem *presbyterion.* His support for the Gentile mission is decisive (15:12-21). He advocates the sending of a letter to diaspora communities (15:23-29), after rejecting the demand that Gentiles be circumcised and observe the law, demanding only those minimal requirements that enable table-fellowship with pious Jews. Acts associates James neither with the agitators in Antioch (15:1) nor with the Pharisaic party in Jerusalem that demanded of Gentiles that they be circumcised and keep the law (15:5). The letter sent by the council does acknowledge that "some from among us" caused the disturbance in Antioch. This statement confirms in substance Gal 2:12, but is even more vague, and the rest of the statement

4

distances the Jerusalem leadership from the agitators, "though with no instructions from us" (Acts 15:24). With regard to the events transpiring in Antioch and Jerusalem, Acts depicts James not as an opponent of Paul but as a mediator between Paul and his attackers.[15]

The final meeting between Paul and James is more ambiguous, to be sure. On his final trip to Jerusalem, Paul and his companions come into the presence of James and all the elders and report on all that God had done through his *diakonia* (an oblique reference to the collection [Rom 15:25-32]?) among the Gentiles (Acts 21:18-19). This echoes Paul and Barnabas' recital at the Jerusalem Council (15:12). The elders respond by glorifying God (21:20), that is, they express their approval of God's activity through Paul (compare Luke 5:26; 7:16; 18:43; Acts 11:18; 13:48). The elders then assert the essential accord between Paul's Gentile mission and the Jerusalem leadership by repeating the decree issued for Gentiles by the council (21:25). No further obligations beyond those stated in 15:23-29 are stated. But Paul's own fidelity to his Jewish heritage is now questioned. Acts does not make the charge come either from James or the elders. Instead, they tell Paul what some of the Jewish believers who are "zealous for the law" are claiming: that Paul has been telling *Jews* to stop circumcising their children or practicing the law (21:20-21). James and the elders suggest that Paul perform a ritual act in the Temple to demonstrate his loyalty to the people and show that he himself follows the law (21:24).

Once more, James (and the elders) appear as mediators rather than attackers. There is no hint of opposition to the Gentile mission, no suggestion that Gentile believers should be circumcised or observe the law. It is only Paul's own teaching and practice as a Jew that is in question. In the Acts portrayal, the question does not arise from James and the elders, but from those "zealous for the law" among Jewish believers. Both the narrative of Acts (16:3; 18:18; 20:16) as well as Paul's own letters, furthermore, show that the charge is false. Paul never advocated Jews abandoning their ancestral customs. He only resisted the demand that Gentiles adopt them.

Does the evidence in Paul contradict the picture in Acts? There are obvious and real difficulties in aligning the account of the Jerusalem Council provided by Acts and that reported by Paul in Galatians.[16] My interest here

---

15. Ben Witherington III calls him "James the Jewish-Gentile Mediator," in *The Brother of Jesus: The Dramatic Story*, p. 109.

16. See the detailed discussion of these literary and historical difficulties in L. T. Johnson, *Scripture and Discernment: Decision-Making in the Church* (Nashville: Abingdon, 1996), 61-80; L. T. Johnson, *The Acts of the Apostles* (Sacra Pagina 5; Collegeville: Liturgical Press, 1992), 258-274.

is only Paul's depiction of James. If Paul himself viewed James as an enemy, he failed to say so. I have already noted how Paul recognizes James as one of the apostles in Gal 1:19, and in 2:9 lists James with Cephas and John as those considered (or considering themselves as) pillars. Although Paul's tone is cool (see also 2:2 and 2:6), he does not question the group's authority, and comes prepared to submit *(anatithēmi)* to them the Gospel he preached among the Gentiles, "lest I am running or have run in vain" (2:2). His claim that they imposed no further obligation on him (2:6) apart from the care of the poor (2:10) and that they gave him the right hand of fellowship in acknowledgement of the legitimacy of his mission (2:9) recognizes their authority to discern and judge. Paul's entire *narratio* to this point makes clear James's place of authority in Jerusalem and his willing fellowship with Paul. Nothing in Paul's remarks can be read as an attack on James. In fact, Paul carefully distinguishes the leadership of the pillars from the "false brethren" who tried to suppress Paul's freedom by forcing the circumcision of Titus (2:3-5). Paul says that despite much opposition neither he nor the Jerusalem leadership gave way to this pressure (2:7-9).

It is against this backdrop that Paul recites the incident at Antioch: Cephas and other Jewish believers (see 2:13) ate freely with Gentile believers until *elthein tinas apo Iakōbou* (2:12). Cephas then withdrew out of fear of *tous ek tēs peritomēs* ("those out of the circumcision"). Paul accuses Cephas, the other Jewish believers of Antioch, and even Barnabas, of hypocrisy (2:13). Paul's main target here is plainly Cephas, whom he confronts "in the presence of all" (2:14). The role of James is less clear. The "people from James" were a catalyst, but were they so as an official delegation sent from Jerusalem? Did they represent James's views or only their own? Did they challenge the practice of fellowship or did Cephas (as Paul suggests) give way of his own accord out of human respect? The most that can be drawn from the account is that the presence of James's representatives posed a challenge to open table-fellowship. This corresponds to the "some from among us" in Acts 15:24, but Paul does not make clear, as Luke seeks to, that "they acted without instructions from" James and the Jerusalem *presbyterion*.

Because of the way the Galatian evidence has been used in reconstructions of Christian origins, two final points concerning Paul's view of James of Jerusalem need to be made with some emphasis. The first is that Paul's *narratio* of past events in Galatians serves to present himself as an example to his readers of steadfastness in the face of opposition: Paul stood by his gift despite false brethren and expects the Galatians to do likewise. Paul does not connect any of the problems he experiences in Galatia to the "false brethren" in Jerusalem, and explicitly distinguishes

James and the other leadership from those false brethren. He does not make James the cause of the troubles in Antioch, and does not connect the dispute at Antioch causally to the issues in Galatia. Even in the harshest reading of Galatians, James of Jerusalem is at most the occasion of a dispute over table-fellowship among Jewish and Gentile believers. James is not connected to any ideological opposition to the Gentile mission, or to any effort to impose circumcision on Gentile converts.

The second point is Paul's statements concerning James in 1 Cor 15:7, where his language suggests that James (as a witness to the resurrection) is an apostle in the Pauline sense (compare 1 Cor 9:1), and where Paul concludes by insisting on the fellowship of all the witnesses with respect to teaching: "whether therefore it is I or they, thus we are preaching and thus you have come to believe" (1 Cor 15:11). Here if anywhere Paul had the chance to distinguish his own preaching from that of the Jerusalem church, if there had been any such fundamental difference. Rather he speaks of what he had received and was handing on (1 Cor 15:1-3). First Corinthians, furthermore, is written well after the events reported by Galatians. If Paul were at enmity with James or the Jerusalem leadership at any point, much less in a constant state of alienation with the mother church, his language never reveals it. Rather, the effort expended in behalf of his great collection (1 Cor 16:1-4; 2 Cor 8 and 9) is cast in terms of a debt that is owed for the spiritual blessing that had been received from "the saints" in Jerusalem (Rom 15:25-32), whom he explicitly distinguishes from the "unbelievers."

If the letter of James is taken as seriously as Acts and Paul as a historical source from the first century, how does it fit into the portrayal of James they give? Remarkably well. The letter presents its inscribed author as a James who addresses the twelve tribes in the dispersion (1:1). This corresponds to the picture given by both Acts and Paul of a James in Jerusalem who exercises some influence among (at least) Jewish-Christians in (at least) Antioch, Syria, and Cilicia (Gal 2; Acts 15). The sense of quiet authority communicated in the simple greeting and hortatory tone of the letter fits the epistle attributed to James and the Council in Acts 15.

The designation "twelve tribes" most naturally suggests Jewish Christian readers.[17] The letter's strong affirmation of the law *(nomos)* supports this suggestion. James speaks of the "perfect law of freedom" (1:25), the

---

17. For the alternative reading of *diaspora* as reflecting a sense of spiritual exile away from a heavenly homeland, see Johnson, *James,* pp. 170-171.

"law of freedom" (2:12), and the "royal law" or "law of the kingdom" (*nomos basilikos*) in 2:8, as that which should be "gazed into" (1:25), "fulfilled" (1:25), and "kept" (2:10) both in its parts and as a whole (2:10). Otherwise, one is a "transgressor of the law" (2:11) who places one's own authority over the law and of God, who alone is lawgiver (*nomothetēs*) and judge (*kritēs*, 4:12). Humans are to live as those who are to be judged by God on the basis of the law of freedom (2:12). And what does James mean by *nomos*? It certainly includes the Decalogue (2:11) and the commandment of love from Lev 19:18 (2:8) — this is the "royal law." James also clearly understands the law of love to be explicated by the moral commands of Leviticus 19:11-18.[18] James also considers *nomos* as a source of moral examples. The image of the "mirror of remembrance" in 1:22-25 makes the "perfect law of freedom" something into which the readers can "gaze" and "remain in," by becoming a "doer of the deed" (*poiētēs ergou*). The Law as text contains examples that the readers can see and imitate: Abraham and Rahab (2:20-25), Job (5:11), and Elijah (5:17-18).

It is equally important to note what James does not include when speaking of *nomos*. First, he does not connect law to circumcision in any fashion. If he were writing to Jewish-Christians, to be sure, circumcision would be assumed. Second, however, we note further that James does not speak of the "works of the law" (*erga tou nomou*), the phrase that Paul uses in his polemics (Rom 3:20, 28; Gal 2:16; 3:2, 5, 10). Neither does James speak of "commandments" (*entolai*) as Paul sometimes does (Rom 7:8; 13:9; 1 Cor 7:19). James recognizes that the law can be thought of in terms of discrete commandments, but rejects that view in favor of one that sees "the whole law" as the object of obedience; breaking a part of the law is breaking the whole law, for obedience is not directed to the specific commandment but to the lawgiver and judge (2:11; see also 4:11-12). Third, James does not connect *nomos* to any form of ritual observance. Besides not mentioning circumcision, he shows no interest in special days or feasts (contrast Gal 4:9-11; 5:2-4, 12; 6:12; Col 2:16), or in dietary or purity regulations (contrast Col. 2:21). James makes no mention of any sort of meal, and certainly betrays no interest in a pure table-fellowship.[19] When James speaks of a "pure religion" that is "unstained from the world" in 1:27, he defines it in terms of control of speech and the care for widows and orphans (1:26-27).

18. See my essay "The Use of Leviticus 19 in the Letter of James," pp. 123-135 in this volume.

19. Despite B. Chilton's efforts to connect James to disputes concerning meals in *A Feast of Meanings: Eucharistic Theologies from Jesus to Johannine Circles* (Leiden: Brill, 1994), 98-108.

In summary, *nomos* in the Letter of James encompasses a set of moral rather than ritual norms established by divine authority and providing the basis for God's judgment of human actions. It focuses on the love of neighbor, and explicates that love through specific attitudes and actions prescribed by Torah. The law also provides narrative examples for imitation, models of *faith* in several dimensions: the obedient deeds of faith shown by Abraham and Rahab, the endurance of faith shown by Job, and the prayer of faith shown by Elijah. What James says about *nomos* cannot be linked to any recognizable program for the protection of Jewish ethnic identity. Still less can it be connected to any "Judaizing" project for early Gentile Christians.

Indeed, focusing on James's language about *nomos* is itself distorting, for it is clear that this composition draws equally from the prophetic and wisdom traditions of Scripture in shaping its message. James refers to the "prophets who spoke in the name of the Lord" in 5:10, and draws from the language and the passion of the prophets particularly in his speech concerning the rich and the poor (1:9-11, 27; 5:1-6), and the necessity of choosing between friendship with the world and friendship with God (4:4-10). Likewise, James makes "wisdom" thematic (1:5; 3:13-16), cites Proverbs 3:34 (4:6), and makes extensive use of motifs that are associated with the wisdom tradition: the testing of virtue (1:2), deliberation in speech (1:19, 26; 3:1-9), the incompatibility of anger and justice (1:20), the necessity of helping those in need (1:27; 2:14-16).

If I have accurately represented the voice of James as expressed in the letter attributed to him, then it must be said emphatically that this voice agrees substantially with the best reading of Luke and Paul with respect to the historical James (and for that matter, with the evidence provided by Josephus as well).[20] The letter can, in turn, be used as the best available, first-hand, evidence for what James of Jerusalem was about. It is in light of this combination of information that we are best able to assess the historical roles of James and Paul.

---

20. In reading Josephus, *Antiquities* 20:200, one must be careful to see what is said and what is not said. Even Witherington draws from Josephus's statement that "those in the city who were most fair-minded and who were strict in the observance of the law" were offended at Ananus's stoning of James, that James himself was pharisaic in his tendencies: "the passage emphasizes that James was a Torah-true, faithfully observant Jew. . . . presumably [the Pharisees] recognized him to be a good and faithful Jew" (*The Brother of Jesus: The Dramatic Story*, p. 149). In fact, however, Josephus says nothing directly about James's practices. He was condemned for having transgressed the law. And Josephus implies that it was the process ("Ananus had not been correct even in his first step") rather than the charge against the person that offended those who were scrupulous about the law.

James and Paul

The evidence found in Acts and Paul's letters resists any attempt to make Paul and James opponents or even rivals in the earliest period of the Christian movement. And the Letter of James lends no support to the hypothesis that the historical James was part of or even the fomenter of an anti-Paul campaign.[21] Indeed, the letter is so conspicuously lacking any trace of anti-Pauline animus, that even the early Tübingen School considered James pseudonymous and part of the harmonizing tendency of early-catholicism.[22] And the most common way of dealing with James and Paul is to consider the letter a mild rebuke to a "misunderstanding of Paul."[23] Even Dibelius, who sought to remove James from any specific historical and social setting by appealing to the genre of "paraenesis," thought that James 2:14-26 could be understood only with reference to an earlier tradition established by Paul.[24] But how should we think about Paul and James if the letter stands — with 1 Corinthians and Galatians, to be sure — as the most important first-hand primary evidence for the historical James?

A first impulse for those who have not, as good historians, been seduced by the importance accorded Paul in the canon of the New Testament into thinking that Paul's historical importance must have been equally central to the early Christian movement, might be to follow J. B. Mayor's lead. Mayor, convinced that James was authentic and therefore among our earliest Christian writings, argued that it is far more logical to suppose that Paul was responding to James than that James was responding to Paul. James, after all, was in Paul's own eyes one of the certified witnesses to the resurrection; James was one of the pillars of the mother church whose approval Paul was not certain of having; James was the leader whose influence, even through emissaries, was sufficient to sway Cephas and Barnabas from their prior course of behavior; James who self-

---

21. Martin Hengel regards James as written by James of Jerusalem, but interprets it throughout as an anti-Pauline polemic, a reading that violently distorts James 2:14-26 and makes the remainder of the letter an entirely implausible exercise; see "Der Jakobusbrief als antipaulinische Polemik," in *Tradition and Interpretation in the New Testament*, ed. G. F. Hawthorne and O. Betz (Grand Rapids: Eerdmans, 1987), 248-278.

22. See F. H. Kern, *Der Character und Ursprung des Briefes Jakobi* (Tübingen: Fues, 1835), 24-36; F. C. Baur, *Paul, the Apostle of Jesus Christ*, 2nd ed., ed. E. Zeller, trans. A. Menzies (London: Williams and Norgate, 1875), 2:297-313; *The Church History of the First Three Centuries*, 3rd ed., trans. A. Menzies (London: Williams and Norgate, 1878), 1:128-130.

23. See, e.g., J. Jeremias, "Paul and James," *Expository Times* 66 (1954/55) 368-371.

24. M. Dibelius, *James: A Commentary on the Epistle of James*, rev. H. Greeven, trans. M. A. Williams (Philadelphia: Fortress Press, 1975), 17-18.

confidently assumed an authority over believers "in the dispersion." In contrast, Paul was by his own admission, "like one born out of season" among the witnesses to the resurrection; Paul had to fight for the recognition of his authority even among churches he himself founded; Paul exercised no discernible influence outside those churches that fell within his circuit; Paul sought the approval and fellowship of the Jerusalem church through his collection.

If James had written to believers in the diaspora on the insufficiency of "faith alone" and had insisted on the necessity of doing "the works of faith," and had pointed to the figure of Abraham as an example of a believer whose faith was tested and brought to fulfillment through the "work" of offering his son, Mayor argues, it might well have been heard by Paul as a challenge, and Paul's language in Galatians particularly might have had the letter of James in mind. In this reading, Galatians would be a "misunderstanding of a Jacobean teaching." Now, I don't think that Mayor is correct, for the reasons I will give below. His position fundamentally falls into the same trap of reading James and Paul only through the narrow lens of James 2:14-26 and Galatians 1–4.[25] But I applaud the historical sensibility that lies behind his thesis. If the Letter of James is taken as a genuine first-generation composition from James of Jerusalem, then the accustomed ways of reading the evidence must be challenged.

Assessment of the respective places of James and Paul in earliest Christianity that takes their respective literary productions seriously must begin with an appreciation of some obvious disparities. Paul has thirteen letters ascribed to him and James only one. Paul writes to many specifically named communities and individuals, while James addresses a general readership. Paul addresses Gentile or mixed congregations he has founded, whereas James addresses Jewish Christians. Paul responds to circumstances in his churches or ministry, while James appears to have no specific crisis in view. It is also obvious that Paul and James each have a range of issues not shared by the other. We find in James no trace of Paul's concern for his own authority, for sexual ethics, for the ordering of worship, for positions advanced by rivals. James, in turn, focuses on the ethics of speech, the care of the poor and needy, and the ministry of healing and reconciliation, with a concentration not found in Paul. It is just as much a

---

25. Mayor argues that it is more likely for Paul out in the mission field to have read a circular letter sent by James to the dispersion than it is for James to be aware of a letter that Paul wrote to churches in Galatia; see J. B. Mayor, *The Epistle of James,* 3rd ed. (London: Macmillan, 1910), xci, clxxxiii-clxxxviii; for a similar argument, see C. Powell, "'Faith' in James and Its Bearing on the Date of the Epistle," *Expository Times* 62 (1950-51) 311-314.

mistake in method to reduce James to a comparison with a portion of Paul as it is to reduce Paul to a comparison with a portion of James, particularly when those comparisons are disconnected from the dominant concerns of each author.

The reason why such comparisons arise is the distinctive way in which James and Paul both converge and diverge in their use of certain kinds of language. To make the comparisons valid, however, it is necessary to move systematically from the general to the specific, from what is common to what appears to be distinctive. I leave aside here the thick texture of language that James and Paul each share as part of the developing Christian *argot:* Jesus as Messiah and Lord, the *parousia* of the Lord, and the rest,[26] and focus only on the similarities and differences between James and Paul in their respective letters.

The first thing to observe is the stylistic resemblance: both authors employ at times the distinctive rhetorical flourishes associated with the diatribe. The stylistic similarity points us to a still more fundamental agreement: James and Paul are both recognizably moral teachers within the Greco-Roman tradition: they have vice-lists with shared elements, call for mutual correction, connect testing and endurance. Most of all, they agree with all moral instructors that identity must be translated into consistent moral behavior: profession must exhibit itself in performance. A natural term to use for such performance is "work" *(ergon).* James uses it for such an effect or action in 1:4 and 3:13, and connects it particularly to the "working out" of faith (1:25; 2:14, 17-18, 20, 21, 22, 24, 25, 26). James *never* connects the term "work" or "deed" to law *(nomos).* Instead, like every other use of the term in the NT outside Paul's letters, he uses it in the sense of moral deed or effort. Of first importance for our comparison, however, is the fact that Paul also uses *ergon* predominantly in this same sense. In his letters, he uses the term some 50 times with this denotation (e.g. Rom 13:3; 14:20; 15:18; 1 Cor 3:13-15; 9:1; 15:58; 1 Thess 1:3), and only 17 times in the more restricted and polemical sense of "works of the law." Paul speaks unembarrassedly about "your work of faith" (1 Thess 1:3) and "the work of faith in power" (2 Thess 1:11). Like James, he would consider it axiomatic that "each person's work *(ergon)* will become manifest" (1 Cor 3:13) and that "each person should test his own work" *(ergon,* Gal 6:4).

As moral teachers within the symbolic world of Torah, James and Paul each affirm *ho nomos* as the revelation of God's will for humans and there-

---

26. For a full discussion of James's immersion in early Christian language see Johnson, *James,* pp. 48-53.

fore the measure for human behavior. Paul agrees in principle with James that the "whole law" must in some sense be kept (Gal 5:3/James 2:10). And if James speaks of the law of liberty and the perfect law and the royal law — meaning thereby the law of love in Lev 19:18 (James 1:25; 2:8), Paul also speaks enthusiastically about the *nomos* as spiritual (Rom 7:14) and "holy and just and good" (Rom 7:12) and "noble" (Rom 7:16). And as moralists in that framework, Paul and James agree that not only knowing but keeping God's law is what matters. It is not James but Paul who declares, "It is not the hearers of the law who are righteous but the doers of the law who will be considered righteous" (Rom 2:13). In the remarkably similar statement in James 1:22-25, James uses the term "word" *(logos)* for what must be both heard and practiced.

Likewise it is Paul rather than James who declares that circumcision "counts" or "profits" *(ōphelei)* only if the law is observed, and that if one is a "transgressor" *(parabatēs)* of the law, then circumcision does not profit (Rom 2:25-27; compare James 2:9-11). Deeds matter, rather than membership or ethnic identity. It is Paul who stresses that neither circumcision nor uncircumcision, but "keeping the commandments of God" (1 Cor 7:19), and insists that the "righteous demand of the law" *(to dikaiōma tou nomou)* is fulfilled by those who "walk in the Spirit" (Rom 8:4). Paul also finds this righteous requirement in the law of love of neighbor, found in Lev 19:18, which "has brought the other law to fulfillment" (Rom 13:8; compare James 2:8). It is this understanding that enables Paul to say in Gal 5:6 that neither circumcision nor its absence matters, but "faith *(pistis)* working itself out *(energoumenē)* through love *(di' agapēs)*."

Both Paul and James have a strong appreciation of God as judge. In Rom 2:6, Paul quotes favorably from LXX Ps 61:12, "he will give to each one according to his deeds *(erga)*," and in the verse preceding says that the wicked are "laying up a treasure of wrath for the day of wrath" (Rom 2:5; see James 5:3!). On the basis of their belief in God as judge, both authors forbid judgment of the neighbor (Rom 14:3, 10, 13). In language reminiscent of James 4:12, Paul asks rhetorically in Rom 14:4, *sy tis ei ho krinōn allotrion oiketēn* ("who are you to judge the servant of another?").

Both authors consider "doubting" *(diakrinomai)* as a hindrance to faithful obedience (Rom 4:20; 14:23/James 1:6). Both, indeed, acknowledge a deeper sort of dividedness in humans. In James it is being "double-minded" *(dipsychos,* 1:8; 4:8). In his discussion of keeping the commandments in Romans 7, Paul speaks of "another law doing battle in my members against the law of my mind" *(en tois melesin mou antistrateuomenon tō nomō tou noos mou,* Rom 7:23), which is strikingly similar to the description of wars deriving *ek tōn hēdonōn hymōn tōn strateuomenōn en tois melesin hymōn,* in James 4:1. Compare also Paul's moral dualism between the "works of the flesh" and the "fruit of the spirit" in Gal 5:16-23 to James's opposition between the wisdom from below and the wisdom from above in James 3:17-18.

Finally, and most critically, James and Paul emphatically agree on the primacy of faith, and agree that being "heirs of the kingdom of heaven" is a matter of God's promise (compare Gal 3:29/James 2:5) and gift (James 1:17; 4:6/Rom 3:24; 5:15) rather than human accomplishment. But it is precisely on these matters that they are often thought to diverge, when James 2:14-26 is compared and contrasted to Galatians 3 and Romans 4. The question must therefore be posed: do James and Paul disagree on the matter of righteousness *(dikaiosynē)* in its relationship to faith and human effort?

In this question above all, the influence of Reformation polemics has had a deleterious and distorting effect, so that a fresh examination is extraordinarily difficult.[27] The polemical placement of Paul and James has had the effect of misreading both.[28] It is important to state from the first, then, that the correct understanding of Paul on the issue of faith and righteousness is as much open to dispute as is the correct understanding of James. In the discussion that follows, readers should be aware that I enthusiastically subscribe to the position that in Paul's arguments in Galatians and Romans, the phrase *pistis Christou* must be understood subjectively rather than objectively: Paul argues that it is the human faith of Jesus that establishes humans in right relationship with God, not the faith of humans in Christ.[29]

---

27. For the narrative of this line of interpretation, see Johnson, *James,* pp. 140-161.

28. It is fascinating to see commentators avoiding the plain grammatical sense of Galatians 2:16, for example, because that plain grammatical sense does not yield the "right" meaning according to traditional understanding of Paul. So the phrase *ei mē,* which in Gal 1:19 must mean "except" ("I did not see another of the apostles, except James the Brother of the Lord"), and is most naturally read as "except" also in Gal 2:16 ("a person is not made righteous out of works of law except through the faith of Jesus Christ") is read as a flat adversative "but rather" (see J. L. Martyn, *Galatians: A New Translation with Introduction and Commentary* [Anchor Bible 33A; New York: Doubleday, 1997], 251; F. Matera, *Galatians* [Sacra Pagina 9; Collegeville: Liturgical Press, 1992], 93-94) or with a bracketed "only" that is then interpreted as "but" (see H. D. Betz, *Galatians: A Commentary on Paul's Letter to the Churches in Galatia* [Philadelphia: Fortress Press, 1979], 117).

29. For a full discussion, see R. B. Hays, *The Faith of Jesus Christ: The Narrative Substructure of Galatians 3:1-4:11,* 2nd ed. (Grand Rapids: Eerdmans, 2002), and L. T. Johnson, "Romans 3:21-26 and the Faith of Jesus," *Catholic Biblical Quarterly* 44 (1982) 77-90. The position that

A full sorting out of the problem must begin with the context of Paul's discussion. In Galatians, Paul is opposing Gentile Christians who want to "Judaize," that is, become circumcised and observe all the commandments of Torah, including the ritual ones (Gal 4:9-10; 5:3, 12). Paul sees their desire for "more" to be in effect the denial of what they have already been given, namely, God's gift in Christ, by which Paul means, "the faith of the Son of God who loved me and gave himself for me" (Gal 2:20; see also 1:4).[30] Paul's rhetoric about "works of the law" (*erga tou nomou*) is therefore specifically fitted to the situation of Gentiles seeking circumcision and the observance of ritual practices, posed in opposition to *pistis Christou,* the faith of Christ. It is in this narrow context that Paul declares that "a person is made righteous not through *erga nomou* except through the faith of Jesus Christ, and we have believed in Christ Jesus so that we might be made righteous *ek pisteōs Iēsou Christou* (Gal 2:16).

Paul therefore sets in opposition *erga nomou* and *pistis Christou* as principles of righteousness before God. He denies that righteousness comes through law (*dia nomou*) apart from faith; rather, it comes through a free gift of Christ (*dōrean,* Gal 2:21). Righteousness derives not from *ergon nomou* but from *akoēs pisteōs* ("hearing of faith," Gal 3:2). It comes not through *nomos* but through *epangelia* ("promise," Gal 3:18). In this argument, Abraham is cited as the example of faith that makes a person righteous in response to God's *epangelia,* and Gen 15:6 is quoted to that effect (Gal 3:6). The principle of faith is thereby established as justifying humans 430 years before the *nomos* was given to Moses (Gal 3:17).

In Romans 4:1-25, Paul's treatment is broadly consistent with that in Galatians 3, but also distinctive.[31] Again, Abraham, "our forefather according to the flesh" (Rom 4:1), is cited within the context established by 3:20, *ex ergōn nomou ou dikaiōthēsetai pasa sarx* ("no flesh is made righteous on the basis of works of law"), and 3:22, that God's *dikaiosynē* is being revealed *dia pisteōs Iēsou Christou eis pantas tous pisteuontas* ("through the faith

---

Paul speaks of the "faith of Jesus" in critical passages does not in the least suggest that "faith in Christ" is not also equally important as the human response of Christians (thus plainly, Gal 2:16b: "and we have believed in Christ Jesus, so that we might be made righteous out of the faith of Christ and not out of works of law").

30. For the religious situation faced by Paul, see L. T. Johnson, "Ritual Imprinting and the Politics of Perfection," in *Religious Experience in Earliest Christianity: A Missing Dimension in New Testament Studies* (Minneapolis: Fortress Press, 1998), 69-103.

31. See H. Boers, *The Justification of the Gentiles: Paul's Letters to the Galatians and the Romans* (Peabody, MA: Hendrikson, 1994), 143-220; see also L. T. Johnson, *Reading Romans: A Literary and Theological Commentary* (Macon, GA: Smith and Helwys, 2001), 69-75.

of Jesus Christ for all who believe").[32] When Paul speaks of *erga* in Rom 4:2, therefore, it is not with respect to moral effort broadly considered, but specifically with respect to the commandments of Torah, and most particularly the requirement of circumcision. This is why Gen 15:6 is used to demonstrate that Abraham was declared righteous *before* he was circumcised (4:10). Again, Paul contrasts *nomos* and *epangelia* (4:13), as well as *nomos* and *klēronomia* (4:14). Abraham is the exemplar of faith for both circumcised and uncircumcised (4:16).

Against this backdrop, how should the disputed passage in James 2:14-26 be read? A number of points can be made in rapid sequence.

The first is that James's entire discussion is not a separate essay but the continuation of James 2:1-13, which has as its theme precisely how *pistis tou kyriou hēmōn Iēsou Christou tēs doxēs* (2:1) must express itself in deeds of love and not be contradicted by acts of discrimination between persons.[33] To rip 2:14-26 out of this context is fundamentally to distort James's argument.

Second, as I have already stated, James's understanding of *nomos* has nothing to do with the issues Paul is debating: James never connects "works" to the law or to circumcision or to any ritual observance.

Third, James is entirely in agreement with Paul in placing faith *(pistis)*, promise *(epangelia)* and inheritance *(klēronomia)* in the same column: they originate in God rather than in human striving (2:1-5).

Fourth, James places in opposition an empty *pistis theou* (here an objective gentitive: faith in God) or an empty *pistis Christou* which amounts to a sort of profession of identity that is purely verbal (2:1, 19) to living *erga pisteōs* ("deeds/works of faith") that make such profession real and performative.

Fifth, James cites Abraham as an example precisely of such "active faith" which is shown by his offering of Isaac (2:21).

Sixth, this *ergon pisteōs* is itself "coworked by faith" *(synergei)* and "perfects faith," that is, brings profession to full realization in performance (2:22).

Seventh, Genesis 22:2-9 is read by James as the textual or narrative "fulfillment" of the declaration made by God that is reported earlier in Genesis 15:6, that Abraham's faith made him to be declared as righteous (James 2:23).

32. See Johnson, "Romans 3:21-26 and the Faith of Jesus"; R. B. Hays, "Psalm 143 and the Logic of Romans 3," *Journal of Biblical Literature* 99 (1980) 107-115; S. Williams, "The Righteousness of God in Romans," *Journal of Biblical Literature* 99 (1980) 241-290.

33. See the full discussion of this entire section, "The Deeds of Faith (2:1-26)," in Johnson, *James,* pp. 217-252.

Eighth, James's statement in 2:24, *ex ergōn dikaioutai anthrōpos kai ouk ek pisteōs monon* ("a person is shown to be righteous on the basis of deeds and not on the basis of faith only"), which has been taken as a direct contradiction of Gal 2:16, does nothing of the sort, for the terms in the two statements have quite distinct referents.

Ninth, James's use of Rahab as a second example of the *erga pisteōs* (2:25-26) demonstrates beyond cavil that his interest is neither in law nor in circumcision, nor even exclusively in Abraham, but in the moral issue of whether belief in God and the faith of Christ is translated into "living action."

A comparison between Paul and James, I suggest, is distorted when reduced to the single topic of righteousness as found in Galatians/Romans and James 2:14-26. The range of similarities and dissimilarities in the two writers is broader and more complex than that of a simple agreement or disagreement on a single point. Each author's language, furthermore, is consistent within the topic each addresses, and there is no compelling reason to suppose that either had the other in mind. And what is most intriguing when placing them on the same plane is the discovery of how much they share as moral teachers within the symbolic world of Torah.

In this essay, I have tried only to clarify that point. I have not yet begun to show what we can learn historically by placing Paul and James into a more positive and energetic conversation within earliest Christianity, a conversation that involves not only their two voices, but those (at least) of the developing Jesus tradition and the Letter to the Hebrews as well. But even this brief discussion has left too little space to do more than touch on some of the other ways in which taking James as an authentic production by James of Jerusalem in the first generation can have importance for history.

James, Hellenistic Judaism, and Jewish Christianity

One of the most important developments in the study of Judaism over the past decades has been the recognition of how thoroughly Hellenistic culture permeated Judaism, both in the Diaspora and in Palestine.[34] If the

---

34. For orientation, see M. Hengel, *Judaism and Hellenism: Studies in Their Encounter in Palestine in the Early Hellenistic Period*, 2 vols., trans. J. Bowden (Philadelphia: Fortress Press, 1974); G. Mussies, "Greek in Palestine and the Diaspora," in *The Jewish People in the First Century*, 2 vols., ed. S. Safrai and M. Stern (Compendium Rerum Iudicarum ad Novum

provenance of James is indeed Jerusalem, and its date before 62, we would then have one of our most important and securely located pieces of evidence for the presence of such Hellenistic Jewish sensibility within Palestine. In the previous sections, I noted the obvious ways in which James fits within the symbolic world of Torah shared by other Jews, and I observed that, like Paul, James also resembles Greco-Roman moral teachers. Here I can briefly elaborate on this fascinating combination.

James is Hellenistic first of all in every dimension of his literary composition. Much of James's diction derives from the Septuagint, but it is far from "translation Greek" in its complex rhetorical effects produced by pleonasm (3:6-7), alliteration (see 1:2-3), parachesis (1:24), and paronomasia (2:4, 20; 4:14). His subtle word-play involving *krisis/eleos/aneleos* in 2:13, his frequent use of word-linkages (1:12-13; 1:26-27; 3:17-18), and his construction of a *sorites* in 1:2-4, make it virtually certain that James was not a translation from a Hebrew or Aramaic original,[35] but was thoroughly Greek from the start. In terms of composition, furthermore, the letter's use of elements of the diatribe, and the paraenetic-protreptic form of his deliberative rhetoric — not to mention his remarkable capacity for *brachylogia* — locate James's writing within the world of Greco-Roman literature.[36]

James also shares the sensibility of Greco-Roman moralists on any number of small points (the testing of the wise, the unity of virtue, the mirror as a source of self-reflection, the tongue as venomous, the charioteer and pilot as images for self-control), and fundamental convictions (that virtue must be tested, that speech must be controlled, that friends correct each other, that wars arise from disordered passions, that speech must be translated into action). More than that, James uses the *topoi* of Greco-Roman moral instruction in order to develop his argument: in 3:13–4:10 he employs the *topos* on envy, in 4:4 and 2:23 the *topos* on friendship, and in 1:19-20, 1:26, and 3:1-9, the *topos* on taciturnity.

At the same time, this thoroughly Hellenistic sensibility takes as its authoritative text the Jewish Scripture, shown must vividly by the fact that the warrant for moral behavior is grounded not in the "honor/

Testamentum, section one; Philadelphia: Fortress Press, 1987), 1040-1064; M. Hengel, "The Interpenetration of Judaism and Hellenism in the Pre-Maccabean Period," in *The Cambridge History of Judaism*, vol. 2, ed. W. D. Davies and L. Finkelstein (New York: Cambridge University Press, 1989), 167-228.

35. See R. P. Martin, *James* (Word Biblical Commentary 48; Waco, TX: Word Publishing, 1988), lxix-lxxvii.

36. For fuller discussion, see Johnson, *James*, pp. 16-24.

shame" motivation found so commonly in Greco-Roman moral discourse but in the power of God to create and to judge. As noted above, James makes use of wisdom and prophetic traditions from Scripture as well as the law. Here we find a complete and seamless merging of Greek and Jewish sensibilities, in the manner of *The Letter of Aristeas, 4 Maccabees, The Sentences of Pseudo-Phocylides,* and Philo Judaeus.[37] But whereas all these writings can safely be located in Alexandrian Judaism, James is located in Jerusalem. And its closest companion within Jewish literature — besides Paul — is *The Testaments of the Twelve Patriarchs.*[38] In the *Testaments,* we find the same use of Greek *topoi* for moral instruction,[39] set within the framework of the law of Israel. We also find the same imagery regarding the involvement of cosmic forces *(pneumata)* in human activity. Most significant, we find in the *Testaments* as well as in James the same combination of sapiential and apocalyptic traditions inextricably interwoven.[40] They share a remarkably similar dualistic appropriation of Greco-Roman ethics within the symbolic world of Torah.

James also shows us a thoroughly Hellenized Judaism that interprets Scripture, not through the sort of allegorical readings that we associate with Alexandrian compositions such as *Aristeas,* Aristobolos, and Philo (or for that matter, Paul and Hebrews), but with specifically Palestinian modes of halachic midrash, with the difference that the text being thus treated is Greek rather than Hebrew. In his distinctive use of Leviticus 19 throughout his composition, James can appropriately be designated a sort of halachic midrash.[41] In this respect, the closest comparisons to James are found in certain passages in the Letters of Paul and in the speeches of Acts.[42]

If James offers us historical evidence for the possible varieties of Judaism within first-century Palestine, no less is it a reminder of the complexity hidden within the catch-all category, "Jewish Christianity."[43] The ex-

37. The full display of parallels as well as dissimilarities is found in Johnson, *James,* pp. 38-43.

38. See Johnson, *James,* pp. 43-46.

39. *The Testament of Simeon,* for example, is entitled in Greek, *Peri Phthonou* (On Envy).

40. See T. C. Penner, *The Epistle of James and Eschatology: Re-Reading an Ancient Letter* (JSNTSup 121; Sheffield: Sheffield Academic Press, 1996).

41. Johnson, "The Use of Leviticus 19 in the Letter of James," pp. 123-135.

42. See L. T. Johnson, *Septuagintal Midrash in the Speeches of Acts* (The Pere Marquette Lecture in Theology 2002; Milwaukee: Marquette University Press, 2002).

43. See, e.g., R. A. Kraft, "In Search of 'Jewish Christianity' and Its 'Theology': Problems of Definition and Methodology," *Recherches de science religieuse* 60 (1972) 81-92; K. Riegel, "Jewish Christianity: Definitions and Terminology," *New Testament Studies* 24 (1978) 410-415.

tended discussion in the first part of this essay suggests that James represents a way of being Jewish and a follower of Jesus that is thoroughly grounded in fidelity to the law but without any specific or special concern for circumcision (as noted, it may simply be assumed) or for any ritual practices. James shows a thoroughly moralizing form of Judaism that recognizes Jesus as Messiah and Lord (1:1; 2:1), lives within the framework of his teachings (see below), and expects his return as judge (5:7-8). If James can be taken as evidence for the messianic movement among Jews in Jerusalem before the Jewish War, then the nature and history of "Jewish Christianity" will need to be reexamined. We need to think in terms of different varieties both of Jewish and Gentile Christians.[44] It should at least give us pause that of all the writings in the New Testament, James has the most profound kinship with the letters of Paul.

James and Early Christianity

I turn finally to the ways in which the Letter of James can serve as evidence for Christianity in Jerusalem before the year 62. Its importance here can scarcely be overestimated, since without this composition, every judgment made about the Jerusalem community must be based solely on inferences drawn from Paul's letters, the descriptions provided by Acts, or by later legendary sources. Concerning James the man, I have suggested that there is far more agreement among Paul, Acts, and this letter, than there is with the later sources. What can we learn about the Christian movement represented by James?

Before seeking positive evidence, we remind ourselves of the necessary methodological cautions. First, James is not describing the church in Jerusalem, but is writing to diaspora communities, and that in general terms. Second, as in all literary texts, we have access only to James's perceptions, not to things as they were. Third, arguments from silence are especially difficult. I have pointed out that James does not speak of circumcision, but this may be simply because he assumes its practice among those he writes, and there is no need to take up the subject. I have also noted that James makes no mention of a sacred meal of any sort, but this cannot be taken as evidence that he or the communities to which he wrote celebrated no sacred meals of any sort. Likewise, it has often been noted

44. R. E. Brown, "Not Jewish Christianity and Gentile Christianity, but Types of Jewish/Gentile Christianity," CBQ 45 (1983) 74-79.

that James makes no reference to the death and resurrection of Jesus or the bestowal of the Spirit (compare Acts!). We cannot conclude that he or his community had no experiences of or convictions concerning these things. Silence is simply silence. The information we get from James concerning Christianity in Jerusalem, therefore, is no less inferential, but it must nevertheless be taken into account.

There are basically five aspects of the Christianity represented by James in his letter that deserve particular attention. In combination, they serve to suggest something about the "Jesus Movement" as continued by James the Brother of Jesus.

First, although the name Jesus occurs only twice (1:1; 2:1), and although James never speaks of the resurrection directly, there is every reason to think that for James, Jesus is not simply a figure of the past but of the present. Jesus is designated both as *christos* and as *kyrios* in 1:1, and James designates himself as *doulos* both of God and of Jesus. Likewise, in 2:1, Jesus is designated as *kyrios tēs doxēs*. The use of "slave," of "Lord" in combination with "God" and the use of "glory," all point to Jesus as resurrected one. This is supported by the references to the *parousia tou kyriou* in 5:7, which is virtually a technical term in the New Testament for the second coming of Jesus, and the *onoma tou kyriou* in 5:14, which again is used most often in the New Testament with reference to the power of the risen Lord. If one can heal in the name of Jesus, and if Jesus is expected as judge, then Jesus now shares in God's life and power.

Second, the distinctive presence of Jesus within James's composition is through the medium of his sayings. The pervasiveness of these sayings, and their thorough integration into James's own discourse, has long been noted.[45] More recent scholarship has sought to identify the sayings, align them with the respective versions in the Gospels, and reach some conclusions concerning what stage of transmission is here represented. It appears more than ever likely that James contains genuine logia of Jesus at a stage earlier than their redaction in the Synoptic Gospels.[46] The Letter of

45. J. H. Ropes, *A Critical and Exegetical Commentary on the Epistle of St. James* (The International Critical Commentary; Edinburgh: T&T Clark, 1916), 39; P. J. Hartin, "James and the Q Sermon on the Mount/Plain," *Society of Biblical Literature Seminar Papers* 28 (1989) 440-457; P. J. Hartin, *James and the Sayings of Jesus* (JSNTSup 47; Sheffield: JSOT, 1991); P. H. Davids, "James and Jesus," in *Gospel Perspectives: The Jesus Tradition outside the Gospels*, ed. D. Wenham (Sheffield: JSOT, 1985), 63-84; D. B. Deppe, *The Sayings of Jesus in the Epistle of James* (Chelsea, MI: Bookcrafters, 1989).

46. See my essay with W. H. Wachob, "The Sayings of Jesus in the Letter of James," pp. 136-154 in this volume.

James, therefore, stands with Paul as our earliest evidence for the transmission and use of the sayings of Jesus in Greek. That James wrote from Jerusalem suggests as well that this transmission and use were taking place there from the start. It can also be noted that James does not cite these sayings as Scripture or refer them to Jesus. While it is possible to argue that this suggests a later mode of incorporation, it is my judgment far more likely that this easy and natural appropriation points to the brother of Jesus standing within the movement and outlook of Jesus himself, and naturally using his brother's language as his own.[47] The Jesus movement was a movement, after all, and it seems to have had its effect on James. Finally, it is striking how the use of the sayings of Jesus intersects James's use of Leviticus 19 throughout the letter,[48] making it more than likely that when James calls the law of love of neighbor in Lev 19:18 the *nomos basilikos* (2:8) he means "the law of the kingdom" that was proclaimed by Jesus (2:5).[49]

Third, James not only contains allusions to the sayings of Jesus, but the entire spirit of his discourse poses a sharp challenge to the *ethos* of the world, a challenge that echoes the ministry of Jesus as recounted by the Synoptic Gospels. Indeed James claims that one must choose between friendship with the world and friendship with God (4:4), and this moral dualism is expressed above all in James's rejection of the rich and the arrogant in favor of the poor and the humble. The moral exhortation in James eschews all conventional notions of honor and shame, pays no attention to the domestic sphere, cares little for sexual issues. It focuses exclusively on moral attitudes and actions, and these are of the most countercultural sort.[50]

Fourth, James nevertheless locates this sectarian outlook not in individuals but in an intentional community. The *ekklēsia* (5:14) or *synagōgē* (2:2) is made up of men and women who use fictive kinship language with each other ("beloved brethren," 1:16; "brother or sister," 2:15). There are leaders who are called "teachers" (*didaskaloi*, 3:1) and "elders of the assembly" (*presbyteroi tēs ekklēsias*, 5:14). The assembly meets together for purposes of judging (2:1-5), as well as for healing and confession of sins (5:14-16). Sparse as it is, this positive information concerning the church con-

---

47. W. H. Wachob, *The Voice of Jesus in the Social Rhetoric of James* (Society for New Testament Studies Monograph Series 106; New York: Cambridge University Press, 2000).

48. Johnson, "The Use of Leviticus 19 in the Letter of James," pp. 123-135.

49. Matt 19:19; 22:39; Mark 12:31; Luke 10:27; see Rom 13:9; Gal 5:14.

50. See my essay "The Social World of James: Literary Analysis and Historical Reconstruction," pp. 101-122 in this volume.

firms in some instances information concerning the first generation of Christianity found in other sources (assembly, argot, leaders, judging), and adds to our knowledge that there were healers (1 Cor 12:9) the description of an actual practice of healing that (even in its wording) echoes the healing ministry of Jesus.[51]

Fifth, James provides us a vision of early Christianity as a community of solidarity. The rejection of discrimination (2:1-5), of the logic of envy (3:13–4:10), as well as the practices of arrogance (4:11–5:6) and resentment (5:9), is matched positively by practices of solidarity: honor toward the poor (2:14-17), simple and unadorned speech (5:12), care for the sick (5:13-15), mutual confession of sins and prayer for each other (5:16), and mutual correction (5:19-20).

This essay is scarcely exhaustive. It suggests only some of the ways in which, working from the premise that the Letter of James is actually written by James of Jerusalem before the year 62, we might begin to re-examine early Christian history. And it suggests that it is already past time for such scholarly reexamination.

---

51. James says that the prayer of faith will "save the sick one, and the Lord will raise him up" (5:14). The combination of *pistis* and *sōzein* echoes the refrain "your faith has saved you" in Mark 5:34; 10:52; Matt 9:22, and especially in Luke (7:50; 8:48; 17:19; 18:42). In Acts, Luke explicitly links "faith" to the power worked by "the name of the Lord" (see James 5:14) in healing (Acts 3:16; 4:9-10; 14:9). The phrase "raise him up," in turn, echoes the description of Jesus' gesture in the Gospel healing stories (Matt 9:5-7; Mark 2:9; 3:3; 5:41; 10:49; Luke 5:23-24; 7:14; 8:54; John 5:8; 11:29).

An Introduction to the Letter of James

The Letter of James is a composition from the first generation of Christianity, possibly composed by the brother of Jesus, the most likely candidate for the one the letter's greeting calls simply a "slave of God and of the Lord Jesus Christ" (1:1). Addressed to the "twelve tribes of the dispersion," it is most naturally understood as written to Jewish Christians outside of ancient Palestine by someone residing within that land. Since the middle of the nineteenth century, scholarship has been evenly divided concerning the authorship of the letter: was it written by that James who was a leader of the church in Jerusalem (Gal 1:19; 2:9; 1 Cor 15:7; Acts 15:13), or was it composed pseudonymously as late as the mid-second century? Those who have paid slight attention to James on its own terms but seek to fit the letter into some scheme of early Christian history have tilted toward pseudonymity. Those who have studied the text carefully have also been persuaded by many small and converging details suggesting it could well have been written by Jesus' brother. The re-

---

This essay is a partial epitome of the introduction to L. T. Johnson, *The Letter of James: A New Translation with Introduction and Commentary* (Anchor Bible 37A; Garden City: Doubleday, 1995), with modifications and — I hope — some improvement by way of afterthought. Full bibliographies are found there. My commentary responds in particular to the magisterial twentieth-century commentary by M. Dibelius, *James: A Commentary on the Epistle of James,* rev. H. Greeven, trans. M. Williams (Hermeneia; Philadelphia: Fortress Press, 1975). Other overall treatments of James that are helpful include J. B. Adamson, *James: The Man and the Message* (Grand Rapids: Eerdmans, 1975); R. B. Ward, *The Communal Concern of the Epistle of James* (Ph.D. dissertation, Harvard University, 1966); T. B. Cargal, *Restoring the Diaspora: Discursive Structure and Purpose in the Epistle of James* (SBLDS 144; Atlanta: Scholars Press, 1995); and R. Wall, *Community of the Wise: The Letter of James* (The New Testament in Context; Valley Forge, PA: Trinity Press International, 1997).

sults of contemporary research tend to support authenticity and an early date.

There are a number of ancient accounts concerning James of Jerusalem, who was martyred in that city in 62 CE. The accounts are so legendary, however, that they give us little historically reliable information. Even if we knew a great deal about this James, and even if we were certain that he wrote the letter, it would be hazardous to interpret the composition from the perspective of authorship. A far better approach to any composition, ancient or modern, is to give close attention to its literary shape. In this essay, James is introduced through such a literary description, which leads to a consideration of the composition's moral and theological concerns, and finally to some brief and tentative remarks about the historical and social situation which these elements suggest.

The Composition's Voice

One of the reasons some scholars have had trouble seeing James as a first-generation composition of Palestinian provenance is the quality of its Greek prose, which employs a variety of rhetorical tropes (alliteration, paronomasia) and at times achieves real elegance (see 1:17). How could a Galilean brother of Jesus write so well? Nor is it simply a matter of syntax and diction. James is aware of Greco-Roman moral commonplaces, and uses them deftly. Some of his essays are masterful miniatures of frequently found discussions on topics such as envy (3:13–4:3), friendship (4:4), and garrulousness (3:1-12). There is no real reason, however, why a Galilean Jew like James could not write such Greek and know such rhetorical and moral tropes. Research in the past decades has shown that Palestine had been hellenized thoroughly since the time of Alexander the Great and that other Jews in Palestine were writing in Greek. Archaeological discoveries confirm the report of the Jewish historian Josephus concerning the city of Sepphoris, only a few miles from Nazareth, as a major center of Greek culture.

James's sentences resemble most those written by ancient moralists. He favors the imperative mode and the kind of brevity often associated with the crafters of moral exhortation. This sort of aphoristic style dominates chapter one and is found in individual statements throughout the letter. Some readers have found in the apparent disconnectedness of James's statements a similarity to that form of Greco-Roman moral exhortation called paraenesis. Other aspects of the paraenetic can be detected in James's appeal to memory (1:23-25) and in his presentation of moral exemplars for imitation (2:21-25; 5:10-11, 16-18). But James has more coherence than appears at a first reading. Portions of the composition are structured in the dialogical style associated with the Greco-Roman diatribe. In the diatribe, an imagined interlocutor is engaged in a give-and-take of rhetorical questions and incisive answers that makes for lively reading. Splendid examples are James 2:14-26 and 3:1-12.

The rhetorical genre of the Hellenistic world that James most resembles, however, is the protreptic discourse, which sought to exhort those holding a profession to behavior consonant with their ideal. In James, this is expressed in terms of practicing the profession of faith, or, putting it in James's own language, not only hearing the word but doing it (1:22). Since letter writing was so widespread a practice in the ancient Mediterranean world, other genres often were put within the framework of the genre "letter." James appears to be an example of this practice. It may be considered a real letter in that it was sent to be read by others (the "twelve tribes of the diaspora"), but it is closer to a literary letter than to the sort of correspondence that represents an exchange of news and views between friends and colleagues.

The combination of these stylistic and generic elements has made James a composition peculiarly difficult to analyze in terms of its literary or rhetorical structure. Suggestions range from the accurate but dull listing of the contents in sequence to fascinating but fanciful architectonic structures. That James contains a series of topically coherent essays is clear to all, though few agree totally on where they begin or end. That aphoristic statements punctuate the essays is also clear, though their literary function remains debatable. That chapter one differs from the rest of the composition because it is aphoristic from beginning to end and touches on so many subjects is also apparent. Putting all these observations together is less easy. A reasonable approach to James's literary structure is to see chapter one as a rhetorical epitome of the succeeding essays. In effect, James 1 uses aphorisms to introduce the themes that are later developed in essay form. By so doing, the epitome also necessarily establishes the basic dualism between God and World that is thematic for the composition as a whole (1:27; 4:4).

An even more obvious accent in James's Greek is biblical. Virtually all the vocabulary in James is found also in the Septuagint, and some of his Semitic constructions, such as the neologism *prosōpolēmpsia* ("respect of persons"/"discrimination") or the expression "doing the word," would make sense only to a reader of Greek who was familiar with the usages in the Septuagint. Scripture provides James with more than diction. James's entire symbolic world is that of Scripture in all its parts. James's positive appreciation of the law *(nomos)* is obvious in his descriptions: it is the "perfect law of liberty" (1:25) and the "royal law" (or perhaps better, "law of the kingdom," 2:8). James explicitly cites from the decalogue and insists that "all the law" must be kept. But what does he mean by "all the law"? There is no indication that James was advocating any sort of "judaizing" program, for the composition is utterly free of any mention of circumcision or other ritual observance. By the "royal law," James means the commandment of love, found in Leviticus 19:18, "You shall love your neighbor as yourself" (2:8). This summary of the law is found also in Paul's letters (Gal 5:14; Rom 13:9), as well as in the Gospels (Mark 12:28-34; Matt 22:35-40; Luke 10:25-28).

What makes James distinctive is his understanding of "all the law." He means loving one's neighbor "according to Scripture" (2:8), that is, as guided by the amplification of that moral norm found in Leviticus 19:11-18. Thus, Leviticus 19:15 forbids partiality in judgment, and James 2:1-11 argues that such discrimination between rich and poor within the community is incompatible with the law of love. James uses Leviticus 19 throughout the letter to provide a basis in Torah for his instructions (see, e.g., 4:11; 5:4, 9).

The prophetic tradition helps shape James's voice well beyond his citation of Isaiah 40:6-7 (1:9-11). His language echoes that of the prophets Isaiah and Amos in his condemnation of the carelessly entrepreneurial merchants (4:13-17) and the oppressively wealthy landowners (5:1-6). In his call to conversion from double-mindedness in 4:7-10, James's words resonate with all the prophetic literature. And in his insistence that God sides with the poor (2:5) and will come in judgment to vindicate them (5:1-9), James contemporizes a central prophetic theme. The wisdom tradition of Scripture continues in James not only thematically in his distinction between the "wisdom from below" and that "wisdom from above" that comes from God (1:5; 3:13-17), but also formally by means of his hortatory style. James can be seen as part of that broad river of wisdom that flowed through and from the ocean of Torah in antiquity, although as we will see momentarily, James is a distinctive and easily discernible current in that flow.

James's voice, in short, combines in distinctive fashion the language of Greco-Roman moralism and the language of Scripture. It is possible to locate his distinctive voice even further by comparing and contrasting it with the traditions already named. We can begin with contrast. If we place

James next to all the wisdom literature of antiquity, both from the side of the Near East and Judaism and from the side of Hellenism, James appears as virtually unique in four major ways. First, James is entirely concerned with morals rather than manners. A large portion of all ancient wisdom instructs the reader on the ways of finding and keeping one's assigned place in the world, using the status markers of honor and shame as motivation. James deals only with moral behavior that is consonant with God's honor. Second, James addresses the intentional community of the assembly (*synagōgē*, 2:2; *ekklēsia*, 5:14) rather than the household *(oikos)*. James shows no concerns for the orderly arrangements of the household that so preoccupy ancient moralists. There is no attention given to the roles and duties of domestic existence; more strikingly, there is no particular attention to sexual behavior (the use of "adulteresses" in 4:4 is symbolic), whether heterosexual or homosexual. Rahab, for example, is identified as a prostitute *(pornē),* but she is portrayed as an example of faith (2:25). Men and women alike are addressed as moral agents within a community; James seeks to reinforce a certain kind of community identity consonant with "the faith of Jesus Christ" (2:1), rather than a domestic tranquility. Third, James is egalitarian rather than hierarchical. Ancient wisdom massively reinforced a stratified view of the world in which the older had more authority than the younger, the free more than slaves, men more than women, the rich more than the poor. James decisively rejects that view of the world. The author is not the "father" of this community and they are not his "little children" (language found even in Paul). He is only a "slave of God and of the Lord Jesus Christ" (1:1). Teachers are not better than others but are held to a more severe judgment (3:1-2). Elders are to be summoned by the weakest in the community and are to respond (5:14-15). They are all "brothers and sisters" (2:14), equally answerable to God and to each other. Fourth, James is communitarian rather than individualistic. Much ancient wisdom was addressed to the individual ("my son") as instruction in social as well as moral improvement. But James opposes any sort of self-advancement at the expense of others. Individuals are called, rather, to a life of mutual gift-giving and collaboration, rather than one of competition and rivalry. In contrast to "the world" that operates on the basis of an envy that leads to murder (3:13–4:3; 5:1-6), James seeks to shape a community that shares its gifts that come from God and restores the life of the sick (5:13-16).

So much of James can be understood within the symbolic world of Judaism that some scholars have questioned whether it began as a Christian composition at all. Perhaps, they say, it was originally a Jewish discourse to which a Christian added the only two references to Jesus (in 1:1 and 2:1) and appropriated it for the church. The suggestion has sufficient superficial appeal to require response. On the one hand, James is certainly not Christocentric in the manner that so many New Testament compositions are. No stories about Jesus are recounted. More significant, James makes no mention of the death and resurrection of Jesus or the sending of the Holy Spirit. But on the other hand, James's language bears unmistakable traces of the developing Christian argot that we find in other early letters. Examples include the pervasive use of kinship language (1:2, 9, 16, 19, etc.), the ambiguous use of the title *kyrios* ("Lord") applicable either to Jesus (2:1) or to God (1:7), the use of *doulos* ("slave") for a leader of the assembly (1:1), the concentration on the distinctive virtues of *pistis* ("faith") and *agapē* ("love"), the absolute use of *to onoma* ("the name") as in the phrase "the name that is invoked upon you" (2:7), the language about "kingdom" and "promise" and "inheritance" (2:5), the use of the Christian neologism *prosōpolēmpsia* ("respecting of persons," 2:1, 9), and, most impressively, the use of the almost technical term *parousia* to designate the Lord's coming (5:7-8). Virtually all these terms can be found in other Jewish literature, but nowhere outside the writings of the Christian movement with equal concentration and in identical combination.

Among other Christian voices, those of Jesus and Paul are the closest to James. Although James is not, as noted, Christological in the usual sense of the term, the writing makes heavy use of Jesus' sayings. The most obvious is the proclamation of love as the "law of the kingdom" (2:8), which is found also in the mouth of Jesus. The detection of these allusions is not easy because so much of James's language echoes Jesus' speech, as when he speaks of the judge standing by the door (5:9; see Matt 24:33), or of having faith without doubting (1:6; Matt 21:21), or when he states that those who endure will be saved (1:12; Matt 10:22), and those who humble themselves will be exalted (4:6-10; Matt 23:12). Four statements are particularly close to the spirit of Jesus as we find it in the Synoptic Gospels: the declarations that the poor receive the kingdom (2:5; see Luke 6:20), that the merciful receive mercy (2:13; Matt 5:7), that the pure of heart and peacemakers are blessed (Jas 4:6, 3:18 and Matt 5:8, 9). And three statements in James are so close to Jesus' sayings in substance and style that the most reasonable surmise is that they in fact derive from Jesus: that God responds to those who ask (1:5; Matt 7:7), that they should not judge lest they be judged (4:11-12, 5:9; see Matt 7:1), that they should not take oaths but speak with a simple yes or no (5:12; Matt 5:34). Close analysis of these statements in comparison with their parallels in the Synoptic Gospels reveals that their form in James is probably closer to the (hypothetical) source Q than to the redacted Synoptic versions, another reason for locating James in the first rather than a later generation of the Christian movement. More important, these multiple and subtle connections to the words of Jesus indicate how for James the "faith of Jesus Christ" is mediated through his teachings.

The most intriguing and problematic relationship is between James and Paul. Analysis of the similarities and differences between them has dominated and distorted much of the study of James, especially since the time of the Reformation. Martin Luther insisted that Paul's teaching on righteousness through faith rather than the works of the law (in Galatians and Romans) and James's discussion of the works of faith (in Jas 2:14-26) represented an irreconcilable contradiction in Scripture. Since in Luther's view Paul represented the truest understanding of the gospel, James was relegated to a secondary position in the canon. Luther's view on this point opposed the entire tradition of interpretation before him and was followed by few of his fellow-reformers. But because of Luther's great influence over that form of German scholarship that came to dominate the critical study of Scripture, James has repeatedly had to seek rehabilitation within scholarship, since ideas about its composition were understood in early Christianity within the context of a supposed ideological opposition between Paul — as the representative of the freedom of the gospel — and James — as the representative of a Judaizing movement.

A better approach to the comparison begins by recognizing the multiple ways in which the literary productions and religious preoccupations of James and Paul differ, rather than reducing the comparison to a handful of verses on each side. A more adequate comparison also takes into account the multiple ways in which Paul and James agree. They share the common Christian symbolic world, though each shapes it differently. They resemble each other stylistically because they both employ the Greco-Roman diatribe. They are both moral teachers, insisting that intellectual assent or verbal profession must be matched by performance. Note that the vast majority of times that Paul uses the term *ergon* in his letters, it has nothing to do with the Law, but means human actions, and he can speak comfortably of "your work of faith" (1 Thess 1:3). Paul and James also share the symbolic world of Scripture, making it natural for them to speak of "law," and to insist on the need to observe God's law. It is Paul rather than James who says "it is not the hearers of the law who are righteous but the doers of the law who will be declared righteous" (Rom 2:13), and it is Paul rather than James who says that circumcision "counts" if the law is observed but does not if it is transgressed (Rom 2:25-27; see James 2:9-11). Both authors agree, furthermore, that what Paul calls "the righteous requirement of the law" is fulfilled by a living faith that expresses itself in self-donative love. So Paul declares, "In Christ Jesus, neither circumcision matters nor uncircumcision, but faith working itself out through love" (Gal 5:6).

Those discussing the disputed passage in James 2:14-16 also need to recognize the differing context of James from Paul's response to the judaizing faction in Galatians. In that letter, Paul defends the adequacy of faith as God's gift against those who insist on the need to practice circumcision and advocate ritual "works of the law." In contrast, James 2:14-26 is actually the climax of an argument that begins in 2:1 concerning the need to act in a manner consonant with "the faith of Jesus Christ." James does not oppose the "faith of Christ" and "works of law" as soteriological principles, but contrasts an empty belief in God (2:19) with a living faith that expresses itself in deeds of faith. Paul and James both use Abraham as exemplar, and they should not be interpreted in contradiction because they address quite different religious and rhetorical situations. The key verse for understanding the Book of James is 2:22, whose significance can be grasped only if translated quite literally. Speaking of Abraham's offering of Isaac, James declares, "You see that faith was co-acting (or 'co-working') his deeds *(ergois),* and faith was brought to completion out of his deeds *(ergōn)."* Faith never becomes something else. It is perfected as faith by the deeds that it performs. And the point for James is not soteriological but intensely moral. James wants readers to grasp that "the faith of Jesus Christ" must be enacted by the acceptance of the poor in the assembly as well as the rich (2:1-5) and must be expressed by the direct care of those in desperate need (2:14-17). It is ludicrous to suppose that either Paul or James, nurtured by the tradition of Torah, should ever think otherwise.

Although James is influenced by Hellenism, Judaism, Jesus, Paul, and the early Christian movement, he speaks in a manner all his own. No reader of James can mistake his distinctive combination of brevity and elegance in style, his liveliness in dialogue, and his vivid use of metaphor. Precisely because James does not deal with the issues of a specific community but takes on universal problems of community life and, even more, the perennial temptations of the human heart, his voice sounds across the centuries with remarkable freshness and vigor. In places, James is matched for stylistic verve only by his colleague Paul and his near-contemporary Epictetus. One reason why James speaks to readers of every age with such immediacy, however, is not merely a matter of style but a matter above all of moral passion and religious conviction.

Moral and Religious Perspectives in James

The earlier comparison between James and other ancient wisdom writings showed James's distinctive interest in morals rather than manners, in an intentional community rather than a household, in equality rather than authority, and in the community rather than the individual. These perspectives suggest that James stands over against a dominant culture rather than as the champion of a ruling elite or the scribal class within a stable, traditional culture. James's moral teaching opposes behavior that has real socioeconomic expression: "Do not the rich people oppress you and themselves drag you into courts? Do they not blaspheme the noble name that is invoked over you?" (2:6-7). The opposition between rich and poor (1:9-11; 2:1-6) is expressed also as the opposition between the arrogant and the lowly (4:6), the oppressor (2:6; 5:1-5) and the innocent/righteous (5:6). James's eschatological framework gives the opposition great urgency: judgment is coming soon (5:9), when the wicked will be punished (5:1-6) and the righteous will be rewarded (1:12).

These oppositions are matched by other sharp moral contrasts between truth and error (1:18; 1:16), war and peace (3:16–4:2), meekness and anger (1:20-21), envious craving and generous gift-giving (4:1-3; 1:17), hearing the word only and doing it (1:22, 25), forgetting and remembering (1:24-25), perfection and instability (1:4, 6-11, 17, 25). Cognitively, the contrasts express the difference between wisdom (1:5; 3:13) and foolishness (1:26). Religiously, they correspond to the contrast between filthiness and purity (1:21, 27; 4:8), blessing and curse (3:9). Cosmically, James puts in opposition saving and destroying (4:12), death and life (1:15), an "indwelling spirit" (4:5) and one which is earthbound and unspiritual (3:15). Such contrasts fit within a spatial imagery of "above and below," and "rising and lowering." James says that "wisdom from above" comes from God (1:5, 17; 3:15). Receiving it demands human "submission" or "lowering," to which God responds with a "lifting up/exalting" (4:7-10). In contrast, James posits a wisdom from below that is "earthbound, unspiritual, demonic" (3:15; 2:19), sponsored by the devil (4:7). Wisdom from below seeks to elevate humans on their own terms through boasting and arrogance (3:14; 4:6). But just as God raises the lowly (4:10), so God resists the arrogant (4:6; 5:6).

The thematic center for this moral and religious dualism appears in James 4:4, "You adulteresses! Do you not know that friendship with the world is enmity with God? Therefore, whoever chooses to be a friend of the world is established as an enemy of God." James contrasts God *(theos)* and world *(kosmos)* as objects of human commitment ("friendship") and says that humans must choose between them. Such a startling statement makes sense only if we see how James consistently speaks of "world" in negative terms, indeed, as opposed to God, as though "the world" were not a place but rather a system of meaning — or value system — by which people might choose to live (see 1:27; 2:5; 3:6). Such choice is expressed in the Book of James in terms of friendship, which in antiquity involved a serious commitment based on a complete sharing of outlook. To be "friends of the world," then, would mean to share completely its view of reality, its way of measuring value, to be of "one mind" with it.

The best access to James's understanding of "the world" as a measure is found in 3:13–4:3, where he elaborates the logic of envy *(phthonos)*. Envy operates within a view of existence that sees it as a zero-sum game, a closed system of limited resources. Being and worth depend on having. Having more means being more. Having less means being less. By this logic — since there is just so much "having" possible — humans are essentially in competition for resources and for the security and worth they provide. The surest way to succeed is to eliminate the competition. The attitude is expressed by those who boast in their capacity to gain profit (4:13-16). It is expressed even more boldly by those willing to kill innocent people by holding back wages due the workers in their fields (5:1-6), thus realizing the ancient conviction that envy leads to murder *(phthonos phonos)*. But it is also expressed by all the ways in which people seek an advantage in order to assert themselves: by partiality in judgment (2:1-4), by refusal to help others (2:14-16), by judging and slandering others (4:12), by murmuring against them (5:9). To act in such fashion is to show oneself a "friend of the world," a world that excludes God from consideration and is heedless either of God's gift or judgment.

In contrast, Abraham perfectly exemplifies what James means by being a "friend of God" (the title he explicitly applies to Abraham in 2:23). By offering his son Isaac, Abraham accepted God's measure rather than the world's. By the measure of the world, Abraham should have clung to his only and beloved son, especially since Isaac was a gift from God, in order to ensure the blessing that God had promised. But Abraham did not see reality as a closed system of limited possibilities. He listened to the God who is the "giver of every good and perfect gift" (1:17) and was willing to give back a gift to the one who "gives a greater gift" (4:6). To be a friend of God, then, means to see reality as gifted constantly by God, and therefore be open to the possibility of sharing possessions and living a life of communion and cooperation, rather than one of individualism and competition.

James's moral teaching, then, is closely tied to his understanding of reality as defined by God. This leads to a short consideration of James's theology. Readers who tend to identify theology with Christology find James deficient, for, as we have seen, his way of appropriating the faith of Jesus is not christocentric in the manner of Paul or Peter. Readers likewise who think of theology in terms of theory or dialectic find James flat and uninteresting, for he directs everything to practical results. But once readers approach James on his own terms, they find a composition that is among the most "theological" in the New Testament. James constantly speaks of *ho theos* ("God") rather than of Jesus or the Holy Spirit (1:1, 5, 13, 20, 27; 2:5, 19, 23 [2]; 3:9; 4:4 [2], 6, 7, 8), sometimes in apposition to *patēr* ("Father"), as in 1:17, 27; 3:9. Several instances of *kyrios* ("Lord") also almost certainly refer to God rather than to Jesus (1:7; 3:9; 4:10, 15; 5:4, 11). In 108 verses, James has at least 24 direct references to God.

James's characterization of *ho theos* is rich and complex. Like all Jews, he agrees that God is one (2:19), but emphasizes that this God is the living one who makes "demons shudder" (2:19) and is the "Lord of Hosts" who redresses oppression (5:4). God is defined in contrast to human weakness and vice: unlike inconstant humans, God has no change or shadow of alteration (1:17); unlike humans who are seduced by desire, God is not tempted by evil (1:13); unlike humans who rage when wronged, God's righteousness has nothing to do with human anger (1:20). James's positive statements about God assert God's powerful presence to creation and humanity. God is not only light but "the father of lights" (1:17), who expresses God's will by a "word of truth" and — in a deeply paradoxical turn — "gives birth" to humans as a kind of first-fruits of creatures (1:18). God has done so by creating humans in God's own image (3:9).

James's God is not distant and uninvolved with creation. God has revealed "the perfect law of liberty" (2:8-11) and will judge humans on the basis of that revelation (2:12). As James puts it in 4:12, "There is one lawgiver *(nomothetēs)* and judge *(kritēs)*, who is able to save *(sōsai)* and destroy *(apolesai)*." God does not leave humans with only a verbal norm. The word of truth is also an "implanted word" that is able to save their souls/lives *(psychos,* 1:21). God has made a *pneuma* ("spirit") to dwell in humans. God is in control of human affairs (4:15) and declares as righteous and as friends those who show faith (2:23). God reveals Godself above all in mercy and compassion, terms that virtually define God (5:11). God promises the crown of life to those who love God (1:12; 2:5); has chosen the poor by the world's measure to be rich in faith and heirs of the kingdom (2:5); regards true religion as visiting orphans and widows in their distress (1:27), even as

God hears the cries of the oppressed (5:4), raises up the sick (5:15), hears the prayers of those who ask in faith (1:5) rather than wickedly (4:3), and forgives the sins of those who confess them to each other (5:15-16).

This is a God who seeks communion with humans, approaches those who approach God (4:8), raises up the lowly (4:10), and enters into friendship with humans (2:23; 4:4). But God also resists the proud and arrogant who exalt themselves by oppressing others (4:6; 5:6). Above all else, James's God is defined in terms of gift-giving. In 4:6, James derives from Proverbs 3:34 ("God resists the arrogant but gives grace to the lowly") the lesson that "God gives more grace/gift" *(meizona de didōsin charin)*. The characterization cannot be accidental, for James's first statement about God in 1:5 is that God "gives to all simply *(haplōs)* and without grudging *(mē oneidizontos)*." And his most solemn statement appears in 1:17, "Every good and perfect gift comes down from above from the father of lights with whom there is no change or shadow of alteration." The three statements together affirm that God's giving is universal, abundant, without envy, and constant. God is that open-system of giving and reciprocity into which humans have been invited.

Human existence, as James understands it, can be expressed in terms of a story involving God and people as characters. The story's past describes what God has already done: God has created the world and all its creatures, making humans into creation's representatives as those bearing God's own image; God has revealed the "word of truth" in the law, the prophets, and in "the faith of Jesus Christ"; God has implanted in people the "word of truth," and the "spirit," and "wisdom from above." The story also has a future, expressed in terms of how God will respond to human fidelity to covenant: God will reward those who are innocent and enduring, who speak and act according to the "royal law of liberty"; God will punish the wicked oppressors who blaspheme the noble name borne by God's people.

The close link between James's moral teaching and his theology is demonstrated by the way in which theological propositions serve as warrants and premises for moral exhortation. James does not simply juxtapose the two sorts of statements. Instead, the theological always functions as the motivator of the moral. James grounds moral life in the relationship of creatures, and above all humans, with God. These theological grounding statements are conveyed by means of participles (1:3, 14, 22; 2:9, 25; 3:1), *gar* ("for") clauses (1:6, 7, 11, 13, 20, 24; 2:11, 13, 26; 3:2, 16; 4:14), and *hoti* ("that/because") clauses (1:12, 23; 2:10; 3:1; 4:3; 5:8, 11). Thus, it is precisely James's affirmation of God as the constant, universal, and ungrudging giver of all good and perfect gifts that grounds his moral imperative that humans live in a community not of competition but of collaboration.

Given James's moral and religious dualism, which demands of everyone a choice between friendship with the world and friendship with God, the composition's most obvious target are those called "double-minded" (1:8; 4:8), who want to be friends with everyone. In 4:4, James uses language that had been used by the prophets to symbolize apostasy from covenant when he addresses his readers as "adulteresses"; if covenant with God is like a marriage, then breaking covenant is like adultery (see Hos 3:1; Ezek 16:38; 23:45; Isa 57:3; Jer 3:9; 13:27). So James regards double-minded Christians as those who claim to live by the standards of the "faith of Jesus" but daily adopt the values and behavior of outsiders, in a kind of spiritual "adultery." They pray, but they do so in doubt (1:8) or for their own gain (4:3). They meet in assemblies, but there practice discrimination against the poor (2:1-4). They express verbal sympathy for the wretched but give no concrete help (2:14-16). With one side of their mouth they bless God but with the other they curse those created in God's image (3:9). James calls the double-minded to simplicity or purity of heart (4:8). He wants them to choose God as friend and to live consistently with that profession, rather than compromising it by behavior more consonant with the logic of envy.

James's final verses in 5:7-20 sketch his understanding of a community that lives by the "faith of Jesus Christ" and in "friendship with God" in a religion "pure and stainless before God." Not surprisingly, given his attention to the ways speech betrays friendship with the world (above all in 3:1-12), James pays particular attention to the speech of such a community. They are to wait patiently for the coming of the Lord and judgment, resisting the temptation of those under oppression to turn on each other in complaint and murmuring (5:7), standing firm until the end, knowing from the example of all the prophets and of Job how God's compassion is expressed toward those who persevere (5:10-11). They are to be a community that is simple in speech, requiring no oaths to support their affirmations or denials because their lives are transparent both to God and to each other (5:12). They are to be a community of mutual correction, turning those who err back to the right path (5:19-20), in effect doing for each other what James in his letter has tried to do for them. In contrast to the world that lives by the rule of competition that says only the fittest survive, a logic that leads from envy to murder, the church is to be a community of solidarity. The weak member can summon the elders and they will come. Far from avoiding the sick, the community gathers to the sick, touching them with healing oil and praying for them (5:14-15). The community heals itself as well by the mutual confession of sins, using speech not as a weapon of self-assertion and arrogance, but as an instrument of self-revelation and mutual vulnerability (5:16). Above all, the community prays in every circumstance to God (5:13, 16), knowing that "the prayer of the righteous is powerful," and having an example in Elijah of how God responds to the prayer of the righteous (5:17). Those who speak and act in this fashion reveal that they truly believe in the God who gives gifts generously, and live as friends of God.

The Circumstances of Composition

For reasons of convenience, I have collapsed author and composition in this essay, referring interchangeably to "its" and "his" voice. Can we go any further in trying to move from a description of the composition to a determination of the circumstances of its composition? I suggested earlier that interpreting the text from the perspective of a putative author was unhelpful. But is it possible to move from what we have learned from the text to a time, place, readership, and author? Yes, but not very far and not with great certainty. The way to the real readers is blocked above all by the general character of James's moral exhortation. He is certainly detailed enough, but his lively vignettes appear as situations that might apply to all communities, rather than a single church. The address to the "twelve tribes of the dispersion" supports such a generalized sense of the readers. Are they ethnically Jewish? Nothing in the writing demands that identification and nothing in the writing disallows it. As 1 Peter demonstrates, Gentile readers also can be addressed as the diasporic people of God. And as the letters of Paul prove, Gentile readers can also inhabit and understand the symbolic world of Torah. If the readers of James are ethnically Jewish, the author sees no need to touch on matters of circumcision or ritual practice. But for that matter, neither do such Jewish moral exhortations as *Wisdom of Solomon* and *Sentences of Pseudo-Phocylides*.

A better way forward may be to assess the cumulative effect of all our literary and thematic observations. If they have been accurate, they can serve to point us in one direction rather than another. That James was written from within the Christian movement is certain. Whether it was written to Jewish Christians cannot be determined. Can we say whether it was written earlier or later?

The best arguments for dating James as late and pseudonymous rather than early and authentically by James of Jerusalem (Brother of Jesus) are its good Greek and its apparent dependence on the Pauline teaching on righteousness through faith. But research has shown that Greek as good as James's was widely attested by Palestinian Jewish writers. And I hope I have shown that there is no need to make James dependent on Paul. It is at least possible that James preceded Paul, if one insists on a conversation between the two. More plausible is the position that they differed on one point because they addressed different questions and resemble each other on many points because they are both Jewish Christians of the first generation who move intimately and instinctively within the world of Jewish Scripture.

Other reasons for dating a composition late include doctrinal development, a claim to tradition, hostility to heretics, increased institutionalization, adaptation to society, and a reduced sense of eschatology. None of these characterize James. The writings of the late first and early second century that have some resemblance to James in language (especially *1 Clement* and *Shepherd of Hermas*) reveal by the rest of their outlook that they are the heirs rather than contemporaries of this far more vivid and original writing.

Among the positive arguments for dating James as early as the first Christian generation, the least powerful is the appeal to the many small details that seem to reflect a Palestinian setting. These are, in fact, impressive. But a number of them could well have been drawn from Scripture, and need not demonstrate local knowledge. A more compelling reason for placing James in the first generation is its marked resemblance to Paul across a wide range of points. They clearly both occupy the symbolic world of Torah as challenged by the "faith of Jesus Christ" in a manner that disappeared by the end of the first century. Still more impressive is the way James's speech is shaped by the sayings of Jesus. And when we realize that the form of some of the more certain allusions is simpler than the redacted form of the sayings found in the Synoptics, then we appreciate that James may be very close indeed to the formative stage of the Jesus traditions. Finally, there is the moral and religious voice of the composition itself. It is impossible to think of this sectarian, rigorous, egalitarian, counter-cultural voice as coming from any stage of the church's life but the earliest. It is literally impossible to think of a Hermas or Clement or Polycarp speaking in this voice. Finally, then, it is the voice of the composition with which we have to do. It may or may not come from James of Jerusalem. But it is, in any case, an original and compelling witness.

A Survey of the History
of Interpretation of James

Just as the origins of the letter of James are obscure, so also is the history of its early reception. Was the author an apostle and identified as the "brother of the Lord" (Gal 1:19)? Did he write for Jewish Christians? Was the "diaspora" of 1:1 literal or symbolic? Did he write early or late? These questions puzzle us as much as they may have puzzled James's first readers. How and when the church first appropriated James is, in fact, unclear. No official canonical list (such as the Muratorian canon) contained the letter until the late fourth century. Eusebius listed James among the "disputed books," although it was "recognized by most" (*Hist. eccl.* 3.25.3). The Paschal Letter of Athanasius (367) and the Council of Carthage (397), however, included James without any hint of indecision.

Substantive objections to James were not made, and its neglect — if such it was — seems to have been benign. The apparent silence between the letter's composition and canonization is difficult to evaluate. The authors of *1 Clement* and the *Shepherd of Hermas* may have known and used it (cf. *1 Clem.* 10 with Jas 2:23; *1 Clem.* 12 with Jas 2:25; *1 Clem.* 30 with Jas 4:6; *Mand.* 9:11 with Jas 3:15; *Mand.* 3:1 with Jas 4:5). But perhaps all three Christian moralists used common paraenetic traditions. Allusions to James in other extant writings of the second and third centuries are even more difficult to decide. None is sufficiently definite to demand James as the source.

The Alexandrian School under Clement and Origen gave the letter its first explicit literary attention. Clement named James among the founders of Christian Gnosis (*Hist. eccl.* 2.1.3-4) in his *Hypotyposes*, a commentary on "all the canonical scriptures," including the disputed ones (*Hist. eccl.* 6.14.1). According to Cassiodorus's *De Institutione Divinarum Litterarum* 8 (*PL* 70:1120), Clement's commentary included James, even though the extant Latin translation does not contain it. Origen called James an apostle and explicitly quoted from and designated the letter as Scripture (see, e.g., *Commentary on John* xix, 6, *PG* 14: 569; *Homilies on Leviticus* 2, 4, *PG* 12: 41; and the *Commentary on Romans* iv, 8, *PG* 14: 989). After Origen, the letter came into wider use and gained authority, as Jerome put it, "little by little" (*De Viris Illustribus* 2, *PL* 23: 639).

The precritical commentary tradition is sparse. Didymus the Blind, who was also head of the catechetical school, wrote — if we except Clement — the first Greek commentary on James (see *PG* 33). Fragments from Didymus and Chrysostom (see *PG* 64) are also found in the *Catena Graecorum Patrum* (ed. J. Cramer [1840]), together with short scholia from Cyril, Apollinaris (fourth cent.), and others. The *Catena* probably dates from the seventh or eighth century; there is some overlap between it and the full commentaries of the tenth century by Oecumenius of Tricca (*PG* 119) and by the eleventh-century Bulgarian bishop Theophylact (*PG* 125). Cassiodorus made an eleven-paragraph summary of James in Latin in his *Complexiones Canonicarum in Epistolas Apostolarum* (*PL* 70), and the Venerable Bede (673-735) produced a full-length commentary in which he, like his predecessors, placed the letter first among the catholic epistles (*PL* 93). Martin of Legio (d. 1021), Nicholas of Lyra, and Dionysius the Carthusian (1402-1471) continued the Latin commentary tradition. Also extant are two Syriac commentaries. The commentary of the ninth-century Nestorian bishop of Hadatha, Isho'dad of Merv (M. Gibson [1913]), is noteworthy for its brevity, its skepticism concerning the letter's apostolic origin, and the note that Theodore of Mopsuestia (whom Isho'dad calls "the Interpreter") knew nothing of the catholic epistles. More extensive and intelligent is the twelfth-century commentary by Dionysius Bar Salibi (I. Sedlacek [1910]), who also complained of the lack of full commentaries on James.

The precritical commentary tradition, resolutely non-allegorical, treated James very much as moral exhortation. Doctrinal preoccupations occasionally surfaced (see, e.g., Oecumenius [6th cent.] on the Trinity in Jas 1:1, *PG* 119: 456). Particular concern was shown for harmonizing James and Paul in the matter of faith and works (Jas 2:14-26), either by distinguishing the condition of the believer before and after baptism (so Oecumenius and Bar Salibi [twelfth cent.]) or by distinguishing kinds of faith (so Theophylact [c. 1150-1225]). One also finds acute linguistic observations, as when Chrysostom noted the apposite use of *makrothymia* in Jas 5:10 rather than the expected *hypomonē* (see *PG* 64: 1049) or when Bar Salibi commented on the various kinds of "zeal" in Jas 3:14.

The patristic and medieval commentary tradition, therefore, is sparse, interdependent, and remarkably uniform. It is also uninformative concerning the role the letter of James may have played in liturgical, homiletical, or didactic settings. Such uses of the text are particularly important for the history of precritical interpretation, since each explicit application of a text to life involves also an implicit understanding of the text itself (cf., e.g., the citation of Jas 2:13 in the *Rule of Benedict* 64, or the discussion of Jas 2:10 in Augustine, *Letter* 167, *PL* 33: 733). Research into such usage has scarcely begun (see L. T. Johnson, 1995), so our knowledge of the letter's pre-critical reception remains partial.

In the fourteenth through the sixteenth centuries, first the Renaissance, then the Reformation stimulated a transition to a more critical reading of James. Three figures established lines of interpretation that have continued to the present: Erasmus, Luther, and Calvin.

Erasmus provided short comments on the verses of James in his *Annotationes* of 1516. In contrast to earlier commentators, he treated James as he would any other ancient author, raising questions concerning attribution, providing alternative manuscript readings, clarifying linguistic obscurities on the basis of parallel usage, and even suggesting textual emendations (reading *phthoneite* for the difficult *phoneuete* in Jas 4:2). The letter's moral or religious teaching was scarcely dealt with.

Luther wrote no commentary on James but exercised considerable influence over subsequent scholarly interpretation. In the preface to his 1522 German Bible, he dismissed the letter as an "epistle of straw" compared to the writings that "show thee Christ." Luther would therefore not include James among the "chief books" of the Canon, although he admired "the otherwise many fine sayings in him." What was the reason for Luther's rejection? James "does nothing more than drive to the law and its works," which Luther found "flatly against St. Paul and all the rest of Scripture." This is the clearest application of Luther's *sachkritik* (content criticism) within the canon; the disagreement between James and Paul on one point removes James from further consideration. The fact that Jas 5:14 was cited in support of the sacrament of extreme unction did not soften Luther's hostility. In this light, the commentary by the Roman Catholic T. Cajetan in 1532 is all the more fascinating. Cajetan also questioned the apostolicity of James and denied that 5:14 could be used as a proof text for extreme unction. But concerning Paul and James on faith, he diplomatically concluded, "They both taught truly."

In contrast to Luther, Calvin wrote a sympathetic commentary on James in 1551. He found the reasons for rejecting the letter unconvincing and saw nothing in its teaching unworthy of an apostle. Although ready to accept Erasmus's emendation at 4:2, he scoffed at those who found a fundamental conflict between Paul and James on faith and works. As in all of his commentaries Calvin brought great exegetical skill to the text, anticipating contemporary sensitivity to the rhetorical skill of James as well as systematically reflecting over its religious significance.

With the obvious modifications caused by the ever-growing knowledge of the first-century world and the cumulative weight of scholarship itself, the basic approaches established by the Reformation continued to dominate scholarship on the letter. The legacy of Calvin continued in those commentaries that, however learned, focused primarily on James as teacher of the church. An outstanding example is the 1640 commentary by the Puritan divine T. Manton. Fully conversant with past and contemporary scholarship (much of it no longer available to us), Manton's approach remains essentially pious and edifying. The German commentary of A. Gebser (1828) is similar in character. He cited many ancient sources to illuminate the text, but above all he gave such extensive citations from patristic commentaries and discussions that his commentary virtually provided a history of interpretation. This tradition can be said to have continued in the commentaries of J. Mayor (1910³) and F. Vouga (1984). In a real sense these commentaries continued the patristic tradition; the meaningful context for understanding James is the Bible. The strength of this approach is its accommodation to the writing's religious purposes. The weakness is its narrowness and scholastic tendency.

The heritage of Luther continued in the historical approach associated with the Tübingen School, in which James was studied primarily as a witness to conflict and development in the early Christian movement. When such scholars as F. Kern (1838) viewed James as written by Paul's contemporary, they saw it as representing a Jewish Christian outlook in tension with Paul's teaching. When such scholars as F. C. Baur (1853-62, 1875) regarded James as a pseudonymous composition, they understood it as a second-century mediation of the conflict between Peter and Paul. In either case James's discussion of faith in 2:14-26 and its apparent disagreement with Paul became the central point for interpretation. L. Massebieau (1895) and F. Spitta (1896), however, maintained that James represented an entirely Jewish outlook; they considered the Christian elements in the letter the result of interpolation into a pre-Christian writing. This approach continued in those (often "rehabilitating") studies that used Paul as the essential key to understanding James (see J. Jeremias [1955]; D. Via [1969]; J. Lodge [1981]). The strength of this approach is its historical sensibility. The weakness is its tendency to reduce James to a few verses and earliest Christianity to the figure of Paul.

The Erasmian tradition sought to place James explicitly within the language and literature of the Hellenistic world. The pioneering monument was the two-volume *Novum Testamentum Graecum* (1752) of J. Wettstein, who brought together a storehouse of parallel illustrative material from both Greek and Jewish sources, a collection all the more tempting because unsorted. The Jewish side of this approach was developed in the commentary of A. Schlatter (1900), who especially emphasized rabbinic parallels. Mayor (1910) also brought together a rich collection of Hellenistic and Christian material. The commentary by J. Ropes (1916) paid particular attention to the letter's diatribal element and singled out the striking resemblances between it and the Testaments of the Twelve Patriarchs. The Erasmian approach found its greatest modern exemplar in the commentary by M. Dibelius (1976). Dibelius combined the best of previous scholarship and brought to the text an acute sense of the appropriate illustrative material, bringing to bear pagan, Jewish, and Christian parallels that placed James squarely in the tradition of paraenetic literature. Most late-twentieth-century scholarship on the letter either derives from or reacts to this magisterial study (cf. L. Perdue [1981]; Johnson [1995]), although studies have also used more Semiotic (see T. Cargal [1993]) and Rhetorical approaches (see D. Watson [1993]). The strength of the Erasmian approach is its textual focus and comparative scope. Its weakness is its ability to miss James's religious dimension entirely.

These assertions would meet with fairly general consent among scholars: James is a moral exhortation *(protrepsis)* of rare passion whose instructions have general applicability more than specific reference. Although not tightly organized, the letter is more than a loose collection of sayings; the aphorisms in chap. 1 establish themes that are developed in the essays in chaps. 2–5. James's Christianity is neither Pauline nor anti-Pauline but another version altogether. It appropriates Torah as the "law of liberty" as mediated through the words of Jesus. James opposes empty posturing and advocates active faith and love. He contrasts "friendship with the world" (living by a measure contrary to God's) and "friendship with God" (living by faith's measure). He wants Christians to live by the measure they profess, and his persuasion has a prophet's power.

BIBLIOGRAPHY

E. Baasland, "Literarische Form, Thematik, und geschichtliche Einordung des Jakobsbriefes," *ANRW* II 25 (1987) 3646-62. F. C. Baur, *The Church History of the First Three Centuries* (1853-62); *Paul, the Apostle of Jesus Christ* (1875²). T. B. Cargal, *Restoring the Diaspora: Discursive Structure and Purpose in the Epistle of James* (SBLDS 144, 1993). J. A. Cramer, *Catena Graecorum Patrum* (1840). P. H. Davids, "The Epistle of James in Modern Discussion," *ANRW* II 25.5 (1987) 36-45. M. Dibelius, *A Commentary on the Epistle of James* (rev. H. Greeven, Hermeneia; ET 1976). A. R. Gebser, *Der Brief des Jakobus* (1828). M. D. Gibson (ed. and trans.), *Horae Semiticae X: The Commentaries of Isho'dad of Merv,* vol. 4, *Acts of the Apostles and Three Catholic Epistles* (1913). F. Hahn and P. Muller, "Der Jakobusbrief," *TRu* 63 (1998) 1-73. J. Jeremias, "Paul and James," *ExpTim* 66 (1955) 368-371. L. T. Johnson, *The Letter of James* (AB 37A, 1995), including full bibliographic entries for all works referred to in the text and not listed in the bibliography; "The Letter of James," *NIB* (1998), 12:175-225. F. H. Kern, *Der Brief Jakobi* (1838). S. Laws, *A Commentary on the Epistle of James* (HNT, 1980). J. G. Lodge, "James and Paul at Cross-purposes: James 2:22," *Bib* 62 (1981) 195-213. L. Massebieau, *"L'épître de Jacques: Est-elle l'oeuvre d'un Chrétien?"* *RHR* 31-32 (1895) 249-283. T. Manton, *A Practical Commentary or an Exposition with Notes on the Epistle of James* (1640). J. B. Mayor, *The Epistle of St. James* (1910³). L. G. Perdue, "Paraenesis and the Epistle of James," *ZNW* 72 (1981) 241-256. J. H. Ropes, *A Critical and Exegetical Commentary on the Epistle of St. James* (ICC, 1916); "The Greek Catena to the Catholic Epistles," *HTR* 19 (1926) 383-388. A. Schlatter, *Die Briefe des Petrus, Judas, Jakobus, der Brief an die Hebräer* (1900). I. Sedlacek (ed.), *Dionysius bar Salibi in Apocalypsim Actus et Epistulas Catholicas* (CSCO 60, Scriptores Syri 20, 1910). F. Spitta, *Zur Geschichte und Literatur des Urchristentums 2: Der Brief des Jakobus* (1896). D. O. Via, "The Right Strawy Epistle Reconsidered: A Study in Biblical Ethics and Hermeneutics," *JR* 49 (1969) 253-267. F. Vouga, *L'Épître de Saint Jacques* (CNT, 2nd ser., 13a, 1984). D. F. Watson, "James 2 in the Light of Greco-Roman Schemes of Argumentation," *NTS* 39 (1993) 94-121.

The Reception of James in the Early Church

The history of the interpretation of James properly begins with its first use in the Church. Unfortunately, the determination of James's first reception is as obscure as the circumstances of its composition. There is no extant evidence for its early liturgical use. We must therefore rely on the appropriation of James by other early Christian writers. So far as we can tell, Origen was the first to cite James explicitly and as Scripture,[1] although Clement, his predecessor in the Alexandrian Catechetical school, may have devoted a commentary to the letter.[2]

Since both Clement and Origen were sensitive to the differences between what was traditionally received and what was not,[3] the Alexandrian sponsorship of James would seem to argue for some prior period of acceptance, at least in their church. The search for positive evidence of James's having been used, however, runs through the briarpatch of post-apostolic literature. Although there are good reasons for thinking that James was known and used by some of these writings, the problems in reaching certainty are severe.[4] The evidence is obscure. Everything depends on its eval-

---

1. Cf. e.g. *Hom. in Ex.* III,3 (PG 12, 316); VIII,3 (PG 12, 355); *Hom. in Lev.* II,4 (PG 12, 418); *Hom. IV in Ps. XXXVI,*2 (PG 12, 1351); *Comm. in Rom.* IV,1 (PG 14, 961); *Comm. in Joh.* XIX,6 (PG 14, 569).

2. According to Eusebius, *HE* VI,14,1, Clement included "all the canonical writings" in his *Hypotyposes.* The extant Latin translation does not include James. According to Cassiodorus's *De Institutione Divinarum Litterarum* 8 (PL 70, 1120), however, the commentary did include James.

3. Cf. Clement of Alexandria, *Stromateis* I.1, 39-42 (PG 8, 700) and III,13 (PG 8,1193), as well as Origen, *De Principiis* I, 8 (PG 11, 120) and IV, 2, 4 (PG 11, 365). Origen also included James in his list of canonical writings, in *Hom. in Jos.* VII, 1 (PG 12, 857).

4. No serious case can be made for James's influence on the letters of Ignatius or of Polycarp, or the Letter to Diognetus, or the apologetic writings of Theophilus, Justin, and

uation. The proper procedure for the evaluation, however, is not itself clear.

Difficulties

The first difficulty comes from the way these writings generally appropriate and use earlier sources. For the most part, only Old Testament citations are formally introduced,[5] although other "scripture" is alluded to, more or less explicitly.[6] New Testament writings are not usually cited as Scripture.[7] Yet as early as Clement, the appropriation of New Testament writings takes place. Clement obviously knows some form of the Gospel tradition,[8] and both knew and used Paul's First Letter to the Corinthians (to which he *does* explicitly refer),[9] and the Letter to the Hebrews.[10] How do we know a New Testament writing is being used when it is not explicitly cited? Two implicit criteria guide readers to such a decision. First, there is the use of language, theme or imagery found previously (so far as we know) only in the NT writing being used. Second, the use of such language must be sufficiently dense and pervasive to suggest dependence.

The second difficulty is more acute in the case of James than for other New Testament writings. James is a form of moral exhortation (paraenesis) which uses traditions already widely attested in both Greek and Jewish moral literature. From the start, then, James is less idiosyncratic in expression and outlook than a writer such as Paul. To complicate

---

Athenagoras. Neither the apocryphal Acts and Gospels nor the writings from Nag-Hammadi show the slightest trace of James's impress. This leaves the Epistle of Barnabas, Didache, 1 and 2 Clement, The Shepherd of Hermas, and possibly the Testaments of the Twelve Patriarchs.

5. Cf. e.g. 1 Clement iii,1; iv,1; viii,2; xxviii,3; Ignatius, *Magn.* xii,1; Polycarp, *Phil.* xii,1; *Ep.Barn.* iv,14; v,2.

6. Thus 1 Clement xxiii,3 has an otherwise unknown "scripture" concerning the "double-minded," which is also reported by 2 Clement xi,2 as a "prophetic word." Hermas, *Vis.* 11,3 refers to the Book of Eldad and Modad as Scripture. The T12P refer repeatedly to the "Book of Enoch" but in a fashion that corresponds to none of the extant Enoch literature: cf. TReub xiv,1; TJud xviii,1; TNaph iv,1; TBenj ix,1.

7. The introduction of Mark 2:7 as "another scripture" in 2 Clement ii,4 is unusual.

8. Cf. 1 Clement xiii,1-2; xlvii,7-8.

9. The explicit reference to 1 Corinthians is in 1 Clement xlvii,1-3. Traces of 1 Cor can be spotted in xxiv,1; xxxiv,8; xxxvii,5; xlix,5.

10. Clement's use of Hebrews is discussed below; for places where its language is discernible, cf. 1 Clement ix,2; x,1-7; xli,1-2; xvii,1; xvii,4; xxxvi,1-5; xliii,1.

matters further, post-apostolic writings such as 1 Clement and The Shepherd of Hermas are also fundamentally paraenetic in character. It becomes difficult to sort out literary dependence in the strict sense from the natural consonances attendant upon writing in the same genre or using the same *topoi*.[11]

Directions

Commentaries have tended to follow the dominant fashion in this matter. The older tendency in New Testament scholarship was to trace literary dependence in ladder-like sequences. Any recurrent phrase was taken as evidence that an earlier document was being employed as a source.[12] J. B. Mayor's classic commentary illustrates this approach to James's influence on subsequent Christian literature. Mayor sedulously lists every verbal or thematic echo as evidence for James's thoroughgoing impact on the early Church.[13] The weakness of the approach is twofold. Not only does it tend to over-detect literary nuances, and thus lose credibility; it also ignores the point mentioned above: some recurrent elements must be attributed to factors other than literary dependence.

The second tendency in New Testament scholarship has been to invoke broad "traditions" to account for the verbal resemblances between writings. Scholars are now schooled to think in terms of *testimonia* or of *haustafeln* available to both Peter and Paul, rather than in terms of borrowing between them.[14] Paraenesis is another, although much looser cate-

---

11. Cf. my "James 3:13–4:10 and the *Topos περὶ φθόνου*," pp. 183-203 in this volume, esp. n. 33.

12. Thus in O. D. Foster, *The Literary Relations of "The First Epistle of Peter"* (Transactions of the Connecticut Academy of Arts and Sciences 17; 1913), 363-538, James appears as a bridge between Ephesians and 1 Peter. For the method applied to the disputed Pauline letters, cf. A. E. Barnett, *Paul Becomes a Literary Influence* (Chicago: University of Chicago Press, 1941). The approach continues in the work of C. L. Mitton, "The Relationship between I Peter and Ephesians," *JTS* 1 (1950) 67-73, and *idem, Ephesians* (New Century Bible; Grand Rapids: Eerdmans, 1976).

13. J. B. Mayor, *The Epistle of St. James*, 3rd ed. (London: Macmillan and Co., 1910), lxvi-lxxxiv. In the process, of course, Mayor provides an indispensable starting point for essays such as the present one. The real weakness of his approach becomes clear when he tries to show the influence of James on other canonical writings (lxxxv-cix). An obvious premise guiding his evaluation of the data was the conviction that James was among the first of the NT writings, composed before the year 50 (cf. p. cl).

14. Cf. e.g. A. C. Sundberg, "On Testimonies," *NovT* 3 (1959) 368-81; P. Carrington, *The*

gory, to which appeal can be made. In the case of James, the commentary of Dibelius best illustrates this second approach. Although Dibelius recognizes the often startling resemblances between James and Hermas, for example,[15] and although he faithfully notes them throughout his commentary,[16] he will not commit himself to any statement concerning possible influence between the two writings, relying instead on a general appeal to a shared paraenetic tradition.[17] Although this approach provides an antidote to the earlier overconfidence concerning the detection of sources, it has drawbacks of its own. First, it downplays the *specific* ways in which even traditional materials can be used and borrowed. Second, it minimizes how thoroughly and self-consciously literary the Christian movement was from the beginning and continued to be in the allusive writers of the second century.[18]

If a serious case is to be made that James was known and used by second-century writers, full account must be taken of the difficulties. The investigator must be careful not to claim too much (everything resembling James comes from him), or too little (nothing resembling James could possibly have come from him). The argument proceeds best not by way of universal statements, but by way of cumulative probabilities. In judgments of literary dependence, moral certainty is the best we can do.

Primitive Christian Catechism (Cambridge: At the University Press, 1940); D. L. Balch, *Let Wives Be Submissive: The Domestic Code in I Peter* (SBLMS 26; Chico: Scholars Press, 1981). In contrast to Foster's alignment, note how the conviction that Peter used shared community traditions affects the commentary of E. G. Selwyn, *The First Epistle of Saint Peter* (London: Macmillan and Co., 1958).

15. M. Dibelius, *A Commentary on the Epistle of James*, rev. H. Greeven, trans. M. A. Williams (Hermeneia; Philadelphia: Fortress Press, 1976), 31.

16. Cf. e.g. Dibelius, pp. 141, 213, 219.

17. Dibelius, p. 32: "it is probably the case that both writings have at their disposal a relatively large store of paraenetic material which *Hermas* passes on in a reworked condition ('expanded paraenesis') and James in the form of sayings."

18. Dibelius, p. 34: "Virtually nowhere can it be shown that an author is dependent upon Jas. for the simple reason that the concepts contained in Jas. are so unoriginal, and so very much the common property of primitive Christianity. In this the essence of paraenesis shows itself once more." This is, of course, circular reasoning. But the premise drives Dibelius to deny (with sometimes tortuous argument) any specific points of resemblance, or, when forced to acknowledge them, to deny their significance.

Narrowing the Possibilities

No firm case can be built on points of resemblance between James and other early Christian writings that are either too isolated within the later composition, or are too widely attested elsewhere. The phrase "double-minded" *(dipsychos),* for example, is distinctive to James 1:8 and 4:8 within the New Testament canon. But its recurrence in 1 Clement xi,2; xxiii,2-3; 2 Clement xi,2-5 and xix,2; Didache ii,4 and iv,4; as well as the Epistle of Barnabas xix,5-7 does not count for much by itself. The incidence in each document is too scattered, and the possibilities of derivation are too great.[19] In some cases, furthermore, the reference for the term seems different than in James.[20] Other examples include the designation of Abraham as "friend of God" in James 2:23 and 1 Clement x,1; xvii,2,[21] and the ideal of impartiality in judgment in James 2:1, Didache iv,3 and Epistle of Barnabas xix,4.[22] Similarly, an axiom such as "love covers a multitude of sins," which appears in James 5:20 as well as 1 Peter 4:8; 1 Clement xlix,5 and 2 Clement xvi,4, cannot stand as independent evidence that these writings used James.

A more difficult decision involves the common use of a *topos.* James 3:13–4:10 is a call to conversion which uses the hellenistic *topos* on envy.[23] Given the nature of a *topos,* it is not surprising to find 1 Clement's exten-

---

19. On the *possible* antecedents for *dipsychos* (apart from James, who is the first documentary evidence for it), cf. O. J. F. Seitz, "The Relationship of the Shepherd of Hermas to the Epistle of James," *JBL* 63 (1944) 131-140; *idem,* "Antecedents and Significance of the Term 'Dipsychos,'" *JBL* 66 (1947) 211-219; and *idem,* "Afterthoughts on the Term 'Dipsychos,'" *NTS* 4 (1957-58) 327-34. Although Dibelius (actually Greeven) greets Seitz's efforts with approval and dismisses Mayor's contention that James originated the term as silly (indicated by an exclamation point), the fact remains that there is no positive evidence for the term's use before James, and the alternative hypotheses remain only that. See also S. E. Porter, "Is *dipsychos* (James 1:8; 4:8) a 'Christian' Word?" *Bib* 71 (1990) 469-498.

20. In 1 Clement xxiii,2, 2 Clement xi,2, EpBarn xix,5 and Did iv,4, the term *dipsychos* seems to mean doubting prophecies, especially concerning the coming judgment, as Dibelius, p. 83, correctly notes. He errs in assuming 1 Clement xi,2 and 2 Clement xix,2 have the same meaning.

21. For the widespread use of the designation, cf. the documentation in Dibelius, pp. 172-173. The fact that the only thing in Irenaeus that could support dependence on James is the two-fold use of this expression is therefore insignificant (*Adversus Haereses* iv,13, 4; iv,16, 1).

22. The same can be said of other isolated points of contact, however interesting they might be in themselves. The notion of "friendship with the world" in opposition to "friendship with God" (James 4:4), for example, is paralleled by 1 John 2:15-17 as well as 2 Clement vi,3-4. Likewise, the prohibition of oaths in James 5:12 is found also in Justin's 1 Apology 1,16 (as well as in Matt 5:34).

23. Johnson, "James 3:13–4:10," 334-341.

sive discussion of envy (chs. iii–vi) having many points of contact with James. Likewise in the Testament of Simeon, subtitled in the Greek text *peri phthonou,* we discover multiple parallels to James 3:13–4:10.[24] It is certainly possible that the three writings employed the hellenistic *topos* independently. But is it a complete coincidence that all three writings place their discussion in the context of a call to conversion?

Although these sorts of resemblance cannot in isolation carry the burden of proof for dependence, they are not meaningless. Their appearance together with more definite evidence adds to the probability that a particular writing knew and used James.

Positive criteria which data must meet before they can be considered evidence for literary dependence are these: 1) an overall similarity in outlook and in language between the writing in question and James, with at least some of the linguistic parallels distinctive; 2) the parallels come from more than one section of James and appear in more than one part of the later writing; 3) the parallels are sufficiently dense and pervasive to suggest dependence and not simply coincidence.[25]

When these negative and positive criteria are applied, there remain only three writings for which the influence of James can plausibly be argued. In order of their probability, they are The Testaments of the Twelve Patriarchs (T12P), 1 Clement, and The Shepherd of Hermas (Hermas).

The Testaments of the Twelve Patriarchs

It may seem odd to include the Testaments among early Christian works, since the dominant scholarly opinion considers them to be pre-Christian Jewish compositions with Christian interpolations.[26] An older opinion has recently been vigorously argued by M. DeJonge, that from the beginning, T12P was a Christian composition.[27] Whether one agrees with his arguments or not, it is certainly the case that in their present redaction, the

---

24. Johnson, "James 3:13–4:10," 344-346.

25. I am proposing here the same method as that developed in my article, "The Use of Leviticus 19 in the Letter of James," *JBL* 101 (1982) 391-401; see below, pp. 123-135.

26. Cf. e.g. the Introduction by H. C. Kee in *The Old Testament Pseudepigrapha,* ed. J. H. Charlesworth, I: "Apocalyptic Literature and Testaments" (Garden City, N.Y.: Doubleday and Co., 1983) 775-780.

27. M. DeJonge, *The Testaments of the Twelve Patriarchs: A Study of Their Text, Composition, and Origin,* 2nd ed. (Assen: Van Gorcum, 1975), esp. 117-128; and idem, ed., *Studies on the Testaments of the Twelve Patriarchs* (SVTP III; Leiden: Brill, 1975).

TI2P can be considered part of early Christian literature.[28] The parallels to James occur, as we might expect, in the paraenetic sections, and have frequently been noted in passing.[29] Are they sufficiently strong to support a literary dependence moving from James to the Testaments?

There are a number of striking individual points of resemblance. James's saying about mercy and mercilessness in 2:13, for example, is found in two parts, in TZeb viii,3 and TGad v,11. The commandment to love the neighbor (James 2:8) appears repeatedly (TIss v,2; TGad vi,1). As in James 5:7-8, the virtue of long-suffering is praised, using the same somewhat surprising term *makrothymia* (TDan v,8; TGad iv,7; TJos xviii,3).[30] Evil speech *(katalalia)* is opposed as vigorously by TGad v,4 as by James 4:11. The "double-tongue" *(diglōssa)* is said to both bless and curse in TBenj vi,5 as well as in James 3:10-11.

Even more impressive is the overarching symbolism of TI2P and James. Humans are subject to the influence of good and bad spirits (TJud xx,1) that "indwell" them (TSim v,1; TDan v,1; TBenj v,2). Humans can "approach God" (TGad vi,2) or "flee to the Lord," which in turn makes the evil spirit flee (TSim iii,1; iii,5; iv,7). All this is virtually identical to James 4:5-8. As in that passage as well, humans face the choice between the God "who gives grace" (TSim iv,5) and the "error of the world" (TIss iv,6; cf. James 4:4).

The cosmic options are spelled out in terms of ethical behavior. On one side is the spirit of envy (TSim iv,6; iv,7) which leads to murder (TSim iii,3) and war (TSim iv,1; James 4:1-2). Envy has an ally in arrogance *(hyperēphania)*, which opposes God (TJud xiii,2; xviii,3; cf. James 4:6). On the other side are lowliness (*tapeinōsis,* TGad v,3) and simplicity of heart *(haplotēs;* TSim iv,5; TLev xiii,1; TIss iii,4; iv,1) dedicated to the Lord. Every form of doubleness (TAsh iii,1; TBenj vi,7) is contrary to this simplicity.

---

28. Cf. the perceptive remarks on this point as well as a review of scholarship in H. D. Slingerland, *The Testaments of the Twelve Patriarchs: A Critical History of Research* (SBLMS 21; Missoula: Scholars Press, 1977), esp. 91-115.

29. Among commentators, particular attention was paid to the "special affinity" between James and the Testaments by J. H. Ropes, *A Critical and Exegetical Commentary on the Epistle of St. James* (ICC; Edinburgh: T&T Clark, 1916), 20-21; cf. also Dibelius, p. 27, and Johnson, "James 3:13–4:10," pp. 341-344.

30. The same expression occurs in *The Testament of Job* 26.6 and 17.10, in R. A. Kraft, et al., eds., *The Testament of Job* (Texts and Translations 5; Pseudepigrapha Series 4; Missoula: Scholars Press, 1974), 50-52. The usage is striking enough for at least one reader to suppose that James 5:11 used TJob! Cf. B.-A. Wacholder, "Job, Testament of," *Encyclopedia Judaica* (1971), 10:130.

There are some striking linguistic as well as thematic parallels. TSim iv,5 seems to echo James 4:1-6, and TDan vi,2 is identical to James 4:7.

Despite these points of contact, there are good reasons for doubting the dependence of T12P on James. The most obvious is the uncertainty whether this text postdated James. In addition, the elements in T12P that parallel James are swallowed up in a much larger proportion of material dedicated to narrative and eschatological components, as well as ethical emphases not found in James. Finally, the points of contact essentially parallel only one passage in James, 3:13–4:10. As noted above, the most striking resemblance of all is found in the Testament of Simeon which, like James, uses the *topos* on envy.

As a whole, then, the T12P does not adequately meet the second positive criterion, that the parallels derive from more than one part of James. The dependence of T12P on James is possible, but not so likely as the case considered next.

1 Clement

Making a firm judgment on the relationship between James and 1 Clement is particularly difficult because of the number and complexity of factors involved. Here is an author who writes with at least two earlier Christian compositions (1 Cor and Heb) either before his eyes or so much in his memory that he can unmistakably echo their language and theme, yet never explicitly cite them. There are places where Clement's use of Hebrews is obvious, because the content and language could come from nowhere else. A prime example is 1 Clement xxxvi,2, where Clement clearly alludes to Heb 1:3-4. Indeed, his whole passage derives from Heb 1-2. Yet a close comparison of the two texts shows that Clement has used his source with considerable flexibility. He elides phrases, transposes words, adjusts tenses, all without comment. The language of Hebrews has become, for the moment, his language.

On the basis of such certain appropriations, it is possible to state that other places in 1 Clement rely on Hebrews. Although the verbal echoes are not so sharp in 1 Clement ix,2-4, for example, the subjects discussed and the sequence of their appearance make it likely that Heb 11:5-7 is being used. We are also able to detect even fainter echoes scattered through the text, as in 1 Clement xvii,1, *hoitines en dermasin aigeiois kai mēlōtais periepatēsan* which recalls Heb 11:37, *periēlthon en mēlōtais, en aigeiois dermasin.*

The possibility that Clement used James in similar fashion is complicated in three ways. First, the language of James is not nearly so distinctive and easily recognizable as that of Hebrews. Second, both Clement and James use the conventions of paraenesis. Clement could have learned them from James but need not have. As I have shown elsewhere, James uses the image of the mirror in 1:23-24 in a way characteristic of paraenesis: to suggest the themes of memory and of models.[31] The image is carried through when he presents the examples of Abraham, Rahab, Job, and Elijah, by the use of verbs of *seeing*. In 1 Clement xxxvi,2, the metaphor of the mirror is also used. Clement provides examples (v,1; xlvi,i; lx,1; lxiii,1) for his readers to imitate (xvii,1) and remember (vii,1). Throughout 1 Clement as well, the metaphor is carried by the use of verbs of seeing (v,3; ix,2; xix,3; xxiv,1; xxv,1; xxxvi,2; cf. esp. xl and liii). The similarity is certainly strong but not conclusive. Third, some though not all of the material in 1 Clement parallel to James is also found in Hebrews or 1 Peter. Despite all these complications, there are striking points of resemblance.

Some of the parallels, of course, have little independent value. We cannot make too much of the fact that care for orphans and widows appears as a sign of repentance (viii,4; James 1:27), or of the single occurrence of the phrase "double-minded" (xxiii,2-3; James 1:8), or of the note that humans are created in the image of God (xxxiii,5; James 3:9), for these are all too widely attested. Nor can we build a great deal simply on the occurrence of the axiom "love covers a multitude of sins" (xlix,5; James 5:20) or of the citation of Prov 3:34, "God resists the proud but gives grace to the humble" (xxx,2; James 4:6). They appear as well in 1 Peter 4:8 and 5:5. The context of this last citation in Clement will, however, deserve our closer attention.

Of greater significance in Clement is a thematic opposition between arrogance and humility very similar to that in James (see, e.g. ii,1; xiii,1; lix,3). In at least one instance, it takes the form of a strong verbal resemblance. In 1 Clement lix,3, we read, *ton tapeinounta hybrin hyperephanon . . . ton poiounta tapeinous eis hypsos kai tous hypēlous tapeinounta*, which recalls James 4:10: *tapeinōthēte enōpion kyriou kai hypsōsei hymas*. The continuation in 1 Clement, *ton apokteinonta kai zēn poiounta* (lix,3) likewise picks up on James 4:12, *ho dynamenos sōsai kai apolesai*.

1 Clement's wording in other places is very close to that of James. 1 Clement xlvi,5, for example, reads *hinati ereis kai thymoi kai dichostasiai kai schismata polemos te en hymin?* which reflects James 4:1: *pothen polemoi kai*

---

31. L. T. Johnson, "The Mirror of Remembrance (James 1:23-25)," *CBQ* 50 (1990) 623-645; see below, 168-181.

pothen machai en hymin? The resemblance is strengthened by the fact that (as noted below) 1 Clement iii–iv so closely parallels James 3:13–4:10, yet this verbal echo occurs outside that passage. Another striking example: James 3:13 has *tis sophos kai epistēmos en hymin? deixatō ek tēs kalēs anastrophēs ta erga autou en prautēti sophias.* This is matched both in form and theme by 1 Clement xxxviii,2: *ho sophos endeiknysthō tēn sophian autou mē en logois all' en ergois agathois.* Although any of these points of contact can be dismissed when taken in isolation,[32] account should be taken of their cumulative effect.

When examining 1 Clement's use of Hebrews, we saw that passages in which there was a high density of verbal and thematic similarity provided the best basis for detecting Hebrews' influence. In 1 Clement, there are three such clusters.

The first is Clement's condemnation of the Corinthians' envy (iii–vi). Here we find a large collection of verbal and thematic parallels to James 3:13–4:10: envy causes social unrest and war (iii,2; vi,4); through envy death came into the world (iii,4); envy causes the murder of brethren (iv,7). These parallels lose some of their distinctiveness because they are found consistently in the hellenistic *topos* on envy. On the other hand, as in the case of TSim, 1 Clement follows the condemnation of envy with a call to repentance in vii,2–viii,5, a combination found elsewhere only in James.

The second set of similarities comes in the treatment of Abraham.[33] The more obvious point of dependence here would be Hebrews, for Clement lists Abraham among heroes of faithful obedience, beginning with Enoch and ending with Rahab (ix,2–xii,8), and introduces the list with language strongly reminiscent of Hebrews 11. Close inspection shows that Clement does not follow Hebrews slavishly. In the case of Abraham, Lot, and Rahab, Clement goes into considerably more detail, and uses the biblical text directly, with multiple citations from Genesis and Joshua.

Is there any indication of a dependence on James in this pastiche? The most interesting deviation from Hebrews is the designation of Abraham as "friend of God" (x,1), which is repeated in xvii,2 (cf. James 2:23). James and Clement both cite Gen 15:6 *verbatim*, whereas Hebrews cites Gen 15:5 but not 15:6 (Heb 11:12). Abraham is praised by Clement for his "faith and hospitality" (x,7), which is carried through the examples of Lot (xi) and

---

32 Cf. Dibelius's dismissal: "The admonition to the wise in I Clem xxxviii,2 resembles James 3:13 more in form than in content" (p. 33). If we had to choose, in fact, the opposite would be the case.

33. 1 Clement xvii,3-4 mentions Job as well, but there is no reason to suspect any influence of James 5:11. The treatment of Rahab in 1 Clement xii is equally close to James 2:25 and Heb 11:31.

Rahab (xii). This emphasis is closer to James's point than to Hebrews'.[34] All three include the sacrifice of Isaac (James 2:21; 1 Clement x,7; Heb 11:17), but only Clement adds in xxxi,2: *tinos charin ēulogēthē ho patēr hēmōn Abraam, ouchi dikaiosynēn kai alētheian dia pisteōs poiēsas?* Not only does this recall James 2:21: *Abraam ho patēr hēmōn ouk ex ergōn edikaiōthē,* but it follows immediately (and serves as exemplar for) the exhortation in xxx,3: *ergois dikaioumenoi, mē logois,* which, in the overall context of James 2:14-26, captures perfectly the sense of *ex ergōn dikaioutai anthrōpos kai ouk ek pisteōs monon* (James 2:24).

A final passage in 1 Clement contains a cluster of parallels to James. It begins in xxix,1, with the exhortation to approach God in holiness of soul and with pure hands raised to him (cf. James 4:7-8). There then follows in 1 Clement xxx,1-5, this sequence: they are to flee evil speech (*katalalia,* James 4:11), evil desire (*epithymia,* James 4:2), adultery (*moicheia,* James 4:4), and arrogance (*hyperēphania,* James 4:6). Then Clement cites Prov 3:34, "God resists the arrogant but gives grace to the lowly" as does James 4:6. More interesting, Clement picks up on the "God gives grace" as does also James 4:6a, and follows with the exhortation to be "lowly-minded" (*tapeinophronountes;* cf. James 4:6).

Clement then again forbids evil speech (*katalalia,* James 4:11), with the statement that they should be justified by deeds and not by words (xxx,3; James 2:24). Clement continues with an exhortation to brevity in speech (xxx,5; James 1:26), and concludes with the statement that whereas arrogance is cursed by God (cf. James 4:16), God blesses gentleness (*epieikeia,* James 3:17), humility (*tapeinophrosynē,* James 4:10), and meekness (*prautēs,* James 3:13). As pointed out above, the example of Abraham as one who shared in this blessing of God by working righteousness and truth through faith is then cited (xxxi,1-2). This is a sequence of thirteen items with the highest degree of thematic and verbal similarity between James and 1 Clement.[35]

Some doubt may remain, but the probability is that Clement knew and used James. The parallels are found in concentrated clusters as well as in scattered verbal echoes. They match in outlook as well as theme. They are found throughout 1 Clement, and are taken from more than one part of James. Even taking into account the generic character of paraenesis

---

34. Cf. R. B. Ward, "The Works of Abraham: James 2:14-26," *HTR* 61 (1968) 283-290.

35. Dibelius's discussion of this passage (pp. 32-33) is so dominated by the false issue of whether Clement was responding to a Pauline teaching that the real pertinence of this sequence of similarities is missed.

and the presence of the same *topos* in both writings, the combination of ethical and religious language is remarkably similar. And in the case of I Clement, the fact that at least two other New Testament writings are used in the same flexible and acknowledged fashion strengthens the argument that he used James.

The Shepherd of Hermas

The resemblance in outlook, theme, and language between James and Hermas is unmistakable. Dibelius paid particular attention to the similarities between James and the *Mandates* section of Hermas,[36] which made his refusal to acknowledge any real dependence all the more puzzling.[37] The evidence, in fact, is considerably stronger than was recognized by Dibelius, and extends beyond the *Mandates*.[38]

Hermas' use of *dipsychos* (cf. James 1:8; 4:8) in all possible forms (even making a verb of it) is extensive.[39] Opposed to double-mindedness is sim-

36. "Here there is found a kinship which goes beyond lexical and conceptual agreement. Extensive and coherent discussions in *Hermas* could be placed alongside isolated admonitions in James and serve as a commentary on the latter" (Dibelius, p. 31). For his emphasis on the *Mandates,* cf. p. 3.

37. So regularly does Dibelius undercut the evidence for literary dependence between James and Hermas, sometimes even at the cost of logic, that the suspicion grows that his own theories of dating and authorship might be having as much influence on his conclusions as did Mayor's premise of an early dating on his conclusions. Despite his denying all other forms of literary dependence in the name of paraenesis, we notice that Dibelius insists that James 2:14-26 is "not conceivable prior to Paul" (p. 23), and "presupposes an acquaintance with definite pauline slogans" (p. 29). Dibelius places the date of James between 80 and 130 (p. 45), which militates against its use either by Clement or Hermas. Dibelius concedes "which [date] of course could be substantially reduced if it were possible to prove that I Clement is dependent on James" (p. 46). He has, of course, made that determination impossible. As for Hermas, Dibelius is consistent if not altogether intelligible. If Hermas can be an "expansion of paraenesis, its application to specifically Christian situations, and at least the Christianization of its framework and arrangement of the traditional materials" (p. 46), why could it not do that in dependence on James as much as on the vague "circumstances of the second century," whatever they were?

38. The study of C. Taylor, "The Didache Compared with the Shepherd of Hermas," *Journal of Philology* 18 (1890) 297-325, includes in pp. 320-325 a helpful analysis of the way Hermas appropriates materials from James.

39. *Vis.* iii,2, 2; iii,3, 4; iii,4, 3; iii,10, 9; iv,1, 4; iv,1, 7; iv,2, 6; *Mand.* ix,1-5; ix,7; ix,9; ix,11; x,2, 2; xi,1; xi,13; xii,4, 2; *Sim.* i,3; vi,2; vii,1; viii,3-5; viii,9, 4; viii,11, 3; ix,18, 3; lx,21, 2. Precisely the extravagance of this use reveals the relatively minor point made by Seitz (cf. note 19, above). Of much greater importance is the larger pattern of use.

plicity *(haplotēs)*.[40] In James 1:5, it is used only of the quality of God's generosity, but the term captures precisely what James means by *adiakritos* (3:17) or "purity of heart" (4:8). In Hermas, as well, the terms are interchangeable. Thus, *Mand* ix,4: *katharison sou tēn kardian apo pantōn tōn mataiōmatōn tou aiōnos toutou* (cf. also *Mand* ix,7) is equivalent to *Mand* ii,7, *en haplotēti heurethē kai kardia sou kathara kai amiantos*.[41] As in James as well, the idea of cleansing the heart is part of the response of repentance, which is perhaps the major theme of Hermas as a whole.[42] Thus, *metanoēsēte . . . hē kardia hymōn genētai kathara kai amōmos* (*Vis* iv,2, 5). Conversion means turning from double-mindedness to simplicity and purity of heart.

The pattern of repentance fits within a cosmological framework virtually identical in substance and expression to that of James. Humans are intimately related to the cosmic forces, represented by God and the Devil. As in James, the "pneumatology" of T12P is focused on these single personified powers. In an exact parallel to James 4:5, *Mand* iii,1 has *to pneuma hō ho theos katoikisen en tē sarki tautē* (cf. also Sim v,6, 5 and v,7, 1). And as in James 4:7, it is the Devil who is to be resisted. The Devil is responsible for double-mindedness (*Mand* ix,9), but need not be feared (*Mand* xii,4, 7). If resisted, he will flee: *ean oun antistathēte autō nikētheis pheuxetai aph' hymōn katēschymmenos* (*Mand* xii,5, 2).[43] Compare James 4:7: *antistēte de tō diabolō, kai pheuxetai aph' hymōn.*

As in James as well, the choice between God and Devil is expressed spatially by the contrast between "from above" and "earthly." *Mand* ix,11 has *hē pistis anōthen esti para tou kyriou kai echei dynamin megalēn. hē de dipsychia epigeion pneuma estin para tou diabolou, dynamin mē echousa.* Compare James 3:15: *ouk estin hautē hē sophia anōthen katerchomenē, alla epigeios, psychikē, daimoniōdēs.* This contrast between "faith" and "wisdom" can be expressed likewise in terms of "spirit," as in *Mand* xi,14: *to pneuma to epigeion.*[44] The choice can also be expressed, as in James 4:4, in terms of "God" and "this world": *hosoi an katharisōsin heautōn tas kardias apo tōn mataiōn epithymiōn tou aiōnos toutou kai zēsontai tō theō* (*Mand* xii,6, 5).[45]

Within this cosmological (religious) framework, the ethical concerns of the two writings are also similar, at times identical. The problem of

---

40. *Vis.* ii,3, 2; iii,1, 9; iii,8, 5; iii,9, 1; *Mand.* ii,1; ii,4, 6; v,2, 2; *Sim.* ix,15, 2; ix,24, 3; ix,31, 4.

41. Cf. also *Vis.* iii,2, 2; *Mand.* iv, 1; iv,4, 3; xii,6, 5; *Sim.* iv,4, 7; v,3, 6; viii,11, 3.

42. Cf. e.g. *Vis.* iv,2, 5; v,7; *Mand.* iv,1, 8-10; iv,2, 2-4; vii,6, 1; and many times more.

43. Cf. also *Mand.* iv,4; vi,2, 7; xii,2; xi,3.

44. Cf. also *Mand.* xi,8; xi,11-12; xi,21.

45. Cf. also *Vis.* iv,3, 2-4; *Sim.* iii,2; v,3, 6; vi,1, 4.

wealth and poverty for Christians pervades both compositions.[46] In James, three aspects of the subject are emphasized: that wealth and poverty are transvalued in the light of faith (1:8-12; 2:5-7); that those involved in the affairs of business lose sight of God's will (4:13-16); and that the luxurious rich have oppressed the poor and can expect to be punished for it in God's judgment (2:6; 5:1-6). Hermas has the same three emphases. First, *ho men plousios echei chrēmata, ta de pros ton theon ptōcheuei* (*Sim* ii,5). Second, those wrapped up in business "and many other occupations of the world" (*Mand* x,1, 4) "also sin much" (*Sim* iv,4, 5).[47] Third, those who live luxuriously must beware *mēpote stenaxousin hoi hysteroumenoi, kai ho stenagmos autōn anabēsetai pros ton kyrion*. This last is very close to James 5:4. It is therefore the more striking that the passage is introduced with *blepete tēn krisin tēn hyperchomenēn* (*Vis* iii,9, 5), just as the corresponding passage in James is followed by *hē parousia tou kyriou engiken . . . ho kritēs pro tōn thyrōn hestēken* (5:9). As in James 1:27, furthermore, the proper use of wealth is spelled out in terms of "visiting orphans and widows" (*Sim* i,8).[48]

In a manner very similar to James 4:11, Hermas condemns evil-speech: *prōton men mēdenos katalalei mēde hēdeōs akoue katalalountos* (*Mand* ii,2). James 3:16-18 connects envy to war and civil unrest; Hermas attributes them to evil-speech in remarkably similar language: *ponēra hē katalalia. akatastaton daimonion estin. mēdepote eirēneuon, alla pantote en dichostasiais katoikoun* (*Mand* ii,3). Evil-speech is a manifestation of double-mindedness (*Sim* viii,7, 21).[49]

Hermas places the same sort of emphasis on "long-suffering" (*makrothymia*) as does James 5:7-10: *ean gar makrothymos esē, to pneuma to hagion to katoikoun en soi katharon estai* (*Mand* v,1, 2).[50] Indeed, in a statement that picks up the same notion of "complete faith" as in James 1:4, we read in *Mand* v,2, 3: *hautē oun hē makrothymia katoikei meta tōn tēn pistin echontōn holoklēron*. The notion of "perfecting faith" in turn (James 1:2-4) occurs in *Mand* ix,10: *hē gar pistis panta epangelletai, panta teleioi, hē de dipsychia mē katapisteuousa heautē pantōn apotynchanei tōn ergōn autēs hōn prassei*.

We have made the transition from the language characteristic of moral discourse to that appropriate to the religious life of the Christian community. Again, we find that Hermas has if anything even more strik-

---

46. Dibelius's sketchy treatment of this issue (p. 32) is confused, with no attention to specific texts.

47. Cf. also *Sim.* ix,20; vi,2, 2; vi,4, 1; vi,5, 4.

48. Cf. also *Mand.* viii,10; *Sim.* ix,26, 2; ix,27, 2.

49. Cf. also *Sim.* ix,23, 2-3; ix,26, 7.

50. Cf. also *Mand.* v,1, 1; v,1, 3; v,1, 6; *Sim.* viii,7, 6; ix,15, 2.

ing agreements both in emphasis and in terminology. In James, faith is closely tied to the effectiveness of prayer; double-mindedness impedes prayer (1:5-6; 4:3; 5:17-18). *Mand* ix,1-4 exactly parallels James 1:5-8: *aron apo seautou tēn dipsychian kai mē holōs dipsychēsēs aitēsasthai ti para tou theou . . . aitou par' autou adistaktōs . . . ean de distasēs en tē kardia sou, ouden ou mē lēpsē tōn aitēmatōn sou . . . houtoi eisin hoi dipsychoi.*[51] *Sim* iv,6, in turn, parallels James 4:3: *pōs, phēsin, ho toioutos dynatai ti aitēsasthai para tou kyriou kai labein, mē douleuon tō kyriō?*

When James speaks of the rich oppressing members of the community in 2:7, he says, *ouk autoi blasphēmousin to kalon onoma to epiklēthen eph' hymas?* The expression "noble name" is unusual, and Dibelius lists it as one of the touches that marks off James's distinctive Christian character.[52] It is all the more striking to find Hermas, then, speaking of apostates from the church in this fashion: *kai blasphēmēsantes en tais hamartiais autōn ton kyrion. eti de kai epaischunthentes to onoma tou kyriou to epiklēthen ep' autous* (*Sim* viii,6, 4; cf. also *Sim* ix,14, 6).

Concerning the power to give life, Hermas and James express the same sentiments in similar language. James exhorts: *dexasthe ton emphyton logon ton dynamenon sōsai tas psychas hymōn* (1:21). Concerning the commandments (*entolai*) *Sim* vi,1, 1 has, *kai dynamenai sōsai psychēn anthrōpou.* In James 4:12, judgment against a neighbor is forbidden with this warrant: *heis estin nomothetēs kai kritēs ho dynamenos sōsai kai apolesai.* In *Mand* xii,6, 3, we read: *phobēthēte ton panta dynamenon sōsai kai apolesai, kai tēreite tas entolas tautas kai zēsesthe tō theō* (cf. also *Sim* ix,23, 4).

Perhaps the most intriguing points of resemblance are these last, because the sentiments expressed in James are seemingly so distinctive, yet are so clearly paralleled in Hermas. James 4:17 condemns sins of omission: *eidoti oun kalon poiein kai mē poiounti, hamartia autō estin.* In *Mand* viii,2, we find: *ean gar enkrateusē to agathon mē poiein, hamartian megalēn ergazē* (cf. also *Sim* x,4, 3). James concludes his letter with a command of mutual correction: *ean tis en hymin planēthē apo tēs alētheias kai epistrepsē tis auton, ginōsketō hoti ho epistrepsas hamartōlon ek planēs hodou autou sōsei psychēn autou ek thanatou* (James 5:19-20). In *Mand* viii,10 there is this command: *eskandalismenous apo tēs pisteōs mē apoballesthai, all' epistrephein kai euthymous poiein, hamartanontas nouthetein* (cf. also *Sim.* x,4, 3 and *Vis.* ix,10).

51. Dibelius, p. 31, calls *Mand.* ix "the best interpretation of James 1:5-8 imaginable," but cavils over the use of a different word for doubting!

52. Dibelius, p. 23. In his discussion of James 2:7, however (pp. 140-141), he makes reference to Hermas's usage without noting that, of all the texts cited, it is the only one to replicate the *onoma epiklēthen*.

Hermas meets all the criteria for deciding in favor of dependence. It shares outlook, themes, and language with James. The similarities are found throughout Hermas, though they are densest in the Mandates. And Hermas uses material from every chapter in James.[53]

Conclusions

Some might object that this essay has reverted to the older style of proving dependence by lining up points of similarity. In fact, the method here has been more rigorous and the conclusions more modest. It is not, after all, claiming a great deal to say that the Testaments could have used James, Clement probably did use James, and Hermas did use James. Given all the literature produced by Christians in the second century, this is not an inflated claim for James's influence. The argument here does, however, put the burden of proof on those who would wish to deny any knowledge or influence of James before Origen.

The case here has been made by the cumulative effect of probability that makes for moral certainty. One can dispute any of the points made, or any series of them. But the cumulative impact, especially when consideration is given to the differences in circumstance, genre and purpose, is substantial. It should especially be noted that the points these writings have most in common are not the commonplaces of hellenistic moral teaching. And if James was not used by T12P, Clement and Hermas, what other writing, Jewish or Christian, antecedent to them, offered just these possibilities in just this language? There is none. James is the obvious and available cause for the effects we have observed.

We can safely conclude, therefore, that if James did not enjoy wide usage in the late first and early second century, he was read and appreciated by some few authors, whose appreciation was shown by their adaptation of his moral teaching for new circumstances.

---

53. We have given close verbal parallels from Hermas to these passages in James: 1:2-4; 1:5; 1:6; 1:8; 1:10; 1:21; 1:27; 2:5; 2:7; 3:8; 3:13; 3:15; 3:16; 4:4; 4:5; 4:7; 4:8; 4:11; 4:12; 4:13-17; 5:4; 5:5; 5:7; 5:9; 5:10; 5:19-20.

Journeying East with James:
A Chapter in the History of Interpretation

This essay is the report of a journey, not across continents or oceans, but through a great body of literature.[1] Paul Theroux, our generation's premier writer of travelogues, reveals the risks as well as the pleasures of the genre.[2] How can the writer know the trip is worth writing about before taking the trip, and how can the journey be experienced in a way that makes writing about it worthwhile? The present expedition is motivated by the desire to better understand the history of biblical interpretation, specifically that concerning the small New Testament writing called the Letter of James.

Largely under the influence of Luther, much of the history of interpretation of this letter since the sixteenth century has revolved around the alleged contradiction between Paul and James on the issue of faith and works, and because of the privileged place given to Paul within critical New Testament scholarship, James's place within earliest Christian literature became for many scholars ever more problematic.[3] A widely used Introduction to the New Testament took up "the theological problem" posed by the "irreconcilable conflict between James and Paul."[4] In what is

---

1. This article originated as one of the Carmichael-Walling Lectures delivered in November 1995 at Abilene Christian University. An abbreviated form of the argument and a small portion of the evidence appear in L. T. Johnson, *The Letter of James* (Anchor Bible 37A; New York: Doubleday, 1995). My thanks to Mark Pitts for his preliminary scouting of the territory, and to Patrick Gray for his help with this form of the paper.

2. Among many others, see *Riding the Iron Rooster: By Train through China* (New York: G. P. Putnam's, 1988), and *The Pillars of Hercules: A Grand Tour of the Mediterranean* (New York: G. P. Putnam's, 1995).

3. For this history, see Johnson, *The Letter of James*, 140-161.

4. W. G. Kümmel, *Introduction to the New Testament*, rev. ed., trans. H. C. Kee (Nashville:

unquestionably this century's most influential commentary on James, Martin Dibelius asserts that only a handful of Greek, Latin, or Syriac commentaries are devoted to this composition and that they were of undistinguished character.[5] An easily received impression is that James was marginal throughout all of Christian history and deserved the demotion it received from Luther. A journey undertaken through such a wasteland would necessarily be a dull one indeed.

The impression of such complete emptiness, however, itself causes one to wonder: did no one in all those centuries treasure James and use it? But if they did, why is there so little evidence for such appreciation? Part of the problem is the way we define biblical interpretation. To a large extent, the history of interpretation is identified with the writing of biblical commentaries. But that equation results from an unexamined bias of critical scholarship. In commentaries, the text is the explicit problem that requires "explaining"; the commentator's task is to solve the textual problem so that the composition is more intelligible. Commentaries both ancient and modern tend to be written by scholars with scholarly preoccupations concerning language, consistency, and coherence. However awkwardly, commentaries — even so-called "pre-critical" ones — fit precisely the understanding of "interpretation" held by critical scholars.

But what would happen if we were to broaden our definition of interpretation? What if we were to consider all the ways in which biblical texts were used in communities of faith throughout the centuries, all the ways biblical texts found their way into compositions other than commentaries: letters, sermons, theological treatises, polemical tractates, hagiographies, monastic rules, and liturgical books? In such *uses* of the text we might find a vast collection of clues as to what the text could "signify" for

---

Abingdon, 1975), 414-416. See also the comment of M. Hengel, "Providentia Dei hat die frühe Kirche in Paulus, nicht in Jacobus *den ἀπόστολος* gesehen," in "Der Jakobusbrief als antipaulinische Polemik," in *Tradition and Interpretation in the New Testament*, ed. G. F. Hawthorne and O. Betz (Grand Rapids: Eerdmans, 1987), 264.

5. M. Dibelius, *A Commentary on the Letter of James,* rev. H. Greeven, trans. M. Williams (Hermeneia; Philadelphia: Fortress Press, 1976), 51-57. Dibelius's treatment of any subject repays close study, because he packs so much learning into such small space. On some subjects he also shows good knowledge of patristic materials, although it is less certain how much derives from direct reading and how much from the highly developed German commentary tradition before him. A. R. Gebser's *Der Brief des Jakobus* (Berlin: Ruecker, 1828), for example — which Dibelius uses frequently — made excellent if far from adequate use of patristic materials.

the believers who cited it. Here it would not be the biblical text which was regarded as problematic and in need of explicit attention, but rather some aspect of life which required interpretation in light of the biblical text. By applying passages to some aspect of the life of faith, however, authors thereby also implicitly interpreted the biblical text itself. Their citations and applications reveal the potential for meaning they considered the biblical text to possess, and in a more spontaneous fashion than could the commentaries of scholars.

The collection of clues is potentially vast, because patristic literature is a continent far larger than the Talmud, and for most biblical scholars it is a territory largely unmapped. Fifteen hundred years of Christian literature lies between the composition of the New Testament and the Reformation. Most of this literature used the Bible with frequency and vigor. The obvious and almost overwhelming problem is how to get any control over such a body of material. In this very respect, however, the Letter of James appears as the perfect research instrument. Because James is small in size and surely not on anyone's list of the central writings of the New Testament, its use should be traceable with relative ease, and provide a manageable amount of data for analysis. This, then, was the impetus for my journey through patristic literature. By examining the uses of the letter of James in Christian writings I hoped to gain a better sense of its significance within the life of the church over a period of fifteen hundred years, and contribute to the history of biblical literature by correcting the narrow focus on the commentary tradition, thus perhaps also expanding the concept of "interpretation" itself.

Outfitting the Journey

There is really only one point of departure for the sort of trip I wanted to take: the great 19th-century collection of ecclesiastical writings published under J. P. Migne, the *Patrologia Graeca* and *Patrologia Latina* which combine to make a set of some 430 volumes. The texts in Migne are rarely critical editions, and those that are have been superseded by later efforts.[6] The

6. Among the collections of patristic critical editions, cf. *Die Griechischen Christliche Schriftsteller der Ersten Jahrhunderte* (Leipzig: 1897-); Corpus Christianorum. Series Latina (Tournolt, 1953-); *Corpus Scriptorum Ecclesiasticorum Latinorum* (Vienna, 1866-); *Corpus Scriptorum Ecclesiasticorum Orientalium* (Louvain, 1903-). All of these series are still in progress with the end not in sight. The series that produces critical editions for all languages, together with copious notes and translations into French, is *Sources Chrétiennes*. The series

process of making better critical editions, unfortunately, is not only slow but always begins with writings everyone regards as "important." For better or worse, Migne remains the essential source for the majority of patristic texts. The collection is arranged chronologically. All the writings attributed to a particular author, spurious or not, are grouped together. Reading Migne from end to end is indeed much like a trip through many centuries and across several lands.

I chose to begin with the Greek writers rather than the Latin for three reasons: first, it is a smaller collection; second, I was interested in how people who continued to speak and write in Greek would read the Greek of James; third, I knew that Western writers from the time of Augustine and Pelagius would inevitably be caught up in the problem of faith and works, and wanted to see if Christian literature in the East was similarly preoccupied. My method of research could not be simpler. The Greek volumes in Migne lack a cumulative Scripture index, but the editors carefully footnoted, page by page, the biblical citations and allusions that they spotted in the text. All I had to do was mindlessly go through each page of the 164 volumes, ending up with some 64 pages filled with some 800 references to verify and analyze in context.

Travel Problems

Like an ambitious train trip that must deal with delays and missed connections, this research expedition through the *Patrologia Graeca* had some technical problems. The most obvious was the difficulty in determining what really was a citation from James and what was only an allusion, or perhaps even a commonplace that may ultimately have derived from James but was no longer clearly connected to it. The obvious example is James 4:6, which reads, "God opposes the proud but gives grace to the humble" (RSV). No line from James is found more frequently in the patristic writings, occurring some forty-seven times.[7] The problem, though, is that James himself is quoting from Proverbs 3:34.[8] Of all the times this

---

began appearing in 1947, and by 1987 had published 339 volumes, but these represent only a tiny fraction of what appears in Migne.

7. The line is introduced in a variety of ways, sometimes with no introduction, thus perpetuating its "proverbial" character.

8. The LXX of Prov. 3:34 reads *kyrios*, while James 4:6 reads *theos*. The majority of patristic uses have *theos*, which may account for the editors' choice of James as source. The problem is further complicated in two ways. First, *kyrios* and *theos* frequently get exchanged both in

line occurs in the patristic writings, indeed, only *once* does the writer himself attribute it to James.[9] Despite such authorial reticence, the editors of Migne attribute it to James every time, so relentlessly that one wonders whether they knew of its occurrence in Proverbs, or of its use also in 1 Peter 5:5! From the context, I was sometimes able to determine to my own satisfaction that in fact the allusion was to James,[10] and at other times that it probably was not.[11] The case of James 4:6 shows how each occurrence needs to be examined individually. It also helps explain the notorious unreliability of even the best scriptural indices.[12] Fortunately, the editors of Migne erred on the side of over-attribution, although even they missed some.[13] Concerning James 4:6, we can be certain that it expressed a sentiment dear to the Greek authors; whether in every case they knew it came from James cannot be proven.

Speaking of citations, one of the diversions on this journey was the variety of ways in which quotations from James were introduced. The first writer to cite James unequivocally and by name is Origen of Alexandria (184-254). He refers to "the letter which circulates under the name of James"[14]

---

the LXX and NT manuscript tradition. Second, Proverbs 3:34 is also quoted by 1 Pet 5:5, once more using *theos*. The difficulty is illustrated in the earliest occurrence, in Clement of Alexandria's *Stromateis* III, 6, 52 (PG 8: 1152). Attacking Gnostics who claim a deeper understanding of the gospel when they forbid marriage, Clement says *legei de autois hē graphē hyperēphanois ho theos antitassetai tapeinois de didōsin charin*. The order of words is slightly different from the LXX, James, or 1 Pet. Yet the use of the NT would seem likely here because every other citation in this chapter is from the NT — except for several from Proverbs (PG 8: 1159)!

9. Antiochus Monachus, *Homilia* XLIV (PG 89: 1573), attributes the passage to James, but in this case the citation uses *kyrios* rather than *theos*.

10. See Origen, *Homilia in Ezechielem* IX, 2 (PG 13: 734); John Chrysostom, *In Psalmum C*, 4 (PG 55: 634); *In Publicum et Pharisaeum* 2 [spurious?] (PG 59:600); Nilus the Abbot, *Epistulae* I, CXLVI (PG 79: 144) — a full and acute reading of the passage in its Jacobean context — and Cyril of Alexandria, *Homilia Paschalis*, XIV, 2 (PG 77: 713). Eusebius, *Commentarium in Psalmos* LXXIV, 7-9 (PG 23: 872), is also possible.

11. See, e.g., Basil, *Commentarium in Isaiam* V, 143 (PG 30: 589); *De Humilitate* 6 (PG 31: 536); *Regulae Brevis Tractatae* XXXV (PG 31: 1105). In *De Consolatione in Adversis* 2, Basil introduces the saying in this fashion, "You find written in Proverbs," yet Migne credits it to James (PG 31: 1699). Cf. also Gregory Nazianzen, *Contra Julianum* I (PG 35:559); Eusebius, *Commentarium in Isaiam* XXIV, 3 (PG 24: 260); Procopius of Gaza, *Commentarii in Isaiam* XIII, 12-16 and XXIV, 1-25 (PG 87: 2084 and 2197), and many others.

12. The *Biblica Patristica* (Paris: Editions du Centre National de la Recherche Scientifique, 1975), 524-525, illustrates the problem. It attempts a complete listing of scriptural citations up to Tertullian, but the majority of entries for James are at best doubtful.

13. The reference to James 2:20 in Philippus Solitarius's *Dioptra* I (PG 127: 712) is missed by the editor, even though it begins the entire treatise.

14. *Commentarium in Johannem* XIX, 6 (PG 14: 569).

and "the brother of the Lord"[15] and "James the Apostle."[16] He even introduces quotations from James as "Scripture."[17] Each author after Origen has his favorite designation. Cyril of Alexandria, for example, prefers the sobriquets "Disciple of Christ"[18] and "Disciple of the Savior."[19] The title "brother of the Lord" is found already in Paul (Gal 1:19).[20] By the time of John Chrysostom in the fourth century, however, it is elevated to "Brother of God" *(adelphotheos)*.[21] Such a dramatically elevated status must be attributed to the Christological controversies of the fourth and fifth centuries which led to an emphasis on the divinity of Christ almost to the loss of his humanity. By an application of what was called the *communicatio idiomatum* (exchange of characteristics), James can be called "brother of God" just as Mary can be called the "mother of God *(theotokos)*."[22] In the Byzantine period, in fact, James's personal exaltation accelerates,[23] until he is termed by one writer simply as "God's brother" *(theadelphos)*.[24] Those who so advanced

15. *Commentarium in Epistulam ad Romanos* IV, 8 (PG 14: 989).

16. *In Exodum Homilia* III, 3 and VIII, 4 (PG 12: 316 and 355); *In Leviticum Homilia* II, 4 (PG 12: 419); *Commentarium in Epistulam ad Romanos* IV, 8 (PG 14: 990), and many times more.

17. *Commentarium in Epistulam ad Romanos* IV, 1 (PG 14: 961); Origen speaks of "divine scripture" when referring to James 5:20, *In Leviticum Homilia* II, 4 (PG 12: 418). He uses the simple name "James" in *Selecta in Psalmos* CXVIII, 153 (PG 12: 1621), and the periphrastic "it is said," *Commentarium in Epistulam ad Romanos* II, 13 (PG 14: 908), "it is written," *Selecta in Psalmos Homilia* III in Ps. XXXVI, 11 (PG 12: 1347), and "it is read," *Selecta in Exodum* XV, 25 (PG 12: 288).

18. *De Adoratione in Spiritu et Veritate* XII (PG 68: 836) and XIV (PG 68: 925-28); *Commentarium in Lucam* VI, 37 (PG 72: 600).

19. *De Adoratione in Spiritu et Veritate* XII (PG 68: 820); *Commentarium in Amos Prophetam* XXXVII (PG 71: 481); *Commentarium in Malachiam Prophetam* XXI (PG 72: 312); *In Epistulam ad Romanos* VIII, 26 (PG 74: 825).

20. The title is used as well by Epiphanius of Salamis, *Epistola ad Johannem* VI (PG 43: 389); Hesychius of Jerusalem, *In Leviticum* IV, 13, 1-7 (PG 93: 930); Athanasius Sinaitus, *Viae Dux* VIII (PG 89: 123); John the Faster *Sermo de Poenitentia* (PG 88: 1920).

21. John Chrysostom, *De Poenitentia* Homilia IX (PG 49: 343); *In Psalmos* CXVIII, 159 (PG 55: 704). Cf. also Gregory Agrigentius, *Explanatio Ecclesiastae* III, 27 (PG 98: 904-905) and V, 4 (PG 98: 965); Theodorus Studitae, *Sermo* LXXXIV (PG 99: 619); Symeon Metaphrastae, *Vita S. Johannis Eleemosynarii* IV, 23 (PG 114: 917); Theophylact of Bulgaria, *Enarratio in Evangelium Marci* VI, 12-13 (PG 123: 549).

22. See Denziger-Schoenmetzer, *Enchiridion Symbolorum* 93 and 139, for examples.

23. Niles the Abbot calls him "great James," *Epistulae* II, CLIX (PG 79: 276); "Holy James," *Epistulae* III, CLXVII (PG 79: 462), and "divine *(theios)* James," *Epistulae* III, CCXXVIII (PG 79: 489). The epithet "divine" occurs also in Caesarius of Cappadocia, *Dialogus* I, 2 (PG 38: 857); Cyril of Alexandria, *Commentarium in Malachiam Prophetam* V (PG 72: 285); Theodorus Studitae, *Sermo* LXVIII (PG 99: 601); Eustratius, *Vita S. Eutychii* (PG 86: 2285); Nicetas Paphlygonis, *Oratio* XX (PG 105: 452).

24. Cf. Symeon of Thessalonica, *Expositio Sacri Symboli* (PG 155: 788 and 804).

his status did not, however, necessarily know or use James more apprecia-
tively. The opposite seems to be true: the weightier the designation the
lighter the use. In some cases, in fact, the author mistakes James for another
writer.[25]

Another sort of difficulty can be mentioned in passing, one that
seems to be an inevitable consequence of rapid travel. Reading only citations of James across this vast literature is a bit like travelling through Eu-
rope and eating only at McDonalds. The sense of repetition and sameness
is unavoidable. The difficulty reminds us that it is impossible to assess the
relative importance of the James citations in a particular writer without
analyzing that same writer's overall use of Scripture, a task considerably
greater than that undertaken by this essay.

Impressions of the Territory

Before reporting on the specific use of James in these patristic writings, I
want to convey three overall impressions of the territory traversed. It is,
first of all, a remarkably stable world. Although the literature was produced in many lands across a span of fifteen centuries, it is all recognizably
part of the same hellenistic culture that despite the vicissitudes of external
events changed internally very little. The Greek language itself remains an
astonishingly steady medium of expression. The overall sensation of permanence, even of fixity, is enhanced by the way later writers continue to
speak of their predecessors, sometimes writing hundreds or even a thou-
sand years before them, as though they were contemporaries.[26] Perhaps in-

---

25. John Chrysostom knew the Letter of James well, yet in the very passage where he
calls its author "brother of God," he cites from 1 Jn 3:18 rather than from James, *In Psalmos*
CXVIII, 159 (PG 55: 704). Later writers make more frequent mistakes. Johannes Xiphilinus
attributes 2:13 to a saying of Jesus, *Orationes post Ascensionem* (PG 120: 1228); Euthymius
Zigabenus attributes 2:26 to "the great Paul," *Commentarium in Marcum* XVI, 18 (PG 129:
849); Theodorus Balsamonis attributes both 2:26 and 1:19 to "Paul the Apostle," *In Epistolam
S. Basilii Canonicam* II, 45 (PG 138: 721) and *Epistola de Rasophoris* 1 (PG 138: 1360). Gregory
Palamas even attributes James 4:4 to Paul, *De Mentali Quietudine* (PG 150: 1056).

26. So naturally does this occur that only occasionally is one jarred by the realization
that Clement of Alexandria, in his *Stromateis,* for example, is citing, extolling, or rebutting
authors (such as Plato and Aristotle) who lived some six centuries before him. Another example: Leo Philosophus, the Roman emperor in 911 (not "Holy Roman Emperor," who is a
barbarian), has his *Orationes* included in Migne, among them one "In Praise of St. John
Chrysostom," who was bishop in Constantinople five hundred years before, *Oratio* XVIII
(PG 107: 228). It is, of course, another feature of that world strange to present-day readers,

evitably, this complex and self-referential literature fell into decline. After John of Damascene, the lack of intellectual rigor is obvious.[27] The Greek Christian writers become primarily preservers rather than creators.

Second, this world is a thoroughly *scriptural* one. No gap is acknowledged between the biblical narrative and empirical reality. The biblical history is the earlier portion of the writers' own story. The chasm between the perceived world and the biblical world which is so fundamental to Western post-enlightenment interpretation is simply not present.[28] All of Scripture, furthermore, is divinely inspired. Because God is the true author of the texts, there cannot be a genuine or fundamental contradiction between them.[29] Apparent contradictions at the literal level can be harmonized by appealing to the spiritual meaning. The spiritual meaning is not always "allegorical"; it can be simply "the intention of the divine author."[30]

Third, the Scripture is construed more as a set of divine oracles than as a collection of compositions. The human authorship and the differences between writings in the collection are never denied. But at the level of spontaneous usage, Scripture functions as a reservoir of oracles.[31] The

---

that the emperor should meddle in religious affairs; see also Emperor Justinian's *Tractatus Contra Monophysitas* written to the monks of Alexandria after 527 (PG 86: 1116). Finally, one notes the perdurance of certain literary forms. The *Loci Communes* of Maximus the Confessor in the mid-seventh century (PG 91) and the *Sacra Parallela* of John Damascene in the mid-eighth century (PG 94) and the *Loci Communes* of Antonius Melissa in the mid-twelfth century (PG 136) are all the same basic work, and they continue the tradition of Greek secular literature reflected in the collections of *topoi* such as Stobaeus's *Anthologium Graecum* (also of the sixth century).

27. A pertinent example is the kind of mistaken scriptural attribution discussed in note 25.

28. See especially H. Frei, *The Eclipse of Biblical Narrative: A Study in Eighteenth and Nineteenth Century Hermeneutics* (New Haven: Yale University Press, 1974), esp. 14-85.

29. Symeon Metaphrastae refers to James as "divinely inspired Scripture," *Certamen S. Martyris Callinici* IV (PG 115: 481), as does Cyril of Alexandria in *De Adoratione in Spiritu et Veritate* VI (PG 68: 472). Cyril expresses the general sentiment when, in his commentary on Romans, he opposes James to Paul and then asks rhetorically, "Do the divinely inspired men speak against each other?" His subsequent argument shows that in fact they do not, *In Epistulam ad Romanos* IV, 2 (PG 74: 781). He again states a general perception concerning Scripture when he calls James the "unlying disciple of the Savior," in *Johannis Evangelium* I, 9 (PG 73: 140).

30. As in Origen, *Commentarium in Epistulam ad Romanos* II, 13 (PG 14: 908).

31. As in Nilus the Abbot, *Peristeria* IV, XV (PG 79: 845): "according to the divine oracle." The perception is revealed and strengthened by such periphrastic introductions as "the mystic doctrine handed down to us," Didymus Alexandrinus, *De Trinitate* II, 6, 6 (PG 39: 524), and "voice of the saint," Cyril of Alexandria, *Commentarium in Amos Prophetam* XV (PG 71: 440); Cyril of Alexandria, *In Johannis Evangelium* X (PG 74: 349).

atomistic conception of the text enables the practice of proof-texting in all its fascinating forms. God speaks in every sentence and in every part of every sentence. The human author's "original intention" and a statement's original literary context are often not considered and are seldom primary. On the other hand, proof-texting is rarely arbitrary. It is governed by conventions of creed or communal practice. Every hermeneutical game has its rules.[32]

Journeying with James

Who Used James?

Two groups of Christian authors made James a favorite source for citations. The evidence overwhelmingly suggests that churches aligned with Alexandria in Egypt used it most vigorously. And wherever they were, monks also made James one of their scriptural resources.

The Alexandrian connection is impressive. It is uncertain whether Clement, the second head of the famous catechetical school in Alexandria, used James.[33] His successor, Origen, was Christianity's first great theologian. Origen listed James in his canon[34] and cited him frequently.[35] After Origen and under his influence, the Alexandrian church made heavy use of James. We have, for example, only a few fragments from the Alexandrian teachers Dionysius, Peter and Alexander, but the extant frag-

32. The elements noted here are remarkably similar to those identified by James L. Kugel in *The Bible As It Was* (Cambridge: Harvard University Press, 1997), 17-23.

33. According to Eusebius, *Historia Ecclesiastica* VI, 14, 1, Clement included "all the canonical writings" in his *Hypotyposes*; and Cassiodorus, *De Institutione Divinarum Litterarum* (PL 70: 1120) says that this included James. The extant Latin translation, however, does not include it. As for citing James, it is certain that Clement never does so by name, even though he does cite by name 1 Pet, 1 Jn, Jude, and the Apocalypse; cf. N. LeNourry, *Dissertatio Secunda de Libris Stromatum* IV, 3 (PG 9: 1094-95). In note 8, I discuss Clement's possible use of James 4:6 in *Stromateis* III, 6, 52 (PG 8: 1152). The only other allusion that could seriously be argued as deriving from James is found in Clement's discussion of righteousness in *Stromateis* VI, 18, 13-14 (PG 9: 397), where his use of *basilikoi* seems to point to James 2:8. Other allusions, as to the "friend of God" (James 2:23) in *Paedagogus* III, 2, 40 (PG 8: 573); III, 8, 25 (PG 8: 613); and *Stromateis* II, 5, 82 (PG 8: 952) could equally be derived from Philo. The decision, however, is difficult. In *Stromateis* IV, 17-18, Clement of Alexandria quotes extensively from 1 Clement (PG 8: 36-86). Could the knowledge of James have reached Alexandria through that connection?

34. Origen, *In Librum Jesu Nave* Homilia VII, 1 (PG 12: 857).

35. For Origen's manner of citation, cf. notes 14-17, above. In his extant writings, Origen cites James some 36 times, referring to 24 verses from every section of the letter.

ments from each author contain references to James.[36] The first extant commentary on James comes from still another head of the catechetical school, Didymus the Blind (313-398).[37] The great theologians and polemicists Athanasius and Cyril found in James an important collection of theological proof-texts. Cyril cites James more frequently than any other Greek ecclesiastical writer.[38]

Next to Alexandria in the use of James are the churches of Palestine, most notably that of Jerusalem.[39] Since by tradition James was the first Bishop of the Jerusalem church, the favor shown him there is perhaps no surprise. Sophronius, Patriarch of Jerusalem from 634, is particularly proprietary, referring to "James, the brother of the Lord, who was once pastor of this flock,"[40] and in another place introducing a citation from "James, the brother of the Lord, and first holder of this seat."[41] This attention to James may also owe something to the strong influence exerted in Palestine by Origen.[42]

---

36. Dionysius Alexandrinus, *Commentarium in Lucam* XXII, 46 (PG 10: 1596); Alexander of Alexandria, *Acta Sincera Sancti Petri* (PG 18: 466).

37. Didymus Alexandrinus, *Enarratio in Epistolam Beati Jacobi* (PG 33: 1749-1754). Didymus quotes James in his theological writings and other scriptural expositions some 23 times, using 16 separate verses.

38. Athanasius (296-373) included James in his influential canonical list (PG 26: 1177). He published a short summary of James in his *Synopsis Scripturae Sanctae* VI, 52 (PG 28: 405-408), and cited James 20 times in addition, using 12 separate verses. Cyril of Alexandria (d. 444) cited James some 124 times, using 39 separate verses. His favorites were James 3:2 (16 times) and 1:17 (16 times). Cyril also contributed heavily to the *catena* with his *scholia* on James; cf. *Catenae Graecorum Patrum in Novum Testamentum,* ed. J. A. Cramer, VIII, Catena in Epistolas Catholicas (Oxford: Oxford University Press, 1840). Among other Alexandrian authors, special mention should be made of Euthalius the Deacon, who issued an edition of catholic epistles ca. 459. For James, he included an interpretive summary of the letter and an analysis of James's Scripture citations (PG 85: 676-677).

39. Cyril of Jerusalem (315-86) includes James in his canonical list in *Catechesis IV De Decem Dogmaticis* 36 (PG 33: 499). Others having their origin in Palestine and using James frequently are Procopius of Gaza (PG 87); Sophronius Patriarch of Jerusalem (PG 87); John Climacus (PG 88); Zachary the Rhetorician (PG 85); Andrew of Jerusalem (PG 97); Hesychius of Jerusalem (PG 93); Epiphanius of Salamis (PG 41-43); John Damascene (PG 94-96); Antiochus Monachus (PG 89); Zachary Patriarch of Jerusalem (PG 86); and Dorotheus, Archimandrite of Palestine (PG 88).

40. *Oratio* I (PG 87: 3206-3207).

41. *Oratio* V (PG 87: 3304).

42. Origen spent the latter part of his life in Caesarea. Pamphilius of Caesarea (240-309) was his ardent student, and in turn was the teacher of Eusebius of Caesarea (260-340), whose admiration for Origen is amply demonstrated in *Historia Ecclesiastica* VI. In *HE* III, 25, 3, Eusebius lists James among the disputed books of the NT rather than among the univer-

Not every regional church shared the Egyptians' enthusiasm for James. The letter is scarcely used at all by Athanasius's Cappadocian colleagues in the fight for orthodoxy. Gregory of Nyssa never mentions James. Gregory of Nazianzen lists James in his canon, but does not quote him.[43] And in all of Basil the Great's voluminous writings, there are only a handful of references to James.[44] Basil's neglect of James is all the more strange since he was a monk and moralist whose sermons should have found ready ammunition in James.[45] The lesson here seems to be that formal recognition does not necessarily lead to enchantment, and that there is always some difference between any author's official canon and real canon.

There is even reason to think that some authors slighted James because he was such a favorite with the Alexandrians. To understand this, we must remember the fierce competition during the fourth and fifth centuries between the theological schools located in the rival patriarchates of Alexandria and Antioch. If the Alexandrians favored the divine side of the salvific equation, the Antiocheans leaned toward the human side. Each thought the other went too far, indeed, all the way to heresy. The more fervently the Alexandrians quoted James in favor of their theological positions, the less attractive James would likely appear to those opposing such positions. There is extant evidence that the great leader of

---

sally acknowledged books. In his other writings, he cites James only rarely, but he does not cavil concerning its status, calling him "the holy apostle" when introducing 5:13, *Commentarium in Psalmos* LVI, 2 (PG 23: 504), and "the scripture" when alluding to 4:11, *ibid.*, C, 5 (PG 23: 1244), and he uses James 5:16 to make an important linguistic point in *De Ecclesiastica Theologica* III, 2 (PG 24: 976).

43. Gregory of Nazianzen (329-389) lists James as the first of the catholic epistles in his *Carminum Liber I Theologica* Sect I (PG 37: 474) and in *Carminum Liber II Historica* Sect II (PG 37: 1597-1598). His allusions to James 4:6 in *Oratio IV Contra Julianum* I (PG 35: 559) and *Oratio XXIII De Pace* III (PG 35: 1156)and *Oratio XLIII in Laudem Basilii Magni* (PG 36: 569) may well not refer to James but to Proverbs 3:34. He appears to refer to James 2:20 "faith without works is dead" in *Oratio XXVI* (PG 35: 1233) and *Oratio XL* (PG 36: 425), but does not mention James by name, and in both cases the phrase appears as an axiom rather than a citation.

44. In addition to the possible allusions to James 4:6 discussed in note 11 above, Basil the Great (330-379) cites James, but not by name, in *Sermo de Contubernalibus* 8 (PG 30: 824) and *Constitutiones Monasticae* XXVI, 1 (PG 31: 1416). He quotes James 2:10 as from "James the Apostle" in *De Baptismo* I, 3 (PG 31: 1529), and James 1:2-3 as from "James in the canonical letter" in the (possibly spurious) *De Consolatione in Adversis* 2 (PG 31: 1689).

45. Most surprising is the fact that Basil finds no use for James in sermons that develop themes identical to those central to James, for example *Quod Deus non est Auctor Malorum* (PG 31: 329-354); *De Invidia* (PG 31: 371-386); *De Invidia et Malevolentia* (PG 32: 1336-1346). Neither does he find a place for James in his *Moralia* (PG 31: 699-870), which cites Scripture for themes so dear to James as temptation and persecution.

the Antiochean school, Theodore of Mopsuestia (350-428), at the very least did not like James, and perhaps even rejected it from the canon.[46]

Monks — who are always moralists — also loved the letter of James, whether they lived in the desert of Egypt, the countryside of Palestine, or the capital city of Constantinople.[47] John Chrysostom (347-407), for example, is usually associated with the Antiochean school, yet because he is fundamentally a moralist and preacher he uses James enthusiastically[48] and even composed a commentary.[49] Monks appreciated James because, like him, they were concerned with the practical living out of Christian ideals. They found in him a clear and challenging support for flight from the world of sin, repentance, the giving of alms, and control of anger and of the tongue.[50]

46. Leontius of Byzantium in his *Contra Nestorianos et Eutychianos* III, 14 (PG 86: 1365) says that Theodore excluded James and the other catholic epistles from his canon. Leontius therefore compares him unfavorably to Marcion, since he truncated the New as well as the Old Testament. Leontius is writing in the sixth century. His opinion may find support in the ninth-century Syriac commentary of Isho'dad of Merv, Bishop of Hadatha, who says regarding all the catholic letters, "Theodorus also, the Interpreter, does not even mention them in a single place; nor does he bring an illustration from them in one of the writings he made; although we see that he brings illustrations not only from the books that are written by the Holy Ghost; but also from the book about Job, and from the Great Wisdom, and from Bar Sira, those that are written by human learning." Cf. *Horae Semiticae X: The Commentaries of Isho'dad of Merv*, ed. and trans. M. D. Gibson, Vol. IV, Acts of the Apostles and Three Catholic Epistles (Cambridge: University Press, 1913), 36. For a sensitive treatment of Theodore's Christology, cf. A. Grillmeier, *Christ in the Christian Tradition* (London: A. R. Mowbray, 1965), 338-368; For his exegetical method, cf. R. A. Greer, *Theodore of Mopsuestia: Exegete and Theologian* (Westminster: The Faith Press, 1961), 86-111.

47. Of monks who made significant use of James, the representation from Egypt is understandably large: Antony (PG 40); Isaiah (PG 40); Serapion (PG 40); Orsiesius (PG 40); Macanus (PG 34); Palladius (PG 65); and Zosimus (PG 78). Others who are either monks themselves or who write for monks are Antiochus Monachus (PG 89); Andrew of Jerusalem (PG 97); Niles the Abbot (PG 79); John Damascene (PG 94); John Climacus (PG 88); and Pachomius (PG 98).

48. Chrysostom quotes James some 48 times, using 20 separate verses.

49. *In Epistolam Sancti Jacobi* (PG 64: 1040-1052).

50. Some outstanding examples: Athanasius, *De Virginitate* (PG 28: 269); Orsiesius, *Doctrina de Institutione Monachorum* XXXI, XLI, and L (PG 40: 883, 887, and 891); Antony, *Sermones ad Monachos* 19 (PG 40: 975), and *Epistola* I, V (PG 40: 980); Isidore of Pelusium, *Epistularum Liber* I, XCIII (PG 78: 248) and II, CLVIII (PG 78: 613); Johannes Carpathius, *Capita Hortatoria* I, 86, Ad Monachos in India (PG 85: 807); Antiochus Monachus, *Homilia (passim)* (PG 89: 1445-1832); Nilus the Abbot, *Epistulae* Lib. III, 73 (PG 79: 421-424); Hyperechius, *Ad Monachos Exhortatio* (PG 79: 1477); Maximus the Confessor, *Loci Communes (passim)* (PG 91: 768-957); Georgius Monachus (Harmartolus), *Chronicon Breve* IV, 251 (PG 110: 928); Antonius Melissa, *Loci Communes (passim)* (PG 136: 769-1212).

How Was James Used?

Patristic biblical interpretation is often thought to be dominated by allegory. I found no evidence that the text of James itself was ever allegorized, although in its literal sense James was sometimes used in allegorical readings of Old Testament texts.[51] The literal sense, however, is put to many uses. Not surprisingly, readers found in this wisdom writing statements of general validity concerning the human condition. James 3:2, "we all fail in many ways," for example, becomes a proverb to be invoked in all the obvious contexts.[52]

In fact, James 3:1-2 provides a fine example of the sort of verse-splitting that is frequent in our authors. As a whole, it reads, "Let not many among you become teachers, my brothers, knowing that we are subject to greater judgment. We all fail in many ways. If anyone does not fail in speech then he is a perfect man able to control the whole body." It is a coherent statement, but rarely if ever is it quoted in full by the patristic writers. Instead, "Let not many become teachers" serves as a general warning for communities.[53] "We all fail in many ways" is applied to human frailty and sinfulness, but not to that of teachers. And the statement about controlling the tongue has its own separate applications.[54]

---

51. See, e.g., Cyril of Alexandria on Ps. 103:15-22 in *De Adoratione in Spiritu et Veritate* XIV (PG 68: 925-928); Origen on James 1:15, *In Leviticum* XII, 3 (PG 12: 538); James 4:6 in *Homilia in Ezechielem* IX, 2 (PG 13: 734); Ezekiel 44:9 is interpreted by Origen according to "allegorias leges" in order to explicate James 2:17 and Romans 2:26-27 in *Commentarium in Epistulam ad Romanos* II, 13 (PG 14: 908). Origen even uses James 1:2 to legitimate the generation of allegorical readings, *In Genesin Homilia* VIII, 10 (PG 12: 209). The most elaborate allegorical uses of James are found in Hesychius of Jerusalem, *In Leviticum* (PG 93: 819-1090).

52. See Origen, *Selecta in Psalmos Homilia IV in Ps. XXXVI*, 2 (PG 12: 1351); Alexander of Alexandria, *Acta Sinceri Sancti Petri* (PG 18: 453-466). It is one of Cyril of Alexandria's favorite verses from James. He refers to it regarding the weakness of human nature in *De Adoratione in Spiritu et Veritate* XV (PG 68: 949) and 14 other times. Cf. also Procopius of Gaza, *Commentarii in Leviticum* XI, 2 (PG 87: 727); Theodorus Studitae, *Epistulae* II, 22 (PG 99: 1188); Arethae of Cappadocia, *Commentarium in Apocalypsin* V (PG 106: 536); Oecumenius of Tricca, *Commentarium in Epistulam I ad Corinthios* III, 12-15 (PG 118: 676); Theophylact of Bulgaria, *Liber de Iis Quorum Latini Incusantur* 16 (PG 126: 248); *Expositio in Prophetam Oseam* I, 7 (PG 126: 585).

53. Cyril of Alexandria, *De Adoratione in Spiritu et Veritate* IV (PG 68: 328); *Commentarium in Lucam* V, 41 (PG 72: 604); *Commentarium in Lucam* XII, 41 (PG 72: 752); *In Johannis Evangelium* Proem (PG 73: 9); Isidore of Pelusium, *Epistularum Liber I* XCIII (PG 78: 248); Procopius of Gaza, *Commentarii in Numeros* XXX, 3 (PG 87: 881); John Damascene, *Sacra Parallela*, R, II (PG 96: 329).

54. Athanasius, *Expositio in Ps. CXVIII* (PG 27: 1208); Caesarius of Cappadocia, *Dialogus*

73

Another text is frequently used for discussions of human frailty. James 1:15 says, "desire when it conceives gives birth to sin and sin when it is grown brings forth death." The statement locates responsibility for human sin in free choice and in concupiscence.[55] By so doing, it relieves God of direct responsibility for sin. The immediately preceding passage in James says, "Let no one when he is tempted say, 'I am tempted by God,' for God cannot be tempted with evil and himself tempts no one. Each one rather is tempted when he is lured and enticed by his own desire" (James 1:13-14).[56] The principle that God does not tempt humans to evil can be employed for such troublesome passages as the testing of Jesus before his death.[57]

James, however, creates the possibility for confusion when he states at the beginning of his letter, "Count it all joy, brethren, if you fall into various testings" (1:2),[58] and a bit later, "Blessed is the man who suffers testing" (1:12).[59] The difficulty, camouflaged by the English translation but

---

III, 140 (PG 38: 1073); Cyril of Alexandria, *In Isaiam* V, 4 (PG 70: 1301); *Fragmenta in Epistolam I Beati Petri* (PG 74: 1013); Procopius of Gaza, *Commentarium in Isaiam* LVIII, 1-21 (PG 87: 2597); Hesychius of Jerusalem, *De Temperantia et Virtute* II, 24 (PG 93: 1520); John Damascene, *Sacra Parallela*, C, XV (PG 95: 1345); Antiochus Monachus, *Homilia* XXII (PG 89: 1501); Maximus the Confessor, *Alia Capita* 18 (PG 90: 1405); *Loci Communes* Sermo XV (PG 91: 813).

55. Origen, *In Leviticum* XII, 3 (PG 12: 538); Athanasius, *Vita et Conversatio S. Antonii* 21 (PG 26: 873); Cyril of Alexandria, *De Adoratione in Spiritu et Veritate* I (PG 68: 148-149); *In Isaiam* I, II, 21 (PG 70: 93); *In Johannis Evangelium* IV, VII (PG 73: 689); Didymus Alexandrinus, *De Spiritu Sancto* 41 (PG 39: 1070); Mark the Hermit, *De Baptismo* (PG 65: 1001); Procopius of Gaza, *Commentarii in Leviticum* XIII, 2 (PG 87: 733); Sophronius of Jerusalem, *Oratio V in Exaltatione S. Crucis* (PG 87: 3304); Hesychius of Jerusalem, *Fragmenta in Psalmos* L, 7 (PG 93: 1202); Olympiodorus of Alexandria, *In Beatum Job* XXXI, 9-10 (PG 93: 324); John Damascene, *Sacra Parallela*, A, XII (PG 95: 1157); Christopher of Alexandria, *Homilia Cui Vita Humana Sit Similis* V (PG 100: 1220).

56. See Didymus Alexandrinus, *De Trinitate* II, 10 (PG 39: 641); Cyril of Jerusalem, *Homilia in Paralyticum* XVII (PG 33: 1152); Epiphanius of Salamis, *Adversus Haereses* III, 2, 59 (PG 42: 753); Palladius, *Apophthegmata Patrum:* De Abbate Sisoe (PG 65: 405); Cyril of Alexandria, *De Adoratione in Spiritu et Veritate* XV (PG 68: 981); Hesychius of Jerusalem, *In Leviticum* I, III, 6-17 (PG 93: 819); John Damascene, *Sacra Parallela*, A, IX (PG 95: 1113); Photius, *Bibliotheca* CCLXXX (PG 104: 345).

57. Dionysius Alexandrinus, *Commentarium in Lucam* XXII, 46 (PG 10: 1596). Origen insists that when God "tests" it is for good rather than for evil, citing James 1:13 in *Selecta in Exodum* XV, 25 (PG 12: 288).

58. The text is cited in straightforward paraenetic fashion by Origen, *In Genesin Homilia* VIII, 10 (PG 12: 209); Basil (spurious?), *De Consolatione in Adversis* 2 (PG 31: 1689); John Chrysostom (spurious?), *De Poenitentia* 2 (PG 60: 685); Antiochus Monachus, *Homilia* LXXVIII *De Patientia* (PG 89: 1668); Theodorus Studitae, *Sermo* LXVIII (PG 99: 601); Germanus II of Constantinople, *Epistula II ad Cyprios* (PG 140: 616).

59. James 1:12 is cited without complication in paraenetic fashion by Athanasius,

evident to Greek readers, is that James uses the same term, *peirasmos,* for both "testing" and "temptation." The Greek interpreters must scramble to reconcile these verses to each other and to other NT passages such as the one in the Lord's Prayer, "Lead us not into temptation" (Matt 6:13). They do this by distinguishing external afflictions, which do come from God to test faith, and internal temptations to sin, which do not come from God but from desire and/or the devil.[60]

In a much less problematic way, chapter five of James provides scriptural warrant for a number of early Christian practices. James 5:13, "Is any among you happy? Let him sing psalms," is used consistently as a justification for just that activity.[61] James 5:14 legitimates the calling of elders to pray over and anoint the sick.[62] James 5:16 at once encourages the prayer of faith[63]

Epistola ad Episcopos Aegypti et Libyae 23 (PG 25: 593); Didymus Alexandrinus, *Expositio in Psalmos* XCII, 4 (PG 39: 1501); Orsiesius, *Doctrina de Institutione Monachorum* L (PG 40: 891); Athanasius Sinaitus, *Interrogationes et Responsiones,* Quaestio IX (PG 89: 416); and others. For an excellent example of a text applied directly to life, cf. the letter of Cyril of Alexandria to the church at Ephesus, which was experiencing persecution: *Homiliae Diversae* VII (PG 77: 1005).

60. This is a "contradiction in Scripture" that is recognized as such and taken seriously by the patristic writers. Among the treatments, see Athanasius, *Epistulae Heorasticae* xiii, 6 (PG 26: 1417); Cyril of Jerusalem, *Catechesis Mystagogica* V, 17 (PG 33: 1121); Maximus the Confessor, *Questiones ad Thelassium,* Quaestio LVIII (PG 90: 594); *Expositio Orationis Domini* (PG 90:908); *Capitum Quinquies Centenorum Centuria* III, 92 (PG 90: 1300); Photius, *Amphilocia* I, 23 (PG 101: 77); Theophylact of Bulgaria, *Enarratio in Evangelium Lucae* XXII, 39-46 (PG 123: 1084); Euthymius Zigabenus, *Commentarium in Mattheum* VI, 13 (PG 129: 240); and a particularly full consideration in Gregory Palamas, *Homilia* XXXII (PG 151: 401-409).

61. Origen, *Selecta in Psalmos* XII, 6 (PG 12: 1205); *ibid.,* XLVII, 7 (PG 12: 1437); *ibid.,* LXV, 4 (PG 12: 1500); *ibid.,* CXIX, 117 (PG 12: 1628); Athanasius, *Epistola ad Marcellinum* 28 (PG 27: 40); *Expositio in Psalmum XLVI,* 6-7 (PG 27: 217); Eusebius of Caesarea, *Commentarium in Psalmos* LVI, 2 (PG 23: 504); Asterius of Anasenus, *Homilia XVII in Psalmum V* (PG 40: 421); John Chrysostom, *De SS Bernice et Prosdoce* 3 (PG 50: 634); *In Epistulam ad Hebraeos* II, Homilia IV (PG 63: 43); and others.

62. Origen, *In Leviticum Homilia* II, 4 (PG 12: 419); John Chrysostom, *De Sacerdotio* III, 6 (PG 48: 644); *In Centurionem* (PG 61: 770); Cyril of Alexandria, *De Adoratione in Spiritu et Veritate* VI (PG 68: 472); Eustratius, *Vita S. Eutychii* VI (PG 86: 2328); Procopius of Gaza, *Commentarium in Leviticum* XIX, 19 (PG 87: 763); John Damascene, *Sacra Parallela,* V, II (PG 96: 188); Theophylact of Bulgaria, *Enarratio in Evangelium Marci* VI, 12-13 (PG 123: 549); Euthymius Zigabenus, *Commentarium in Marcum* VI, 12 (PG 129: 808); Antonius Melissa, *Loci Communes* I, XVII (PG 136: 825); Gregory Palamas, *Homilia* XXXI (PG 151: 400).

63. See Athanasius Sinaitus, *Interrogationes et Responsiones,* Quaestio XX (PG 89: 532); *Oratio de Sacra Synaxi* (PG 89: 836); Maximus the Confessor, *Capitum Quinquies Centenorum Centuria* III, 80 (PG 90: 1296); Hesychius of Jerusalem, *In Leviticum* I, IV, 22-31 (PG 93: 829); John Damascene, *Sacra Parallela,* D, VII (PG 95:1364); *ibid.,* E, VII (PG 95: 1440); Theodorus Studitae, *Sermo* CVII (PG 99: 647); *Epistulae* II, 17 (PG 99: 1173); Eustratius, *Vita S. Eutychii* VI

and the mutual confession of sins.[64] Finally, James 5:20 justifies the practice of mutual correction in the community.[65]

Proof-texting can appear to be mechanical or arbitrary, but it some-times reveals unexpected insight into the text of James. An example is the patristic use of James 2:13, "judgment is without mercy to those who have not done mercy, but mercy overcomes judgment." We may at first wonder why this text is used by several writers to interpret the parable of Lazarus and Dives (Luke 16:19-31). There is a fairly obvious connection, of course. When the rich man cries out from Hades to father Abraham for mercy, the patristic commentators could exclaim, "*Now* he asks for mercy when it is too late for repentance!"[66] But the citation of 2:13 is appropriate in a less obvious sense as well. We remember that the Greek word for mercy is *eleos,* and that *eleos* was commonly used in early Christianity for alms and almsgiving. With few exceptions,[67] indeed, James 2:13 is used in a direct, paraenetic sense, to support the giving of alms to the needy.[68] Under-

(PG 86: 2234); Zachary Patriarch of Jerusalem, *Epistola* (PG 86: 3232); Symeon of Thessalonica, *Responsa ad Gabrielem Pentapolitanum* (PG 155: 917).

64. Origen, *Expositio in Proverbia* XXXVIII, 51 (PG 17: 244); Epiphanius of Salamis (spurious), *Homilia III in Resurrectione Christi* (PG 43: 472); Palladius, *Apophthegmata Patrum: De Abbate Marco Aegypto* (PG 65: 304); John the Faster, *Poenitentiale* (PG 88: 1891); *Sermo de Poenitentia* (PG 88: 1920); Athanasius Sinaitus, *Interrogationes et Responsiones,* Quaestio VI (PG 89: 373); Hesychius of Jerusalem, *In Leviticum* I, IV, 22-31 (PG 93: 829); *ibid.,* II, VI, 8-12 (PG 93: 855); John Damascene, *Sacra Parallela,* M, III (PG 96: 112).

65. Origen, *In Leviticum Homilia* III, 4 (PG 12: 418); Didymus Alexandrinus, *De Trinitate* III, 1 (PG 39: 776); Isaias Abbas, *Orationes* XXV, 14 (PG 40: 1183); John Chrysostom, *In Psalmos* CXVIII, 158 (PG 55: 704); (spurious) *Quod Oporteat Eum* (PG 61: 785); Cyril of Alexandria, *Commentarium in Sophoniam Prophetam* XIV (PG 71: 969); *De Recta Fide ad Reginas* (PG 76: 1220); John Damascene, *Sacra Parallela,* A, XLVIII (PG 95: 1257); *ibid.,* O, XXIX (PG 96: 305); Andrew of Jerusalem, *Oratio* XIX (PG 97: 1245); Theodorus Studitae, *Epistulae* II, CXVI (PG 99: 1385); *ibid.,* II, CXXXIV (PG 99: 1432); Symeon Metaphrastae, *Certamen S. Martyris Callinici* IV (PG 115: 481); Antonius Melissa, *Loci Communes* I, XVII (PG 136: 825); Gregory Palamas, *Vita S. Petri Athonite* V, 27 (PG 150: 1020).

66. John Chrysostom, *De Lazaro et Divite* 2 (PG 59: 595); *Homilia de Eleemosyna* IX (PG 64: 441); Nilus the Abbot, *Peristeria* IV, XV (PG 79: 845); Johannes Xiphilinus, *Orationes post Ascensionem* (PG 120: 1228).

67. The verse is used to refer to judgment in Basil, *Sermo de Contubernalibus* 8 (PG 30: 824); John Chrysostom, *Contra Virginum Corruptores* (PG 60: 741); (spurious) *In Illud, Memor Fui Dei* (PG 61: 696); *In Epistolam ad Philemonem* III, 2 (PG 62: 717); and Mark the Hermit, *De Lege Spirituali* CXIV (PG 65: 920). John Damascene uses the text to exhort the emperor Theophilus to show mercy, *Epistola ad Theophilem Imperatorem* 26 (PG 95: 380).

68. In addition to the four writings listed in note 66, cf. also Athanasius, *De Titulis Psalmorum* XL, 2 (PG 27: 810); Caesarius of Cappadocia, *Dialogus* III, 140 (PG 38: 1061); John Chrysostom (spurious), *In Decem Virgines* I (PG 59: 528); *De Poenitentia* (PG 60: 767); Cyril of

standing this, we better perceive why the text was applied to Lazarus and Dives, for the rich man had ample opportunity to show mercy (give alms) to the beggar at his gate and had refused.

The text in James accords beautifully with the literary and religious point of Luke's parable in its original context. When we place James 2:13 in its own original context, furthermore, we discover that it forms with 2:12 the hinge between James's essay against discriminatory judgment in matters involving the poor (2:1-11), and his insistence on the necessity of acting out one's faith with deeds (2:14-26), a section he opens with the example of sharing possessions with the needy, that is, the giving of alms.[69] With their continuing appropriation of the term in the tradition, the polyvalence of the term *eleos* was more obvious to the ancient Greek readers than to us. However odd (to our eyes) their point of entry, their reading provides access to a rich understanding of James's text and of Christian existence as well.

Two Favorite Texts

James 2:20-26: Faith and Works

This section of James is among the most heavily quoted by the Greek writers. Once again, some parts of the text are splintered off for separate application. A handy text to throw at opponents is 2:19: "You believe that God is one; you do well, even the demons believe, and shudder." The point, of course, is that the right *kind* of belief is necessary.[70] Likewise, the statement that Abraham's belief was reckoned righteousness to him, and that he was called "friend of God" (James 2:23) has a life of its own.[71]

Alexandria, *De Adoratione in Spiritu et Veritate* VII (PG 68: 528); Isidore of Pelusium, *Epistularum Liber* I, CDXCII (PG 78: 449); Maximus the Confessor, *Loci Communes,* Sermo VII (PG 91: 768); Hesychius of Jerusalem, *Fragmenta in Psalmos* XL, 4 (PG 93: 1193); John Damascene, *Sacra Parallela,* E, VIII (PG 95: 1461); *Homilia* IV (PG 96: 640); Gregory Agrigentius, *Explanatio Ecclesiastae* V, IV (PG 98: 965).

69. The connection is made by Cyril of Alexandria, *Homilia Paschalis* XI, 4 (PG 77: 645); cf. also John Damascene, *Sacra Parallela,* E, VIII (PG 95: 1481).

70. Cyril of Alexandria, *In Isaiam* V, III (PG 70: 1269); *In Johannis Evangelium* VI, I (PG 73: 928); *ibid.,* X (PG 74: 368); Photius, *Bibliotheca* CCXXII, 39 (PG 103: 817); Gregory Agrigentius, *Explanatio Ecclesiastae* III, XX (PG 98: 888); Symeon of Thessalonica, *Expositio de Sacri Symboli* (PG 155: 804).

71. Clement of Alexandria, *Paedagogus* III, II, 40 (PG 8: 573); *ibid.,* III, VIII, 25 (PG 8: 613); *Stromateis* II, V, 82 (PG 8: 952); Cyril of Jerusalem, *Catechesis* V, *De fide et Symbolo* (PG 33: 512);

When the passage as a whole is considered, two aspects of the Greek writers' treatment deserve attention.[72] First, there is the implicit recognition that James was not opposing faith in the Messiah and the works of Torah such as circumcision, and was therefore not directly contradicting Paul's principle of justification by faith. Rather, these writers understood that James used the terms "faith" and "works" precisely as Greek moralists spoke of "word" and "deeds." James's contrast was between verbal profession and lived behavior, between empty talk and fruitful action. Because for the most part these writers were also moralists who continued the same tradition, James's exhortation appeared to them as the most obvious common sense.[73]

Second, when the verbal differences between James and Paul become a matter for discussion, the patristic writers do not oppose the statements, as Luther did. Rather they harmonize them by distinguishing the points of reference. Paul, they said, addressed the faith that leads to conversion

---

Epiphanius of Salamis, *Adversus Haereses* III, 2, 6 (PG 42: 707); Origen, *Commentarium in Johannem* XX, 23 (PG 14:592); *Commentarium in Epistulam ad Romanos* IV, 3 (PG 14: 970); Cyril of Alexandria, *In Johannis Evangelium* V, V (PG 73: 860); Macanus of Egypt, *Regula ad Monachos* IV (PG 34: 972).

72. In speaking of the "passage as a whole," I mean primarily the gist: "faith without works is dead." This occurs in James 2:26 and in 2:17, but the version most often cited is in 2:20, where the *koine* ms tradition reads *pistis chōris tōn ergōn nekra estin,* even though modern critical editions (probably correctly) prefer *argē* to *nekra* in 2:20. Given the haphazard mode of citation and the destiny of this passage to become an axiom, any one of the verses or none of them may have been in a particular writer's mind.

73. The unselfconscious application of James 2:20/26 in exhortation is found in Origen, *In Librum Jesu Nave Homilia* X, 2 (PG 12: 881); *Selecta in Psalmos* XXX, 6 (PG 12: 1300); *Commentarium in Johannem* XIX, 6 (PG 14: 569); *Commentarium in Epistulam ad Romanos* VIII, 1 (PG 14: 1159); Athanasius, *De Virginitate* (PG 28: 269); Antony, *Sermones ad Monachos* 1 (PG 40: 964); John Chrysostom, *De Poenitentia* Homilia IX (PG 49: 343); *De Verbis Apostoli* I, 10 (PG 51: 281); *In Mattheum Homilia* LII (PG 56: 931); *In Pascha* II (PG 59: 727); *In Epistolam ad Philemonem* II, 1 (PG 62: 709); Cyril of Alexandria, *Commentarium in Micheam Prophetam* XXXVI (PG 71: 693); *Commentarium in Malachiam Prophetam* XLIII (PG 72: 357); *In Johannis Evangelium* IX (PG 74: 253); *ibid.,* X (PG 74: 349); Isaias Abbas, *Orationes* XXI, 8 (PG 40: 1163); Isidore of Pelusium, *Epistularum Liber* IV CCXXVI (PG 78: 1321); Maximus the Confessor, *Questiones ad Thelassium* Quaestio LIV (PG 90: 521); *De Charitate* I, 59 (PG 90: 968); *Mystagogica* V (PG 91: 677); Sophronius of Jerusalem, *Oratio* I (PG 87: 3206-3207); Symeon Junior, *Oratio* III (PG 120: 335); *Oratio* XXII (PG 120: 428); *Divinorum Amorum Liber* XV (PG 120: 530); Euthymius Zigabenus, *Commentarium in Johannem* XVI, 18 (PG 129: 849); Athanasius Sinaitus, *Oratio de Sacra Symboli* (PG 89: 836); Johannes Carpathius, *Capita Hortatoria* II, XXXVI (PG 85: 817); Eustratius, *Vita S. Eutychii* V (PG 86: 2321); Oecumenius of Tricca, *Commentarium in Epistolam II S. Petri* I, 3-9 (PG 119: 584); Theophylact of Bulgaria, *Enarratio in Evangelium Johannis* XV, 1-3 (PG 124: 193).

before baptism, whereas James addressed the faith of Christians already baptized.[74] Paul therefore was correct in saying that no works of Torah could bring one to faith in the Messiah. But James was also correct in affirming that Christian belief needed to be expressed in more than words.[75] Far from calling James into question (as it did for Luther) the discrepancy appears to enhance James's authority. Indeed, both Origen and Cyril in their commentaries on Romans explicate Paul in the light of James![76]

I discovered, in fact, a short exchange of letters between Julian, the monophysite bishop of Halicarnassus (d. after 518) and Severus, the monophysite Patriarch of Antioch (465-538). Julian raises the question concerning the contradiction in Scripture posed by these passages, and Severus responds. His harmonizing resolution is exquisitely argued, with careful attention not only to the argument in James and in Paul but also to the narrative sequence of Genesis upon which both Paul and James are dependent.[77] The author decides, quite rightly, that what James means by the works of faith is what Paul means as well, citing Galatians 5:6, "faith working through love." The strongest contrast to Luther in this whole discussion is the governing premise, stated by the author this way: "The Holy Writings and the Fathers have always handed on to us a harmonious teaching."[78]

---

74. See Origen, *Commentarium in Epistulam ad Romanos* II, 12 (PG 14: 900). That James's exhortation was addressed specifically to the baptized is emphasized by John Damascene, *De Fide Orthodoxa* IV, IX (PG 94: 1121); Theophanis of Sicily, *Homilia* XXVIII (PG 132: 617); John of Antioch, *Oratio de Disciplina Monastica* (PG 132: 1120); Philippus Solitarius, *Dioptra Rei Christianae* I (PG 127: 712); Euthymius Zigabenus, *Panoplia Dogmatica* XI (PG 130: 453).
ction is argued particularly well by Isidore of Pelusium, *Epistularum Liber*
). The letter begins with a citation and takes its theme from James 2:24.
remarks in Origen, *Commentarium in Epistulam ad Romanos* II, 12; II, 13;
; IX, 24 (PG 14: 900, 908, 961, 970, 989-990, 1159, 1226); Cyril of Alexan-
tomanos IV, 2; VII, 16; VIII, 26 (PG 74: 781, 812, 825); also Theophylact of
Evangelium Johannis IX, 30-33 (PG 124: 57), and especially *Expositio in*
', 6 (PG 124: 1012), where, without being named as such, James 2:20 is
nt of Galatians 5:6, "faith working through love"; and *Expositio in*
:6 (PG 125: 156).
Selecta ex Historiae Ecclesiasticae section XIX, compiled by the 6th cen-
iop Zachary the Rhetorician, whose origin was in Palestine (PG 85:

he ultimate expression of this "harmonious teaching" is the combi-
s to emerge already in the fourth century and becomes a frequently
ut works is dead, so are works without faith dead." Some form of
d in Gregory Nazianzen, *Oratio* XXVI (PG 35: 1233); *Oratio* XL (PG

James 1:17: Every Good and Perfect Gift

For the Greek authors, however, the primary *locus theologicus* is James 1:17, which reads, "Every good gift and every perfect gift comes down from above, from the father of lights with whom there is neither change nor shadow of alteration." Even a quick parsing reveals the verse's potential for exploitation. The adjective "every" denotes universality but also connotes exclusivity: God gives every good gift, and no one else does. The word "from above" *(anōthen)*, as in the Gospel of John, suggests an origin in God. The title "Father of Lights" is also congenial to Johannine theological symbolism and to the creedal tradition of "God from God, light from Light." The phrase "without change or shadow of alteration," finally, points to the immutability of God — and, equally importantly — to the changeless and therefore spiritual character of the "good and perfect gifts" that come from God.

We find the text used first in theological arguments, properly so termed — that is, with arguments concerning the nature of the Godhead itself. As expected, it appears in passages asserting the unchangeability of God[79] and the universal beneficence of God.[80] The text plays an important role in trinitarian theological arguments, being used to assert the full divinity of the

---

36: 425); John Chrysostom, *In Genesin I, Homilia* II, 5 (PG 53: 31); *In Psalmum CXVIII*, 48 (PG 55: 685); Cyril of Alexandria, *De Adoratione in Spiritu et Veritate* XIV (PG 68: 924); *Homilia Paschalis* IX, 6 (PG 77: 601); Maximus the Confessor, *Liber Asceticus* 34 (PG 90: 940); Athanasius Sinaitus, *Interrogationes et Responsiones* Quaest. I (PG 89: 329); Basil of Seleucia, *Oratio* XXXIX, 6 (PG 85: 452); Procopius of Gaza, *Commentarii in Leviticum* XI, 2 (PG 87: 727); John Damascene, *Vita Barlaam et Joasaph* XI (PG 96: 949); *ibid.*, XIX (PG 96: 1033); Symeon Junior, *Oratio* IV (PG 120: 341); *Oratio* VII (PG 120: 356); Theophylact of Bulgaria, *Enarratio in Evangelium Johannis* VI, 28-30 (PG 123: 1297); Callistus et Ignatius Xanthopopulorum, *Opuscula Ascetica* 16 (PG 147: 664); Johannes Cantacuzenias, *Contra Mahomatem Apologia* (PG 154: 660); Philotheus the Patriarch, *Laudatio Trium Doctorum* (PG 154: 788).

79. See Origen, *In Numeros Homilia* XVIII, 1 (PG 12: 712); John Damascene, *De Imaginibus, Oratio* I (PG 94: 1240); Gregory Acindyni, *De Essentia et Operatione Dei* 6 (PG 151: 1200).

80. The range of "gifts" is considerable, from the Pauline "gifts of the Spirit" in Origen, *Commentarium in Epistulam ad Romanos* IX, 24 (PG 14: 1226), to the "gift" of the episcopacy, in Symeon of Thessalonica, *De Sacerdotio* (PG 155: 965). Cf., variously, Antony, *Sermones ad Monachos* 7 (PG 40: 967); Mark the Hermit, *De Baptismo* (PG 65: 1028); *Disputatio cum Causidico* IV (PG 65: 1075); Cyril of Alexandria, *De Adoratione in Spiritu et Veritate* XI (PG 68: 772); *Commentarium in Amos Prophetam* LVI (PG 71: 513); John Damascene, *Sacra Parallela*, X, I (PG 96: 341); *De Fide Orthodoxa* IV, XV (PG 94: 1165); Eustratius, *Vita S. Eutychii* I (PG 86: 2285); Pantaleon of Constantinople, *Sermo* IV (PG 98: 1264); Theophylact of Bulgaria, *Oratio in Praesentationem B. Mariae* 10 (PG 126: 141).

Son, the second person of the Christian Trinity.[81] Even more often, the passage is used in arguments asserting the divinity of the Holy Spirit.[82]

The Letter of James refers to Jesus only twice (1:1; 2:1), but in the Alexandrian school, James 1:17 was put on active duty in Christological arguments to assert that, even in his humanity, Jesus was fully divine.[83] In this connection, the fact that both James and John use *anōthen* to mean "origin in God" has significance: Jesus is not the appearance of a lesser demiurge, but "God from God."[84] Cyril of Alexandria, in particular, makes frequent use of two other passages from James in Christological arguments. James 2:1 is used (rather oddly) because it implies that Jesus shares the same glory (that is, status) as the Father.[85] James 4:12 is used because it asserts, "there is one lawgiver and judge." And since the gospel attributes both legislative and judging functions to Jesus, the passage in James stands as warrant for the equality in status of Jesus and God.[86] Much of this argument was addressed against the extreme Antiochean

81. Athanasius, *Epistola ad Afros Episcopos* 8 (PG 26: 1044); Caesarius of Cappadocia, *Dialogus* I, 2 (PG 38: 857); Cyril of Alexandria, *Commentarium in Lucam* XXII, 19 (PG 72: 908); *De SS Trinitate Dialogus* II (PG 75: 782); Cyril of Jerusalem, *Catechesis* VII (PG 33: 609); Maximus the Confessor, *Quaestiones et Responsiones* Quaestio L (PG 90: 469).

82. Didymus Alexandrinus, *De Trinitate* II, 6, 3 (PG 39: 513); *ibid.,* II, 6, 6 (PG 39: 524); *ibid.,* II, 6, 8 (PG 39: 532); Athanasius, *Epistola I ad Serapionem* 26 (PG 26: 592); Cyril of Alexandria, *De SS Trinitate Dialogus* III (PG 75: 841-844); *De Recte Fide ad Reginas* (PG 76: 1255); *De Recte Fide ad Reginas* (PG 76: 1289); Athanasius Sinaitus, *Viae Dux* XIII (PG 89: 225); Euthymius Zigabenus, *Panoplia Dogmatica* XII (PG 130: 717); *ibid.,* XII (PG 130: 869); Johannes Vecus, *Refutationes adversus D. Andronici Canateri* (PG 141: 528); Dominicus Bessarionis, *Refutatio Marci Epheseni* (PG 161: 188); Georgius Trapezuntius, *De Processione Spiritus Sancti* (PG 161: 772).

83. See Cyril of Alexandria, *Glaphyrorum in Genesin* VI (PG 69: 325); *In Epistolam II ad Corinthios* III, 4-6 (PG 74: 929); *Adversus Nestorianum* V, IV (PG 76: 229); *De Recte Fide ad Reginas* (PG 76: 1255); *ibid.* (PG 76:1289); Andrew of Jerusalem, *Oratio* IX (PG 97: 1013); John Chrysostom, *In Mattheum* Homilia XXXIX (PG 56: 847); Nicetas Paphlygonis, *Oratio* I (PG 105: 25).

84. See Cyril of Alexandria, *In Johannis Evangelium* II, II (PG 73: 268); *De SS Trinitate Dialogus* I (PG 75: 704); *ibid.,* IV (PG 75: 872); John Chrysostom, *In Mattheum* Homilia IV, 4 (PG 56: 657).

85. Cyril of Alexandria, *In Johannis Evangelium* IV, I (PG 73: 549); *Thesaurus de Sancta et Consubstantiale Trinitate* (PG 75: 509); *ibid.* (PG 75: 636); *De SS Trinitate Dialogus* VI (PG 75: 1029); *Quod Unus Sit Christus* (PG 75: 1321); cf. also Euthymius Zigabenus, *Panoplia Dogmatica* XV (PG 130: 976).

86. The usage began with Didymus Alexandrinus, *De Trinitate* I, 15 (PG 39: 313); *ibid.,* I, 29 (PG 39: 416); *ibid.,* III, 28 (PG 39: 944), and it was a favorite of Cyril of Alexandria, *De Adoratione in Spiritu et Veritate* XIII (PG 68: 881); *In Psalmum XCIX*, 3 (PG 69: 1257); *De SS Trinitate Dialogus* III (PG 75: 812); *ibid.* (PG 75: 821); *ibid.* (PG 76:1268); *ibid.* (PG 76: 1419). The logic of the argument is revealed in *Commentarium in Amos Prophetam* XV (PG 71: 440).

emphasis on Jesus' humanity called Nestorianism. Not surprisingly, the extreme Alexandrian position itself was soon enough also called the heresy of monophysitism.[87]

James 1:17 was used in many other contexts. It supported the divine origin of mystical illumination,[88] personal transformation,[89] and the working of miracles.[90] It is used as an invocation, the Christian equivalent of calling on the Muses. Humans cannot speak about these great mysteries, but with divine aid they can, because "every good and perfect gift. . . ."[91] In the same way, the text is employed hermeneutically. God is the one who inspired the scriptural texts. Therefore, God's Spirit is required to understand them, because "every good and perfect gift. . . ."[92] James 1:17 is such a favorite text throughout this tradition that we are not really surprised to find it enshrined in the liturgy of the Eastern Church. The last citation from Scripture heard by the faithful before departing the church in every celebration of the Eastern Liturgy — down to our own day — is this declaration from James, "Every good and perfect gift comes down from above, from the father of lights, with whom there is neither change nor shadow of alteration."[93]

---

87. See Grillmeier, *Christ in the Christian Tradition*, 363-368.

88. It is noteworthy that the very first line of (Pseudo-) Dionysius (the Aereopagite), *De Coelestia Hierarchia* I, 1 (PG 3: 119) is an (unacknowledged but clear) citation of James 1:17, and it forms the very basis of his theology, which was deeply influential on the mystical tradition of the medieval West; cf. J. F. Ben M. de Rubies, O.P., *Dissertatio* in PG 3: 57-95, and in particular the points of influence on Aquinas, cols. 88-90.

89. For the knowledge of God and illumination in prayer, cf., e.g., John Chrysostom, *In Psalmum CXVIII*, 33 (PG 55: 683); *Oratio Secunda* (PG 63: 925); John of Raythu, *Scholia in Scalam Paradisi* IX ad Gradum 27 (PG 88: 1247); Nicetas Pectoratus, *Practicorum Capitum* I, 100 (PG 120: 897-900); Theophylact of Bulgaria, *Expositio in Epistulam S. Judae* 19 (PG 126: 101); Gregory Palamas, *Homilia* XXXIV (PG 151: 436); *Homilia* XXXV (PG 151: 437).

90. Anon., *Vita S. Clementis Romae*. The narrative is attributed to St. Ephraim in the text itself (PG 116: 183).

91. As an invocation, cf. Cyril of Alexandria, *In Johannis Evangelium*, proem (PG 73: 9); Athanasius Sinaitus, *In Hexaemeron*, praef. (PG 89: 851); Maximus the Confessor, *Questiones ad Thelassium*, praef. (PG 90: 248); Andrew of Jerusalem, *Oratio* XIX (PG 97: 1209); John Damascene, *Dialectica*, praef. (PG 94: 524); *De Institutione Elementarii*, praef. (PG 95: 100); Stephen of Constantinople, *Vita S. Stephani Junioris* (PG 100: 1073); Johannes Vecus, *Epistola ad Joannem Papam* (PG 141: 944).

92. As a general hermeneutical principle, cf. Cyril of Alexandria, *In Joannis Evangelium* IV, III (PG 73: 605); Maximus the Confessor, *Questiones ad Thelassium* Quaestio LIX (PG 90: 605); with reference to the understanding of Scripture, cf. John Damascene, *De Fide Orthodoxa* IV, XVII (PG 94: 1177); Athanasius Sinaitus, *In Hexaemeron*, praef. (PG 89: 851).

93. For the Alexandrian Liturgy spuriously attributed to Basil, in which James 1:17 ap-

Conclusion

Excursions such as this one show that further such trips must be undertaken if the full history of interpretation is to be appreciated, not only for James, but for all biblical texts. We cannot be content only with the commentary tradition. In pre-critical interpretation, a far richer body of material is to be found in ecclesial *uses* of the text than in scholarly examinations of it. Such empirical research would also provide a better test for theories of interpretation. It is one thing to study Origen's or Augustine's argument how a text *ought* to be interpreted. It may be something else to discover how in fact they interpreted it by actual use. Even for the tiny Letter of James, more needs to be done. This study covers only the Greek writers. There remain the 271 volumes of Latin Fathers, the Syriac writers, and the Western medieval authors. All of this usage, finally, needs to be correlated with the formal commentary tradition.[94] More such travelogues can be written.

pears at the end, cf. PG 31: 1656; for its continuing use, cf. J. Raya and J. de Vinck, *Byzantine Liturgy* (Tournai: Desclée et cie, 1958), "Prayer behind the Ambo," pp. 110-111.

94. In addition to the commentaries listed by Dibelius, 262, namely Didymus Alexandrinus (PG 39: 1749-1754), Oecumenius (PG 119: 452-509), and Theophylact (PG 125: 1132-1189), one should add the *Fragmenta* of Chrysostom (PG 64: 1040-1052), the *Fragmenta* of Hysechius of Jerusalem (PG 93: 1389-1390), as well as the extensive interpretive comments found in Euthalius of Alexandria (PG 85: 676-677) and Symeon Metaphrastae (PG 115: 200-217).

How James Won the West:
A Chapter in the History of Canonization

The process by which the Letter of James reached canonical status in the Latin-speaking church of the Western Roman Empire appears at first to be sudden and inexplicable. Though known and used fairly early in the Greek church of the East, James is usually considered to have been largely unknown in the West. How then did James go so quickly from an obscure and apparently noncanonical status to a secure position in the New Testament? Even one involved in the process seemed a bit puzzled. In a short passage devoted to James the Brother of the Lord, Jerome remarks concerning the letter that it may have been edited by someone other than James, and that it gained recognition in the church only "little by little."[1] It is this puzzle of incremental authority and sudden canonicity that requires closer scrutiny.

In brief, I will argue first that the non-use of James has been exaggerated, and that closer analysis reveals that James was an important writing in the local Roman church from the end of the first century. I will argue, second, that James's secure place in the canon was won by his being sponsored vigorously by three writers who were ascetics, allies of Damasus of Rome, and admirers of Origen.

---

1. Jerome, *De Viris Illustribus* 2 (PL 23: 639).

This essay began as one of the Carmichael-Walling Lectures, delivered in November 1995 at Abilene Christian University. Some elements appear also in an abbreviated form in L. T. Johnson, *The Letter of James* (Anchor Bible 37A; Garden City: Doubleday, 1995).

The Pertinence of Canonicity

The comparative study of religions confirms that the concept of canon is not uniformly present or important in all traditions.[2] But for Christianity, the canon of Scripture is a critical element in its self-definition for at least four reasons. First, Christianity produced an impressive amount of literature from its inception, exchanged and collected it, and established something like a formal and closed canon within a remarkably short time.[3] Second, the bulk of this literature engaged and reinterpreted the Scriptures of Judaism, so that the combination of shared texts and diverse interpretation was critical to the separation of Christianity from its mother tradition and led to a continuing debate over which texts made up Torah and in what version.[4] Third, it can be argued that in Christianity, the process of canonization and the process of self-definition were virtually identical, since the issue of which writings represented the authentic and original character of Christianity was at the heart of the decisive battle with Gnosticism and Marcionism in the second century.[5] Fourth, in Irenaeus of Lyons' response to Gnosticism, the establishment of the canon of Scripture was part of the threefold strategy of orthodox self-definition, together with the rule of faith and the episcopal succession, so that to resolve subsequent controversies, Christian leaders would meet in council to debate these same texts in order to define and refine their beliefs and practices.[6]

For Christianity, therefore, the canon of Scripture is an essential element in self-definition. In private, all the apocryphal gospels ever written can be read, but only these twenty-seven small compositions serve as the public documents of the community. They alone are to be read publicly at worship to shape the consciousness of the community. They alone are considered authoritative for continuing debates over how the church

---

2. See, e.g., W. A. Graham, *Beyond the Written Word: Aspects of Scripture in the History of Religions* (Cambridge: Cambridge University Press, 1987); J. Z. Smith, "Sacred Persistence: Toward a Redescription of Canon," *Imagining Religion* (Chicago: University of Chicago Press, 1987), 36-52.

3. For the basic process, see H. Y. Gamble, *The New Testament Canon: Its Making and Meaning* (GES: Philadephia: Fortress, 1985).

4. For the New Testament as a midrashic engagement with the texts of Torah, see L. T. Johnson, *The Writings of the New Testament: An Interpretation,* 2nd ed. (Minneapolis: Fortress, 1999); for a good sense of the dispute over the proper form of the text (Hebrew or Greek), see substantial portions of Justin, *Dialogue with Trypho.*

5. See, e.g., E. Pagels, *The Gnostic Gospels* (New York: Random House, 1979), 57-83.

6. See Irenaeus of Lyons, *Adversus Haereses* III, 1-4 (PG 7: 843-857).

should respond to God in present circumstances.[7] The opinions of theologians past and present are significant only as they give insight into these writings. And because the canon plays this critical role in the continuing process of Christian self-definition, the question of how these particular writings came to be included, while others were not, is understandably an important one.

Because official canonical lists from bishops and synods do not appear before the late fourth century, it is sometimes thought that canonization began at that point. But official lists ratify the results of a much longer, more natural, and more organic process. From the sending of Paul's letters on, we observe how writings were exchanged between communities and built into local collections. A much more difficult and critical stage came when, in the face of Marcion's challenge to truncate the traditional collection, and Gnosticism's threat to expand the authoritative Scripture with countless new compositions, the church (in the person of writers like Tertullian and Irenaeus) began consciously to select the traditional writings over against new challenges, and as a result began to "name their sources" in a manner previously unattested. It became suddenly necessary to identify which writings attributed to Paul were being cited, which Gospels were being taken as authoritative.

This process was made explicit by writers such as Eusebius and Augustine, who adduced certain criteria, such as apostolicity, correspondence with the rule of faith, and citation by earlier writers.[8] All of these are criteria for historical priority, asserting that the canonical writings testify to the primordial expression of the faith. Citation by earlier writers is the main "hard" criterion, since it is difficult to prove a writing existed by such and such a time if no writer prior to that time ever quoted it. In effect, these criteria represent after-the-fact rationalizations for an earlier process that had proceeded much less self-consciously.

These, however, were the sort of criteria that Luther used in his rejection of James from the proper books of the Bible. Like Erasmus,[9] Luther denied apostolic authorship for James and declared that to be the reason why James had been rejected by the ancients.[10] Most of all, James was un-

---

7. For further remarks on the role of canon in ecclesial hermeneutics, see L. T. Johnson, *Scripture and Discernment: Decision Making in the Church* (Nashville: Abingdon Press, 1996).

8. See Eusebius, *Historia Ecclesiastica* III, 23-25; Augustine, *De Doctrina Christiana* II, 8.

9. Erasmus, *Annotationes in Epistolam Jacobi* in *Opera Omnia*, vol. 6 (Leiden: Vanden, 1705), 1038.

10. See "The Babylonian Captivity of the Church," *Luther's Works*, vol. 36: *Word and Sac-*

acceptable because it contradicted Paul on the question of faith and works, and, in Luther's phrase, "drives us back to the law."[11] The editor of Luther's "Preface to the New Testament of 1522," where these sentiments appear, refers us back to Eusebius, who says, concerning James, "It is to be noted that its authenticity is denied," and gives as his reason, "few of the ancients quote it."[12] Close analysis of Eusebius's statement, however, shows that it was descriptive rather than prescriptive. He acknowledges that some question James's authenticity, but he himself does not question it, for in another place where he cites James he refers to him as "the holy apostle."[13] He therefore lists James among the disputed writings rather than among the rejected ones, and says, "nevertheless we know that these letters have been used publicly with the rest in most churches *(pleistais ekklēsiais)*."[14]

Nevertheless, lack of citation of James by early Christian writers is regularly taken by some scholars as evidence that the composition was not written by James the Brother of the Lord from Jerusalem in the first generation of the Christian movement, but was rather composed pseudonymously in response to a generalized Paulinism perhaps as late as the middle of the second century.[15] As a result, James is seen as a witness not to the earliest stage of the faith but rather to a developed and (in the eyes of many) an already declining one. Its inclusion in the canon therefore appears again as arbitrary, raising questions both about its authority and about the integrity of the canonical process as a whole. In effect, was not Luther correct in demoting James to apocryphal status?

---

rament II, ed. A. R. Wentz (Philadelphia: Muhlenberg Press, 1959), 118-119; also the "Preface to the New Testament of 1522," *Luther's Works,* vol. 35: *Word and Sacrament* I, ed. E. T. Bachmann (Philadelphia: Muhlenberg Press, 1959), 395.

11. "Preface to the New Testament of 1522," pp. 396-397.

12. Eusebius of Caesarea, *Historia Ecclesiastica* II, 23, 25.

13. Eusebius, *Commentarium in Psalmos* LVI, 2 (PG 23: 503).

14. Eusebius, *Historia Ecclesiastica* II, 23, 25.

15. Adolf von Harnack dated James no earlier than 120-140, with its title being appended as late as the third century; see *Geschichte der altchristliche Literatur bis Eusebius* Teil 2: *Die Chronologie* (Leipzig: Hinrichs'sche Buchhandlung, 1897) 2: 486-91. More recently, Burton Mack mapped early Christian literature and placed James with the Letter of Diognetus, under "location uncertain," between 120 and 150; see Burton, *The Lost Gospel: The Book of Q and Christian Origins* (San Francisco: Harper, 1993), 259.

The Shape of the Problem

In the East, the enthusiastic sponsorship of James by Origen (185-254),[16] and the entire Alexandrian tradition after him,[17] fairly well assured the canonization of the composition at least in the rest of the Greek-speaking empire.[18] Origen gives no hint that his appreciation of James was a novelty, and despite the originality of his mind, he was extremely careful to distinguish between tradition and his own positions,[19] so we are justified in assuming a prior use of James at least in the Alexandrian church before him.

The first Alexandrian writer of whom we have substantial evidence is Clement (ca. 150-215). He assumed the leadership of the catechetical school in Alexandria from his teacher Pantaenus around 190 and ceded it to Origen around 202. Clement also was concerned to distinguish what came from tradition and what did not, and in the case of writings, the apocryphal from the received.[20] If we could be sure that Clement knew and used James in his writings, then we could push its reception in the Alexandrian church back to at least 180 (when Pantaenus seems to have started teaching there). Unfortunately, the evidence for Clement is mixed. His extant writings contain a number of phrases that *could* be from James,[21] although only one of them seems to demand some knowledge of

16. Origen lists James as canonical in *In Librum Jesu Nave* VII, 1 (PG 12:857), knows the author as "the brother of the Lord" in *Commentarium in Epistulam ad Romanos* IV, 8 (PG 14: 989), as well as "James the Apostle" in *In Exodum Homiliae* III, 3 (PG 12: 316), and refers to the writing as "scripture" in *In Leviticam Homiliae* II, 4 (PG 12: 418). In his extant works, he cites James some 36 times, using 24 verses from the letter.

17. The fragments of the Alexandrian teachers Dionysius, Peter, and Alexander all contain citations of James (PG 10: 1596 and PG 18: 466). Didymus the Blind wrote a commentary on the letter (PG 39: 1749-1754). Athanasius and Cyril both use James extensively. James appears in Athanasius's canonical list in his Paschal Letter of 364 (*Epistula* XXXIX [PG 26: 1177]).

18. For the difficulties faced by the letter (together with other catholic epistles) in the Syriac church before the Peshitta, see J. S. Siker, "The Canonical Status of the Catholic Epistles in the Syriac New Testament," *JTS* n.s. 38 (1987) 311-33.

19. See *De Principiis* I, 8 (PG 11: 120) and IV, 2, 4 (PG 11: 365).

20. See *Stromateis* I, 1, 39-42 (PG 8: 700) and III, 13 (PG 8: 1193).

21. E.g., Clement may allude to James 4:6 in *Stromateis* III, 6, 52 (PG 8: 1152), but since the same line appears also in Prov 3:34 and 1 Pet 5:5, it is impossible to know whether Clement got it from James. The same difficulty of multiple possible sources applies to Clement's speaking of unclean spirits who "tremble" *(phrissousin)* at the sight of the baptized (*Excerpta ex Theodoto* 4, 77; excerpt 3 [PG 9: 693]), and calling Abraham "friend of God" (*Paedagogus* III, 2, 40 [PG 8: 573], *Stromateis* II, 5, 82 [PG 8: 952]).

that composition,[22] and he never cites James by name, the way he does
1 Peter, 1 John, Jude, and the Apocalypse.[23] Several of the possible allusions
to James, furthermore, occur in a section of the *Stromateis* where Clement
is obviously dependent on an earlier Clement, the elder from Rome who
wrote to the Corinthians around the year 95.[24] This other Clementine
connection will be noted again.

It is possible, on the other hand, that Clement of Alexandria actually
wrote a small commentary on James. According to Eusebius, Clement
composed a work called the *Hypotyposes,* "in which he has set forth his interpretations of the scriptures and his traditions."[25] And he continues,
"he has given concise explanations of all the canonical scriptures, not
passing over even the disputed writings, I mean the epistle of Jude and the
remaining catholic epistles."[26] Since Eusebius himself considers James to
be the first of the Catholic Letters,[27] it would seem logical that James
would be among the writings on which Clement commented. Such was
the opinion of Cassiodorus as well.[28] The extant fragments of the
Hypotyposes, unfortunately, contain no portions of James. Nevertheless,
Clement may have included it. I say this because Eusebius quotes explicitly from Books 6 and 7 of the *Hypotyposes* when discussing traditions of
James of Jerusalem's death and ministry.[29] Since according to him Clement's work contained both commentary on texts *and* traditions, his citing
Clement's traditions on James would seem to suggest that Clement com-
mented on the text of the letter as well. But, as I said, we have no extant evidence. We are therefore not able to push the reception of James in the
East back earlier than Origen.

The situation in the Western part of the empire appears at first to be
even starker. If we look in the obvious places, it is almost impossible to

---

22. In *Stromateis* VI, 18, 13-14 (PG 9: 397), Clement provides a demonstration from
"scripture" *(graphē),* beginning with Matt 5:20, concerning a righteousness that exceeds
that of the Pharisees, but then spelling it out in terms of Lev 19:18, which of course is also
found in James 2:8; what makes this most interesting is that Clement declares that unless
they act this way, they will not be *basilikoi,* that is, "kingly." The usage is so unexpected, and
is so close to James's reference to Lev 19:18 as the *nomos basilikos* in 2:8, that an allusion is
here likely, in my view.

23. See L. LeNourry, *Dissertation Secunda De Libris Stromatum* IV, 3 (PG 9: 1094-1095).

24. See *Stromateis* IV, 17-18 (PG 8: 1311-1328).

25. Eusebius, *Historia Ecclesiastica* VI, 13, 2.

26. Eusebius, *Historia Ecclesiastica* VI, 14, 1.

27. Eusebius, *Historia Ecclesiastica* II, 23, 25.

28. Cassiodorus, *De Institutione Divinarum Litterarum* (PL 70: 1120).

29. See Eusebius, *Historia Ecclesiastica* II, 1, 3-7.

catch a glimpse of James before the late fourth century. Among the apologists of the second century, James seems unknown.[30] In Irenaeus, there is no real trace of James's influence.[31] In the works of Tertullian and Cyprian of Carthage, there is nothing that can certainly be attributed to James.[32] In all the writings of Ambrose, there is scarcely a trace of James.[33] Outside the church in Rome, the earliest clear use of James is the citation of James 1:17 by Hilary of Poitiers (356-358).[34] Hilary was an admirer of Origen, as his commentaries on Matthew and the Psalms indicate.[35] Even more striking, James is absent from the Muratorian canonical list, which is traditionally located at Rome around 170, even though that list recognizes Jude and two of the Johannine letters as well as the Apocalypse.[36] James is also missing from an African canonical list called the Cheltenham or Mommsenian Canon, dated around 360.[37]

Then, quite suddenly, within a two-decade period, James appears everywhere in the West. Athanasius, the fierce opponent of Arianism, published his famous paschal letter with its canonical list in 367, and it contained James.[38] In the See of Rome, Damasus became pope in 366, and he proved to be an ally of Athanasius, and equally committed to the defense of the anti-Arian position. He was also a consolidator of papal authority in the West. It is perhaps no surprise, then, to find James appearing in the canonical list of Damasus in 382.[39] But James also appears in the canon of

30. No trace of James's distinctive language appears in Aristeas, Justin Martyr, Theophilus, Tatian, Athenagoras, or the *Letter to Diognetus*. The incidental traces found in other post-apostolic literature are discussed in L. T. Johnson, *The Letter of James* (Anchor Bible 37A; New York: Doubleday, 1995), 68-72.

31. There is only the twofold reference to Abraham as "friend of God," in *Adversus Haereses* IV, 3, 4 (PG 7: 1009) and IV, 16, 1 (PG 7: 1016).

32. In Cyprian, there is nothing at all. In Tertullian, there is only the reference to Abraham as "friend of God" in *Adversus Judaeos* 600:2 (PL 2: 638).

33. There is a possible allusion to James 4:8 and 2:5 in Ambrose's *Expositio in Lucam* (PL 15: 1669 and 15: 1859). The absence is more striking, given his discussion of justification by faith in *Epistula* LXXVIII (PL 16: 1323-1325).

34. Hilary of Poitiers, *De Trinitate* IV, 8 (PL 10: 101).

35. See *The Oxford Dictionary of the Christian Church,* 2nd ed., ed. F. L. Cross and E. A. Livingstone (Oxford: Oxford University Press, 1974), 649.

36. See A. Souter, *The Text and Canon of the New Testament,* rev. ed., ed. C. S. C. Williams (London: Duckworth, 1954), 191-193.

37. Souter, pp. 195-196.

38. Athanasius, *Epistula* XXXIX (PG 26: 1177).

39. That a canon was issued under Damasus, and later edited and expanded under Gelasius and Hormisdas, is argued by C. H. Turner, "Latin Lists of the Canonical Books," *JTS* old series 1 (1899) 554-60. The position that this was only an extract from a sixth-century

the Council of Carthage in 397, even though no trace of James's use by any African writer can be detected before this time.[40] James is listed again in the canon of Innocent I in 405.[41] And from the fifth to the sixteenth century, James is securely part of the canon in the Latin church.

The Use of James in the Roman Church

While it is true that no certain citation of James appears in second-century literature, that is only part of the truth. There is a very strong possibility that James was known and used by the authors of two writings composed in Rome before the middle of the second century, namely *The First Letter of Clement* and *The Shepherd of Hermas*. Before presenting the positive evidence supporting this case, however, the difficulties in making it should be acknowledged.

The first difficulty is the way the writings of the early second century appropriate earlier sources. For the most part, only Old Testament citations are formally introduced,[42] although other "scriptures" are alluded to more or less explicitly.[43] New Testament writings are not usually cited as Scripture.[44] Yet the appropriation of New Testament writings is clearly happening. It is obvious, for example, that *1 Clement* knows some form of the Gospel tradition,[45] and used 1 Corinthians (to which he explicitly refers),[46] as well as the Letter to the Hebrews.[47] The detection of such appropriation,

---

Decretum Gelasianum, which circulated in some MSS independently under the name of Damasus, is argued by E. von Dobschütz, *Das Decretum Gelasianum de Libris Recipiendis et Non Recipiendis* (Leipzig, 1912). The argument I make here tends to confirm, by other than purely text-critical means, the position of Turner.

40. For the Latin text, see Souter, p. 204.

41. Innocent I, *Epistula* VI, 7, 13 (PL 20: 502).

42. See, e.g., *1 Clement* 3:1; 4:1; 8:2; 18:3; Ignatius, *Magnesians* 12:1; Polycarp, *Letter to the Philippians* 12:1; *Epistle of Barnabas* 4:14; 5:2.

43. *1 Clement* 23:3 has an otherwise unknown "scripture" concerning the double-minded, which is also reported by *2 Clement* 11:2 as a "prophetic word." The *Shepherd of Hermas, Vis* 3, 4 refers to the Book of Eldad and Modad as "scripture."

44. The introduction to Mark 2:7 as "another scripture" by *2 Clement* 2:4 is unusual.

45. See *1 Clement* 13:1-2; 46:7-8.

46. The explicit reference to 1 Corinthians is in *1 Clement* 47:1-3. Traces of 1 Corinthians can be found also in 24:1; 34:8; 37:5; 49:5.

47. For the use of Hebrews, see *1 Clement* 9:2; 10:1-7; 12:1-2; 17:1, 4; 36:1-5; 43:1. See also P. Ellingworth, "Hebrews and 1 Clement: Literary Dependence or Common Tradition?" *BZ* n.s. 23 (1979) 262-269; D. A. Hagner, *The Use of the Old and New Testaments in Clement of Rome* (NovTSup 34; Leiden: Brill, 1973), 179-237.

therefore, must rely on the evaluation of linguistic signals: language, themes, or imagery appears in a writing which finds precedent (so far as we know) only in a certain NT writing, and does so with sufficient density and pervasiveness to suggest dependence of one writing on another.

In the case of James, however — and this is the second difficulty — such detection is made more difficult by the fact that James is a moral exhortation, or protrepsis, that uses traditions otherwise widely attested in both Greco-Roman and Jewish moral literature. And to make things even more complicated, writings such as *1 Clement* and *Shepherd of Hermas* are also hortatory in character. This makes it difficult to sort out literary dependence in the strict sense from the natural consonance of compositions using the same genre or *topoi*.[48]

The older tendency in scholarship was to assert literary dependence everywhere. Any recurrent phrase could stand as evidence that an earlier document was being used as a source.[49] In the case of James, J. B. Mayor's great commentary sedulously lists every verbal and thematic echo as evidence for James's thoroughgoing impact on the early church.[50] The problems with this approach are obvious. It tends to over-detect literary nuances, and it fails to account for the use of shared traditions. By claiming too much, the method loses credibility.

A second tendency among scholars has been to assert broad traditions to account for the verbal and thematic resemblance between compositions. Similarities between Paul and 1 Peter, for example, are attributed to the use of common materials rather than to literary dependence.[51] Appeal can also

48. It is clear, for example, that *1 Clement* makes use of the standard examples and connections found in the *topos* on envy everywhere in Greco-Roman and Jewish literature, as well as in James 3:13–4:10, complicating the question of possible derivation of those tropes *for Clement* from James; see my essay "James 3:13–4:10 and the *topos* περὶ φθόνου," pp. 182-201 in this volume, esp. p. 189, n. 33.

49. A classic example is O. D. Foster, *The Literary Relations of "the First Epistle of Peter"* (Transactions of the Connecticut Academy of Arts and Sciences 17; 1913), 363-538. James appears as a bridge between Ephesians and 1 Peter. For the same approach, see A. E. Barnett, *Paul Becomes a Literary Influence* (Chicago: University of Chicago Press, 1941), and C. L. Mitton, "The Relationship between 1 Peter and Ephesians," *JTS* n.s. 1 (1950) 67-73.

50. J. B. Mayor, *The Epistle of St. James,* 3rd ed. (London: Macmillan and Co., 1910), lxvi-lxxxiv. The weakness of the approach is shown especially when Mayor tries to show James's influence on other canonical writings (pp. lxxxv-cix), which is based on his premise that James was composed before 50 and one of the earliest NT writings (see p. cl).

51. Notice, for example, how the conviction that Peter used shared traditions affects the commentary of E. G. Selwyn, *The First Epistle of Saint Peter* (London: Macmillan and Co., 1958), in contrast to Foster's approach.

be made to a literary genre like parenesis or the farewell discourse to account for similarities between compositions. In the case of James, the classic commentary of Martin Dibelius best illustrates this second approach. He recognizes the often startling resemblances between James and Hermas, for example,[52] and faithfully notes them throughout his commentary.[53] But he refuses to recognize any possible dependence between the writings, appealing instead to a shared parenetic tradition.[54] This approach provides an antidote to the earlier overconfidence concerning the detection of sources, but it has drawbacks of its own. First, it tends to neglect the *specific* ways in which even traditional materials can be borrowed and used, and therefore tends to ignore the specificity of language that points to possible dependence. Second, it minimizes the thoroughly literary and self-referential character of the Christian movement from the beginning.[55]

To make a credible case, then, that second-century compositions knew and used James, it is not enough to locate specific phrases that occur both in James and in these writings, even when they are otherwise unattested, such as the expression "double-minded" *(dipsychos)*,[56] although even in this

52. M. Dibelius, *A Commentary on the Epistle of James,* rev. H. Greeven, trans. M. A. Williams (Hermeneia; Philadelphia: Fortress Press, 1976), 31.

53. Dibelius, pp. 141, 213, 219, etc.

54. "It is probably the case that both writings have at their disposal a relatively large store of paraenetic material which *Hermas* passes on in a reworked condition ('expanded paraenesis') and James in the form of sayings" (Dibelius, p. 32).

55. Dibelius, p. 34, states: "Virtually nowhere can it be shown that an author is dependent on Jas for the simple reason that the concepts contained in Jas are so unoriginal, and so very much the common property of primitive Christianity. In this the essence of paraenesis shows itself once more." This is not only an example of circular reasoning, but it also obviously fails to deal with the highly distinctive *language* James uses to express what are sometimes (not always) shared concepts. This premise leads Dibelius to deny, sometimes with tortuous argument, any specific points of resemblance, or, when forced to acknowledge them, to dismiss their significance.

56. Within the NT canon, *dipsychos* is found only in James (1:8 and 4:8). There is, furthermore, no evidence of its occurrence before James, despite the efforts of O. J. F. Seitz, "The Relationship of the Shepherd of Hermas to the Epistle of James," *JBL* 63 (1944) 131-40; "Antecedents and Significance of the Term *'dipsychos'*," *JBL* 66 (1947) 211-219; and "Afterthoughts on the Term *'dipsychos'*," *NTS* 4 (1957-58) 327-334. That James is the source of the expression is argued by S. E. Porter, "Is *dipsychos* (James 1:8; 4:8) a 'Christian' Word?" *Bib* 71 (1990) 469-498. Still, it is better to be cautious concerning the occurrence of the isolated term in passages such as *1 Clement* 11:2; 23:2-3; *2 Clement* 11:2-5; 19:2; *Didache* 4:4; and *Epistle of Barnabas* 19:5-7. The same is true of such expressions as "friend of God" applied to Abraham (James 2:23) found in *1 Clement* 10:1; 17:2, the ideal of impartiality in judgment (James 2:1) found in *Didache* 4:3 and *Epistle of Barnabas* 19:4, and the expression "love covers a multitude of sins" (James 5:20), found in 1 Peter 4:8 as well as in *1 Clement* 49:5, *2 Clement* 16:4.

case it is pertinent to ask where such writings would have learned the expression except from James. In order to assert the use of James by one of these writings, three positive criteria must be met: (1) there is an overall similarity in outlook and language between this writing and James, with at least some of the linguistic parallels being distinctive if not unique; (2) the parallels come from more than one section of James, and appear in more than one part of the second-century writing; (3) the parallels are sufficiently dense and pervasive to suggest dependence rather than coincidence.

1 Clement meets these criteria impressively. In addition to scattered points of parallel language,[57] *1 Clement* establishes a thematic opposition between arrogance and humility very similar to that in James,[58] which in one place also takes the form of a strong verbal parallel.[59] There are also sentences in *1 Clement* that match James in both language and meaning.[60] In addition, there are three sections of *1 Clement* in which there is a particularly high density of verbal and thematic resemblances to James. The first is Clement's condemnation of the Corinthians' envy (*1 Clement* 3-4): as in James 3:13–4:10, we see that envy causes social unrest and war, brought death into the world, and causes the murder of the brethren. These elements, it is true, are commonly found in the *topos* on envy, but in *1 Clement* the condemnation of envy is followed by a call to conversion (7:2–8:5), a combination otherwise found only in the *Testament of Simeon* 4:4 and the Letter of James. Second is Clement's treatment of Abraham (9:2–12:8), which, while having some resemblances to Hebrews as well, on critical details comes closer to the portrayal of Abraham in James 2:20-26. Third is a section of *1 Clement* running from 29:1 to 31:1-2 in which there is a sequence of thirteen items with the highest degree of thematic and verbal similarity to James.[61]

There is, then, the strong probability that *1 Clement* knew and used James. If the data are so impressive that an argument can be made that James used *1 Clement*,[62] they are even more convincing for the dependence of *1 Clement* on James.[63] If this is so, then a composition that certainly was

---

57. See the examples in the previous note.

58. See *1 Clement* 2:1; 13:1; 59:3.

59. Compare *1 Clement* 59:3a to James 4:10, and 59:3b to James 4:12.

60. Compare *1 Clement* 46:5 to James 4:1, and *1 Clement* 38:2 to James 3:13.

61. For full data on this and the previous points, see L. T. Johnson, *The Letter of James* (Anchor Bible 37A; New York: Doubleday, 1995), 72-75.

62. See F. Y. Young, "The Relation of 1 Clement to the Epistle of James," *JBL* 67 (1948) 339-345.

63. See also Hagner, *The Use of the Old and New Testaments in Clement of Rome*, pp. 248-256.

written from the church at Rome, probably around the year 95, testifies to the presence of James and its assumed authority in that local church.

That the *Shepherd of Hermas* was also written from Rome in the first half of the second century is attested by the Muratorian Fragment, which attributes the writing to a brother of Pius, the bishop of Rome from 140 to 154.[64] The resemblance in outlook, theme, and language between James and *Hermas* is remarkable and has often been noted.[65] Martin Dibelius is so appreciative of these parallels that his refusal to acknowledge dependence in this case seems based more on his presuppositions than on the evidence. If *Hermas* is, as Dibelius notes, "an expansion of paraenesis, its application to specifically Christian situations, and at least the christianization of its framework and arrangement of the traditional materials,"[66] why should we not accept here a direct dependence on James, rather than the (unsupported) hypothesis of shared parenetic materials with the same distinctive linguistic characteristics?

The points of contact include the use of *dipsychos* in all its possible permutations, including as a verb, and its being placed (as in James 4:8) in direct opposition to purity and simplicity of heart, which is accomplished, as in James (4:8-10), by repentance. *Hermas* shares the same cosmology as James, and the same contrast between a wisdom from above and one from below. Its ethical preoccupation with poverty and wealth matches precisely that in James, as does its focus on evil speech.[67] The demand for simplicity and lack of double-mindedness in prayer in *Hermas* Mand. 9:1-4 and James 1:5-8 is so alike that Dibelius is moved to declare *Hermas* to be "the best interpretation of James imaginable."[68] But isn't the best explanation of such an "interpretation" the use of James by *Hermas*? Finally, there is a series of statements in which the sentiment and the language alike are so similar that the dependence of the later writing on the earlier is virtually demanded.[69] Indeed, the evidence in *Hermas* is so strong

---

64. See the Muratorian Canon in Souter, p. 193.

65. The way in which *Hermas* appropriates materials from James is demonstrated by C. Taylor, "The Didache Compared with the Shepherd of Hermas," *Journal of Philology* 18 (1890) 297-325. With reference to the Mandates, Dibelius (p. 3) notes: "Here there is found a kinship which goes beyond lexical and conceptual agreement. Extensive and coherent discussions in *Hermas* could be placed alongside isolated admonitions in James and serve as a commentary on the latter."

66. Dibelius, p. 46.

67. For specific references, see Johnson, *The Letter of James,* pp. 75-78.

68. Dibelius, p. 31.

69. Compare James 2:7 to *Hermas* Sim. 8:6,4; James 1:21 to *Hermas* Sim. 6:1,1; James 4:12

that the burden of proof is shifted: if James is *not* the source of such distinctive language, then what is?

If this analysis is correct, then there are two writings from the Roman church, dated circa 95 and 150, that, without citing James by name (which was, as we have seen, rarely done for any NT writing at this time), make extensive use of this composition in their respective moral exhortations.

The evidence for the continued use of James in this local church is slender and suspect. There is extant an encyclical letter from Urban I (ca. 230) which begins with a mixed citation from James 2:14 and 3:2, introduced by "James the Apostle says."[70] Sometime before 250, Novatian's tractate on the Trinity contains an allusion to James 1:17.[71] In a series of letters from Stephanus (before 257), there is an allusion to James 2:13.[72] An even clearer allusion to James 2:13 appears in a spurious composition attributed to Hippolytus of Rome (after 260). There is a lengthy and explicit citation of James 3:1-8 attributed to "James the Apostle" in a letter from Pope Marcellus (308-309).[73] Finally, there is a possible allusion to James 5:9 in an encyclical letter from Liberius (352-366), the immediate predecessor to Damasus.[74] There is, therefore, some evidence for the knowledge and use of James in the Roman church from the late first century up through the fourth century.

The Three Doctors

Despite the importance of the Roman church, its use of James locally would not itself have been sufficient to secure the place of James in the canon. Had not three teachers who were all monks (or near enough), who were all aligned with Damasus and who were also all admirers of Origen, sponsored James so enthusiastically, it might not have won general acceptance in the West.

Rufinus (345-410) is the least well known of the three. Born in Aquileia, he went to school in Rome, where he became friends with Jerome. Around

---

to *Hermas* Mand. 12:6,3; James 4:17 to *Hermas* Mand. 8:2; James 5:19-20 to *Hermas* Mand. 8:10. For the specific language, see Johnson, *The Letter of James,* pp. 78-79.

70. Urban I, *Epistula ad Omnes Christianos* (PG 10: 135). The problem with this and the other "papal" letters cited is that they are among the "False Decretals," undoubtedly medieval forgeries. I include them simply because, even if spurious, they associate James with Rome in an intriguing way.

71. Novatian, *De Trinitate* IV, 1 (PL 3: 919).

72. Stephanus, *Epistulae Decretales* (PL 3: 1042).

73. Marcellus, *Epistula ad Episcopos Antiochenae Provinciae* (PL 7: 1094-1095).

74. Liberius, *Epistula ad Omnes Generaliter Episcopos* (PL 8: 1402).

372, he went to Egypt and visited the monks there. He studied for several years with Didymus the Blind (313-398), himself a disciple of Origen, who also happened to have written a commentary on James.[75] Rufinus was in Jerusalem living as a monk during the same period that Jerome was there (381-397). Rufinus's admiration for Origen was so great that he was thought to have been an Origenist. He translated into Latin Origen's *First Principles,* as well as a number of his commentaries. He also translated Eusebius's *Historia Ecclesiastica,* from which he undoubtedly learned of Eusebius's views on James.[76] In any case, Rufinus explicitly lists James as canonical in his commentary on the Apostles' Creed, calling him both "apostle and brother of the Lord," and concluding the list, "These are the ones the fathers have closed within the canon and from which they wished assertions of our faith to stand."[77] When Rufinus fell into dispute with Jerome over his understanding of Origen, he quoted against his new adversary James 3:1, "not many of us should become teachers!"[78]

St. Jerome (342-420) was also a native of Aquileia, who spent time in Rome as well as great periods of time in Palestine as an ascetic. He is of tremendous importance for the wider acceptance of James, simply because, with Origen, he was regarded as the supreme authority on Scripture. Indeed, his explicit debt to Origen is acknowledged in a letter he wrote to Augustine.[79] He also shared Origen's esteem for the Letter of James, remarking in a letter to Paulinus how the catholic epistles "declare as much mystically as succinctly,"[80] and he quotes James frequently in a variety of his writings as "the apostle James."[81] Most of all, of course, Jerome's influence is found in the fact that he included James among the NT writings, when, acting as secretary to Pope Damasus and instructed by him in 382 to provide a better Latin translation of the Bible, he produced his Vulgate version.

But why did Jerome include James in his improved translation? Here we come to what is properly a third line of argument concerning the use

---

75. Didymus, *Enarratio in Epistolam Beati Jacobi* (PG 39: 1749-1754).

76. For these biographical details, see *The Oxford Dictionary of the Christian Church,* p. 1207.

77. Rufinus, *Commentarius in Symbolum* 36 (PL 21: 374).

78. Rufinus, *Apologia Contra Hieronymum* I, 19, 31 (PL 21: 557).

79. Augustine, *Epistula* 75 (PL 33: 251-263).

80. Jerome, *Epistula* 53:8 (PL 22: 548).

81. For the explicit introduction, see *Dialogus adversus Pelagianos* II, 5, 10-15; II, 18, 6; for other citations from James, see, e.g., *Tractatus de Psalmo CXVIII* 2; *Homilia in Lucam* XVI, 19-31; *Commentarium in Matthaeum* I, 5, 22; *Dialogus adversus Pelagianos* I, 20, 1-19; II, 13, 30; II, 14, 40; II, 18, 20; III, 14, 33.

of James in the West, namely the fact that it had already been translated from the Greek into Latin in a variety of versions that are known collectively as Old Latin. If, as some critics have argued, the text lying in back of the Bobbio MS (fifth century) and Corbey MS (ninth/tenth century) actually went back to third-century translations produced in Africa, such dissemination of James would have considerably preceded its earliest known citation by an African writer.[82] As J. H. Ropes has observed, James does not always, in such MSS, appear with other biblical writings.[83] But this may, in fact, be an example of what Jerome himself described as James gathering authority "bit by bit." The presence of James in Old Latin NT MSS, the probable use of James by the local Roman church, especially its bishops, since the second century, the listing of James as canonical by Damasus his sponsor in 382, and the strong tradition of James's inclusion in the canon in the school of Origen; these all must have combined to make the inclusion of James in the Vulgate, and therefore its acceptance as part of Scripture for the Western church, seem almost inevitable.

There remains North Africa, which had seemingly made no use of James before the fourth century. North Africa in turn brings us to Augustine of Hippo (354-430), the youngest but also ultimately the most influential of our three doctors. It is undoubtedly through his influence that James finally won this last piece of the West and helped shape a millennium of Christendom. Augustine rose rapidly through ecclesiastical ranks after his long-delayed conversion, becoming a priest in 391, a coadjutor bishop in 395, and bishop of Hippo in 396. Augustine was almost obsequious in his admiration for Jerome, as their star-crossed but fascinating correspondence indicates. Their letters make clear that both teachers found Origen to be a significant authority in matters scriptural.[84] His letters also attest to Augustine's enthusiastic recognition of James as Scripture,[85] as does his inclusion of James in the canonical list provided by *On Christian Doctrine*.[86]

---

82. See J. Wordsworth, "The Corbey St. James (ff) and Its Relation to Other Latin Versions, and to the Original Language of the Epistle," *Studia Biblica: Essays in Biblical Archaeology and Criticism*, ed. S. R. Driver et al. (Oxford: Clarendon Press, 1885), 134-136.

83. J. H. Ropes, "The Text of the Epistle of James," *JBL* 28 (1909) 103-129.

84. See, e.g., Augustine, *Epistulae* 40 (PL 33: 154-158) and 75 (PL 33: 251-263).

85. He, too, quotes James 3:2 to Jerome, as Rufinus had; see *Epistula* 73 (PL 33: 249-250). For other citations of James in his correspondence, see, e.g., *Epistulae* 82 (PL 33: 285); 137 (PL 33: 516); 140 (PL 33: 549, 574); 147 (PL 33: 602); 149 (PL 33: 632-633); 153 (PL 33: 657); 157 (PL 33: 678, 691); 162 (PL 33: 707); 167 (PL 33: 732-742); 177 (PL 33: 766); 186 (PL 33: 820); 189 (PL 33: 857); 205 (PL 33: 947); 214 (PL 33: 970-971); 250 (PL 33: 1067); 266 (PL 33: 1090).

86. *De Doctrina Christiana* II, 13 (PL 34: 41).

Augustine even wrote a short commentary on James, although it is not extant.[87] His many citations of James in other compositions suggest some of the things that might have been in that *expositio,* and show how the developing Western tradition of interpreting James was remarkably close to that in the Eastern church. On numerous occasions, for example, Augustine combines Gal 5:6 and James 2:19-26 in a harmonizing resolution of the issue of faith and works.[88] That Augustine saw no conflict between James and Paul is obvious. He uses James 4:6 to interpret Rom 1:20,[89] and concludes his treatise on "Grace and Free Will" with a catena of verses from James 1:5; 3:17; and 3:14-17![90] Like Greek patristic writers, Augustine used James 1:13 to assert that God did not tempt humans, and 1:14 to blame human passions for temptations and sin.[91] Like Eastern writers, Augustine used 1:17 to assert the unchangeableness of God[92] and to declare that God is the source of all righteousness.[93] Augustine also offers a full discussion of James 2:10 in light of the Stoic principle of the unity of all virtue,[94] and sermonic expositions of James 1:19-22[95] and 5:12.[96]

In the light of the development I have traced, the canon that includes the Letter of James published by the Council of Carthage in 397 (one year after Augustine became sole bishop of Hippo and an ever greater influence together with his ally Bishop Aurelius of Carthage) takes on even greater significance. Not only does it show James finally winning the West, but it suggests something of the process by which this happened and the network of communication that enabled it. Canon 39 begins,

87. *Retractiones* II, 32 (PL 32: 643-644) lists among his *opuscula* an "expositio epistulae Jacobi ad duodecim tribus."

88. See *De Fide et Operibus* XIV, 23 (PL 40: 212); *De Trinitate* XV, 18 (PL 42: 1083); *De Gratia et Libero Arbitrio* VII, 18 (PL 44: 892); *Discourse 2 on Psalm 31, 1-26* (PL 36: 259); and the newly discovered *Epistula* *2:6.

89. *De Spiritu et Littera* 20 (PL 44: 212).

90. *De Gratia et Libero Arbitrio* 46 (PL 44: 912). Notice also the way Augustine concludes his "incomplete" *Literal Interpretation of Genesis* with a citation of 3:9, attributed to "the authority of the apostle James" (XVI, 62 [PL 34: 246]).

91. For 1:13, see *Epistula* 162 (PL 33: 707) and 205 (PL 33: 947); *Tractatus in Evangelium Johannis* 43, 5 (PL 35: 1707); *De Gratia et Libero Arbitrio* 2, 3 (PL 44: 883). For 1:14, see *De Gratia et Libero Arbitrio* 4, 8 (PL 44: 887).

92. *De Trinitate* I, 1 (PL 42: 821); see also the "incomplete" *Literal Interpretation of Genesis* (PL 34: 334).

93. *De Spiritu et Littera* 11, 22, and 63 (PL 44: 207, 214, and 242); *Epistula* 147:46 (PL 33: 617) and 214:4 (PL 33: 970); *De Gratia et Libero Arbitrio* VI, 15 (PL 44: 890).

94. *Epistula* 167 (PL 33: 733-742).

95. *Sermo* 179 (PL 38: 966-972).

96. *Sermo* 180 (PL 38: 972-979).

"nothing is read in church under the name of the divine scriptures except the canonical writings." It then lists the Old Testament, and our present canon of twenty-seven writings, including James, concluding, "For the confirmation of this canon, the church across the sea [— we understand this to be the Roman church —] is to be consulted."[97]

The argument depends on a frustratingly small amount of data and a willingness to take a position on some difficult and obscure points. But the process by which James came to enjoy an unquestioned place in the canon of the Western church until the time of Luther must have been close to the one here suggested. The argument is that James was written sufficiently before the year 95 to have been employed by writers in the Roman church by the end of the first century and that this local usage, together with Rome's alliance with Alexandria and three great doctors' admiration for Origen, helped secure James its place.

---

97. For the Latin text, see Souter, p. 204.

The Social World of James:
Literary Analysis and Historical Reconstruction

In the history of New Testament scholarship, the name Wayne A. Meeks inevitably and appropriately will be associated with the social analysis of early Christianity. Both by his writing and by his teaching, Meeks has demonstrated that a "sociological" approach to the New Testament is not a scholarly fad but a fundamental contribution to historical knowledge. His seminal contributions to the discussion of Christianity's social world have revealed the rich possibilities of the approach and have helped secure at the very least a conviction that earliest Christianity can no longer be understood simply in terms of a "history of ideas." But Meeks's own highly successful forays into the analysis of early Christian social realities have also suggested certain intractable limitations on what this approach can yield by way of real knowledge.

In *The First Urban Christians,* for example, Meeks built on his own and others' previous studies to provide a rich profile of the Corinthian congregation during the years of Paul's work there.[1] By combining the close analysis of the Corinthian correspondence with archaeological evidence, and reading these texts for signs of social structures and relationships, Meeks was able to illuminate not only the social realities underlying the

---

1. Wayne A. Meeks, *The First Urban Christians: The Social World of the Apostle Paul* (New Haven: Yale University Press, 1983). See also, for example, W. A. Meeks, "Social Functions of Apocalyptic Language in Pauline Christianity," in *Apocalypticism in the Mediterranean World and the Near East,* ed. D. Hellholm (Tübingen: Mohr-Siebeck, 1982); idem, "The Image of the Androgyne: Some Uses of a Symbol in Earliest Christianity," *HR* 13 (1974) 165-208; E. A. Judge, "The Social Identity of the First Christians: A Question of Method in Religious History," *Journal of Religious History* 11 (1980) 201-217; A. J. Malherbe, *Social Aspects of Early Christianity* (Baton Rouge: Louisiana State University Press, 1977); G. Theissen, *The Social Setting of Pauline Christianity: Essays on Corinth,* trans. J. Schutz (Philadelphia: Fortress, 1982).

specific problems dealt with by Paul but also something of the umbrella of meaning that provided an ideological framework for the nascent Christian movement. So brilliant was his achievement that it may have raised unrealistic expectations of accomplishment elsewhere.

Meeks would be the first to acknowledge that the success of his Corinthian analysis depended on an unusual combination of factors: a successfully excavated and archaeologically rich urban setting that was also described in ancient literature; a correspondence that not only dealt with specific problems in the community but did so with an unparalleled degree of particularity and specificity, down to the naming of names; and, finally, the existence of other Christian literature (Acts, Romans) which helped locate this correspondence chronologically and confirm some of the social realities suggested by 1 Corinthians. To a remarkable degree, in fact, Meeks's analysis focused almost exclusively on the Corinthian congregation, with evidence from other Pauline letters and communities offered mainly by way of corroboration.

Where a like combination of converging evidence is lacking, sociological analysis of early Christianity can easily mean a return to a slightly more complex version of the history of ideas, with the use of sociological/developmental models filling in for the lack of genuine data.[2]

Think what our knowledge of the Corinthian church itself would really amount to, if 1 Corinthians — so rooted in the real and urban world — were no longer extant. 2 Corinthians could lend itself to any number of "mirror readings" concerning Paul's rivals, as in fact it has.[3] R. Hock has offered a slight foothold in reality by sketching the background to debates concerning payment for services among Hellenistic philosophers, which helps make sense of Paul's language in 2 Corinthians 10-12.[4] But otherwise, 2 Corinthians and the other Pauline letters tend to be read as evidence for theological debates between "Paul and his opponents," with

2. An early advocate of an explicit commitment to such models was J. G. Gager, *Kingdom and Community: The Social World of Early Christianity* (Englewood Cliffs, N.J.: Prentice-Hall, 1975); for the options, see H. E. Remus, "Sociology of Knowledge and the Study of Early Christianity," *SR* 11 (1982) 45-56.

3. The most elaborate and influential example has been D. Georgi, *The Opponents of Paul in Corinth* (1964; Eng. trans. Philadelphia: Fortress, 1985); see also C. K. Barrett, "Paul's Opponents in II Corinthians," *NTS* 17 (1971) 233-254. Criticism of this approach is found in C. J. A. Hickling, "Is the Second Epistle to the Corinthians a Source for Early Church History?" *ZNW* 66 (1975) 284-287, and in C. R. Holladay, *Theios Anēr in Hellenistic Judaism: A Critique of the Use of This Category in New Testament Christology* (SBLDS 40; Missoula, Mont.: Scholars Press, 1977).

4. R. F. Hock, *The Social Context of Paul's Ministry* (Philadelphia: Fortress, 1980), 50-65.

the letters themselves being chopped into ever finer pieces and arranged in sequence to supply the appropriate reconstruction of the "stages" of such debates.[5]

The recent attempt by J. Neyrey to read Galatians in terms of anthropological concepts such as "witchcraft" shows the intrinsic limitations of social-scientific approaches for Pauline letters where rich supporting evidence is lacking: his readings are fascinating and suggestive, but cannot reach much beyond that.[6] When it comes to the disputed Pauline letters, the evidence is even thinner. M. MacDonald's study of institutionalization in Pauline churches, for example, is forced to make the production of pseudonymous letters itself the major evidence for that particular stage of institutional development![7]

It seems clear that the more we move from occasional literature such as letters to compositions intended for a wider readership, the more the factors of rhetoric and literary artistry necessarily interpose themselves between the contemporary reader and the social world that may have been presumed by the composition. Likewise, when the text itself reveals little specific information about its social world, the investigator becomes more dependent on theoretical models concerning social groups and their development. The sheer multiplicity of possibilities suggested for the various "communities" presupposed or addressed by the Gospels raises severe doubts concerning the usefulness of the search.[8]

5. On 2 Corinthians, see the recent attempt along these lines by A. de Oliveira, *Die Diakonie der Gerechtigkeit und der Versöhnung in der Apologie des 2 Korintherbriefes: Analyse und Auslegung von 2 Kor 2,14–4,6; 5,11–6,10* (NTAbh n.F. 21; Münster: Aschendorff, 1990); for other Pauline Letters, see J. Tyson, "Paul's Opponents in Galatia," *NovT* 10 (1968) 241-254; R. Jewett, "Conflicting Movements in the Early Church as Reflected in Philippians," *NovT* 12 (1970) 361-390; W. A. Meeks and F. O. Francis, *Conflict at Colossae,* rev. ed. (SBLSBS 4; Missoula, Mont.: Scholars Press, 1975).

6. J. Neyrey, *Paul in Other Words: A Cultural Reading of His Letters* (Louisville: Westminster/John Knox, 1990), 181-206.

7. M. Y. MacDonald, *The Pauline Churches: A Socio-Historical Study of Institutionalization in the Pauline and Deutero-Pauline Writings* (SNTSMS 60; Cambridge: Cambridge University Press, 1988), 86-97; somewhat similar is the argumentation of M. Wolter, *Die Pastoralbriefe als Paulustradition* (FRLANT 146; Göttingen: Vandenhoeck & Ruprecht, 1988), 115-130. As I noted in my review of MacDonald's study in *JAAR* 58 (1990) 716-719, her work has the significant virtue of methodological clarity and consistency; in my view, however, that very quality makes even more doubtful the validity of the development as she exposes it.

8. I have tried to suggest some of the difficulties for finding a "community" behind the Gospel narratives in "On Finding the Lukan Community: A Cautious Cautionary Essay," in *Society of Biblical Literature 1979 Seminar Papers,* ed. P. J. Achtemeier (Missoula, Mont.: Scholars Press, 1979), 87-100.

Not that stunning invention is impossible. By his use of sociological categories concerning sectarianism, Meeks himself masterfully exploited the possibilities of such a theoretical model for unlocking the intricate rhetoric of a narrative text.[9] No one acquainted with Meeks's analysis of the Fourth Gospel's textual ironies as reinforcing the sectarian views of Johannine Christianity can, I suspect, ever totally shake the force of that reading. Yet even so great an accomplishment did not significantly add to our knowledge of John's social world, although it immeasurably sharpened our appreciation of its ideology and literary rendering.

More pedestrian attempts to derive from the layered texture of John's narrative or from the sequential arrangement of the Gospel and Johannine letters a "history" of Johannine Christianity must be viewed as interesting but nonconclusive paper chases rather than history.[10] Beyond the signals obvious to any careful reader — that this literature reflected experiences of being embattled from without and divided from within; that such division sharpened its symbols into polar opposites; that the causes of embattlement from without and division from within involved the central figure of Jesus — efforts at reading a "history" out of such fragmentary sources become less plausible the more highly they are developed. Once more, access to the social world of John or his readers is blocked by the lack of controls offered by a convergence of diverse sources from a specific time and place, as well as by the literary character of the texts.[11]

These observations on the possibilities and problems of reconstructing the social world behind New Testament writings bring me in a chastened mood to the real topic of this essay. What, if anything, can be determined from the Letter of James about the social world of its author or readers? Can the Letter of James be rooted in history at all? If so, by what means or with what benefit to the understanding of the letter? On the one hand, we are offered hope because James is so obviously enmeshed in the realities of life and practical wisdom. On the other hand, our hope is

9. W. A. Meeks, "The Man from Heaven in Johannine Sectarianism," *JBL* 91 (1972) 44-72.

10. For example, J. L. Martyn, *History and Theology in the Fourth Gospel* (rev. ed.; Nashville: Abingdon, 1979); idem, *The Gospel of John in Christian History* (New York: Paulist, 1978); R. E. Brown, *The Community of the Beloved Disciple* (New York: Paulist, 1979); J. Painter. "The Farewell Discourses and the History of Johannine Christianity," *NTS* 27 (1980-81) 525-43.

11. Chances are obviously improved if the book of Revelation is taken seriously as a source for the history of Johannine Christianity: see, e.g., E. Schüssler Fiorenza, "The Quest for the Johannine School: The Book of Revelation and the Fourth Gospel," in *The Book of Revelation: Justice and Judgment* (Philadelphia: Fortress, 1985), 85-113.

qualified by the realization that James's no-nonsense practicality is never clothed with the sort of specific information we desire. In the remainder of this essay I propose to survey some of the ways the social world of James might be approached and assess the chances of success offered by each.

A Social World Suggested by Traditional Authorship

The most encouraging possibilities would seem to be offered by the identity of the author, if we could assume that James "the Brother of the Lord" — universally considered the "James" of the letter's greeting[12] — was the real and not simply the eponymous author. What we would gain by this supposition is a writer whose position and importance as a pillar of the church in Jerusalem are attested by other New Testament writers,[13] and

12. See the very full discussions in J. B. Mayor, *The Epistle of St. James* (3rd ed.; London: Macmillan, 1910), i-lxv; J. H. Ropes, *A Critical and Exegetical Commentary on the Epistle of St. James* (Edinburgh: Clark, 1916), 53-74; M. Dibelius, *James: A Commentary on the Epistle of James,* rev. H. Greeven, trans. M. A. Williams (Hermeneia; Philadelphia: Fortress, 1976), 11-21; R. P. Martin, *James* (WBC 48; Waco, Tex.: Word, 1988), xxxi-lxix.

13. Paul lists James as a witness to the resurrection in 1 Cor 15:7, and may include James in his passing reference to those who traveled with a woman/sister: "the rest of the apostles and the brothers of the Lord and Cephas" (1 Cor 9:5). In Galatians, Paul recounts having seen James in Jerusalem on his trip to that city ἱστορῆσαι Κηφᾶν ("to visit Cephas"), although his language does not make clear whether he regards him as one of the apostles (1:19; compare the language in 1 Cor 15:7). James is included first in his list of those "reputed to be pillars" (δοκοῦντες στῦλοι εἶναι) in that city who made agreement with Paul concerning the allocation of mission work (2:9). Finally, there are the mysterious "people from James" (τινας ἀπὸ Ἰακώβου) who catalyze the problem between Paul and Cephas in Antioch (2:12). In contrast to Mark 6:3 and Matthew 13:55, who mention James among Jesus' brothers in a somewhat negative context (see J. D. Crossan, "Mark and the Relatives of Jesus," *NovT* 15 [1973] 81-113), Luke makes no certain mention of this James (see the ambiguity of Luke 6:16; Acts 1:13) until Peter's escape from prison in Acts 12:1-17: before "departing to another place," he told the assembly to "inform James and the Brothers of these things" (12:17). The language, together with that in 1 Cor 9:5, suggests the picture of James at the center of a special group called "brothers of the Lord" (see also Acts 1:14). James appears twice more in Acts as spokesperson for the Jerusalem church, first at the Apostolic Council, where his response to the debate concerning circumcision of Gentile converts is definitive (Acts 15:13-21), and second at Paul's final trip to Jerusalem, where James and the elders with him recommend that Paul deflect charges concerning his rejection of the law and circumcision for Jews by performing a symbolic act of solidarity (21:18-25). Finally, the author of the Letter of Jude identifies himself as "servant of Jesus Christ and brother of James" (Jude 1:1; compare Mark 6:3; Matt 13:55).

who is sufficiently prominent in the public affairs of Jerusalem to have his martyrdom in 62 noted as well by Josephus.[14] By this means we would gain as well the sort of geographical and chronological controls otherwise so difficult to come by in the analysis of New Testament literature. Geographically, the greeting to "the twelve tribes in the dispersion" (1:1) would be unproblematic if written by one residing in Jerusalem,[15] as would the assumption that his readers were, indeed, fellow Jews "holding the faith of our Lord Jesus Christ" (2:1). References to "Gehenna" (3:6), "fig-tree, olives, grape-vine" (3:12) or the "early and late rain" (5:7) might even be taken as spontaneous evidence for the influence of local conditions.[16]

Chronologically, connecting the letter to James the brother of Jesus makes more plausible the simple social structures and activities suggested by the text. The letter contains no sign of the institutional complexities that are supposed to be the marks of a community developing over time. The gathering of the community can be called the συναγωγή ("assembly or

14. Josephus, *Antiquities* 20.200. In contrast to an older criticism that tended to reject the authenticity of the notice (see F. C. Baur, *Paul, the Apostle of Jesus Christ,* 2nd ed., ed. E. Zeller, trans. A. Menzies [London: Williams & Norgate, 1875], 1:160), more recent scholars have tended to credit it; see the discussion, with literature, in J. P. Meier, *A Marginal Jew: Rethinking the Historical Jesus,* vol. 1: *The Roots of the Problem and the Person* (New York: Doubleday, 1991), 58-59, 72-73. James's death is also recounted (with variations) by the account from Hegesippus found in Eusebius, *Church History* 2.23, and in the Nag Hammadi writing the *Second Apocalypse of James* 61-62.

15. An alternative to the straightforwardly geographical understanding of "diaspora" (διασπορά) is to understand it as symbolizing the Christian condition of being "exiles, aliens, and sojourners" with respect to their heavenly homeland (compare especially 1 Pet 1:1; 2:11; 2 Cor 5:1-10; Gal 4:26; Phil 1:21-24; 3:20-21). And the opposition between faith and a certain understanding of "the world" is certainly central to James (see 2:5; 4:4). See my essay "Friendship with the World and Friendship with God: A Study of Discipleship in James," pp. 202-220 in this volume. But the two levels of meaning are compatible.

16. For commentaries that consider James of Jerusalem to be the author of this letter it is characteristic to entertain the possibility of "real life" perceptions behind passages such as 3:12 (see Mayor, *Epistle,* p. 124; Martin, *James,* p. 121; J. B. Adamson, *The Epistle of James* [NICNT; Grand Rapids: Eerdmans, 1976], 129), whereas commentaries holding for pseudonymous authorship lean entirely on literary sources (Dibelius, *James,* pp. 204-205). Mayor (*Epistle,* p. cxliii) is convinced that the supposition of early authorship is "confirmed by incidental allusions to the early and latter rains (v. 7), to the effect on vegetation of the burning wind (i.11), to the existence of salt and bitter springs (iii.11), to the cultivation of figs and olives (iii.12), and to the neighborhood of the sea (i.6, iii.4)." The case of γεέννη ("Gehenna") in 3:6 is particularly interesting. Since it does not occur in the LXX and is absent as well from Philo and Josephus or any other New Testament writings except the Gospels, it seems in particular to suggest a knowledge of local Palestinian usage (see J. Jeremias, γεέννη, *TDNT* 1:657-658).

synagogue"; 2:2) as well as ἐκκλησία ("assembly or church"; 5:14).[17] As for authority figures, the author designates himself simply as a δοῦλος ("servant") of God and the Lord Jesus Christ (1:1) before modestly receding behind his message. He demands no further recognition from his readers and asserts no further role among them, with the exception of carrying, with fellow teachers, the burden of "a greater judgment" (3:1).[18] Otherwise, the letter speaks of the "elders of the church" (πρεσβύτεροι τῆς ἐκκλησίας) who are to be called to pray over the sick.[19] Apart from this collegial leadership — if, in fact, πρεσβύτεροι ("elders") here suggests a position of official leadership rather than age — there is no indication of a formal structure, with only a passing warning against many seeking to become "teachers" because of the inherent dangers of that role (3:1-2).[20] Such minimal structure fits well within what little we know of the diaspora synagogue in Judaism.[21] The same can be said about the straightforward activities of the community mentioned by the text: judging cases (2:1-4), assisting the needy (1:27; 2:14-17), teaching (3:1-2), praying and singing (5:13), anointing the sick (5:14), and practicing mutual correction (5:16, 19).[22]

If James the brother of the Lord wrote the letter sometime around the

17. Compare the use of ἐπισυναγωγή in Heb 10:25. Although the terms ἐκκλησία and συναγωγή would come in some contexts to signify opposition between Christianity and Judaism (see Justin, *Dialogue with Trypho* 134.3), there also continues a more flexible usage in which the terms are virtually interchangeable: see Ignatius, *Polycarp* 4.2 (or the combination of συνέδριον/ἐκκλησία in *Tral.* 3.1); *Shepherd of Hermas, Mand.* 11.9, 13-14; Justin, *Dialogue with Trypho* 63.5.

18. The title of δοῦλος ("servant") for leaders is attested in several places in the first-generation Christian literature (Rom 1:1; 2 Cor 4:5; Gal 1:10; Phil 1:1; Col 4:12; 2 Tim 2:24; Titus 1:1; 2 Pet 1:1; Jude 1; Rev 1:1).

19. According to Acts, the leadership of elders was found not only in Jerusalem (15:2, 4, 6, 22-23; 21:18) but also in "diaspora" churches of the first generation (14:23; 20:17). Although it is popular to dismiss this portrayal as anachronistic for Pauline churches (see, e.g., F. Prast, *Presbyter und Evangelium in nachapostolischer Zeit: Die Abschiedsrede des Paulus in Milet (Apg 20, 17-38) im Rahmen der lukanischen Konzeption der Evangeliumsverkündigung* [Stuttgart: Katholisches Bibelwerk, 1979]), the evidence of 1 Tim 4:14; 5:1, 17, 19; and Titus 1:5 should not altogether be disregarded, nor that of 1 Pet 5:1, 5.

20. For the διδάσκαλος (also ὁ διδάσκων, ὁ κατηχῶν) as a first-generation position within the assembly, see Acts 13:1; Rom 12:7; 1 Cor 12:28-29; Gal 6:6; Eph 4:11. For teaching as a possible double-duty for the elder, see 1 Tim 5:17.

21. See Josephus, *Antiquities* 14.260; the inscriptional evidence has been gathered by L. H. Kant, "Jewish Inscriptions in Greek and Latin," *ANRW* 2.20 (1987) 692-698.

22. For the range of activities in the synagogue, see Josephus, *Antiquities* 4.211; *Against Apion* 2.10; *Life* 294-302; Philo, *Life of Moses* 2.216; *Special Laws* 2.62; *b. Ber.* 6a; *Ber.* 64a; *Ket.* 5a; *B. Meṣ.* 28b; *Pes.* 101a; *Yeb.* 65b.

middle of the first century, other aspects of this composition also make sense. It has frequently been noted that, despite mentioning Jesus by name only twice (1:1; 2:1), this letter appears to know and make use of the Jesus sayings traditions (see, e.g., 1:5, 9, 12; 2:5, 8; 5:9, 12).[23] At the same time, the letter combines a profound appreciation for wisdom (1:5; 3:13-18),[24] together with a vivid sense of the nearness of the παρουσία ("coming") of the Lord for judgment (2:12-13; 3:1; 4:11-12; 5:7-9).[25] Although I have misgivings about some of the ways in which the hypothetical document Q has been hypostatized, it is striking that just this combination of features (a concentration on the sayings of Jesus and his return as judge) is taken in Q as characteristic of a distinctively Palestinian form of earliest Christianity.[26]

23. See, e.g., M. Shepherd, "The Epistle of James and the Gospel of Matthew," *JBL* 75 (1956) 40-51; P. Minear, "'Yes and No': The Demand for Honesty in the Early Church," *NovT* 13 (1971) 1-13; P. J. Hartin, "James and the Sermon on the Mount/Plain," in *Society of Biblical Literature 1989 Seminar Papers*, ed. D. J. Lull (Atlanta: Scholars Press, 1989), 440-57.

24. See B. R. Halston, "The Epistle of James: 'Christian Wisdom'?" in *Studia Evangelica* 4 (1968) 308-314; J. A. Kirk, "The Meaning of Wisdom in James: Examination of a Hypothesis," *NTS* 16 (1969) 24-38.

25. There are three lines of evidence supporting the position that the coming of the Lord in 5:7-9 refers to the return of Jesus rather than the visitation of God. (1) The term παρουσία occurs only four times in the LXX and always in the secular sense (Neh 2:6; Judith 10:18; 2 Macc 8:12; 15:21; 3 Macc 3:17). The use in *Testament of Judah* 22:2 for "the appearing of the God of righteousness" may be an interpolation. In the New Testament, the term can be used in the secular sense (1 Cor 16:17; 2 Cor 7:6-7; 10:10; Phil 1:26; 2:12), but its dominant usage is as virtually a *terminus technicus* for the return of the Son of Man (Matt 24:3, 27, 37, 39; 1 Cor 15:23; 1 Thess 2:19; 3:13; 4:15; 5:23; 2 Thess 2:1, 8; 1 John 2:28; 2 Pet 1:16). (2) The use of the verb ἐγγίζω ("draw near") in the perfect tense to express "the Lord is near" is similar to the usage in Mark 1:15; Matt 3:2; 4:17; 10:7; Luke 10:9, 11; Rom 13:11; 1 Pet 4:7; Phil 4:5; Rev 1:3; 22:10. (3) The statement of 5:9b, "the judge is standing at the doors" (πρὸ τῶν θυρῶν), seems to fit within the development of the cluster of statements found in Mark 13:28-29; Matt 24:32-33; and Rev 3:20.

26. Already James Ropes had observed, "James was in religious ideas nearer to the men who collected the sayings of Jesus than to the authors of the Gospels" (*James*, p. 39). It is striking to observe the complete lack of any references to James in the analyses of Q which describe precisely those preoccupations that have long been associated with James: the theme of judgment in a context of wisdom and prophecy; see, e.g., R. A. Edwards, *A Theology of Q: Eschatology, Prophecy, and Wisdom* (Philadelphia: Fortress, 1976). It is especially startling when the argument about Q is precisely its similarity to other wisdom traditions and therefore its comfortable fit within early Palestinian Jewish Christianity; see J. S. Kloppenborg, *The Formation of Q: Trajectories in Ancient Wisdom Collections* (Studies in Antiquity & Christianity; Philadelphia: Fortress, 1987). The link with James called out to be made, and has been recently by P. J. Hartin (*James and the Q Sayings of Jesus* [JSNTSup 47; Sheffield: JSOT Press, 1991]), reaching conclusions concerning the provenance of James similar to those in the present essay (see esp. pp. 220-244).

Even with such a simple and straightforward hypothesis, of course, great caution would need to be exercised in drawing conclusions from the text about James's social world.[27] In the first place, the self-presentation of the document itself suggests a broad readership, and one not located in the same place as the author (1:1)! Throughout the diaspora, furthermore, readers could live in a variety of social situations. Such specific and lively examples as that provided in 2:1-7 must, therefore, be handled gingerly. They can reflect general or typical situations just as easily as they could local ones known to the author.[28] Similarly, language that seems to derive from knowledge of local meteorology and horticulture might equally come from the reading of Torah,[29] or acquaintance with popular moral traditions.[30] The language of "rich and poor" in James is likewise complex and not easily reducible to conclusions about the economic status of the readers.[31] James's frequent and fluent use of *topoi* from Hellenistic philosophy equally resists simplistic conclusions concerning the social situation being addressed;[32] it is surely a mistake, for example, to take James 4:1-2

27. The most obvious error in method is to deduce from the circumstances of the author the situation of the readers.

28. This, of course, is the point made emphatically by Dibelius, *James,* pp. 2, 46. Yet it is perhaps noteworthy that the analysis that has provided the fullest understanding of even a hypothetical social context for Jas 2:1-7 finds its basis in specifically Jewish traditions: see R. B. Ward, "Partiality in the Assembly," *HTR* 62 (1969) 87-97.

29. For the "early and late rain," in 5:7, see LXX Deut 11:14; Hos 6:4; Jer 5:24; Joel 2:23; Zech 10:1.

30. Despite the broad resemblance of 3:12 to Matt 7:16//Luke 6:44, Dibelius (*James,* pp. 204-205) lists an impressive number of Stoic parallels; see also Mayor, *Epistle,* p. 125.

31. An adequate analysis of this language complex requires: (a) making appropriate distinctions between terms for the "poor" (πτωχοί, 2:2, 3, 5, 6) and the "rich" (πλούσιοι, 1:10, 11; 2:5, 6; 5:1), which naturally bear an economic sense, and terms for "lowliness" (ταπεινός, etc., 1:9, 10; 4:10) and "exaltation" (ὕψος, 1:9; 4:10), which may have an economic sense but need not; (b) determining the ways such language may serve to demarcate community boundaries (e.g., 2:5-7; 5:1, 6); (c) correlating such language with the various characters and activities described in the letter: Is the "rich man" who enters the assembly (2:2) a member of the community or an outsider (2:6)? Is the rich man who "[boasts] in his humiliation" (1:10) a member of the community or an outsider (1:11)? Are those who thoughtlessly engage in commerce (4:13-15) and oppress day-laborers (5:1-5) the wicked outsiders, or insiders who have been seduced by the measurement of "the world" (4:4)? Likewise, what do we make of the ability of members of the community to feed and clothe the needy (2:14-16)? It is easier to affirm that the author and his readers shared the ideology of the poor than it is to deduce from that a realistic appreciation of the actual economic conditions within which they lived.

32. See my own attempts to identify some of these *topoi* of Hellenistic moral teaching in "James 3:13-4:10 and the *Topos* περὶ φθόνου," pp. 182-201; "The Mirror of Remembrance:

out of its literary context, that is, of a *topos* on envy, to conclude that the author was responding to Zealot activity in first-century Palestine.[33]

Despite such warnings, it is obvious that the hypothesis of authorship by the historical James of Jerusalem at least provides the *possibility* for genuine investigation into the social world of the composition.[34] It may be appropriate, therefore, to ask why that hypothesis is now so seldom entertained. There is certainly nothing in the letter that prevents its having been written from Palestine in the middle of the first century. All the usual criteria for positing a late dating for New Testament writings are absent: there is no institutional development, no sense of tradition as a deposit, no polemic against false teachers, no highly developed Christology, no delay of the parousia. On the face of it, everything in the letter suggests an early dating rather than a late one.

The rejection of traditional authorship is based on a perceived conflict between what we think we know of the "historical James" from other sources and the evidence suggested by this letter. Sometimes the distinctive Greek style of the letter has been cited as a factor against its being composed by James of Jerusalem,[35] but that argument has no real weight; it is now universally acknowledged that Palestine was thoroughly Hellenized and that writers from there could write sophisticated Greek.[36] The real problem has to do with what is believed to be the attitudes and actions of the "historical James" concerning the question of circumcision and the keeping of the Law of Moses. Although it is rarely stated in such

---

James 1:22-25," pp. 168-181; "Taciturnity and True Religion: James 1:26-27," pp. 155-164, all in this volume.

33. See M. T. Townsend, "James 4:1-14: A Warning Against Zealotry?" *ExpTim* 87 (1975) 211-13.

34. Notice, for example, that by working with traditional authorship Mayor is able to locate the poor in the Christian communities of the diaspora, and the rich oppressors in their Jewish compatriots (*Epistle,* pp. cxxxviii-cxli); whatever one thinks of his argument, his premise at least enables the inquiry.

35. "Nor does the language of our text point to an author who spent his life as a Jew in Palestine" (Dibelius, *James,* p. 17).

36. Thus, Dibelius himself adds a footnote (*James,* p. 17 n. 42) that cancels the opinion just cited; see also J. N. Sevenster, *Do You Know Greek?* (NovTSup 19; Leiden: Brill, 1968), 3-21; M. Hengel, *Judaism and Hellenism: Studies in Their Encounter in Palestine during the Early Hellenistic Period,* trans. J. Bowden (Philadelphia: Fortress, 1974), 56-106. But the habit is hard to break. Even after answering the objections to James's ability to write such Greek, Martin (p. lxxiii) is compelled to add: "on the several grounds of the letter's style, its Jewishness in tone and content, its post-Pauline ambience . . . it seems hardly to have been written as it stands by James of Jerusalem." So Martin invokes a two-stage theory of composition (p. lxxvii).

bald terms, James is taken to be not only a representative of Jewish Christianity but specifically the source of the so-called judaizing movement that was fundamentally hostile to Paul's Gentile mission.

Challenge to Traditional Authorship

The essential body of evidence comes from the only firsthand source contemporary with James, Paul's Letter to the Galatians. In the *narratio* that forms the first part of his argument in Galatians,[37] Paul mentions James three times. When Paul went up the first time to Jerusalem after his conversion, he visited Cephas, "but I saw none of the other apostles except James the Lord's brother" (Gal 1:19). When he went up by way of revelation after fourteen years with Titus, "James and Cephas and John, who were reputed to be pillars, gave to me and Barnabas the right hand of fellowship, that we should go to the Gentiles and they to the circumcised" (Gal 2:9). So far, nothing but Paul's acknowledgment of James's position and James's reciprocal acknowledgment of Paul's. Then, when recounting his altercation with Cephas in Antioch, Paul attributes Peter's change of behavior and "insincerity" to the arrival of "certain men from James": before they came, Cephas had eaten with Gentiles, but after they came, he withdrew from such fellowship (Gal 2:12).

Now the difficulty of this text for learning much at all about the "historical James" is obvious. Paul's dispute is with Cephas, not with James, nor even the men from James. Nor does Paul suggest that the "men from James" were on an official mission from that leader. The way these comments get turned into a portrayal of James as Paul's opponent is, first, by identifying the "false brethren" who threatened Paul's liberty in Gal 2:4 with these "men from James," as representatives of a circumcising party, and, second, by connecting "those unsettling" the Galatians by advocating circumcision (Gal 5:12) with emissaries sent out by James.[38] By an even

37. For the rhetorical function of the *narratio,* see H. D. Betz, *Galatians* (Hermeneia; Philadelphia: Fortress, 1979), 58-62, 83.

38. See Baur, *Paul, the Apostle of Jesus Christ,* 1:122-23 n. 1; 1:136; the men from James are "his declared foes and opponents" (1:203); Baur is circumspect, however, in attributing the troubles in Galatia directly to James, although Paul's opponents there represent James's party (1:250-257). More recently, see M. Hengel, *Acts and the History of Earliest Christianity,* trans. J. Bowden (Philadelphia: Fortress, 1980), 112-126. See also his argument for the early dating of James and its character as a contemporary and sustained if indirect polemic against Paul, in "Der Jakobusbrief als anti-paulinische Polemik," in *Tradition and Interpreta-*

further extrapolation, Paul's "opponents" in Philippi and Corinth as well are then connected to a coherent program of repression ultimately deriving from the Jewish Christianity of the Jerusalem church over which James ruled.[39]

It should be obvious that these connections are not required by the text of Galatians. If Paul himself saw his problems either in Jerusalem or in Galatia as stemming from James, he was remarkably reticent and roundabout in his complaint. In fact, James may well not have had anything to do with Paul's troubles in either place. The tone of Paul's comments in Gal 1:19 and 2:9 is entirely positive (as, for that matter, is his reference to James in 1 Cor 15:7). But once Galatians is read this way, then the evidence of Acts 12:17; 15:1-21; and 21:17-26 is taken not as a historically accurate portrayal of cooperation between James and Paul but as a partially successful cover-up for a relationship characterized by mutual hostility.[40] Then, the admittedly legendary account in Hegesippus concerning the death of James[41] is taken at least as confirmation of James's place in the "Jerusalem Caliphate"[42] and, together with an unreasonably high valua-

---

tion in the New Testament: Essays in Honor of E. Earle Ellis, ed. G. F. Hawthorne with O. Betz (Grand Rapids: Eerdmans, 1987), 248-278.

39. See Baur's discussion whether the "Christ Party" in Corinth might be explicitly associated with James; he seems almost convinced, but of course the demands of his system require that there be only two real "parties," so James is associated with the Jewish Christianity of Peter (*Paul, the Apostle of Jesus Christ,* 1:265); see also the discussion of the "superapostles" in 2 Corinthians, and James's association with them (1:277). For a more recent rendering of this view, see P. Achtemeier, *The Quest for Unity in the New Testament Church* (Philadelphia: Fortress, 1987), 59-61.

40. An essential part of Baur's reconstruction of the conflict between the Pauline and Jewish-Christian parties, of course, is the destruction of the credibility of Acts in the key passages dealing with Paul's relationships with Jerusalem (*Paul, the Apostle of Jesus Christ,* 1:110-121, 125-126 n. 1, 129). See Achtemeier, *The Quest for Unity,* pp. 29-55.

41. That the account in Eusebius, *Church History* 2.23 is filled with patently fictitious elements is obvious to anyone who carefully examines it (see the comments of Dibelius, *James,* pp. 15-17; and Martin, *James,* pp. xlviii-liv). What is more surprising is the hold it has on scholars' imaginations: "This legend from Hegesippus cannot be considered a serious rival to the short, clear, and prosaic statement of Josephus. However, it is valuable as evidence of Jewish Christian piety, and moreover it sketches the image of the 'just' James which was current in certain circles of Jewish Christianity" (Dibelius, *James,* p. 17).

42. Other primary texts support the picture of James's special role. See the account in Eusebius (derived from Clement's *Hypotyposes*) concerning the installation of James on the "throne of the bishopric of the church in Jerusalem" by the apostles themselves; Clement had also made James a direct recipient of "the tradition of knowledge" (γνῶσις) from Jesus after the resurrection, a portrayal that accords exactly with that in the Nag Hammadi writings associated with James (see Eusebius, *Church History* 2.1.2-5). There is also the fragmen-

tion of the Pseudo-Clementine literature, is thought to reflect the character of Jewish Christianity in some sort of continuity with an earlier historical reality.[43]

A number of observations need to be made about this reconstruction of the "historical James" as an opponent of Paul. The first is that it is even on its own terms a fragile restoration, dependent more than it might like to think on presuppositions concerning the rival "parties" in early Christianity derived from the Tübingen school,[44] and requiring the connection of a good many pieces that need not be connected at all.[45] Second, the dis-

---

tary passage from *The Gospel of the Hebrews* (cited by Jerome in *De Viris Illustribus* 2) that appears to make James the first witness of the resurrection. For the language of "caliphate," see, e.g., K. Aland, "Der Herrenbruder Jakobus und der Jakobusbrief: Zur Frage eines urchristlichen Kalifäts," *TLZ* 69 (1944) 97-104.

43. "The Ebionites are generally regarded as mere heretics, but their connection with the original Jewish Christianity is unmistakable. Thus their view of the Apostle Paul is no isolated phenomenon" (F. C. Baur, *Church History of the First Three Centuries*, 2 vols. [London: Williams and Norgate, 1878-79], 1:90). More recently, see H. J. Schoeps, *Theologie und Geschichte des Judenchristentums* (Tübingen: Mohr-Siebeck, 1949), 69. The parts of the extraordinarily complex collection called the Pseudo-Clementine literature that are regarded by advocates of such views as deriving from the Ebionites and reflecting early perceptions are the *Epistula Petri ad Jacobum* and the *Contestatio* (Schoeps, *Theologie*, p. 50). The major sections that contain the most explicit polemic against (supposedly) Paul under the guise of Simon Magus are *Recognitions* 1.43-72 (including a role played by "the enemy" in the death of James, 70-71) and *Homilies* II, 16; XI, 35; XVII, 13-19. The identification of those called Ebionites (Irenaeus, *Adversus Haereses* 1.26.2; Origen, *Contra Celsum* 2.1) is essential for Baur's position. But see L. Keck, "The Poor among the Saints in the New Testament," *ZNW* 56 (1965) 109-129; idem, "The Poor among the Saints in Jewish Christianity and Qumran," *ZNW* 57 (1966) 54-78. The historicity of the Ebionites' "flight from Jerusalem" to Pella — essential to making the connection between this group and the Jerusalem community — has been challenged. G. Lüdemann has described it as a legend serving to legitimate this version of Jewish-Christianity; see "The Successors of Pre-70 Jerusalem Christianity: A Critical Evaluation of the Pella Tradition," in *Jewish and Christian Self-Definition*, ed. E. P. Sanders (Philadelphia: Fortress, 1980), 1:161-73.

44. For a critique of the entire premise that undergirds so much of the Tübingen project and remains as a staple of historical reconstructions, namely, the theological distinction between the "Hellenists" and the "Hebrews" in the Jerusalem church, with the figure of Stephen providing the necessary bridge between the "Hellenists" and Paul (as still in Hengel, *Acts and the History of Earliest Christianity*, pp. 71-80), see now C. C. Hill, *Hellenists and Hebrews: Reappraising Division within the Earliest Church* (Minneapolis: Fortress, 1992); among other things, Hill argues for the fictional character of the Hegesippus story that has proven so influential in shaping the image of James (pp. 184-191); argues that the Jerusalem church on the basis both of Acts and of Galatians is shown by our best sources to be in fundamental agreement with Paul (pp. 143-147); and claims that James is explicitly not an opponent of Paul (pp. 183-192).

45. For more neutral discussions of "Jewish-Christianity" that recognize the complexi-

covery of the Nag Hammadi writings shows us that the figure of James could be developed in quite a different direction by later parties seeking legitimation in the founding figures of the Christian movement. In the Nag Hammadi writings, James is not connected to circumcision or the observance of the Law or hostility toward Paul. The place of honor held by James in this Gnostic collection suggests that, like other eponymous figures in earliest Christianity, he was capable of various exploitations.[46] We are thereby given the salutary reminder that the "James" of Hegesippus and the "James" of the Pseudo-Clementines are not necessarily any closer to the historical James than is the "James" of the Nag Hammadi Library.

Third, and most critically, the Letter of James — at the very least one of the earliest witnesses concerning James — simply does not support this picture. Despite the lingering influence of Luther's dictum that James "drove you back to the law,"[47] contemporary readers are increasingly coming to agree with Calvin that such an opinion was a form of "absurdity."[48] James's references to the "perfect law, the law of liberty" (1:25), we now see, have nothing to do with a demand for circumcision or the keeping of ritual commandments. Nothing in James could possibly be construed as part of a judaizing program, much less one directed against Paul. Rather, James's understanding of "the royal law" (2:8) involves the keeping of the Decalogue and the moral commandments of Lev 19:11-18.[49] James takes the same moralizing approach to the Law as we find in such Jewish parenetic texts as the *Testaments of the Twelve Patriarchs* and the *Sentences of Pseudo-Phocylides*.[50] Far from being a point-by-point rebuttal of Paul's

---

ties of categorization and historical identification, see J. Daniélou, *Théologie du Judéo-Christianisme* (Bibliothèque de Théologie; Tournai: Desclée, 1958), 17-98; S. K. Riegel, "Jewish Christianity: Definitions and Terminology," *NTS* 24 (1977-78) 410-415.

46. James the Righteous is called one "for whose sake heaven and earth came into being" and is recommended as a leader after Jesus' departure in *Gospel of Thomas* 12. He appears with Peter as the source of a "secret book" revealed by the Lord in the *Apocryphon of James,* and as a Gnostic teacher in the *First Apocalypse of James* and the *Second Apocalypse of James.*

47. See the preface to the Letters of James and Jude in his "Preface to the New Testament" of 1522, in *Luther's Works,* vol. 35: *Word and Sacrament* I, ed. E. T. Bachmann (Philadelphia: Muhlenburg Press, 1959), 395-397.

48. J. Calvin, *Commentaries on the Catholic Epistles,* trans. and ed. J. Owen (Grand Rapids: Eerdmans, 1948), 314-315.

49. See my essay "The Use of Leviticus 19 in the Letter of James," pp. 123-135 in this volume.

50. The resemblances to the *Testaments* were noted especially by J. H. Ropes, *James,* pp. 20-21; see also my essay "James 3:13–4:10 and the Topos περὶ φθόνου," pp. 182-201 in this volume. See also M. de Jonge, "Light on Paul from the *Testaments of the Twelve Patriarchs?*" in *The*

teaching in Gal 2:15-16, James's discussion of "faith and works" in 2:14-26 uses those terms in quite a different fashion,[51] elaborating the moralist's concern that profession be enacted by specific deeds (compare Jas 3:13), and agrees substantially with the position stated by Paul in Gal 5:6.[52]

Remarkably, however, despite three substantial objections to the standard historical reconstruction of James of Jerusalem, the portrayal still has sufficient influence to make scholars uncomfortable with the notion that the jerry-rigged portrait is wrong, and that this letter may actually represent the straightforward views of the historical James. Instead, it is simply assumed that something in the traditional picture must be right and that the Letter of James must come from a later, pseudonymous author. Despite a grudging admission that James and Paul were talking about two different sorts of things, scholars have not been able to rid themselves of the besetting sin of virtually all historical reconstructions of earliest Christianity, namely, *that Paul has to figure in the equation some-*

Social World of the First Christians: Essays in Honor of Wayne A. Meeks, ed. L. M. White and O. L. Yarbrough (Minneapolis: Fortress Press, 1995), 100-115. On Pseudo-Phocylides, see P. W. van der Horst, *The Sentences of Pseudo-Phocylides* (SVTP 4; Leiden: Brill, 1978), 126, 295; idem, "Pseudo-Phocylides and the New Testament," *ZNW* 69 (1978) 202.

51. The main problem with the putative James-Paul opposition on this point is that it simply refuses to take into account the full range of meaning in *either* author. Paul is reduced to parts of Galatians/Romans, and James is reduced to 2:14-26. Yet it is obvious that Paul in those places is arguing a contrast between ἔργα τοῦ νόμου ("works of the law") and πίστις Χριστοῦ ("faith of Christ"), whereas James is arguing that πίστις θεοῦ ("faith of God") requires expression in ἔργα πίστεως ("works of faith"). Thus, James says in 2:22, "*faith* coworked his works and out of the works *faith* was perfected." The connections in each author, furthermore, are more complex than the discussion usually takes into account. The use of ἔργον in Jas 1:4 and 3:13 must be considered. Equally, Paul's use of ἔργον is much wider than often supposed (see Rom 13:3, 12; 14:20; 15:18; 1 Cor 3:13-15; 9:1; 15:58; 16:10; 2 Cor 9:8; 11:15; 1 Thess 1:3; 5:13; 2 Thess 2:17). If the entire Pauline corpus is considered, over 50 occurrences of ἔργον fit perfectly with the meaning in James, whereas only 17 fit Paul's narrower polemic purpose. Note that Paul can speak without embarrassment about "your work of faith" (ἔργον τῆς πίστεως) in 1 Thess 1:3 and of the "work of faith in power" (ἔργον πίστεως ἐν δυνάμει) in 2 Thess 1:11; and if we can make bold to use the Pastorals, Titus 1:16, "They claim to know God but deny him by their works," accords perfectly with Jas 2:19.

52. This is the conclusion reached by an exquisitely argued letter written by Severus, the Monophysite patriarch of Antioch (ca. 465-538), to a Julian, who was probably the Monophysite bishop of Halicarnassus (d. after 518); see Zachary the Rhetorician, *Capita Selecta ex Historiae Ecclesiasticae,* sect XIX (*PG* 85: 1176-1178). The entire patristic and medieval tradition concerning the apparent contradiction was that there was none, a view nowhere more trenchantly conveyed than by Erasmus, "Verum Paulus illic opera vocat observationem Legis Mosaice, hic sentit de officiis pietatis et charitatis"; see *In Epistolam Jacobi* in *Opera Omnia* (1516; repr. London: Gregg, 1962), 6:1031.

where. Although it is a historical fallacy of the plainest sort to infer from Paul's canonical importance data relevant to his historical importance, scholars continue to read whatever is different from Paul with reference to Paul, rather than allow it to stand as simply different.[53]

Pseudonymous Authorship and the History of Ideas

Deciding for pseudonymous authorship does not by itself mean abandoning hope for finding the social world of James, but it makes the quest more difficult, if only because the number of variables automatically increases. In reality, the decision to regard James as pseudonymous has tended to place James not in a specific social context but within a temporal development of ideas. If the letter is not by the historical James but by a pseudepigrapher, then it must be not only later than James but also later than Paul. Why? Not because there are any indications within the text of the letter itself that suggest a situation inconsonant with that of the first generation, but because Paul is the only stable point of reference available. And if the letter cannot be taken as a response of the historical James to the historical Paul, then it must represent a response of a certain kind of Christianity to a certain brand of Paulinism.

The conflict model used by the Tübingen school is demonstrated by F. Kern's 1835 study of James. Although he designates James as a "sittliche-paraenetische" letter,[54] he nevertheless works to place it within the movements of early Christianity. To do this, he aligns two major themes of the letter: that dealing with the rich and poor and that dealing with faith and works. By this means he locates the intended recipients of the letter as second-generation Jewish Christians who are being marginalized by Gentile Christians.[55] James's teaching of faith and works is, therefore, some-

53. See, e.g., E. Lohse, "Glaube und Werke: Zur Theologie des Jakobusbriefes," *ZNW* 48 (1957) 1-22. In the light of my remarks below about Dibelius's inconsistency it should be noted that he clearly saw the fallaciousness of trying to pull Paul into every equation: "Yet, only too easily we fall into the error — which, to be sure, is fostered by the character of the materials preserved from the early Christian period — of thinking that Paul influenced every branch of early Christianity. This is, in fact, an error . . ." (*James*, p. 118).

54. See F. H. Kern, *Der Character und Ursprung des Briefes Jacobi* (Tübingen: Fues, 1835), 5.

55. See Kern, *Character*, pp. 24, 36; Kern argues that James had to know Paul's letters even though it is not a direct attack on the person of Paul (p. 25), and that on the issue of righteousness Luther was correct: James and Paul are incompatible (pp. 11-17, 44). The similarity of James to the Letter of Clement and the Pseudo-Clementines suggests a time after the apostolic age but before the writing of the Pseudo-Clementines (p. 86). Note here the as-

thing of a *rapprochement* between these competing parties.[56] Likewise F. C. Baur (who expressly approved Kern's reading) considered the Letter of James — though incompatible with Paul's teaching on righteousness[57] — to be part of that synthesizing movement that helped shape catholic Christianity.[58] In the same tradition, Hans Joachim Schoeps refuses to consider James in his elaborate reconstruction of "Jewish Christian Theology," but in an excursus devoted to the letter, he defines it as a post-apostolic writing of "Jewish Christian but not Ebionite" character and of basically an "antignostic" tendency.[59] More recently, J. Jeremias argued in similar fashion that James's teaching on faith and works was intended to correct a misunderstood and misused Paulinism.[60]

Whatever the merit of these respective positions, their inadequacy for enriching our understanding of James's social world is obvious. Because they need Paul as a control, they isolate within James only that aspect which can be brought into conversation with Paul, namely, the section on faith and works (2:14-26). Not only does this perpetuate the fallacy of treating Paul as the essential pivot point for all early Christian history; it distorts James's discussion in 2:14-26 by treating it as a "response" to a theoretical position putatively held by Paul, rather than as an integral part of James's own argument. Finally, by making 2:14-26 the only section of James of compelling interest, it fails to take into account those other features of James's text that might prove instructive precisely concerning the "world" inhabited (or at least imagined) by this text.

Social Setting Through Genre?

The magisterial commentary by M. Dibelius placed its entire interpretive weight on a decision concerning the genre of James. Dibelius regarded the epistolary format as nothing more than a formal adornment. James was re-

---

sumption of continuity between the Jerusalem church of the first generation ("the poor among the saints," Rom 15:26; Gal 2:10) and the later group identified as "the Ebionites." It is not shocking that Kern made the identification; but despite work such as that noted in n. 43, above, the equation is still sometimes made as if it were obvious; see Hengel, *Acts and the History of Earliest Christianity,* p. 118.

56. Kern, *Character,* p. 38.

57. Baur, *Paul, the Apostle of Jesus Christ,* 2:297-313.

58. Baur, *The Church History of the First Three Centuries,* 1:128-130.

59. Schoeps, *Theologie und Geschichte des Judenchristentums,* pp. 343-349.

60. J. Jeremias, "Paul and James," *ExpTim* 66 (1955) 368-371.

ally a form of *parenesis.*[61] This meant, for Dibelius, that James was a relatively structureless compendium of wisdom traditions with no specific reference to time or place. Topics are taken up as much because they are the expected topics for the genre as because they addressed specific social situations.[62] It was possible to describe certain broad aspects of James's outlook, such as that concerning wealth and poverty,[63] but the characterizations were ideational rather than social. In effect, Dibelius's decision on genre seemed to cut James off from any connection to the real world, allowing it to float in the sea of generalized wisdom traditions with little distinctive character of its own. Given his overall commitment to the exegetical consequences of this generic decision — so much so that he treated each unit atomistically, disallowing in principle the possibility of contextual analysis[64] — it is surprising to find Dibelius still insisting on James's connection to Paul in 2:14-26, proving how powerful that particular assumption has been![65]

Recently, however, L. Perdue has taken the generic analysis of James in the opposite direction. He has suggested that the genre of James might actually provide a sort of back-door entry to the social world of the writing. Perdue agrees with the designation of James as *parenesis.*[66] But he is convinced that this literary genre, as a subset of wisdom literature such as we find it reaching back into antiquity,[67] demands a certain kind of social

61. See Dibelius, *James,* p. 1.

62. Ibid., pp. 3-5.

63. In Dibelius's lengthy discussion ("Poor and Rich," pp. 39-45), he sketches the piety of the "poor of the Lord," within which James stands. But despite his earlier warning (p. 11) that "the admonitions in James do not apply to a single audience and a single set of circumstances: *it is not possible to construct a single frame into which they all fit*" (his emphasis), the legacy of Kern and Baur remains strong. Dibelius suggests that the "most likely place" where this pauperistic piety would have survived was in the churches of diaspora Judaism "where the consistency of Paul is alien" (p. 43).

64. Dibelius, *James,* pp. 2-3. He could scarcely be more emphatic. With original italics, he declares (p. 6): *"It seems to me that the literary evaluation of Jas depends completely upon the resolution of this question,"* and in his exegesis he sticks to that principle (see, e.g., pp. 207-208).

65. Just how deeply conflicted Dibelius was can be indicated by his painful discussion on pp. 17-18, where he insists that Jas 2:14-26 "cannot be comprehended without the previous activity of Paul . . . yet the letter presupposes not only Paul's formulation of the question about the Law but also the resolution of Paul's struggles regarding the Law," and pp. 29-30, where he must argue that the passages in James which seem to have an obvious affinity with Paul (e.g., Jas 1:2-4 and Rom 5:3-5) are to be explained on a basis other than a knowledge of Paul's letters.

66. L. G. Perdue, "Paraenesis and the Epistle of James," *ZNW* 72 (1981) 241-246.

67. L. C. Perdue, "The Death of the Sage and Moral Exhortation: From Ancient Near Eastern Instructions to Greco-Roman Paraenesis," *Semeia* 50 (1990) 81-109.

setting. Specifically, the formality of "father to son" transmission of wisdom so typical of wisdom/parenetic texts fits the state of liminality (and therefore danger) that occurs in moments of transgenerational change. Parenetic literature provides a medium for safe passage across such moments of crisis.[68] With this sort of rough-and-ready equivalency model, the identification of James as parenetic would seem to demand its production at such a moment in the history of Christianity, and its function as an instrument of resocialization and relegitimation of the social world of the readers. Perdue suggests a situation when the author is either separated from the readers (and must write a letter) or about to leave them because of age and approaching death (a farewell address).[69]

When I read Perdue's first effort along these lines, I was not convinced,[70] primarily because I considered parenetic literature more diverse in character and capable of being fitted to a variety of social situations. I doubted that direct conclusions could be drawn from genre to social world.[71] Recently, however, more careful attention has been paid to these connections. J. G. Gammie has pursued the variety in *literary* (material and formal) characteristics within wisdom/parenetic writings.[72] And L. G. Perdue has greatly refined his analysis of the *social worlds* of parenesis, recognizing that parenesis can function variously within them for purposes of conversion or socialization or legitimation. In such situations, parenesis serves to establish or confirm order.[73]

But it is Perdue's perception of some parenetic texts as serving a "conflict" function that is particularly interesting. In these cases, parenesis

68. L. G. Perdue, "Liminality as a Social Setting for Wisdom Instruction," *ZAW* 93 (1981) 114-126.

69. Perdue, "Paraenesis and the Epistle of James," pp. 250-251.

70. I commented on it negatively in "Friendship with the World and Friendship with God," p. 204, n. 13, and "The Mirror of Remembrance," p. 168, n. 1, both in this volume.

71. See, e.g., A. J. Malherbe, *Moral Exhortation: A Greco-Roman Sourcebook* (Library of Early Christianity; Philadelphia: Westminster, 1986), 23-29. For Malherbe's views on the relationship between literary production and social settings, see *Social Aspects of Early Christianity*, 2nd ed. (Philadelphia: Fortress, 1983), 29-59. Malherbe had in view A. Deissmann's famous thesis. An attempt to derive something of an "implicit sociology of letter writing" (p. 87) has recently been essayed by S. K. Stowers on the basis of the ancient classifications of letter types; see "Social Typification and the Classification of Ancient Letters," in *The Social World of Formative Christianity and Judaism*, ed. J. Neusner, P. Borgen, et al. (Philadelphia: Fortress, 1988), 78-89.

72. J. G. Gammie, "Paraenetic Literature: Toward the Morphology of a Secondary Genre," *Semeia* 50 (1990) 41-77.

73. L. C. Perdue, "The Social Character of Paraenesis and Paraenetic Literature," *Semeia* 50 (1990) 19-26.

serves to "subvert" the broader cultural values (those of the *Gesellschaft*) in order to reaffirm the values of an inner group that has withdrawn from that larger society (as a *Gemeinschaft*). Here "a different social reality is constructed, and efforts are undertaken to protect it from the threat of outside worlds," clearly a "sectarian position." Perdue locates the Letter of James as an example of such subversive parenesis.[74] Although he does not himself explicitly make a connection between James and Q, it is striking that Perdue lists as another example of such "conflict" parenesis "the sayings source Q, produced by an early Christian community before the fall of Jerusalem."[75] Thus, the genre analysis tends to confirm the connection between James and the early Palestinian traditions about Jesus suggested earlier.

To some extent, Perdue is pursuing the principle already enunciated though not systematically applied by Dibelius, namely, that an author's "voice" can be heard even in parenetic literature through analysis of the "selection and arrangement of traditional thought and of the new emphasis which he gives to it,"[76] as well as his own conviction that the way toward the analysis of social function is through comparative analysis.[77] But that project might be pushed much further. What might we learn if we *systematically* compare James to other recognizably parenetic/wisdom writings across the cultural spectrum of the Mediterranean world, as a way of checking what James might be expected to include but does not, and what it does include that might not be anticipated?

Among the distinctive (though not necessarily unique) characteristics of James that emerge from this comparison is the letter's focus on a community *ethos* rather than simply individual behavior,[78] on moral behavior

---

74. Ibid., pp. 26-27; in this article, his type distinctions make the final determination concerning James more convincing than in "Paraenesis and the Epistle of James," pp. 255-56.

75. Perdue, "Social Character of Paraenesis," p. 14.

76. Dibelius, *James,* p. 21.

77. "Any suggestions about conceivable social settings for the parenesis of James must necessarily be inferential and analogical, based on a variety of other paraenetic texts" ("Paraenesis and the Epistle of James," p. 247).

78. The group is always being addressed in James even when individual cases are being considered; the exhortation in the majority of ancient parenetic texts is to the individual: see, e.g., *Instruction of the Vizier Ptah-Hotep (ANET,* pp. 412-414); *Instruction for King Meri-Ka-Re (ANET,* pp. 414-418); *Instruction of King Amen-Em-Het (ANET,* pp. 418-419); *Instruction of Prince Hor-Dedef (ANET,* p. 419); *Instruction of Ani (ANET,* pp. 420-421); *Instruction of Amen-Em-Opet (ANET,* pp. 421-424); *Counsels of Wisdom (ANET,* pp. 426-427); *Words of Ahiqar (ANET,* pp. 427-430); the book of Proverbs; Qoheleth; Sirach; the *Sentences of Pseudo-Phocylides;* Pseudo-

rather than on manners,[79] on an ethics of solidarity rather than of competition.[80] But equally worth considering are the elements typical of
parenesis that are entirely lacking in James. It is not remarkable that
James should use kinship language, for it is universal in wisdom writings.[81] What is remarkable is that James lacks completely any generational
kinship language such as is found even in Paul.[82] Instead, James's use of
kinship language is entirely egalitarian.[83] Far from reflecting the tensions
of generational change, James lacks even the conventional use of generational language. It is also remarkable that James should find no need to
speak of sexual ethics[84] or of marriage,[85] since these are, once more, common fare in parenesis, including the parenetic sections of other early New
Testament letters.[86] Nor does James take up the subject of the care and

---

Isocrates, *To Demonicus;* the *Sentences of Sextus;* and the *Sentences of Syriac Menander.* A partial
exception is the *Testaments of the Twelve Patriarchs.*

79. See Prov 23:1-9; Sir 4:27-31; 7:14; 9:18; 31:12-30; 32:1-9; *Words of Ahiqar* x.142ff.; *Counsels
of Wisdom* 20; *Sentences of Syriac Menander* 11-14, 57-62, 99-101, 148-153, 181-184; *To Demonicus* 15,
20, 27, 41; *Sentences of Sextus* 149, 157, 164, 252, 265; *Sentences of Pseudo-Phocylides* 81-82, 98, 123,
147-148, 156-158, 211-212; *Instructions of Vizier Ptah-Hotep* 139; *Instruction of Amen-Em-Het* 1.4-5;
Instruction of Ani 6.1; 7.7; *Instruction of Amen-Em-Opet* 9, 23.

80. That one of the motivations for being "wise" is to be a greater success in the world
than others is frequently implied, but nowhere more obvious than in Pseudo-Isocrates, *To
Demonicus* 2, 3, 13, 15, 17, 21, 24, 26, 32, 33, 35, 38; nothing could be at greater odds to such "pursuit of nobility" than the lowly-mindedness encouraged by James (4:7-10).

81. The transmission of wisdom from father to son is, of course, the standard *mise-en-
scène* of parenesis, from the most ancient works *(Instruction of the Vizier Ptah-Hotep)* to works
close in time to James *(Testaments of the Twelve Patriarchs),* and enables the play on the convention in Pseudo-Isocrates, *To Demonicus* 1-3, 9-10.

82. Thus, it is Paul's claim to be the "father" of the community that legitimates his moral
instruction (1 Cor 4:15; 1 Thess 2:11); see also his language about individuals like Onesimus
(Phlm 10) and Timothy (Phil 2:22). It is not surprising that the most obviously "parenetic" of
the letters attributed to Paul explicitly employs this kinship *topos* (2 Tim 1:2; 2:1).

83. James never designates himself or anyone else as "father," but identifies his readers
consistently as "brothers" (1:2, 9; 2:1, 14, 15; 3:1, 10, 12; 4:11; 5:7, 9, 10, 12, 19) or as "beloved
brothers" (1:16, 19), the only exception being the reference to the sister in 2:15.

84. For commandments concerning sexual ethics, see *Sentences of Pseudo-Phocylides* 3,
198; Sir 7:24-25; 9:1-9; 25:21-26; 26:11-12; Prov 2:16-22; 6:24-32; 7:10-27; 9:13-18; Pseudo-Isocrates,
To Demonicus 15, 21; *Sentences of Sextus* 60, 67, 70, 71, 73, 75, 102, 139, 240, 346, 449; *Testament of
Reuben* 4:1–6:5; *Sentences of Syriac Menander* 170-172, 240-249; *Instruction of Ani* 3.13.

85. For discussions of marriage, see *Sentences of Syriac Menander* 45-51, 118-122; *Instruction
of Prince Hor-Dedef;* Sir 7:25-26; 26:1-9, 13-18; 40:19; Prov 5:15-20; 31:10-31; *Instruction of Vizier
Ptah-Hotep* 320-340; *Counsels of Wisdom* (Obverse 23); *Sentences of Pseudo-Phocylides* 3, 175-197,
201-206; *Sentences of Sextus* 235-239; *Instruction of Ani* 3.1; 8.4; 9.1.

86. See Rom 13:13; 1 Cor 5:1-5; 6:12-20; 7:1-24; Eph 5:21–6:4; Col 3:18-25; 1 Thess 4:4-5; 1 Tim
2:9-15; Titus 2:3-5; Heb 13:4; 1 Pet 3:1-7.

disciplining of children so frequently found in such literature.[87] In a word, the sort of topics that work for the establishing of order and socializing people within it tend to be absent from James.

Taken together with the characteristics sketched earlier in this essay. these deviations from the generic norm help support the suggestion that James is not simply a compendium of wisdom themes or a free-floating piece of parenesis, but a vivid exhortation that emerges from and addresses real human beings in specific social settings. Everything in the letter and everything lacking from the letter help confirm the impression that this social world was one shared by a leader of the Jerusalem church and Jewish messianists of the diaspora during the first decades of the Christian movement.[88]

---

87. See, e.g., *Words of Ahiqar* 6.79, 7.106, 9.138; *To Demonicus* 14, 16; *Sentences of Pseudo-Phocylides* 207-217; Prov (LXX) 10:1-8; 13:1-2; 30:11-14; Sir 3:1-16; 7:28; 16:1-5; 30:1-6; *Sentences of Sextus* 254, 256-257; *Sentences of Syriac Menander* 5-6, 9-10, 20-24, 94-98, 194-212; *Instruction of Vizier Ptah-Hotep* 565-595; *Instruction of Meri-Ka-Re* 55-60; *Instruction of Ani* 7.17.

88. Readers familiar with the history of scholarship on James will recognize that the basic points in my argument, although responding to more recent contributions to the discussion, do not differ dramatically from the ones laid out so simply by G. Kittel, "Der geschichtliche Ort des Jakobusbriefes," *ZNW* 41 (1942) 71-105.

The Use of Leviticus 19 in the Letter of James

The family resemblance between the Letter of James and *The Sentences of Pseudo-Phocylides* has long been recognized. Both are paraenetic writings from the first century of our era, studded with imperatives dealing with practical life rather than theory. Both, in some fashion, use Leviticus 19 in their paraenesis. James, in fact, cites Lev 19:18b accurately from the LXX in 2:8: ἀγαπήσεις τὸν πλησίον σου ὡς σεαυτόν. The way he places this citation in the context of προσωπολημψία (2:1, 9) has led most readers to acknowledge that, at least here, James made use of Lev 19:18b within its original context (Lev 19:15).[1] Marty[2] and Dibelius,[3] indeed, suggested a possible *dependence* of James on some form of Jewish paraenesis based on Leviticus 19, such as Pseudo-Phocylides. Strangely, after their comments on 2:8, neither commentator pursued this insight further.

The most recent translator of and commentator on Pseudo-Phocylides, Pieter van der Horst, has also noticed the resemblance of that

---

1. Cf., e.g., J. B. Mayor, *The Epistle of St. James*, 3rd ed. (London: Macmillan and Co., 1910), cxi, 78; J. H. Ropes, *A Critical and Exegetical Commentary on the Epistle of St. James* (ICC; New York: Scribner's, 1916), 186; A. Meyer, *Das Raetsel des Jakobusbriefes* (BZNTW 10; Giessen: A. Töpelmann, 1930), 140 n. 5; F. Mussner, *Der Jakobusbrief* (HTKNT 13; Freiburg: Herder, 1964), 115; C. L. Mitton, *The Epistle of James* (London: Marshall, Morgan and Scott, 1966), 80, 89, 92; J. Adamson, *The Epistle of James* (Grand Rapids: Eerdmans, 1976), 108; R. B. Ward, "Partiality in the Assembly," *HTR* 62 (1969) 90; O. J. F. Seitz, "James and the Law," SEII (=TU 87 [1959]) 476.

2. J. Marty, *L'Epître de Jacques* (Paris: Felix Alcan, 1935), 69.

3. M. Dibelius, *James* (Hermeneia; Philadelphia: Fortress, 1976), 142. Dibelius also recognized the resemblance of James 5:12 to Pseudo-Phocylides 16 (p. 248), and James 5:4 to Pseudo-Phocylides 19 (p. 238 n. 46).

writing to James, both in parallel expressions,[4] and in tone.[5] The likelihood of literary dependence is negligible. The resemblance, however, involves more than a sharing of parallel expressions. It is due, at least in part, to an *analogous* use of Leviticus 19.

That Pseudo-Phocylides used Leviticus 19 in a rather systematic fashion is the consensus of those who have studied him. After an opening couplet (lines 1-2), and a poetic reworking of the Decalogue (lines 3-8),[6] Pseudo-Phocylides 9-21 depends heavily on Leviticus 19.[7] There is no citation of or allusion to Lev 19:18b, but several other verses from Lev 19:12-19 can be spotted beneath their poetic transformation.[8] Such a thorough use of this section of the law has not yet been recognized in the case of James. Yet there are grounds for thinking that, in even clearer fashion than Pseudo-Phocylides, James used the LXX of Lev 19:12-18 as a whole in his work of Christian exhortation. A look at the way Leviticus 19 appears in Pseudo-Phocylides can help us discern its presence in James.

The Use of Leviticus 19 in Pseudo-Phocylides

The LXX text of Leviticus 19 does not leap off the page of Pseudo-Phocylides; it is subtle enough in its presence, in fact, to have escaped detection until the analysis of the Jewish scholar Jacob Bernays.[9] The reason is simply that the language is transformed. A word can be recognized here, perhaps part of an idiom there, but otherwise it is a matter of thematic rather than verbal allusions. The clearest clue to the text of Leviti-

4. P. van der Horst, *The Sentences of Pseudo-Phocylides* (SVTP 4; Leiden: Brill, 1978), 126, 295; and "Pseudo-Phocylides and the New Testament," *ZNW* 69 (1978) 202, where he lists the Jacobean passages 3:1ff., 3:6, 5:4, and 5:12 as parallel to Pseudo-Phocylides 20, 27, 19, and 16.

5. "Pseudo-Phocylides and the New Testament," p. 202.

6. Van der Horst, *Sentences*, p. 66; cf. J. Bernays, *Über das Phokylideische Gedicht. Ein Beitrag zur hellenistischen Literatur* (Jahresbericht des jüdische-theologischen Seminars "Fraenckelschen Stiftung"; Berlin: Hertz, 1856), xxi.

7. Bernays, pp. xxii-xxiv; van der Horst, *Sentences*, pp. 117-118, 124-126, 292. M. Rossbroich, *De Pseudo-Phocylides* (Münster: Theissingsche Buchhandlung, 1910), 31 n. 2, and 33, disputes a systematic use of Leviticus 19, but then acknowledges allusions to it in Pseudo-Phocylides 12-14, on pp. 33-38.

8. So van der Horst sees Pseudo-Phocylides 10 referring to Lev 19:15 (*Sentences*, pp. 117-118); Pseudo-Phocylides 16 to Lev 19:12 (*Sentences*, p. 124); Pseudo-Phocylides 19 to Lev 19:13 (*Sentences*, p. 126); and Pseudo-Phocylides 21 to Lev 19:16 (regarding this last as doubtful, *Sentences*, p. 292).

9. Cf. the history of research in van der Horst, *Sentences*, p. 66.

cus 19 is found at Ps.-Phoc. 10, μὴ κρῖνε πρόσωπον, which manifestly derives from the Septuagintalism πρόσωπον λαβεῖν, which in turn translates נשא פנים. The term is used for favoritism in judging, and is classically expressed in Lev 19:15: οὐ λήψῃ πρόσωπον πτωχοῦ. Again, one can glimpse beneath Ps.-Phoc. 19, μισθὸν μοχθήσαντι δίδου, the phrase μισθὸς τοῦ μισθωτοῦ in Lev 19:13. But generally, verbal allusions are less evident than thematic ones.

This suggests a heuristic guideline. Where we can show a cluster of allusions from one document to another, it is easier to argue for the probable presence of other allusions in passages which, considered alone, might seem at first unlikely candidates. The certain presence of one makes a second more plausible. Two in the same spot render suspicion of a third less absurd. So, in Ps.-Phoc., the presence of μὴ κρῖνε πρόσωπον in line 10 increases dramatically the chances of line 9's πάντα δίκαια νέμειν μὴ δὲ κρίσιν ἐς χάριν ἕλκειν depending on Lev 19:15, οὐ ποιήσετε ἄδικον ἐν κρίσει. Likewise, although μὴ δ᾽ἐπιορκήσῃς μητ᾽ ἀγνὼς μήτε ἕκοντι (Ps.-Phoc. 16) is not verbally identical to οὐκ ὀμεῖσθε τῷ ὀνόματί μου ἐπ᾽ ἀδίκῳ (Lev 19:12), given the clustering effect, it almost certainly represents an allusion to it.

Another consideration is thereby suggested. So dense is the cluster of allusions to Leviticus 19 in Ps.-Phoc. 9-21 (compared with the rest of the writing), and so disparate the topics the cluster contains, that one is moved to see Leviticus 19 precisely as an organizing principle for this section of the work. There is no a priori reason why the condemnation of perjury, partiality and oppression should appear so closely together in a work otherwise so scattered in exhortation as this one. The clustering, one suspects, is created at least in part by dependence on Leviticus 19. The probability of this is increased significantly by the virtual certainty of the Decalogue forming the basis for lines 3-8.

Finally, the determination that Leviticus 19 has been used in this fashion by Pseudo-Phocylides has had considerable impact on discussions of the nature and purpose of the work. Since Bernays, its "Jewish" character has generally been acknowledged, but the precise delineation and direction of that character remains a matter of debate.[10] The importance of Pseudo-Phocylides for this examination is that it provides a helpful analogy for the use of Lev 19 in the Letter of James.

---

10. Cf. the discussion in Bernays, pp. xxv-xxxvi; Rossbroich, pp. 102-103; van der Horst, *Sentences*, pp. 72-76.

The Certain Use of Leviticus 19 by James

James certainly knew and made use of the LXX of Leviticus 19. As stated above, he quotes Lev 19:18b accurately from the LXX in 2:8. What is more striking is the way that he places this in the framework of partiality in judging, showing a clear allusion to Lev 19:15. Furthermore, as in the case of Pseudo-Phocylides, James combines the reference to Leviticus 19 with a citation of part of the Decalogue: "For he who said, 'do not commit adultery,' also said, 'do not kill'" (2:11), following the order of commandments found in one manuscript tradition of the LXX for Deut 5:17-18 and Exod 20:13ff.[11] There can be little doubt, therefore, that James was aware of the levitical context of the "Royal Law." The *textual* implications for James's understanding of ὅλος ὁ νόμος (2:10), and κατὰ τὴν γραφήν (2:8) become intriguing.

There is another virtually certain (and generally noted) allusion to Lev 19:13 in James 5:4: ἰδοὺ ὁ μισθὸς τῶν ἐργατῶν τῶν ἀμησάντων τὰς χώρας ὑμῶν ὁ ἀπεστερημένος ἀφ' ὑμῶν κράζει. . . .[12] In this verse, James characteristically (cf. 2:23's combination of Gen 15:6 and 2 Chron 20:7) melds Isa 5:9 (LXX) to the Lev 19:13 reference. The reason for claiming an allusion to Lev 19:13 here in the first place, however, should be noted. The language of James 5:4 is no closer to Lev 19:13 than to Deut 24:14 or Mal 3:5. In fact, Mal 3:5 (ἀποστεροῦντας μισθὸν μισθωτοῦ) is closest verbally to James 5:4. The allusion to Lev 19:13 seems secure, nevertheless, because of the cluster effect. We know of the deliberate allusions in 2:1, 8 and 9, and can therefore more readily assume James's use of the levitical allusion here. To this point, then, we have a direct citation and two verbal allusions. Is there evidence for further use of Leviticus 19 by James? There is good reason for considering 4:11, 5:9, 5:12 and 5:20 all as thematic allusions to Lev 19:12-18. The first three passages share formal characteristics, and so will be considered before 5:20.

11. Cf. Dibelius, p. 147 n. 122; Seitz, "James and the Law," pp. 474-475.

12. Dibelius, p. 238 n. 46; Mayor, pp. cxi, 158; Ropes, p. 288; Mitton, p. 179; Adamson, p. 186; Mussner, p. 196; A. Schlatter, *Der Brief des Jakobus* (Stuttgart: Calwer, 1932), 31; J. Michl, *Die Katholischen Briefe,* 2nd ed. (RNT 8/2; Regensburg: F. Pustet, 1968), 57.

Further Allusions to Leviticus 19 in James

General Remarks

The most striking feature of the passages we are to consider is their formal resemblance. It is this structural similarity which first directs the reader's attention to a possible connection to Lev 19.

(1) Of all the negative commands in James (1:7, 13, 16; 2:1, 11; 3:1; 4:11; 5:9, 12), two are third person imperatives (1:7, 13), one is merely rhetorical (1:16), and one is a direct citation from Scripture (2:11). This leaves 2:1, 3:1, 4:11, 5:9 and 5:12 as second person plural, present prohibitions, introduced by μὴ. This alone reminds us of Leviticus 19 with its repeated prohibitions (οὐ with the future).

(2) All these passages make explicit mention of the *law* and/or *judgment* in their immediate context, and these references serve as warrants for the prohibitions. For 2:1, cf. ἐλεγχόμενοι ὑπὸ τοῦ νόμου ὡς παραβάται . . . παραβάτης νόμου . . . διὰ νόμου ἐλευθερίας μέλλοντες κρίνεσθαι . . . κρίσις ἀνέλεος (2:9-13). For 3:1, μεῖζον κρίμα λημψόμεθα. For 4:11-12, καταλαλεῖ νόμου καὶ κρίνει νόμον . . . ὁ κρίνων τὸν πλησίον. For 5:9, ἵνα μὴ κριθῆτε . . . ἰδοὺ ὁ κριτής. For 5:12, ἵνα μὴ ὑπὸ κρίσιν πέσητε.

It is important to note that, apart from the mention of the law of liberty in 1:25, the royal law in 2:8, and the use of κριτής in 2:4, these passages contain all the references to law and judgment in the Letter of James. In the case of 2:1, 9; 3:1; 4:11; 5:9 and 5:12, therefore (and only in these cases), we find a negative command, together with a sanction either explicitly or implicitly connected to judgment under the law.

The first of these commands contains all the elements in the fullest fashion. The prohibition of 2:1 is followed by the explanation of the pertinence of the law in 2:8-11, and the statement concerning judgment under the law of liberty in 2:12-13. The formal pattern is more impressive in this case since 2:1 begins the series of thematic essays which characterizes James after the aphoristic first chapter, and since in this first instance, there is the direct citation of Lev 19:18b in 2:8.

No claim is being made here for any allusion to Leviticus in James 3:1, so no further mention will be made of it. The formal notes shared by 4:11, 5:9 and 5:12, together with 2:1, 9, suggest a definite family relation between the passages: these prohibitions entail judgment under the law. Is there further cause for seeing in them a connection to Lev 19? The case has already been made for 2:1, 9, so we can turn to 4:11, 5:9 and 5:12 in some detail, before considering 5:20.

The Individual Passages

(1) 4:11: μή καταλαλεῖτε ἀλλήλων, ἀδελφοί. This short prohibition, with its extensive sanction and warrant (4:11b-12) is strikingly similar to Lev 19:16, as some commentators have already seen.[13] The likelihood of allusion is made stronger by James's shift to πλησίον in 4:12 in place of ἀδελφός.[14] This is used elsewhere by James only in the levitical citation of 2:8, and is found at the conclusion of the passage to which allusion is being made, Lev 19:16: οὐ πορεύσῃ δόλῳ ἐν τῷ ἔθνει σου . . . τοῦ πλησίον σου. In spite of Dibelius's demurral,[15] furthermore, it is likely, in view of the elaborate statement about slandering and judging the law, that James does have in mind a concrete commandment, namely the command to love in Lev 19:18b, precisely as explicated by the commandment of 19:16.

The important question with regard to this verse is whether we have a real thematic allusion to Lev 19:16. There is clearly no close verbal resemblance, just as there is not in the allusion to Lev 19:16 spotted in Ps.-Phoc. 21.[16] Although καταλαλεῖν means generally to speak boisterously against another,[17] and although its appearance in NT vice lists does not in itself lend greater specificity to it (cf. 2 Cor 12:20; Rom 1:30; 1 Pet 2:1), its use in the OT justifies its understanding as secret speech against another, or slander.[18]

This is seen most clearly in LXX Ps 100:5 (τὸν καταλαλοῦντα λάθρα τοῦ πλησίον αὐτοῦ), Ps 49:20 and Wis 1:11, and is further supported by the use in 1 Clem 30:3, 35:5, and, above all, Hermas, *Man* 2:2-3 and *Sim* IX,26,7. When placed in the context of "judging a neighbor," καταλαλεῖν certainly means "to slander," for such judgment is always involved in secret, hostile speech. What about Lev 19:16? Although the Greek may be translated "Thou shalt not walk deceitfully among thy people" (taking the prepositional phrase as adverbial), it represents here the Hebrew לא תלך רכיל which means, "do not go about as a slanderer," and is elsewhere similarly translated (cf. Jer 9:3). Between Lev 19:16 and James 4:11, the fit is not airtight, but is, nevertheless, remarkably snug. Four points converge to support the probability of an allusion here: a) the negative command; b) its

13. Cf. the margin of Nestle-Aland, 25th edition; Marty, p. 165; Mitton, p. 166.

14. Dibelius, p. 228; Mussner, p. 187. There is variation in both. James has ἀδελφός . . . πλησίον; Lev 19:16, ἐν τῷ ἔθνει σου . . . πλησίον.

15. Dibelius, p. 228.

16. Van der Horst, *Sentences*, p. 292.

17. Cf. Liddell-Scott-Jones, s.v.

18. G. Kittel, "καταλαλέω," *TDNT* 4:4.

content; c) the reference to "the neighbor"; d) its attachment to observance of the law.

(2) 5:9: μὴ στενάζετε, ἀδελφοί, κατ᾽ ἀλλήλων. This is the most tenuous of the possible allusions to Leviticus 19 in James, and is advanced here only tentatively. I suggest that it is a thematic allusion to Lev 19:18a, which immediately precedes the "Law of Love": καὶ οὐκ ἐκδικᾶταί σου ἡ χείρ, καὶ οὐ μηνιεῖς τοῖς υἱοῖς τοῦ λαοῦ σου ("And thy hand shall not avenge thee, and thou shalt not be angry with the children of thy people"). Note that anger and revenge are both prohibited. But can James 5:9 seriously be read as a thematic allusion to this? At first glance, it is not encouraging. Στενάζειν, after all, means simply to groan or sigh, and some commentators take it in as banal a fashion as possible.[19]

Two aspects of the verse, however, give the reader pause. First, the construction στενάζειν κατὰ τινων is somewhat unusual,[20] and reminds us of 4:11, καταλαλεῖν ἀλλήλων. The κατὰ renders the verb considerably more transitive. Second, the sanction ἵνα μὴ κριθῆτε seems excessive, if there is only a question of sighing. As in 4:11 and the other verses we are considering, the issue of judgment is explicit.[21] 5:9, therefore, poses three questions: how strongly are we to understand στενάζειν, against whom is it directed, and why is the injunction so forcefully supported?

The "do not grumble" of the *RSV* should have the strength at least of the *KJV*'s "grudge not against one another." But even if στενάζειν be granted maximal force, a further difficulty is presented by its being directed κατ᾽ ἀλλήλων, when the appropriate objects of grumbling would appear to be those outside the community.[22] Nevertheless, and again despite Dibelius,[23] a contextual reading of 5:9 gives us the best chance of grasping the sense of this verse, and therefore of its possible connection to Lev 19:18a.

James 5:7-11 must be seen as a response to 5:1-6. The οὖν of the exhortation in 5:7 is based on the statement of nonresistance which concludes

19. "James 5:9 charges Christians so to order their mutual relations that they have no cause for sighing against one another. The reference is to inner sighing, not to open complaints." J. Schneider, "στενάζω," *TDNT* 8:603.

20. Although κατατενάζω appears in LXX Exod 2:23, Jer 22:23, Lam 1:11.

21. Mitton, p. 187, and Adamson, p. 191, see a resemblance between 4:11 and 5:9.

22. Cf. A. Feuillet, "Le Sens du mot Parousie dans l'evangile de Matthieu. Comparaison entre Matt xxiv et Jac V.1-11," in *The Background of the New Testament and Its Eschatology*, ed. W. D. Davies and D. Daube (Cambridge: Cambridge University Press, 1956), 280-281.

23. "This verse is quite isolated, so there is no need to find some sort of connection between the warning not to 'grumble against one another,' and the preceding saying" (Dibelius, p. 244).

5:6b. The overall context for 5:9, therefore, is one of response to oppression by οἱ πλούσιοι (5:1). It should also be noted that 5:7-11 is exceptionally well structured. There is an alternation of imperatives concerning attitudes (be patient, strengthen your hearts, do not grumble, receive examples), and the imperatives ἰδού (5:7, 9, 11) which provide the grounds for the attitudes. They are to be patient *until* (ἕως), just as the farmers are patient *until* (ἕως, 5:7). They are not to complain *because* the judge is near; they are to receive examples *because* they show the blessedness of endurance (5:9, 11). 5:9 fits neatly and cogently between "the parousia of the Lord has approached" and "the judge stands before the door."

Within this context of oppression and exhortation the attitude of μακροθυμία recommended to the congregation and the exhortation to strengthen their hearts represent a characteristic response to tribulation (cf. 2 Cor 6:6; Eph 4:2; 2 Tim 3:10; and Acts 18:23; Rom 16:25; 2 Thess 2:17; 1 Pet 5:10), particularly that which precedes the Lord's coming in judgment (cf. 1 Thess 3:13). Here, the two attitudes point the same way: in spite of the affliction suffered by the innocent, they are to allow God to do his work. They are not to usurp his role of making judgment against oppression. They are to be long-suffering and firmly fixed.

How should μὴ στενάζετε be understood, then? The use of στενάζειν in the LXX is confined to the sense of sighing or groaning, not surprisingly in situations of suffering. There are places, however, in which the groaning is in response to oppression such as that pictured by James (cf. Job 30:25, Isa 59:11; Lam 1:21; Ezek 26:15; 1 Macc 1:26). The classic instance is the complaint of the Israelites in Egypt: κατεστέναξαν οἱ υἱοὶ Ἰσραήλ . . . καὶ εἰσήκουσεν ὁ θεὸς τὸν στεναγμὸν αὐτῶν . . . (Exod 2:23, cf. 6:5). The "complaint" of the people was raised, not against each other, but to the Lord, for his hearing. In 5:9, then, the author forbids his readers' taking out their resentments at oppression and trouble on each other. They are not to assume the role of judges and vindicate themselves, either against the outsider who oppresses or against each other. Vindication belongs to the Lord (Deut 32:35-36) who is now ready to judge the oppressors without the community and the grumblers within (5:9b). If they assume his prerogative of judging (by their complaint against each other) they will themselves be judged. Within this context, James 5:9 is thematically close to Lev 19:18a. There, revenge and wrath against a fellow Israelite are forbidden. Here, that grumbling against each other which arises from resentment and is equivalent to seeking vindication on one's own terms rather than the Lord's. It must be granted that this argument for a thematic allusion in 5:9 is the most fragile of those I am suggesting. But the strange features of the verse, coupled with the formal resemblances to the other passages considered, make the suggestion at least possible.

(3) 5:12: μὴ ὀμνύετε . . . ἵνα μὴ ὑπὸ κρίσιν πέσητε. In this prohibition, there is not only a thematic but also a verbal allusion to Lev 19:12, which reads οὐκ ὀμεῖσθε τῷ ὀνόματί ἐπ' ἀδίκῳ, καὶ οὐ βεβηλώσετε τὸ ὄνομα τοῦ θεοῦ ὑμῶν. Certainly the resemblance to Lev 19:12 is clearer in the case of James than in Ps.-Phoc. 16.[24] The Leviticus text has been recognized by some as one of the texts which form the general background for James 5:12, but no direct allusion has been suggested, so far as I know.[25] Failure to see an allusion here is surprising, and is undoubtedly due to the fact that 5:12 so emphatically calls attention to itself as a possible saying of Jesus, and has been studied primarily in relation to Matt 5:34-35.[26] Although other passages of the Law pertain to the issue of swearing (cf. Num 30:2; Deut 23:21), James is by far closest to Lev 19:12 in vocabulary and form. The cluster principle is again important here. Knowing that James had recourse to Lev 19:12-18 several other times in this letter makes a decision in favor of an allusion here easier to reach.

(4) 5:20: γινωσκέτω ὅτι ὁ ἐπιστρέψας ἁμαρτωλὸν ἐκ πλάνης ὁδοῦ αὐτοῦ σώσει ψυχὴν αὐτοῦ ἐκ θανάτου καὶ καλύψει πλῆθος ἁμαρτιῶν. After the negative commands comes this positive one, which corresponds to Lev 19:17b, also positively stated: ἐλεγμῷ ἐλέγξεις τὸν πλησίον σου, καὶ οὐ λήψῃ δι' αὐτὸν ἁμαρτίαν. The notions of "covering sins" and "bearing sin" in each case are connected to the correction or reproval of a neighbor. The relation between the verbs ἐπιστρέφω and ἐλέγχω is close, with the first denoting the completion of what the second intends (cf. James's use of ἐλέγχω in 2:9). The thematic allusion seems clear, but has remained virtually unattended.[27] As with 5:12, another factor has probably proven dis-

---

24. The clearest connection between James and Pseudo-Phocylides here lies in the repeated μήτε . . μήτε and the threat of divine retribution. Matt 5:34-35 repeats the μήτε four times and lacks the explicit note of judgment. In Lev 19:12, the ἐγώ εἰμι κύριος ὁ θεὸς ὑμῶν has an equivalent function. In *Sentences,* p. 124, van der Horst sees an allusion to Lev 19:12 in Pseudo-Phocylides 16, and in "Pseudo-Phocylides and the New Testament," p. 202, he sees one between Pseudo-Phocylides 16 and James 5:12 (also *Sentences,* p. 295). But neither he nor Dibelius (who also sees the relation to Pseudo-Phocylides 16) finds any connection between James 5:12 and Lev 19:12.

25. Cf. Marty, p. 199; Mussner, p. 213, E. Kutsch, "Eure Rede aber sei ja ja, nein nein," *EvT* 20 (1960) 208. P. Minear, "Yes or No, the Demand for Honesty in the Early Church," *NovT* 13 (1971) 2, connects Lev 19:12 to Matt 5:34-35, but not directly to James 5:12.

26. Cf. esp. Kutsch, pp. 206-218, and Minear, pp. 1-13.

27. H. Van Vliet, *No Single Testimony* (Utrecht: Kemink En Zoon, 1958), I, 54-57, accurately notes the allusion and its function.

tracting, namely the resemblance between 5:20, on the one hand, and Prov 10:12 and 1 Pet 4:8, on the other. It must be said, however, that apart from the notion of "hiding" (found in all three), and that of "a multitude of sins" (shared with 1 Pet), James 5:20 is *functionally* much closer to Lev 19:17b.

Dibelius had little use for attempts to find structure in James. This outlook led him to remark, "Any of the admonitions in James would be as good a conclusion as 5:19f."[28] That judgment is less than sound in any case, for the last verse of James extends as challenge to the reader the task James had set for himself in addressing his reader (cf. 1:16). But if we have in 5:20 a thematic allusion to Lev 19:17b, it is all the more an appropriate conclusion, forming a positive frame with 2:8 around the prohibitions of 2:1, 4:11, 5:9 and 5:12. The implications of the royal law of love are spelled out not only in avoidance, but also in care.

Conclusions

(1) Beginning with some clues derived from the use of Leviticus 19 in Pseudo-Phocylides, I have shown that in addition to the direct citation from Lev 19:18b in 2:8, the Letter of James contains certainly four, and possibly six further verbal or thematic allusions to Lev 19:12-18. Arranged according to the order of Leviticus, and with the least likely allusions marked with asterisks, they are:

(1)	Lev 19:12	James 5:12
(2)	Lev 19:13	James 5:4
(3)	Lev 19:15	James 2:1, 9
(4)	Lev 19:16	James 4:11
(5)	Lev 19:17b	James 5:20*
(6)	Lev 19:18a	James 5:9*
(7)	Lev 19:18b	James 2:8

The only verse from this section of Leviticus which is missing is 19:14.[29] The evidence, therefore, strongly suggests that James made conscious and sustained use of Lev 19:12-18 in his letter. The text of Leviticus did not

28. Dibelius, p. 2.

29. Also absent are the apodictic commands of Lev 19:11, although their substance is touched on in James 3:13–4:10.

guide the order of his exposition, nor did it, by any means, exhaustively dictate the contents of his message. But the clear thematic connections, together with the formal characteristics involving law, judgment and prohibition shared by many of these passages, point this way: that James regarded the "Royal Law" by which Christians were to live, and the "Law of Liberty" by which they were to be judged, as explicated concretely and specifically not only by the Decalogue (2:11), but by the immediate context of the Law of Love, the commands found in Lev 19:12-18.

(2) Awareness of James's use of Leviticus 19 can lead to exegetical consequences. For example, consternation has always been caused by the apparent dislocation of 4:11, 5:9 and 5:12. The solitude of 5:12 is only exacerbated by its introduction, πρὸ πάντων, which is even more problematic here than in the counterpart passage in 1 Pet 4:8. Commentators have suggested an interpolation,[30] a gloss,[31] and various epistolographic solutions.[32] Dibelius, typically, despairs of any resolution, "Since this verse has no relationship with what precedes or follows, nothing can be determined about the significance of the phrase, 'above all.'"[33] Dibelius is correct in this case concerning the unattached state of 5:12. Can the verse have found its way into the text at least partially by way of the inertia created by the use of the other Leviticus passages by James? This would certainly not be enough in itself, for James did not use Lev 19:14. Nor can there be any doubt that 5:12's relation to a saying of Jesus had importance for James. But there is this intriguing speculation: Lev 19:12 stands first in the list of injunctions used by James to explicate the law of love. Can this ordinal position in Leviticus have played a role in the incongruous continuance of πρὸ πάντων in 5:12? Such a solemn opening would better suit the whole listing of Lev 19:12-18 than just this isolated command in James 5:12.

More pertinently, if James read and understood the law of love explicitly within the context of Lev 19:12-18, we are also better able to understand James 2:8-13. It is not the βασιλικός of 2:8 which is most puzzling in this section, but the precise relation between "fulfilling the law" and "according to the Scripture." Unquestionably, the μέντοι of v. 8 and the δὲ of v. 9 must be seen as correlative. This means that the conclusion of v. 9, ἐλεγχόμενοι ὑπὸ τοῦ νόμου ὡς παραβάται should correspond to the νόμος

30. Cf. Mayor, p. 165.

31. G. Rendall, *The Epistle of James and Judaic Christianity* (Cambridge: Cambridge University Press, 1927), 68.

32. Mitton, p. 191; Ropes, p. 300; Mussner, p. 211; cf. also F. O. Francis, "The Form and Function of the Opening and Closing Paragraphs of James and I John," *ZNW* 61 (1970) 125.

33. Dibelius, p. 242.

of v. 8. Furthermore, the phrase which precedes the citation from Lev 19:18b, κατὰ τὴν γραφήν, is not a typical introduction to a Scripture citation. Its only other NT use is in 1 Cor 15:3-4, and there it does not introduce a citation. James uses other forms of introduction. One wonders, therefore, if the κατὰ τὴν γραφήν might refer to more than just Lev 19:18b.

What follows from these observations is this: keeping the law of love involves observing the *commandments* explicated by the Decalogue (2:11) and Lev 19:12-18 in their entirety. Given the connection James draws between Lev 19:18 and Lev 19:15 in 2:9, this conclusion appears certain. Breaking the prohibition against partiality is breaking the law of love, for that prohibition is one of its explications.[34] The emphasis of 2:8, therefore, should be, "If you *really* keep the royal law, *according to the Scripture* (that is according to the dictates of the Scripture), 'you shall love your neighbor as yourself,' you do well." For James, Lev 19:12-18 provides an accurate explication of that law of love which should obtain in the church.

(3) A further point should be made. James regards Lev 19:12-18 as an *accurate* exposition of the demands of love, but not, by itself, an *adequate* one. These commandments enter James as filtered through the Christian tradition. In remarkable fashion, precisely these halachic statements are colored by explicit dominical references. Partiality is incompatible with "the faith of our glorious Lord Jesus Christ" (2:1). The law of love from Lev 19:18b is characterized as βασιλικός not only because of its "excellence," but because it is the "law of the kingdom" (the use of βασιλεία in 2:5 is decisive for this) first enunciated by Jesus (cf. Matt 19:19; 22:39; Mark 12:31; Luke 10:27; Rom 13:9; Gal 5:14). The prohibition of slander and judging not only recalls Jesus' command against judging (Matt 7:1), but is sanctioned by the truth that there is but one κριτής (4:12), which points us to 5:9b. The coming of the judge in 5:9b, in turn, can only, in the light of 5:8, refer to the coming of Jesus (cf. the use of παρουσία and ἐγγίζω), and the language of 5:9b itself recalls synoptic traditions (Matt 24:43; Luke 12:39; cf. also Rev. 3:20). The prohibition of oaths has clear connection to the dominical saying in Matt 5:34-35. The ideal of fraternal correction (5:20) reflects a saying of Jesus (Matt 18:15; Luke 17:3).

In James, the value of Leviticus is affirmed for the church by reading it in the light of the Christian tradition which began with the words of Jesus. Because of certain excesses along these lines,[35] one hesitates to use

---

34. For the opposite position, cf. Dibelius, p. 142.

35. Cf., e.g., M. Gertner, "Midrashim in the New Testament," *JSS* 7 (1962) 267-292. His attempt to show that James is a midrash on Psalm 12 is misdirected.

the term *midrash* in any but the clearest of cases, but this is really what James is doing by his use of Leviticus 19. In the passages I have isolated, James engages in halachic midrash. The text is Lev 19:12-18. The perspective on the text is provided by the understanding of life and law given by the experience of Jesus Christ. James has long been seen as a NT representative of the wisdom and prophetic traditions. He reshapes as well the inheritance of Torah.

(4) Finally, a note on the possible historical significance of this use by James of Leviticus 19. In his introduction to *The Sentences of Pseudo-Phocylides,* van der Horst suggests that the late rabbinic tradition concerning the role of Leviticus 19 as a summary of, or counterpoint to the Decalogue, to be read in the assembly, may be supported by the evidence of systematic use of this chapter of Leviticus by Pseudo-Phocylides.[36] If my reading of the levitical allusions in James is accurate, James would be another first-century witness for such a role.

36. Van der Horst, *Sentences,* pp. 66-67.

The Sayings of Jesus in the Letter of James
(with Wesley Wachob)

The task of this essay is to assess the intertexture of several sayings attributed to "James a servant of God and of the Lord Jesus Christ" (Jas 1:1).[1] Put differently, our interest is the apparent use of Jesus' sayings that appear in the Letter of James. Whether its specific rhetorical category finally be called paraenesis or protrepsis, the Letter of James is certainly a form of wisdom literature that appropriates cross-cultural traditions without explanation, apology, or explicit citation. Determining the precise provenance of any specific expression within James is commensurately difficult, since there are usually too many possibilities. The sayings of Jesus themselves present a similar problem: what parts of the gospel tradition can be said to come from Jesus, and what parts from other sources? Asking about the presence of Jesus sayings in the Letter of James is therefore an invitation to a hazardous and necessarily tentative examination.

James offers some small help in the way it makes use of Leviticus 19. The quotation of Lev 19:18 in Jas 2:8 is the letter's only direct and explicit citation of "scripture" (γραφή). Yet other places in James strongly suggest allusions to Lev 19:11-18: sometimes the wording is close, sometimes not. The important methodological point, however, is this: the clear and explicit citation of one passage legitimates the search for others and makes the detection of each incrementally more plausible. Close analysis shows that James's use of Lev 19:11-18 is considerable: Lev 19:12 = Jas 5:12; Lev 19:13 = Jas 5:4; Lev 19:15 = Jas 2:1, 9; Lev 19:16 = Jas 4:11; Lev 19:17b = Jas 5:20; Lev 19:18c = Jas 2:8.[2] Lev 19:11 and 19:14 are not verbally echoed but the sub-

---

1. On the intertexture of texts, see esp. V. K. Robbins, *Exploring the Texture of Texts: A Guide to Socio-Rhetorical Interpretation* (Valley Forge: Trinity Press International, 1996), 40-70.
2. See my essay "The Use of Leviticus 19 in the Letter of James," pp. 123-135 in this volume.

stance of their commands is covered by Jas 2:14-16 and 3:13–4:10 respectively.[3] A similar procedure will be followed in this essay: the surest candidate for a saying of Jesus within James will receive the greatest attention, for the simple reason that securing it makes the possibility of the presence of other sayings more likely.

For more than two centuries some scholars have held that James uses a tradition of Jesus' sayings in his letter. They base their conclusion on the perception that a number of the sayings attributed to James have a striking affinity to Jesus logia. Further, as M. Dibelius observed,[4] some of these parallels are similar to Jesus logia in form, style, and convictions. Recently, these scattered opinions have been given the fullest possible airing by D. B. Deppe,[5] who studied the twenty-five most frequently mentioned parallels and concluded that at least eight of them are conscious allusions to Jesus' sayings:

1. Jas 1:5 = Q^M 7:7 = Q^L 11:9 = *GThom* §92, §94
2. Jas 4:2c-3 = Q^M 7:7 = Q^L 11:9 = *GThom* §92, §94
3. Jas 2:5 = Q^M 5:3 = Q^L 6:20b = *GThom* §54
4. Jas 4:9 = Q^M 5:4 = Q^L 6:21b = *GThom* §69b
5. Jas 4:10 = Q^M 23:12; Q^L 14:11
6. Jas 5:2-3a = Q^M 6:20 = Q^L 12:33b = *GThom* §76b
7. Jas 5:12 = Q^M 5:34-37
8. Jas 5:1 = Q^L 6:24-25

The present essay focuses on only six sayings: four that Deppe calls "conscious allusions" (Jas 5:12; 1:5 and 4:2c-3; 2:5) and two others that are among the twenty-five sayings he mentions, but not (in his view) "conscious allusions" (Jas 2:8 and 13).

James 5:12 = Matthew 5:34-37

Apart from Jesus and James, no one else in the Old or New Testament categorically prohibits oaths. Oaths are, in fact, regarded as an acceptable

---

3. L. T. Johnson, *The Letter of James* (AB 37A; Garden City: Doubleday, 1995), 31.

4. M. Dibelius, *James: A Commentary on the Epistle of James*, rev. H. Greeven, trans. M. Williams (Hermeneia; Philadelphia: Fortress, 1976), 28.

5. D. B. Deppe, *The Sayings of Jesus in the Epistle of James* (dissertation, Amsterdam; Chelsea, MI: Bookcrafters, 1989), 219-220, 222-223. See also W. H. Wachob, "The Relationship Between the Epistle of James and Q" (unpublished paper presented to the Southeastern Regional 1988 SBL Meeting, Macon, GA).

and important part of life in both Testaments (Gen 22:16; Exod 13:5; 22:10-11; Num 14:16; Deut 6:13; 1 Kgs 8:31-32; Jer 12:16; Matt 23:16-22; Luke 1:73; Acts 2:30; Rom 1:9; 2 Cor 1:23; Gal 1:20; Phil 1:8; Heb 6:13-20; Rev 10:6). There is, to be sure, criticism within Judaism of frequent and flagrant swearing (Lev 5:4; Num 30:3; Deut 23:22; Sir 23:9-11; Philo, *Decalogue* 84-95; *m. Nedarim; m. Šebu.* 4:1). Such critiques are found elsewhere in the *Umwelt* (e.g. Epictetus, *Enchr.* 33.5). The aversion to swearing even led some in the ancient world, like the Pythagoreans, to prohibit oaths (see Diog. Laert. 8.22; Iambl. *Vit. Pyth.* 47). Such interdictions, however, are based on different ideas than those grounding Jesus' and James's prohibitions of oaths.[6] And, while there was a prohibition of oaths among (one branch of) the Essenes, the evidence is complicated by the fact that the Dead Sea sect required an entrance oath (see Josephus, *J.W.* 2.8.6 §135; 2.8.7-8 §139-43; *Ant.* 15.10.4 §370-372; cf. 1QS 5:8; 1QH 14:17; CD 15:5, 8-12; 16:1-5). The distinctiveness of Jesus and James with regard to oaths, therefore, is striking.[7] A comparison of James's prohibition of oaths (Jas 5:12) with the one attributed to Jesus in Matt 5:34-37 shows that they have sixteen Greek words in common:

$$\ldots\mu\grave{\eta}\;\grave{o}\mu[\;]\ldots\mu\acute{\eta}\tau\epsilon\;\tau[\;]\;o\grave{v}\rho\alpha\nu[\;]\ldots\mu\acute{\eta}\tau\epsilon\ldots\tau[\;]\;\gamma[\;]\ldots\mu\acute{\eta}\tau\epsilon\ldots[\;]\;\tau\omega$$
$$\delta\grave{\epsilon}\ldots\dot{v}\mu\tilde{\omega}\nu\ldots\nu\alpha\grave{\iota}\;\nu\alpha\grave{\iota}\ldots o\grave{v}\;o\breve{v}\ldots$$

James's prohibition ("do not swear") features the present imperative active, second person plural (μὴ ὀμνύετε), while the Matthean version has the aorist infinitive active (μὴ ὀμόσαι) with the adverb ὅλως. In Matt 5:34c and 35a the first two μήτε-phrases ("neither by the heaven . . . nor by the earth") have ἐν, the dative article and noun, a Semitic usage;[8] the third μήτε-phrase in Matt 5:35c ("nor by . . .") has εἰς + an anarthrous noun in the accusative case. In Jas 5:12a the first two μήτε-phrases have the accusative article and noun, which is ordinary classical usage,[9] and the third μήτε-phrase also features the accusative case: ἄλλον τινὰ ὅρκον. Both Jas 5:12b and Matt 5:37a have the imperative third person singular

---

6. Dibelius, *James*, p. 248 n. 41.

7. Concerning the criteria of authenticity, the prohibition of oaths satisfies the criterion of dissimilarity. If we may regard Jas 5:12 as a Jamesian performance of a saying of Jesus, then we have multiple attestation, for Matthew and James are most probably independent sources for this logion. The prohibition also satisfies the criterion of embarrassment, since both the Old Testament and New Testament accept and honor the swearing oaths.

8. See BDF §149, §220; N. Turner, *A Grammar of New Testament Greek*, vol. 3 (Edinburgh: T. & T. Clark, 1963), 252-253.

9. See H. W. Smyth, *Greek Grammar* (Cambridge: Harvard University Press, 1956), §1596.

of εἰμί ("but let be"), though the forms are different (ἤτω and ἔστω, respectively). And where James has τὸ ναὶ . . . καὶ τὸ οὔ . . . ("your yes . . . and [your] no . . ."), the compound (articular) subject of the verb, followed by a compound (anarthrous) predicate, ναὶ . . . οὔ ("yes . . . no"), Matt 5:37a has as its subject λόγος ὑμῶν ("your word"), and an anarthrous, asyndetic and emphatic ναὶ ναὶ, οὔ οὔ ("yes yes, no, no") as the predicate.[10] The fact that there are grammatical and syntactical variations in these performances is anything but surprising, since "recitation of a saying using words different from the authoritative source" was a common practice in the culture of the Greco-Roman age, including early Christianity.[11] Besides, the variations here do not hide what the two texts have in common. In fact the Jamesian performance is overwhelmingly regarded as the surest example of James's use of the sayings of Jesus.[12] For example, H. Koester says, "In Jas 5:12 there can be no doubt that James is quoting the same injunction that Matthew used in the third [sic!; should read fourth] antithesis of the Sermon on the Mount. James has preserved an earlier form."[13]

The Matthean performance of Jesus' prohibition of oaths occurs as part of a (so-called[14]) antithesis, which, within the Sermon on the Mount,

---

10. The lack of the article in Matt 5:37a does not prevent the statement from having the same meaning as that of Jas 5:12. Dibelius (*James*, pp. 250-251), as well as H. Koester (*Ancient Christian Gospels: Their History and Development* [London: SCM Press; Philadelphia: Trinity Press International, 1990], 73-75), suggests (on the basis of *1 Enoch*) that 5:37a should be understood as providing a milder and acceptable "oath formula" (as opposed to those in 5:34c-36). But it is better to understand the second yes and no in 5:37a as emphatic. See W. D. Davies and D. C. Allison, Jr., *A Critical and Exegetical Commentary on the Gospel according to Saint Matthew* (ICC; Edinburgh: T. & T. Clark, 1988), 538; H. D. Betz, *The Sermon on the Mount: A Commentary on the Sermon on the Mount, including the Sermon on the Plain (Matthew 5:3–7:27 and Luke 6:20-49)* (Hermeneia; Minneapolis: Fortress, 1995), 271. Moreover, that the emphatic "yes, yes and no, no" is synonymous with simple "yes and no" is corroborated by Paul's usage in 2 Cor 1:17-18. See P. Minear, "'Yes and No': The Demand for Honesty in the Early Church," *NovT* 13 (1971) 1-13.

11. See Robbins, *Exploring the Texture of Texts*, pp. 41-48; and idem, *The Tapestry of Early Christian Discourse: Rhetoric, Society and Ideology* (London and New York: Routledge, 1996), 96-143.

12. Of the sixty authors listed by Deppe (*The Sayings of Jesus in the Epistle of James*, 141 n. 500), fifty-nine of them include Jas 5:12. K. A. Credner (*Einleitung in das Neue Testament* [Halle: Waisenhauses, 1836]), the only exception, omitted it accidentally, according to Deppe.

13. Koester, *Ancient Christian Gospels*, p. 74.

14. Although Matt 5:21-48 is usually referred to as "the antitheses," this is, as E. P. Sanders (*The Historical Figure of Jesus* [London: The Penguin Press, 1993], 201) argues, an inac-

is a rhetorical argument that supports the thesis that Jesus has come "not to abolish the law and the prophets, but to fulfill them" (Matt 5:17).[15] The argument may be outlined as follows:

A testimony of the ancients based on the law:	Do not swear falsely (5:33).
A contrary judgment by Jesus based on the law:	Do not swear at all (5:34b);
Three parallel examples:	by heaven, by earth, by Jerusalem (5:34c, 35a, 35c);
Reason (in three parallel statements):	heaven, earth, Jerusalem belong to God (5:34d, 35b, 35d).
A fourth example:	Do not swear by your head (5:36a);
Reason:	you cannot even make one hair black or white (5:36b).
A judgment by Jesus based on the law:	Let your yes be yes, and your no, no (5:37a);
Reason:	anything more is evil (5:37b).[16]

The antithetical character of Jesus' prohibition of oaths in Matthew is due to its juxtaposition to an authoritative judgment based on the law "by the men of old" (Matt 5:33). The latter judgment is not a quotation of the law; rather, it appears to be "a Hellenistic-Jewish halakah"[17] or summary based on the law (esp. Lev 19:12; cf. Exod 20:7; Num 30:3-15: Deut

---

curate designation. Antithesis in form does not necessarily mean opposition in content. "This section of Matthew has often been cited as showing Jesus' 'opposition' to the law. But heightening the law is not opposing it, though I have shown elsewhere (pp. 210-11) it implies a kind of criticism. If intensification were against the law, then the main groups of Judaism, the Pharisees and the Essenes, were systematic breakers of the law. But in fact no ancient Jew thought that being super-strict was illegal, nor did the author of Matthew" (p. 212).

15. G. A. Kennedy, *New Testament Interpretation Through Rhetorical Criticism* (Chapel Hill and London: University of North Carolina Press, 1984), 42. Of the six so-called antitheses in the Sermon on the Mount (= SM), the fourth (Matt 5:33-37) begins a second set of three antitheses. See the analyses and discussions in Betz (*Sermon on the Mount*, pp. 259-274), Davies and Allison (*Matthew*, pp. 533-538), and U. Luz (*Matthew 1-7* [Minneapolis: Augsburg, 1989], 310-322).

16. B. L. Mack, *Rhetoric in the New Testament* (Guides to Biblical Scholarship; Minneapolis: Fortress, 1990), 83.

17. Betz, *Sermon on the Mount,* p. 264.

23:21-23). Its probable meaning is, "You have heard that it was said to the men of old: 'All your oaths are to be true.'"[18] To this judgment Jesus authoritatively responds with a different, intensifying judgment, "But I say to you, 'do not swear at all'" (Matt 5:34b). Jesus' judgment is also based on the law and is not contradictory to it: the person who does not swear obviously would not transgress the law which forbids swearing falsely.[19]

James's instruction occurs at the beginning of a section of the letter that has an undeniably pragmatic and linear relation to earlier advice concerning speech, but does so with specific emphasis on speech acts within the ἐκκλησία (5:14). In James, as in the SM, the judgment about oaths seeks to persuade its addressees to refrain from an action (the swearing of oaths) and to perform an action (speaking frankly, truthfully) in the immediate future.

Jesus' prohibition of oaths is amplified and illustrated by four μήτε–sentences, each of which features a ὅτι–clause as its rationale or basis. The first three sentences (5:34c-35) are parallel and symmetrical; the fourth (5:36) breaks the pattern and flow of the previous three. As illustrations of the tendency to avoid using God's name in swearing, however, they are all examples of the effort to reduce the binding character of oaths, accentuating Jesus' conviction that all oaths are equally serious (cf. Matt 23:16-22).[20]

The formal similarity of the threefold repetition μὴ . . . μήτε . . . μήτε . . . μήτε in Jas 5:12a and μὴ . . μήτε . . . μήτε . . . μήτε . . . μήτε in Matt 5:34-36 is impressive. The formal similarity is only strengthened by the fact that the fourth μήτε clause in Matt 5:36, which is so markedly different from the three in Matt 5:34c-35, is probably a secondary addition. Nor should it be overlooked that the meaning of James's third and climactic μήτε ἄλλον τινὰ ὅρκον ("nor any other sort of oath") corresponds to the qualification of μὴ ὀμόσαι by ὅλως ("at all") in Matt 5:34.[21]

---

18. Davies and Allison, *Matthew*, p. 534. It appears that the halakah in 5:33 is closest to Lev 19:12 (but cf. Ps.-Phocylides, *Sent.* 16), where not fulfilling oaths sworn in the name of God is a grievous act of perjury. The amplifications support this by arguing that all oaths used in place of the Holy Name are nevertheless binding (Davies and Allison, *Matthew*, p. 536; E. P. Sanders, *Jewish Law from Jesus to the Mishnah: Five Studies* [London: SCM Press; Philadelphia: Trinity Press International, 1990], 53).

19. Sanders, *Jewish Law*, p. 55. He further says: "The position that oaths should not be taken at all implicitly criticizes the law, however, for catering to human weakness" (p. 55; see esp. pp. 51-57).

20. Davies and Allison, *Matthew*, p. 536; Sanders, *Jewish Law*, p. 55; and esp. Betz, *Sermon on the Mount*, pp. 266-270.

21. A. H. McNeile, *The Gospel according to St. Matthew* (London: Macmillan, 1915), 67; Johnson, *James*, p. 328.

The similarity of form and content in these two performances is undeniable and raises the question of the relationship of James and Matthew. Most scholars correctly agree that neither James nor Matthew knows the other,[22] so the question of a common source presents itself, along with the issue of which performance, James's or Matthew's, has priority.

Our analysis suggests that Matt 5:36 is most probably a secondary element; furthermore, the three μήτε–clauses in James are the better, smoother performance: in Matt 5:34b the adverb ὅλως makes the subsequent explanations redundant, while James's placement of the limiting phrase, "any other sort of oath," is a rather logical extension and intensification of the prohibition. Matthew's "by Jerusalem" is also probably redactional, though it is uncertain whether the redaction is pre-Matthean (SM) or Matthean.[23] The final clauses in both texts (Matt 5:37b and Jas 5:12b) are most likely redactional statements, as well. In short, although we cannot always argue that the briefer version is the more original, the specific elements of Matthew's longer version support the conclusion that his redactional interests are at work, and that the form of Jas 5:12b may be closer to Jesus' original saying.

With regard to the last point, Justin Martyr's performance of this prohibition is crucial (*1 Apol.* 1.16.5). Like the one in Matthew, it is contextually attributed to Jesus; it reads: "Do not swear at all (μή ὀμόσητε ὅλως), but let your yes be yes and your no be no (ἔστω δὲ ὑμῶν τὸ ναὶ ναὶ καὶ τὸ οὒ οὒ; anything more than this is from evil (τὸ δὲ περισσὸν τούτων ἐκ τοῦ πονηροῦ). The first and last of these three clauses are virtually identical to Matt 5:34b and 37b; the only differences are the form of the verb in the first clause and the ellipsis of the verb in the last. The second clause, however, is identical to Jas 5:12b, except for the verb ἔστω (which agrees with Matthew). One may argue that Justin's performance is a harmonization of the performances of Matthew and James.[24] On the other hand, one can argue that while Justin clearly depends on Matthew, his agreement with James in the second clause is due to the fact that the Jamesian form is

22. Pace M. H. Shepherd, "The Epistle of James and the Gospel of Matthew," *JBL* 75 (1956) 40-51.

23. The tension between the categorical prohibition of oaths in the pre-Matthean SM (Matt 5:34-37) and Matt 23:16-22 makes it possible that the understanding of oaths in the SM is not that of the final redactor of Matthew (see Deppe, *Sayings of Jesus,* p. 137; Betz, *Sermon on the Mount,* pp. 213-214).

24. A. J. Bellinzoni, *The Sayings of Jesus in the Writings of Justin Martyr* (Leiden: Brill, 1967), 65.

broadly and independently known; indeed, it is the Jamesian form of this clause that is replicated throughout early Christianity, even in texts that are presumably quoting Matt 5:37a.[25]

Since Luke does not share this material with Matthew, most scholars do not include the prohibition in Q. This simply shows the limits of our knowledge of Q: Luke could have chosen not to include it, if he and Matthew read a shared version; alternatively, Matthew and Luke could have had different versions of Q, with Q-Matthew containing the prohibition. H. D. Betz's hypothesis that both the SM and the SP were pre-synoptic sources suggests that the SM is the primary source for Jesus' prohibition of oaths. Perhaps the antithesis before us appeared in both Q-Matthew and in the SM.[26] James, on the other hand, does not appear to be dependent either upon Q or the written Gospels.[27] Nevertheless, it is quite possible — perhaps probable — that James was familiar with a collection of sayings in which Jesus categorically prohibited oaths. In other words, James was familiar with a collection of Jesus logia similar to those in the pre-Matthean SM and/or Q-Matthew.

Our analysis supports the hypothesis that most probably Jas 5:12 is an independent source for the prohibition of oaths attributed to Jesus in Matt 5:34-37, and that — in agreement with Koester — the saying in James reflects an earlier stage of the tradition than the one in the Matthean SM.[28] The high probability that James in 5:12 recontextualizes without attribution a saying of Jesus also increases the probability that other, less obvious, echoes might have the same source.

James 1:5, 4:2c-3 = Q^M 7:7, 11 = Q^L 11:9, 13 = GThom §92, §94

Jas 1:5 Εἰ δέ τις ὑμῶν λείπεται σοφίας, αἰτείτω παρὰ τοῦ διδόντος θεοῦ πᾶσιν ἁπλῶς καὶ μὴ ὀνειδίζοντος καὶ δοθήσεται αὐτῷ. Jas 4:2-3 οὐκ ἔχετε διὰ τὸ μὴ αἰτεῖσθε ὑμᾶς, αἰτεῖτε καὶ οὐ λαμβάνετε διότι κακῶς αἰτεῖσθε, ἵνα ἐν ταῖς ἡδοναῖς ὑμῶν δαπανήσητε.

---

25. D. C. Duling, "Against Oaths: Crossan Sayings Parallels 59," *Forum* 6.2 (1990) 99-138, here 133.

26. Betz, *Sermon on the Mount*, esp. pp. 42-88. "The conclusion is most likely," says Betz, "that Matthew as well as Luke found the SM and the SP, respectively, in their recension of Q (Q^Matt and Q^Luke)" (p. 44).

27. W. D. Davies, *The Setting of the Sermon on the Mount* (Cambridge: Cambridge University Press, 1964), 403-404.

28. Koester, *Ancient Christian Gospels*, pp. 74-75.

Both Jas 1:5 and 4:2c-3 have a parallel in Matt 7:7, 11 = Luke 11:9, 13. The latter verses are the beginning and ending statements in pericopae (Matt 7:7-11 = Luke 11:9-13) which concern prayer. While some scholars argue for a complex tradition-history behind these synoptic texts,[29] others hold, with better reason, that they defy a history of traditions analysis and conclude that they are unified sections.[30]

In Matthew and Luke, respectively, a three-part exhortation (Matt 7:7 = Luke 11:9) is followed by a three-part rationale (Matt 7:8 = Luke 11:10) which is confirmed by two examples, both of which are arguments from analogy (Matt 7:9-10 = Luke 11:11-12) and warrant the inferred conclusion (Matt 7:11 = Luke 11:13). Moreover, five occurrences of αἰτέω and six formations from δίδωμι — weld the individual parts into unified elaborations.[31]

Shared by Matthew and Luke and almost identical in wording, these elaborations are, according to most scholars, derived from the common source Q.[32] On the other hand, the differences in the wording and order of Matt 7:9-10 (bread/stone and fish/snake) and Luke 11:11-12 (fish/snake and egg/scorpion), are significant and difficult to explain as either evangelist's redaction. Consequently, a growing number of scholars argue that Matthew and Luke had different recensions of Q and/or other sources.[33] This position is further strengthened by the fact that the pericopae have different contexts and functions in Matthew and Luke. The Lukan pericope fits easily within a large instruction on prayer which begins with the Lord's Prayer (Luke 11:1-13). In contrast, the Matthean pericope, which is part of the SM, seems, at first glance, only loosely connected to its surroundings. Certainly it makes a complete argument for praying confidently, but the function of Matthew's elaboration is less an instruction on prayer than an argument using prayer to emphasize God's generosity. In other words, the primary function of the prayer elaboration in Matt 7:7-11

---

29. J. D. Crossan, *In Fragments: The Aphorisms of Jesus* (San Francisco: Harper & Row, 1983), 95-104.

30. Luz, *Matthew 1-7*, pp. 420-425; Davies and Allison, *Matthew*, pp. 677-685. The best and most complete discussion is in Betz, *Sermon on the Mount*, pp. 501-508.

31. On "elaboration," see Mack, *Rhetoric in the New Testament*, pp. 31-49, 81-85; and esp. Robbins, *Exploring the Texture of Texts*, pp. 40, 52-59.

32. J. S. Kloppenborg, *Q Parallels: Synopsis, Critical Notes and Concordance* (Sonoma: Polebridge, 1988), 86-89.

33. See I. H. Marshall, *Commentary on Luke* (Grand Rapids: Eerdmans, 1978), 466; Davies and Allison, *Matthew*, p. 681; G. Strecker, *The Sermon on the Mount* (Abingdon: Nashville, 1988), 11-13; Luz, *Matthew 1-7*, pp. 46-49; and Betz, *Sermon on the Mount*, esp. pp. 42-44.

is to argue that the children of the Father in Heaven should generously give to others (cf. 7:12).[34]

A clue to the secondary emphasis on prayer in Matt 7:7-11 may be reflected in the partial parallels to Matt 7:7 found in the *GThom* §92 and §94 (the latter has a partial parallel in Matt 7:8; and with *GThom* §93; cf. Matt 7:6). These parallels have been overlaid with gnostic emphases and are unrelated to prayer. Likewise, the partial parallels in The Gospel of the Hebrews and in POxy 654 §1 (which is similar to *GThom* §2), while attesting to the widespread popularity of the saying in view, are not necessarily related to prayer and are but faint reminiscences of the elaboration in Matt 7:7-11. The history of tradition is opaque.[35]

In Matt 7:7-11 = Luke 11:9-13 it is only in the final statements (Matt 7:11 = Luke 11:13) that "asking and receiving" ("seeking" and "knocking") are clearly related to prayer. Nonetheless, even if the prayer-connection here is due to secondary interpretation, there is nothing in the history of tradition that violates the integrity of these synoptic sections. In other words, already in the sources used by the evangelists these pericopae were unified wholes. It is certainly conceivable that the original elaboration goes back to Jesus.[36]

Against this background, let us look at Jas 1:5 and 4:2c-3. Both concern prayer and share the pertinent lexical terms: αἰτείτω . . . καὶ δοθήσεται (Jas 1:5) and αἰτεῖτε καί . . . λαμβάνετε (Jas 4:3; cf. Matt 7:8 = Luke 11:10).[37] Additionally, in Jas 1:5 the reference to God as "the God who gives to all liberally and does not upbraid," though clearly different from Matthew's ("our Father, the one in the heavens, [who] will give good things to those who

34. See esp. Betz, *Sermon on the Mount,* pp. 423-428, 500-508. The Golden Rule (Matt 7:12), which epitomizes "the law and the prophets," not only supports this assessment of Matt 7:7-11 but, as Betz argues (see esp. *Sermon on the Mount,* pp. 508-519), is (1) also the hermeneutical key for understanding the third section of the SM (Matt 6:19–7:11), and (2) a framing device that, with Matt 5:17-18, interpreted the Law in terms of fulfilling the love command. In Jas 2:1-13 we are in the same milieu as the SM, for "those who love God" (Jas 2:5) are those who obey the Torah (Jas 2:10 = "the royal law," Jas 2:8), which, summarized in the love-command (Jas 2:8; cf. Lev 19:18), coheres with the "faith of Jesus [himself]" (Jas 2:1). See below in the remarks on the parallel between Jas 2:5 and Matt 5:3 = Luke 6:20b.

35. Whether the *Gospel of Thomas* depended on Matthew or on presynoptic tradition is uncertain; cf. also John 14:13-14; 15:7; and 16:24 (see Betz, *Sermon on the Mount,* pp. 426, 503-504; Marshall, *Luke,* p. 466; Davies and Allison, *Matthew,* pp. 674-675, 678-680, 682).

36. Luz, *Matthew 1–7,* p. 421; also R. W. Funk and R. W. Hoover, eds., *The Five Gospels: The Search for the Authentic Words of Jesus* (New York: Macmillan, 1993), p. 155.

37. In Jas 1:5 αἰτέω occurs once; δίδωμι twice. In Jas 4:2c-3 αἰτέω occurs three times; δίδωμι does not occur but its synonym λαμβάνω occurs once. See Philo, *Migr. Abr.* 121.

ask him") and Luke's ("the Father, the one from heaven [who] will give the Holy Spirit to those who ask him"), is a linguistic performance that captures the essence of the emphasis on God's generosity in the Jesus logion. Thus, it appears that in Jas 1:5 the author has recited, in his own words, the essence of both the fundamental exhortation (Matt 7:7 = Luke 11:9) and the fundamental conclusion (Matt 7:11 = Luke 11:13) of the saying of Jesus in Matt 7:7-11 = Luke 11:9-13.

Most scholars hold, with good reason, that the Matthean performance, with its reference to "good things," is more original than Luke's reference to the "Holy Spirit." This is extremely significant in light of the connections that James makes with the "wisdom from above" (3:17), which is one of the good and perfect gift(s) which come down from God the Father (1:17). Indeed, it is because God the Father is a generous giver of "good things" that one is exhorted in Jas 1:5 to pray with confidence for "wisdom." The pragmatic relations between James's sayings reveal a network of presuppositions that resonate with the saying of Jesus in Matt 7:7-11 = Luke 11:9-13. There is more than enough to suggest that Jas 1:5 is a Jamesian recitation of a saying attributed to Jesus. Moreover, it appears that Jas 1:5 is closer to the pre-Matthean saying in Matt 7:7, 11.

The lexical terms and the prayer theme in Jas 4:2c-3 recall the language of Jesus in Matt 7:8 = Luke 11:10. On the other hand, some have argued that here James is not using a saying of Jesus. Apart from its lack of attribution to Jesus, the argument against Jas 4:2c-3 is basically this: James, here, is dealing with unanswered prayer (he juxtaposes an unqualified form in 4:2 with a qualified form in 4:3); the format of Jas 4:3 is negative (while the format of Matt 7:8 = Luke 11:10 is positive); and there are grammatical variations in the texts (James has the indicative, rather than imperative, mood, and he shifts voices: middle to active to middle, in 4:2c-3). None of these arguments is persuasive. James here seems to use the active and middle voices interchangeably (see 1 John 5:14-16 and cf. 1 John 3:22); neither the differences in the grammar of Jas 4:2c-3, nor the negative format of Jas 4:3 can disqualify this as a Jamesian recitation of the Jesus logion in Matt 7:8 = Luke 11:10. Moreover, the unity, coherence, and emphasis in Jas 4:2c-3 cohere with the integrity of its grammar, form, and content.

James 2:5 = Q^M 5:3 = Q^L 6:20b = *GThom* §54

James 2:5 is one of James's most important parallels to a Jesus logion. It has a strategic function within Jas 2:1-13, which is a well-defined and complete elaboration of the theme introduced in Jas 2:1; namely, that "the faith of our Lord Jesus Christ" is incompatible with acts of partiality.[38] From a rhetorical perspective, it appears that James has adapted a Jesus-beatitude (Matt 5:3 = Luke 6:20b) and partially recited it for his own persuasive purposes.

Besides Jas 2:5, there are four other performances of the saying in question. These are Matt 5:3; Luke 6:20b; *GThom* §54; and Polycarp, *Phil.* 2:3. All five performances share two key terms: "the poor" and "the kingdom." Moreover, all five performances exploit the common terms to produce sentences that feature one common denominator — "God's kingdom is promised to the poor." Apart from this, however, Jas 2:5 is observably different from its four parallels in attribution, form, content, style, and function. For example, the parallels to Jas 2:5 are beatitudes, specifically attributed to Jesus. In addition, they are also enthymemes, rhetorical syllogisms: each consists of a conclusion (a macarism) and a premise (a ὅτι clause), with, as is typical of enthymemes, one premise unstated and tacitly assumed. Because of these differences, and because it emphasizes God's concern for the poor, some scholars separate Jas 2:5 from its context and conclude that it simply states a "principle of the traditional piety of the poor."[39]

There is no doubt that both the OT and Jewish literature reflect the notion that God has a special concern for the poor, and Jas 2:5 clearly evokes "the traditional piety of the poor."[40] On the other hand, as Deppe reminds us, "there are no references in the OT, intertestamental literature, or the Talmud specifically saying that God is giving the kingdom to the poor."[41] This

---

38. W. H. Wachob, *"The Rich in Faith" and "The Poor in Spirit": The Socio-Rhetorical Function of a Saying of Jesus in the Epistle of James* (doctoral dissertation, Atlanta: Emory University, 1993: forthcoming in SNTSMS; Cambridge: Cambridge University Press); Johnson, *James*, p. 56.

39. Koester, *Ancient Christian Gospels*, p. 74.

40. H. D. Betz (*Essays on the Sermon on the Mount* [Philadelphia: Fortress, 1985], 34) rightly asserts that Q^M 5:3 also "derives from the Jewish 'piety of the poor.'" See L. T. Johnson, *Sharing Possessions: Mandate and Symbol of Faith* (OBT 9; Philadelphia: Fortress, 1981), 79-116.

41. Deppe, *Sayings of Jesus*, p. 90. He further says (*Sayings of Jesus*, pp. 90-91): "The decisive clue for the presence of a saying of Jesus lies in the fact that the word 'kingdom' is not Jamesian vocabulary: Jas 2:5 is the only occurrence of this term in the epistle. Certainly the employment of a term particularly associated with the preaching of Jesus is evidence that James is alluding to the same saying quoted in Matt 5:3 and Luke 6:20. This is confirmed by the fact that even critical exegetes like Dibelius and Laws admit the probability that Jas is consciously referring to a logion previously spoken by Jesus." He refers to Dibelius and

fact alone warrants the conclusion that the most likely source for Jas 2:5 is not the traditional piety of the poor but the teaching of Jesus.

Strong support for this conclusion is found in the following facts. First, the term kingdom appears only here in James, although significantly, βασιλικός occurs immediately in 2:8. Second, this term, which is so distinctive in the language of Jesus, appears in a statement about God that is marked by, subsumed under, and intimately connected to Jesus' own faith (Jas 2:1).[42] Third, previous research has shown that the historical example in Jas 2:5 achieves its rhetorical meaning and function by recalling Jesus' own faith as the measure for the elect community's faith.[43] Fourth, the introduction of historical example in Jas 2:5 ("Has not God promised . . . ?") presupposes that, like Jesus' faith which it recalls, it is already known to James's addressees. In sum, looking at the letter of James as a protreptic wisdom discourse, we find that the first and fundamental supporting proof (Jas 2:5) of the argumentative unit in Jas 2:1-13 is a statement — about God's action with reference to "the poor" — which recalls Jesus' own faith (Jas 2:1) in language that resonates with the texture of a well-known wisdom saying of Jesus in which the poor are promised God's kingdom.[44]

A closer look at the intertextual relations of these five performances only increases the probability that Jas 2:5 is a recitation of a Jesus-beatitude. Recent Q-studies claim that Matt 5:3 = Luke 6:20b belonged to the formative stage in the development of the Synoptic Sayings Source.[45]

Greeven (*James,* p. 132), and S. Laws (*The Epistle of James* [HNTC; San Francisco: Harper & Row, 1980], 103-104).

42. For the suggestion that the reference to Jesus' faith in 2:1 functions as a "global allusion" that evokes the whole of what our author perceives Jesus to have believed, said, and done, see Wachob (*"The Rich in Faith" and "The Poor in Spirit,"* p. 263). For the term "global allusion," see R. Alter, *The Pleasures of Reading in an Ideological Age* (New York: Simon & Schuster, 1989), 124.

43. Wachob, *"The Rich in Faith" and "The Poor in Spirit,"* pp. 134-243.

44. Wachob, *"The Rich in Faith" and "The Poor in Spirit,"* pp. 244-329. Because the entire letter presupposes a unity of purpose and action for God and the Lord Jesus Christ (cf. 1:1), this argument presumes a congruence between the faith of the Lord Jesus Christ and God's choice of the poor to inherit the kingdom, and supports the thesis that Jesus' faith and acts of partiality are contrary and incompatible to each other (p. 188).

45. See J. S. Kloppenborg, *The Formation of Q: Trajectories in Ancient Wisdom Collection* (SAC; Philadelphia: Fortress, 1987), 171-173, 174-245. The sayings in this stratum (Q 6:20b-49; 9:57-62 + 10:2-16, 21-24; 11:2-4, 9-13; 12:2-12, 22-34; 13:24-30) comprise "clusters or 'speeches'" that are governed by "sapiential themes and devices" and "are directed at the Q community in support of its radical mode of existence." Thus, Kloppenborg classifies Q 6:20b as a "wisdom saying"; on the other hand, Koester (*Ancient Christian Gospels,* pp. 136-138; esp. 149-171)

Supposedly, this stratum of Q was comprised mainly of wisdom sayings, some of which are also found in the *Gospel of Thomas*. Among the latter is *GThom* §54.[46] The source of this wisdom saying, however, seems not to have been Q itself but most likely a cluster of sayings that also belonged to Q. Both Paul and the author of *1 Clement* (chap. 13) appear to have known this cluster of sayings.[47] This is significant, because Polycarp, *Phil.* 2:3 also suggests an intertextual relation to *1 Clem.* 13:2 (and probably also to the Gospels of Matthew and Luke).[48] If these scholarly hypotheses regarding the development of the Jesus tradition are correct, then the Jesus logion alluded to in Jas 2:5 is an early, widely known and exploited saying of Jesus.

Recent research on the intertexture of Jas 2:5 has shown that there is a difference in the perspectives respectively of Q^L 6:20b, *GThom* §54, and Polycarp, *Phil.* 2:3, and of Q^M 5:3 and Jas 2:5.[49] While all of the latter, except Jas 2:5. are enthymemes, and therefore logical arguments, the reasoning within Q^L 6:20b, *GThom* §54, and Polycarp, *Phil.* 2:3 is different from that in Q^M 5:3. And while all five performances, except (perhaps) *GThom* §54, are dependent upon their respective contexts for their meaning and function, Q^M 5:3 and Jas 2:5 have different rhetorical and theological functions than do Q^L 6:20b, *GThom* §54, and Polycarp, *Phil.* 2:3.[50]

For example, the similar performances of Q^L 6:20b and *GThom* §54 pronounce blessings on people in an ascribed state of socio-economic

---

classifies it as a "prophetic saying." The reader notes that such research presupposes that Q went through several redactional stages; see Kloppenborg (pp. 89-262, 317-328) and Koester (pp. 133-171).

46. Koester (*Ancient Christian Gospels*, p. 87) finds that forty-six of the seventy-nine sayings shared by the *Gospel of Thomas* and the Synoptic Gospels are Q sayings (see his list and discussion, pp. 86-95).

47. Koester, *Ancient Christian Gospels*, p. 137.

48. Koester, *Ancient Christian Gospels*, pp. 19-20; also idem, *Synoptische Überlieferung bei den apostolischen Vätern* (TU 65; Berlin: Akademie, 1957), 114-120. Also see W. R. Schoedel, *Polycarp, Martyrdom of Polycarp, Fragments of Papias* (The Apostolic Fathers 5; London: Nelson, 1967), 12.

49. According to Wachob, *"The Rich in Faith" and "The Poor in Spirit,"* pp. 326-327 n. 162: "Q^{Matt} 5:3 and Jas 2:5, as the sayings of Jesus and James, respectively, recall the traditional Jewish piety of the poor. Though in different ways, both sayings address 'the Poor of God,' that is, those who in their actions love God by obeying God's law. In neither of the latter are the socially and economically impoverished promised the kingdom on the basis of their situation (as they are in Q^{Luke} 6:20b and *Gos. Thom.* 54). In Q^{Matt} 5:3 and Jas 2:5 the kingdom is the incentive, the reward, of those whose actions conform to the law of God (as it is not in Q^{Luke} 6:20b, *Gos. Thom.* 53, and Pol. Phil. 2:3)."

50. For a complete discussion of Polycarp, *Phil.* 2:3, see Wachob, *"The Rich in Faith" and "The Poor in Spirit,"* pp. 317-319.

poverty. In other words, what Koester says of Luke 6:20b, namely, that it "blesses the situation in which those to whom Jesus' message comes happen to be,"[51] is also true of GThom §54.[52] But this is not the case in Q^M 5:3 and Jas 2:5 — in neither of these sayings are the socially and economically impoverished promised God's kingdom on the basis of their situation. On the contrary, both Q^M 5:3 and Jas 2:5 argue that the kingdom is the incentive, the reward, of those whose actions conform to the Torah as interpreted by Jesus and summarized in the love command.[53] In their respective contexts, "the poor in spirit" (Q^M 5:3) and "the rich in faith" (Jas 2:5) designate people (not of an ascribed status but) of an achieved status. Both of these sayings recall the traditional piety of the poor; and each saying, in its own manner, addresses "the Poor of God." James, in particular, plays on the fact that his addressees are for the most part socio-economically impoverished ("the poor before the world"), but Jas 2:5 manipulates their ascribed status from the perspective of the Jewish piety of the poor. In no sense does James suggest that God's kingdom belongs to the socio-economically poor as a reward for their earthly poverty. The poor are chosen by God, for God, that they might be rich now in obedience to God and therefore receive the promised reward, God's kingdom. In Jas 2:5, "rich in faith" is synonymous with "loving God," and both are functionally equivalent to fulfilling the Torah of God, summarized in the love command.

Deppe[54] reminds us of Spitta's assertion "that if one could somehow show Jas 2:5 to be dependent upon a logion of Jesus, then one could legitimately be convinced that James throughout his epistle alludes to Jesus' sayings."[55] This has been done.[56] It is beyond dispute that in Jas 2:5 the author of James is reciting a saying of Jesus very much like that in Q^M 5:3, so that "the poor in spirit" of Q^M 5:3 are "the rich in faith" of Jas 2:5.

---

51. Koester, *Ancient Christian Gospels*, p. 156.

52. Wachob, *"The Rich in Faith" and "The Poor in Spirit,"* pp. 315-317.

53. Betz, *Essays on the Sermon on the Mount*, p. 34; and Wachob, *"The Rich in Faith" and "The Poor in Spirit,"* pp. 325-329.

54. Deppe, *Sayings of Jesus*, p. 90.

55. F. Spitta, "Der Brief des Jakobusbrief," in *Zur Geschichte und Literatur des Urchristentums*, vol. 2 (Göttingen: Vandenhoeck & Ruprecht, 1896), 164.

56. Wachob, *"The Rich in Faith" and "The Poor in Spirit."*

James 2:8 and Matthew 22:39; Mark 12:31; Luke 10:27

James 2:8-11 is a four-part argument based on the written law; the argument is adduced as a judgment, an authoritative witness, that supports the theme introduced in Jas 2:1. In Jas 2:8 the author clearly activates an antecedent text from the LXX, exploiting seven of the twenty-four words in Lev 19:18. Actually, Jas 2:8 is but the third clause in (the four clauses of) Lev 19:18. James marks it with a citation formula as an authoritative text (γραφή), and recites it verbatim. Technically, Jas 2:8 is an "abbreviation" (συστέλλειν) of Lev 19:18; and the Jamesian performance of the love-commandment is properly a rhetorical "recitation" (ἀπαγγελία) of an ancient authority.[57]

Is James aware of the prominence of the love-commandment in the teaching of Jesus?[58] In support of the argument that James is not only citing Lev 19:18 but also alluding to a logion of Jesus is the fact that Jas 2:8 has an unmistakable rhetorical connection to the mention of "Jesus' faith" in Jas 2:1; this is a strong indication that — as those who "hold the faith Jesus" — both James and his addressees are aware of Jesus' use of the love-commandment. Moreover, Betz is certainly correct in saying that "early Christianity was historically united on the fact that Jesus taught the fulfillment of the Torah in the love-commandment."[59] The parallels to Jas 2:8 in Matt 22:39; Mark 12:31; and Luke 10:27 bear this out. On the other side, however, the abundance of Jewish and Christian sources that corroborate the use of Lev 19:18 as a summary of the whole law (e.g. Hillel in *b. Šabb.* 31a; R. Aqiba in *Gen. Rab.* 24.7 [on Gen 5:1][60]; and also Matt 5:43; 19:19; Mark 12:31 = Matt 22:39 = Luke 10:27; Rom 13:9; Gal 5:14; *Did.* 1:2; *Barn.* 19:5)[61] makes the argument that James was specifically alluding to a logion of Jesus more difficult to sustain.

---

57. Theon, *Progymnasmata*, ed. C. Walz (Rhetores Graeci 1; Stuttgart: Cortae, 1832), 139-142; J. R. Butts, *The Progymnasmata of Theon: A New Text with Translation and Commentary* (doctoral dissertation, Claremont Graduate School, 1987), 204-205.

58. On James's use of Leviticus 19, see my essay "The Use of Leviticus 19 in the Letter of James," pp. 123-135 in this volume; and for a rhetorical analysis of language in Leviticus 19 and the love commandment intertext of Jas 2:8, see Wachob, *"The Rich in Faith" and "The Poor in Spirit,"* pp. 253-260.

59. Betz, *Essays on the Sermon on the Mount*, p. 37; also Davies, *Setting of the Sermon on the Mount*, pp. 405-413.

60. See H. L. Strack and P. Billerbeck, *Kommentar zum Neuen Testament aus Talmud and Midrasch*, 5 vols. (Munich: Beck, 1965), 1:356-358.

61. Cited in H. D. Betz, *Galatians: A Commentary on Paul's Letter to the Churches in Galatia* (Hermeneia; Philadelphia: Fortress, 1979), 276 n. 34.

Nevertheless, it can be asserted that in the context of a wisdom discourse that is addressed to Christian Jews (1:1) and pointedly embraces "the faith of our glorious Lord Jesus Christ," it is hard to imagine that judgments connecting the poor, the promised kingdom, the royal law, and the love-commandment could have been heard without thinking of Jesus' words and deeds.

James 2:13 = Q^M 5:7 = Q^L 6:36

The problem of determining whether this aphorism is reliant on a Jesus logion is even more severe. All commentators agree that the conception expressed in this verse is conventional in Jewish thought and literature from the prophets to the rabbis (Sir 29:1; *T. Zeb.* 5:1; cf. Tob 4:10-11).[62] For example, J. H. Ropes notes that its performance in "Jer. Baba q. viii, 10, 'Every time that thou art merciful, God will be merciful to thee; and if thou art not merciful, God will not show mercy to thee,'" is very close to the performance in Jas 2:13.[63] Betz correctly sums up the evidence: "for all branches of Judaism the exercise of mercy was one of the preeminent religious and social duties. This duty was based on the belief that God is a God of mercy. Early Christian theology continued this tradition in a variety of ways."[64]

The criterion of dissimilarity would also apparently rule out Q^M 5:7 = Q^L 6:36 as a saying of Jesus, given its conventional character both within Judaism and early Christianity (*1 Clem.* 13:1-2). Similarly, with respect to Jas 2:13, the well-worn argument and widely accepted view is that James draws on Jewish tradition rather than a Jesus saying. The Jamesian performance certainly reflects thinking similar to the thought emanating from the pre-Matthean SM.[65]

---

62. Cited in Dibelius, *James*, pp. 147-148.

63. J. H. Ropes, *A Critical and Exegetical Commentary on the Epistle of St. James* (ICC; Edinburgh: T. & T. Clark, 1916), 201.

64. Betz, *Sermon on the Mount*, p. 133, see esp. nn. 313-315.

65. Betz (*Essays on the Sermon of the Mount*) has argued that the SM derives from a Jewish-Christian group in which law and gospel are strongly intertwined (p. 35). "In the SM, Jesus is regarded as the authoritative teacher and interpreter of the Jewish Torah" (p. 91). "According to the SM, Jesus' authority depends upon that of the Torah, though naturally in accordance with his particular interpretation" of it (p. 92). "The Torah taught by Jesus is nothing less than the way revealed by God which corresponds to his kingdom and which leads one into it ([Matt] 7:13-14)" (p. 95). Moreover, as Koester (*Ancient Christian Gospels,*

Jesus may well have said something like the sayings attributed to him in Q^M 5:7 = Q^L 6:36.[66] Converging lines of evidence (multiple attestation) and the argument from coherence — both of which are more important than the criterion of dissimilarity — based on, for example, the parable of the good Samaritan (Luke 10:30-37) and the command to love one's enemies Q^M 5:44 = Q^L 6:27) certainly support that possibility. The saying coheres with numerous other texts in the tradition which indicate that Jesus' interpretation of the law emphasized justice and mercy. But the road from possibility to probability is a long one, and cannot be traveled for Jas 2:13 with the available evidence.

In this analysis, we have deliberately been minimalist, seeking to avoid sweeping generalizations and grandiose claims, and placing our analysis within the broader scholarly conversation concerning the sayings of Jesus. We argue that there are four passages in James where not simply an echo of Jesus' teaching but a specific use of his words is to be found. The strength of the evidence supporting this claim is shown by contrast with the two passages that we have considered but rejected. We do not deny that Jas 2:8 and 2:13 could have derived from Jesus logia, only that the evidence is insufficient so to assert. The same goes for the other passages in Deppe's extensive list; there is no intrinsic reason why the author of James should not have been so deeply influenced by the teaching of Jesus that his inflections in each of these cases also echoed what had been said by Jesus. But we cannot show it.

The isolation of four passages as performances of Jesus logia, however, is by no means insignificant, especially since, in each case, a further argument can be sustained that the form of the saying in James is closer to the form of tradition commonly hypothesized as Q than to the final redaction of Matthew and Luke.[67] On this point, the instinctive assessment of Ropes[68] has been substantiated by all subsequent analysis. The most

---

p. 171) has correctly observed, "the author of this epistle [James] and the redactor of Q who produced the Sermon on the Mount belong to the same Jewish-Christian milieu; both share the decision that the followers of Jesus belong to law-abiding Israel and that fulfillment of the law, though without any emphasis upon circumcision and ritual law, is the appropriate interpretation of the teachings of Jesus."

66. Funk and Hoover, *The Five Gospels,* pp. 296-297, designate Q^M 5:7 = Q^L 6:36 gray. "Gray" means, "Jesus did not say this, but the ideas in it are close to his own" (p. 36). However, it should be pointed out that often "gray" indicates wide disagreement among the members of the Jesus Seminar.

67. P. J. Hartin, *James and the Q Sayings of Jesus* (JSNTSup 47; Sheffield: JSOT Press, 1991), 140-217, 220-244.

68. Ropes, *James,* pp. 38-39.

logical conclusion to draw about the composition of James, given this finding, is that it took place in a setting that was temporally and geographically close to an early stage of the developing tradition. The authors of this essay differ on the judgment concerning authorship. Johnson thinks that the author may very well have been James, the Brother of the Lord;[69] Wachob thinks that an anonymous teacher wrote in the name and ethos of James, the Brother of the Lord, and used the Jesus sayings as a way of strengthening his own instruction.[70] They agree, however, on the following judgment: the use of an early form of the Jesus tradition suggests that the Letter of James was written either before the composition of the Synoptic Gospels, or at the very least before their version of Jesus' teachings became standard.

---

69. Johnson, *James,* pp. 89-123.
70. Wachob, *"The Rich in Faith" and "The Poor in Spirit."*

Taciturnity and True Religion:
James 1:26-27

The careful attention to speech in the Letter of James reveals its roots in the wisdom traditions of the ancient world. Like other Hellenistic moralists, James insists that speech find consistent expression in deeds (1:22-25; 2:14-26).[1] Of equal importance, however, are speech-acts themselves. The way James shares, yet also differs from, the perceptions of his world concerning proper speech is the focus of this chapter offered in fond tribute to a teacher who exemplifies, ὡς ἐν ἐσόπτρῳ (as in a mirror), the virtues here discussed.[2]

The ancient world agreed that the wise person was also taciturn. Silence was generally better, and always safer, than speech. Brevity in speech was preferred to loquacity. The evidence is everywhere: in the Wisdom literature of the OT (LXX),[3] Hellenistic Jewish[4] and other Jewish

---

1. "In the first place I require that the consistency of men's doctrines be observed in their way of living." Plutarch *Stoic. Rep.* 1 (Mor. 1033B). In addition to the passages in Stobaeus's *Anthologium* II, 15 (Hense 185-196), see also Seneca *Ep.* 20.1; Diog. Laert. 1.53; and 9.37; Plut. *De Prof. Virt.* 14 (Mor. 84B); Philo *Vit. Mos.* 1.6.29; 2.8.48; *Spec. Leg.* 2.14.53; *Congr.* 13.67; *The Sentences of Sextus* 177; *Did.* 2.5, as well as the references in my essay "Friendship with the World and Friendship with God: A Study of Discipleship in James," p. 219 n. 66 in this volume.

2. Like the other students of Abraham J. Malherbe, I have enjoyed and benefited from the Malherbian apothegms, delivered in his inimitable style. In this essay, I emulate Professor Malherbe's scholarly example of making appropriate distinctions in order to clarify specific traditions.

3. The biblical passages (LXX) include Prov 10:8, 14, 19, 31; 11:12-13; 12:13, 18; 13:3; 14:3; 15:2; 17:27-28; 18:4, 6-7; 21:23; 29:20; Eccl 5:1-2, 6; 10:14; Wis 1:11; 8:12; Sir 1:22-24; 4:23, 29; 6:33; 7:14; 8:3; 9:18; 11:8; 13:12-13; 19:5-12, 16; 20:1, 5-8, 18, 27; 21:26; 22:27; 23:8; 32:4, 8. The widespread use of the theme in the ancient Near East is shown by *The Instructions of Shuruppak* 21 and 130 (*ANET* 595); *Instructions of Ptah-Hotep* 535 and 575 (*ANET* 414); *Instructions for King Meri-ka-re* 30 (*ANET* 415); *The Instruction of Ani* 4.1 (*ANET* 420); *The Instruction of Amen-Em-Opet* 3.15; 11.15; 22.15 (*ANET* 422-424); *The Words of Ahiqar* 7.95-110 (*ANET* 428-429).

writings,[5] and early Christian literature.[6] The topic was so widely discussed by Greek writers that it was anthologized under several different rubrics.[7]

In the NT, James gives most direct expression to this ideal: "Let every one be quick to hear, slow to speak, slow to anger" (Jas 1:19). He devotes considerable (if complex) attention to the power and peril of speech in 3:1-12.[8] The person who can control the tongue, he says, is "perfect" (τέλειος [3:2]).[9] His statements seem at home within the standard distinction between the laconic and loquacious, in which short is always better than long.[10]

Another of James's statements, however, is more puzzling: "If anyone

4. Cf., e.g., *The Sentences of Pseudo-Phocylides* 20; 57; 69; 123-124. Among many places in Philo are *Fug.* 16.136; *Som.* 2.40.262-270; 2.42.276; *Det. Pot. Ins.* 13.42; 27.10; *Spec. Leg.* 2.14.50; *Abr.* 3.20; *Mut. Nom.* 41-42.240-243; *Leg. All.* 3.53.155; *Plant.* 42.176.

5. See *'Abot* 1:5, 9, 11, 15, 17; 3:14; 5:7, 12; and *'Abot R. Nat.* 13, 22, 26, 37; also *The Sentences of the Syriac Menander* 311, 312, 313.

6. *1 Clem.* 21.7; 30.4; Ign. *Phld.* 1.1; *Eph.* 15.1-2; *Barn.* 19.7-8; Herm. *Vis.* 2.3; *Mand.* 11.12. Striking similarities to James can be found in *The Sentences of Sextus* 155-157; 162a; 163b; 171; 185; 253a; 350-351; 361; 366; 426-427; 430-432.

7. Stobaeus's *Anthologium* contains pertinent entries in these chapters: Περὶ σιγῆς (["concerning silence"] 3.33; Hense, 678-82); Περὶ τοῦ εὐκαίρως λέγειν (["concerning speaking at the appropriate time"] 3.34; Hense, 682.87); Περὶ βραχυλογίας (["concerning taciturnity"] 3.35; Hense, 687-690); and Περὶ ἀδολεσχίας (["concerning garrulity"] 3.36; Hense, 690-698). Many passages, particularly from historians and rhetoricians, are considered by C. Schnayder, *De Antiquorum Hominum Taciturnitate et Tacendo* (Traveaux de la Société des Sciences de Wroclaw 56; Wroclaw, 1956). Among the noteworthy passages not contained in the above sources are Diog. Laert. 1.35, 69, 70, 88, 92, 104; 9.2; Lucian *Demon.* 64; Plut. *Lib. Educ.* 14 (Mor. 10F); and those discussed below. For the continuation of the ideal in Western monasticism, cf. A. G. Wathen, O.S.B., *Silence: The Meaning of Silence in the Rule of St. Benedict* (Cistercian Studies Series 22; Washington, D.C.: Cistercian Publications, 1973), esp. 109-176.

8. The NT has much to say about appropriate and inappropriate modes of speech as in Matt 6:7; Col 3:8; Eph 5:4; 1 Tim 1:6; Titus 1:10) but little about speech as such. The term ἡσυχία in 1 Thess 4:11 and 2 Thess 3:12 refers to the quiet life. Paul's use of σιγάω (to be silent) in 1 Cor 14:28-30 is purely functional. The notable exception is the silence imposed on women in the assembly (1 Cor 14:34; 1 Tim 2:11-12).

9. For a careful discussion of the exegetical problems in Jas 3:1-12, with a rich selection of material illustrating the metaphor of "reining the tongue," see M. Dibelius, *A Commentary on the Epistle of James*, rev. H. Greeven; trans. M. Williams (Hermeneia; Philadelphia: Fortress, 1976), 181-206; and J. B. Mayor, *The Epistle of St. James*, 3rd ed. (London: Macmillan, 1910), 107-125. Neither supplies the best parallel to James's assertion concerning the "perfection" of someone who controls speech; it is in Philo *Poster. C.* 24.88 (cf. also *Migr. Abr.* 13.73).

10. A variety of terms are used for both "laconic" and "loquacious," the most common being βραχυλογία *(brevitas)* and ἀδολεσχία *(garrulitas)*. For the rough equivalent of σιγᾶν and σιωπᾶν (to be silent), cf. Schnayder, *Taciturnitate*, p. 51 n. 41; for that between *silere* and *tacere*, cf. Wathen, *Silence*, pp. 13-19.

thinks that he is religious [θρησκός], not curbing his tongue [χαλιναγωγῶν γλῶσσαν] but deceiving his heart, this person's religion [θρησκεία] is vain [μάταιος]" (Jas 1:26).[11] Why and how should speech be connected to authentic religion?

Jas 1:26 raises the question of why silence was preferred to speech, the pithy to the prolix. This chapter surveys the rationalizations given in Hellenistic moral literature[12] and examines James against that background. The relative rarity of explicit rationalization should not be surprising. Perceptions that are pervasive often appear to those holding them to be so obvious and experientially confirmed as to require no theoretical support. Enough evidence remains available to suggest a fairly intricate web of perceptions governing the preference for concision in speech. A line of at least implicit logic can be traced through the three realms of the rhetorical, the ethical, and the religious.

Silence and Speech in the Hellenistic World

Brevity Is Best

In rhetorical discussions, the quality of speech known as βραχυλογία (*brevitas* [conciseness]) holds an honored, but for the most part minor, place. Aristotle does not use the term. In several places, he does assert that in style, "the mean" (τὸ μέσον) between the overly concise and overly diffuse (ἀδολέσκη) is to be observed (*Rh.* 3.2.3; 3.12.6; 3.16.4). He recognizes that brevity communicates knowledge quickly (3.11.9) and that "laconic apothegms and riddles" have their uses.[13] Cicero scarcely adverts to *brevitas* when discussing figures of thought and speech (*De Or.* 3.53.202). Only slightly more attention is given by the author of *Rhetorica ad Herennium,* who links *brevitas* to the figure aposiopesis.[14] Quintilian de-

---

11. Θρησκός is a hapax legomenon, but θρησκεία is common, having perhaps a slight emphasis on cultic observance (cf. BAGD 363). Thus, Philo opposes εὐσέβεια and ὁσιότης to θρησκεία in *Det. Pot. Ins.* 7.21. The "vain" character of religion (μάταιος) can also be read as "foolish," suggesting a wisdom/folly contrast in the statement, which reinforces the connection of taciturnity to wisdom (cf. Liddell-Scott, s.v.).

12. The largest number of exhortations to silence or brevity lack explanation. The fullest discussions are found in the Greek materials. I concentrate on them, noting passim points of agreement or disagreement in Jewish literature.

13. His phrasing is: τὰ Λακωνικὰ ἀποφθέγματα καὶ αἰνιγματώδη, Arist. *Rh.* 2.21.8.

14. *Rhet. Her.* 4.54.67-68. *Brevitas* has this admiring definition: "Brevitas est res ipsi

clares that the "praise awarded to perfect brevity is well deserved" because it expresses a great deal in a few words, but he warns that failure to achieve such perfection results in obscurity (*Inst.* 8.3.82). In his extensive treatise on rhetoric, he gives meager attention to βραχυλογία (expressions not linked by conjunctions or other grammatical connectors) as a form of asyndeton (9.3.50; cf. 9.3.99). Brevity is considered only in passing as well by "Longinus," who characterizes garrulousness as a sign of old age and who, like Aristotle, recommends a middle ground between excessive brevity and prolixity in speech (*Subl.* 9.14; 42.1-2; cf. also Philostr. *Vit. Ap.* 8.2).

In contrast, the treatise "On Style" attributed to Demetrius pays considerably more attention to brevity. Demetrius thinks lengthy sentences appropriate to an elevated style, but when they grow too long, garrulousness results (*Eloc.* 4.204, 212-14). In the same way, sentences that are too short fail to make an impression on hearers (1.4). Demetrius nevertheless shows unusual fondness for βραχυλογία. He attaches three qualities to brevity.

First, short sentences are forceful (δεινός). Excessive length paralyzes intensity, but βραχυλογία, because it packs "much meaning in a brief form[,] is more forcible" (Demetr. *Eloc.* 5.241; trans. Roberts in LCL; cf. also 5.274).[15] Like Longinus, Demetrius considers garrulousness a sign of old age, occurring then "because of their weakness." In contrast, the people he associates with βραχυλογία are the vigorous Lacedaemonians (1.7).

Second, because of its force, brevity is appropriate to apothegms and maxims. It thereby reveals great skill in speakers or writers by "putting much thought in little space." Demetrius cites two sorts of examples. From the Spartans, he quotes the response to the tyrant Philip, "Dionysius at Corinth." From the pre-Socratic sages, he cites the apothegms "Know thyself" and "Follow God" (*Eloc.* 1.9; cf. also 5.241).

Third, Demetrius says that brevity leads to a certain inevitable ambiguity. This makes it useful for symbolism. The hearer is forced to supply interpretation (*Eloc.* 5.242). In this respect, βραχυλογία resembles aposiopesis (5.253, 264). Demetrius can thus call the statement "Dionysius at Corinth" an "allegory" (2.102).

---

tantummodo verbis necessariis expedita" ("Conciseness is the expressing of an idea by the very minimum of essential words" [trans. Caplan in LCL]). Plutarch's characterization comes very close. He states that the orator Phocis had βραχυλογία and was considered the most clever in speaking because "his speech contained the most meaning in the fewest words" (*Praec. Ger. Reip.* 7 [Mor. 803E]).

15. The same connection between βραχυλογία and δύναμις is made by Philo *Rer. Div. Her.* 21.102.

As the art of rhetoric developed, it left behind βραχυλογία except as one figure of speech or thought among others.[16] But the rhetorical sources still contain intriguing traces of another way of viewing brevity. Garrulousness is a sign of age and weakness. Brevity represents youth and power. Is there, in these associations, a nostalgia for perhaps an earlier time, when speech was the sign of a certain kind of character rather than a matter of making proofs (Philo *Plant.* 38.157-58)? The examples of the sages and Spartans would make us suspect that it was not the professional speakers, but rather the professedly virtuous, who would treasure βραχυλογία as the ideal mode of speech.

Speech as Self-control

The moralist was concerned with βραχυλογία as a sign of character. The connection between style and character is suggested by Demetrius in his discussion of epistolary style, because letters are an "image of one's soul" and enable the reader to "see the character of the writer." One epistolary virtue is brevity, but its exaggeration is sententiousness (Demetr. *Eloc.* 4.227-32).[17]

Seneca makes the most explicit connection between virtue and style. In one place he argues that the style not only of individuals but also of peoples at a particular time reveals private and public character (*Ep.* 114.2). A luxurious life-style is reflected in overly ornate (or even preciously clipped) speech (114.9-14, 17). Not surprisingly, Seneca recommends care for the soul as a prerequisite for appropriate speech. When the soul is sound and strong, "the style too is vigorous, energetic, manly; but if the soul loses its balance, down comes all the rest in ruins [illo sane ac valente oratio quoque robusta, fortis, virilis est; si ille procubuit, et cetera ruinam sequuntur]" (114.22; trans. Gummere in LCL).

Elsewhere, Seneca argues that speech should be unadorned and plain. Above all, it should be controlled: "Quomodo autem regere potest quae

---

16. Dio Chrysostom, for example, acknowledges the reputation of Lysias for brevity and simplicity but does not recommend him for imitation (*Or.* 18.11). Dio was confident that speech could express everything (12.64-65). His philosopher need "never keep silence" or be at a loss for words (71.1). With the exceptions noted below, Philo often expressed the same sentiments concerning the power of speech. Cf. *Jos.* 44.269; Philo *Migr. Abr.* 14-15.78-81; *Det. Pot. Ins.* 35.129-31.

17. Advice and proverbs are appropriate to letters, but maxims and exhortations are not (Demetr. *Eloc.* 4.232).

regi non potest? [But how can that speech govern others which cannot it-self be governed?]" (*Ep.* 40.4). Speech that runs too fast or too elaborately reveals a loss of self-control and with it, the loss of modesty (*pudor* [40.13]). Seneca concludes with the clearest possible connection between speech and the sage: "Just as a less ostentatious gait becomes a philosopher, so does a restrained style of speech, far removed from boldness. Therefore the ultimate kernel of my remarks is this: I bid you be slow of speech [tardiloquum esse te iubeo]" (40.14).[18]

Taciturnity, then, is associated with the philosophical life. The pre-Socratic sages,[19] and in particular the Pythagoreans, are consistently char-acterized by silence and βραχυλογία.[20] The necessity of silence for becom-ing wise is obvious: one must hear in order to learn. Silence is the precon-dition for the learning of wisdom.[21] Garrulous people can become neither wise nor virtuous simply because they never stop talking (Sir 8:3; Plut. *De Garr.* 1 [Mor. 502C]).

Silence is also safer. If one does not speak, then one cannot misspeak. Silence is therefore a protection against error. It is the mute symbol of perfection.[22] Once something is spoken, furthermore, it enters the public

---

18. The connection between style and character is made with equal force by Plut. *De Prof. Virt.* 7 (Mor. 79B); *Lib. Educ.* 9 (Mor. 6B-7B); *Quomodo Adul.* 12 (Mor. 33F).

19. See the sayings in Diogenes Laertius attributed to Thales (1.35); Chilon (1.69-70); Bias (1.88); Cleobolus (1.92); Anacharsis (1.104), and Heracleitus (9.12). Note as well Diogenes Laertius's own characterizations of Chilon, βραχυλόγος τε ἦν (1.72); Zeno, βραχυλόγος ἦν (8.8), and Heracleitus (9.7). Similar characterizations are found in Plut. *Pyth. Or.* 29-30 (Mor 408E-409D) and *De Garr.* 17 (Mor. 511B). Zeno's heroic refusal to divulge names to the tyrant made a great impression; cf. Plut. *De Garr.* 8 (Mor. 505D); Philo *Omn. Prob. Lib.* 16.108; *Det. Pot. Ins.* 48.176.

20. The Pythagoreans demanded a five-year period of silence as part of initiation (Diog. Laert. 8.10), and silence was a well-known aspect of the Pythagorean regimen (Lucian *Demon.* 64). The maxims of Pythagoras are fine examples of βραχυλογία (cf. Diog. Laert. 8.17). Apollonius of Tyana was a spectacular representative of this tradition (Philostr. *Vit. Ap.* 1.1; 1.14; 6.11). Philostratus repeatedly refers to the βραχυλογία of the sage (*Vit. Ap.* 1.17; 4.33; 5.32; 7.35), and the letters attributed to Apollonius both discuss and manifest that style (cf., e.g., *Ep.* 8). Cf. also B. E. Perry, *Secundus the Silent Philosopher* (Philological Monographs 22; Ithaca: Cornell University Press, 1964), esp. 69.

21. Zeno says, "The reason why we have two ears and only one mouth is that we may lis-ten the more and talk the less," Diog. Laert. 7.23; cf. also 1.92; Luc. *Demon.* 51; Philostr. *Vit. Ap.* 6.11; Plut. *De Garr.* 2 (Mor. 502E); Prov 17:27-28; Sir 6:33; 11:8; Philo *Rer. Div. Her.* 3.10-13; *'Abot* 5.12; *Sentences of Sextus* 171, a-b.

22. Cf. Diog. Laert. 7.26; Epict. *Ench.* (in Stobaeus 3.35, 10); Apollonius of Tyana *Epp.* 81-82; Plut. *Lib. Educ.* 14 (Mor. 10F); *Rect. Aud.* 4 (Mor. 39C); *De Garr.* 23 (Mor. 515A); Prov 12:13; 13:3; 21:23; Sir 20:18; 22:27; Philo *Fug.* 14.136; *Som.* 2.40.262-70; *Det. Pot. Ins.* 13.42.

realm. Its consequences cannot be controlled (see Plut. *Lib. Ed.* 14 [Mor. 10F]; Wis 1:11). The results of loose speech can be disastrous both for speaker and hearers. The speaker is discredited[23] and the listeners put in peril.[24]

In the Hellenistic world, self-control (ἐγκράτεια) was an inarguable virtue. Emotions and their expression in speech ought to be directed by reason.[25] Lack of self-control (ἀκρασία) is a vice. It is revealed above all in drunken speech[26] and in speech driven by anger.[27] People who speak when angry not only show lack of self-control and thereby shame themselves;[28] they also can do real injustice to others.[29]

Rhetoricians define βραχυλογία in terms of compression, and the moralists define it in terms of self-control. Together, these definitions point to power and authority in speech. It is therefore not surprising to find alongside the sages the Lacedaemonians of old as the exemplars of taciturnity.[30] Their "laconic" speech was literally proverbial.[31] By exten-

23. Prov 10:18; 12:13; 13:3; 18:6-7; Sir 9:18; 20:5, 8; 23:8; Epict. *Diss.* 4.13.11, 17; Plut. *Cap. Util.* 8 (Mor. 90C); *De Garr.* 4-7 (Mor. 504C-F); 16 (Mor. 510D); Philo *Spec. Leg.* 1.9.53; *Fug.* 34.191; *Mut. Nom.* 43.247; *Det. Pot. Ins.* 47.174.

24. See Prov 18:6; Plut. *Lib. Educ.* 14 (Mor. 10F); *Cohib. Ira* 4 (Mor. 455B); *De Garr.* 3 (Mor. 503C); 7 (Mor. 504F-505A).

25. Cf. Diog. Laert. 1.70; 1.104; 7.24; Philostr. *Vit. Ap.* 6.11; Epict. *Ench.* 33.1-2; Plut. *Lib. Educ.* 14 (Mor. 10B); *Cap. Util.* 7-8 (Mor. 90B-C); *De Garr.* 3 (Mor. 503C); 9-11 (Mor. 506D-507F); 14 (Mor. 510A); 17 (Mor. 510E); Philo *Spec. Leg.* 2.14.50; *Conf. Ling.* 13.53-55; *Cong.* 14.80; *Det. Pot. Ins.* 19.68; *The Sentences of Sextus* 253b; 294; 429-30.

26. Cf. Diog. Laert 1.69; Plut. *De Garr.* 4 (Mor. 503E-540C); Philo *Leg. All.* 3.53, 155; *Plant.* 42.176.

27. Cf. Prov 29:11; Eccl 7:9; Sir 1:22-24; Diog. Laert. 1.70; 8.23; Luc. *Demon.* 51; Plut. *Cap. Util.* 8 (Mor. 90C); *Cohib. Ira* 3 (Mor. 454F); 7 (Mor. 461C); 16 (Mor. 464B-C); *Lib. Educ.* 14 (Mor. 10B); Philo *Leg. All.* 3.42-44, 123-28.

28. In contrast, the person who controls speech maintains dignity and modesty; cf. Plut. *De Garr.* 4 (Mor. 504b); *Cap. Util.* 8 (Mor. 90D); *De Prof. Virt.* 10 (Mor. 80E-81B); Philo *Conf. Ling.* 10.37; Sen. *Ep.* 40.13. Those, in turn, who can make their meaning clear even without words are even more to be admired (Plut. *De Garr.* 17 [Mor. 511C]).

29. Plut. *Cohib. Ira* 9 (Mor. 457D); 14 (Mor. 462C); *Sera* 5 (Mor. 551A).

30. Cf. Thuc. 4.12.16; Hdt. 4.77; 7.135; 7.226; Arist. *Rh.* 3.21.8; Demetr. *Eloc.* 1.7; 2.102; Dio Chrys. *Or.* 12.55; Plut. *De Garr.* 17 (Mor. 510F); *Lyc.* 19.1-4; *Apophth. Epameinodes* 16 (Mor. 193D); Charillus 1 (Mor. 189F): When Charillus the king was asked why Lycurgus enacted so few laws, he replied that "people who used few words had no need for many laws." Cf. also *Apophth. Lac.* Charillus 1 (Mor. 232C). In Plutarch, the view is nostalgic; cf. *Inst. Lac.* 42 (Mor. 239F). Clement of Alexandria also attaches brevity to the Lacedaemonians in particular, *Stromateis* 1.14.42-43.

31. Cf. the examples in Plut. *Apophth. Lac.* Agis 7 and 9 (Mor. 215E-F), and Diaphon 2 (Mor. 232E), as well as *Inst. Lac.* 39 (Mor. 239C); *Lyc.* 20.1-6.

sion, it seems natural as well that brevity should be a quality of lawgivers.[32]

Religious Silence and Speech

Two religious rationalizations appear in the Hellenistic literature. Silence is legitimated by the Mysteries, and brevity by the Delphic Oracle.

Because the Mysteries demanded silence of their initiates,[33] silence itself could, by extension, take on a sacred quality.[34] In the Pythagorean tradition, this is clearly the case.[35] And following from the religious value of silence, the reception of teachings could also have a religious connotation. The sayings of a sage or legislator were like oracles.[36] Finally, the Mysteries can be understood as providing a religious legitimation for the keeping of human secrets.[37]

The practice of taciturnity — and its legitimation — centers on the shrine of Pythian Apollo at Delphi. The connections are complex and interwoven. In the first place, the oracles delivered by the prophetess at the shrine were themselves marked by βραχυλογία. As a result, they were also obscure (sometimes notoriously so).[38] Around the shrine at Delphi, fur-

32. Cf. Philostr. *Vit. Ap.* 1.17; Luc. *Demon.* 51; Plut. *Praec. Ger. Reip.* 14 (Mor. 810D). Plutarch says that those who receive a royal and noble education "learn first to be silent, and then to speak," *De Garr.* 9 (Mor. 506C).

33. Hdt. 2.171; Plut. *De Def. Or.* 14 (Mor. 417C); Philo *Cher.* 14.48.

34. τὸ σεμνὸν καὶ τὸ ἅγιον καὶ τὸ μυστηριῶδες τῆς σιωπῆς ("the solemn, holy, and mysterious character of silence"), Plut. *De Garr.* 17 (Mor. 510E) trans. Helmbold in LCL; also Philostr. *Vit. Ap.* 3.26; Plut. *De Prof. Virt.* 10 (Mor. 81E).

35. Cf. Philostr. *Vit. Ap.* 1.1; 6.11. Philo is fond of defining Judaism in terms of its "lesser and greater mysteries" (*Vit. Mos.* 1.11.62). Consistent with the symbolism attached to the Mysteries in the Greek world, he repeatedly invokes silence as one of their chief components, as in *Op. mund.* 1.14; *Fug.* 16.85-86; *Sac. A. C.* 15.60; *Cher.* 12.42; *Vit. Cont.* 10.75. In particular, read *Sac. A. C.* 16.62.

36. Philostr. *Vit. Ap.* 6.11; Plut. *Is. et Os.* 10 (Mor. 354F). For Philo, Moses spoke like a prophet in oracles (*Vit. Mos.* 1.10.57). He learned the secrets of the holy mysteries and revealed them to those with purified ears (*Gig.* 12.54). Even the translators of the LXX were like prophets and priests of the Mysteries (*Vit. Mos.* 2.7.40).

37. "Men of olden times established the rites of initiation into the mysteries, that we, by being accustomed to keeping silence there, may transfer that fear which we learned from the divine secrets to the safekeeping of the secrets of men," Plut. *Lib. Educ.* 14 (Mor. 10F); also *De Garr.* 8 (Mor. 505F). Schnayder, *Taciturnitate*, p. 51 n. 42, touches on this in passing.

38. Plut. *Pyth. Or.* 29-30 (Mor. 408E-409D). Among the many examples of obscure oracles, the most notorious may be the one that told Croesus he would destroy a mighty em-

thermore, were inscribed the gnomic sayings of the Seven Sages. Visitors, when confronted with them on the way to consult the god, found themselves forced to reflect and interpret these sayings:[39] "Know thyself" (Diog. Laert. 1.40), "Nothing too much" (1.4), and most intriguingly, "Follow God."[40]

In the most obvious way, therefore, a person who used brevity in speech imitated the sages and, more impressively, "imitated the god" as well, in this case the Pythian Apollo.[41] Plutarch explicitly aligns the apothegms of the sages and the oracles of the god, even noting that both were formerly delivered in verse but, in his day, only in prose (*Pyth. Or.* 18, 24 [Mor. 402F, 406E]).

The tripod that was used when delivering prophecies at Delphi also excited comment and speculation among visitors (Plut. *Ei ap. Delph.* 2 [Mor. 385D]). The symbol of the tripod was portable. The Seven Sages, according to one tradition, were supposed to have passed the tripod to one another in succession, according to the command of the Delphic Oracle that the one who was most wise should have the tripod (Diog. Laert. 1.28, 82). Because the tripod ended up at Delphi, we are to assume that Apollo is always most wise. The association of tripod, prophecy, wisdom, and βραχυλογία occurs frequently in the literature.[42]

Finally, the Greeks most renowned for their βραχυλογία were also most widely known for their devotion to the Delphic Oracle.[43] There is even a tradition that has Lycurgus's Spartan Constitution revealed by the

---

pire (Hdt. 1.53) and the one assuring the Athenians that they would be saved from the Persians by a "wooden wall" (Hdt. 7.139-143; 8.51).

39. Plut. *Ei ap. Delph.* 2-3 (Mor. 385D-E). For the legend of the sages meeting at Delphi, cf. Diog. Laert. 1.41.

40. For the attribution of ἔπου θεῷ to Pythagoras, cf. Stobaeus *Anth.* 2.7.16 (Hense, 49), as well as Iamb. *Vit. Pyth.* 28.137. Diverse traditions make Pythagoras himself the Apollo of Delos (Diog. Laert. 8.10), or have him worshiping exclusively at Apollo's altar (8.13), or receiving his doctrines from the Delphic priestess Themistoclea (8.21).

41. For "following God" as the "imitation of God," cf. Plato *Tht.* 176B-D; *Phdr.* 248A; Epict. *Diss.* 1.12.8; Plut. *Sera* 5 (Mor. 550D).

42. As priest of Apollo at Delphi, Plutarch might be expected to have more than ordinary interest in this symbolism, and such is the case: cf. *Sera* 17 (Mor. 560D); 29 (Mor. 566D); *Conv. Sept. Sap.* 10 (Mor. 154A); *Ei ap. Delph.* 6 (Mor. 387C-D); *Pyth. Or.* 24 (Mor. 406D); *De Def. Or.* 7 (Mor. 413B). But traces can be found also in Hdt. 1.144; 4.179. Philostratus likens one who prophesies (as did Apollonius) to the Delphic Oracle, clasping the tripod to the breast and uttering oracles (*Vit. Ap.* 3.42). His taciturn sage is himself said to speak ὥσπερ ἐκ τρίποδος (as from a tripod [*Vit. Ap.* 1.17]).

43. Cf., e.g., Hdt. 1.51; 1.66; 1.67; 5.42-43; 5.62-63; 5.91; 6.52; 6.57; 6.66; 6.76; 6.86; 7.220; 7.239; 8.114; 8.141; Thuc. 2.7.55; 3.11.92; 4.13.118; 5.15.17.

oracle itself.[44] Seers, sages, and Spartans come together at Delphi. For such as these, "following God" in speech means the practice of taciturnity, for "the god himself [is] fond of conciseness and brevity in his oracles [φιλοσύντομός ἐστὶ καὶ βραχυλόγος ἐν τοῖς χρησμοῖς]" (Plut. *De Garr.* 17 [Mor. 511B]; trans. Helmbold in LCL).

Speech and Religion in James

The Shared Tradition

Much of what James says about speech fits comfortably within the conventions of Hellenistic wisdom. At the rhetorical level, James deserves high marks for his own βραχυλογία. Although Jas 3:1-12 is one of James's longer "essays," it is a marvel of brevity, compressing a variety of conventional motifs with unconventional conciseness.[45]

Many of the Hellenistic ethical concerns are also found in James. He links speech and character. He emphasizes the importance of hearing. Speech should be slow. Incontinent speech he connects to anger, and anger to the doing of injustice (Jas 1:19-20). He thinks control of speech particularly important for the sage (διδάσκαλος [3:1]). He uses the stereotypical metaphors: the rudder of a ship, the bit for a horse, the taming of wild animals.[46] Equally commonplace are statements on the tongue's disproportionate power to do both good and evil (3:5, 9-12).[47]

In several decisive ways, however, James differs from the standard treatment of speech. He is, for one thing, far more pessimistic. Hellenistic moralists recognize the difficulty in controlling speech but do not really doubt its possibility.[48] In contrast, James denies that anyone can truly control speech (Jas 3:8).[49] He also heightens the tongue's potential for evil.

44. Hdt. 1.65; Plato *Leg.* 1.624A; 632D; Plut. *Lyc.* 5.3; 6.5. To complicate matters still further, Plutarch in one place suggests that Lycurgus was also influenced by Thales (4.2)!

45. Compare Jas 3:1-12 with Plutarch's *De Garrulitate,* a compendium of the themes here under review, marred only by its own garrulousness (cf. esp. Mor. 511F-515A)!

46. Cf. the fine collection of passages in Dibelius, *James,* pp. 185-190.

47. In most dramatic fashion, Prov 18:21 says, "Life and death are in the power of the tongue." Cf. also Anacharsis in Diog. Laert. 1.105 and Bias in Plut. *Rect. Aud.* 2 (Mor. 38B); also *Lib. Educ.* 14 (Mor. 10B); *De Garr.* 8 (Mor. 506C).

48. Cf. Diog. Laert. 1.69; Plut. *De Garr.* 1 and 19 (Mor. 502E and 511F).

49. Cf. Dibelius, *James,* p. 191. The sentiment closest to James is found in Sir 19:16: "Who has not sinned with his tongue?"

He personifies the tongue as though it were indeed completely independent: "It boasts of great things" (3:5). He also makes the tongue a cosmic force. It is a "world of wickedness," a fire that is "lit from Gehenna" (3:6). This mention of Gehenna introduces the most important difference between James's treatment of speech and that of Hellenistic wisdom: in James, the religious valuation of speech is distinctive, more fundamental to his exhortations, and more pervasive.

James's Distinctive Approach

The first and most startling thing one notices in turning to James from the Hellenistic materials is that he entirely lacks the religious motivations found in those writings. He makes no mention of the Mysteries or of the Delphic Oracle. James's monotheism is not sufficient reason for his abstinence, for Philo appropriated both themes into his system. James's entire outlook is distinctive. He has a relational or, perhaps better, a covenantal perspective, in which the speech and actions of humans are fundamentally qualified by the speech and action of the God who chooses to be involved with humans.

Three elements in the essay of Jas 3:1-12 provide important clues to James's perspective. First, the "double-mindedness" (cf. 1:8; 4:8) of human speech is manifested by the same tongue, both blessing God and cursing humans (3:9). The cursing of people is wrong, because they are "created in the image of God." This is an assertion that is derived from something other than the observance of behavior. Second, when James mentions Gehenna, he not only invokes the symbolic world of Torah but also points to the conviction that the rule of God in the world is opposed by the devil. This theme is developed in the call to conversion that immediately follows the essay on the tongue (3:13–4:10).[50] Third, teachers who fail in speech are not simply "foolish," failed sages. They are instead liable to a "greater judgment," obviously from God (3:1).

These small touches alter the reader's view of James's traditional material. They direct us to the central religious polarity in James between the "wisdom from above," which leads to "friendship with God," and the "wisdom from below," which manifests itself in a "friendship with the world" (Jas 3:13-16; 4:4).[51] All human activity, certainly including speech, is lived within these competing norms and allegiances.

---

50. Cf. my essay "James 3:13–4:10 and the *Topos* περὶ φθόνου," pp. 182-201 in this volume.
51. Johnson, "Friendship with the World," pp. 202-220.

The theological weighting is present as well in Jas 1:19-20, the passage with which this essay began. James's command to be "quick to hear, slow to speak, slow to anger," is classically Hellenistic. So also, as we have determined, is the connection between rash speech, anger, and the doing of injustice. Notice, however, that for James, it is *human* anger that does not work *God's* justice. The two levels of activity are intertwined with an intensity that would be unsettling to a Plutarch.[52]

James's commandment, furthermore, is framed by two statements that show that taciturnity is more than a matter of self-control. In Jas 1:18, readers are told that they have been given birth by a "word of truth" (λόγῳ ἀληθείας) that has made them "first-fruits of creation." In 1:21, they are ordered to "receive with meekness the implanted word [τὸν ἔμφυτον λόγον] that is able to save your souls." Human speech is qualified by reference to the creating and saving word of God. God's word determines a form of identity and behavior not measured by the world or its wisdom.

James's transcendental reference point is stated succinctly in Jas 2:12. "So speak and act as those who will be judged by the law of freedom." By the law of freedom, James means the law of love (2:8), derived from Lev 19:18 and explicated by the Decalogue, the scriptural context of Lev 19:12-18, and the words of Jesus.[53] Thus, James categorically condemns slander (4:11), mutual grumbling (5:9), and the taking of oaths (5:12). As in 3:1, these sins of speech bring a person under God's judgment (see the warrants in 4:12; 5:9; 5:12).

Less directly, but no less emphatically, James condemns speech that distorts the proper relationship between humans and God:[54] arrogantly boasting about human projects without reference to God's will (Jas 4:15); claiming that temptation has its source in God (1:13); and praying with a double mind, either with doubt (1:5-6) or "wickedly" as a means of self-gratification (4:3). James likewise condemns religious language that does not manifest itself in moral action. It is useless to pronounce a benediction ("Go in peace") while denying to the needy the food or clothing that they require (2:14-16). This is precisely to bless God and curse humans made in God's image (3:9). In James's covenantal perspective, religion and ethics are inseparable. The line from claiming to be religious to "visiting orphans and widows" is a direct one (1:26-27).

52. But cf. Plut. *Cohib. Ira* 16 (Mor. 464B-D).

53. Cf. my essay "The Use of Leviticus 19 in the Letter of James," pp. 123-135 in this volume.

54. Two passages that touch on the same concern, though in very different fashion, are Eccl 5:1-2 and Philo *Spec. Leg.* 2.2.7.

James has few positive instructions on speech. He prefers listening and acting. But he does add a few characteristic commands: say "if God wills" and mean it (Jas 4:15), and let your "yes be yes and your no be no" (5:12). Most of all, he stresses the speech that builds the community. In every circumstance, members of the community are to pray and sing (5:13). When a brother or sister is ill, the elders are to be called for the prayer and anointing of the sick person (5:14). They are to confess their sins to one another and pray for one another (5:16). They are to turn a brother or sister from the path of error back to the truth (5:20). These are the uses of speech that match the measure of friendship with God and express the wisdom from above. Without them, even the claim to be "religious" is a dangerous failure to "control the tongue" (1:26).[55]

---

55. Johnson, "Friendship with the World," pp. 202-220; B. C. Johanson, "The Definition of 'Pure Religion' in James 1:27 Reconsidered," *ExpTim* 84 (1973) 118-119.

The Mirror of Remembrance:
James 1:22-25

Although the Letter of James is generally regarded as a form of parenesis,[1] it appears at first to lack some features often found in such moral exhortation. Of maxims it has an abundance, in the form of short commands. But parenesis usually attaches such maxims to a model or paradigm which is presented for imitation.[2] The example (or paradigm/model) provides a living framework which the maxims fill in with their specific directives. The imitation of the model is also closely connected to the use of memory.[3] Parenesis is not new teaching but the reminding of instruction already learned. So in James's "Do you not know," there is an intended rebuke — the readers *should* have known (4:4).

1. James was identified as "sittlich-paraenetisch" at least as early as F. H. Kern, *Der Brief Jacobi* (Tübingen: Fues, 1838), 37; M. Dibelius argued that parenesis was a *Gattung*, but did not elaborate its form beyond calling it "a text which strings together admonitions of general ethical content" (in *A Commentary on the Epistle of James*, rev. H. Greeven [Hermeneia; Philadelphia: Fortress, 1976], 1-7, esp. 3). The attempt to align parenesis with a specific social setting by L. G. Perdue ("Paraenesis and the Letter of James," *ZNW* 72 [1981] 241-256) is not convincing.

2. For the display of these elements, see A. J. Malherbe, "Hellenistic Moralists and the New Testament," in *Aufstieg und Niedergang der römischen Welt* (II/26; ed. W. Haase and H. Temporini; Berlin: de Gruyter, forthcoming); and more succinctly, idem, *Moral Exhortation: A Greco-Roman Sourcebook* (Library of Early Christianity 5; Philadelphia: Westminster, 1986), 124-129.

3. 2 Timothy and 2 Peter are NT writings which illustrate these components in impressive fashion. For 2 Timothy, see L. T. Johnson, "II Timothy and the Polemic Against False Teachers: A Reexamination," *JRelS* 6/7 (1978-79) 1-26. Particularly rich parallel material on the *exemplum* is provided by B. Fiore, *The Function of Personal Example in the Socratic and Pastoral Epistles* (AnBib 105; Rome: Biblical Institute, 1986), esp. 26-100. For 2 Peter, see L. T. Johnson, *The Writings of the New Testament: An Interpretation* (Philadelphia: Fortress, 1986), 449-450. Notice in particular the element of "forgetting" in 2 Pet 1:9; 3:5,8, as in James 1:24.

But the themes concerning model, memory, and imitation so often found in parenesis seem at best vestigial in James. He does point his readers to the *hypodeigma* of the prophets in 5:10, but leaves the allusion undeveloped. In 1:24 he mentions, apparently casually, "forgetting" what one has seen in a mirror. To contemporary readers, the phrase is both isolated and obscure. The problem of obscurity is directly connected to that of isolation.

When these two passages are joined together with several others, we begin to perceive how James links the elements of memory, imitation, and model in a distinctive fashion. The key passage is that concerning the mirror in 1:22-25. By grasping the force of James's metaphor, we better appreciate how it establishes connections to other parts of the writing and how James follows the conventions of Hellenistic parenetic literature.

I will first analyze the passage in its immediate context, then demonstrate the proper understanding of the metaphor in the light of Hellenistic parallels, and finally show the way it points to specific models for imitation. The point of the analysis is threefold: to sharpen the perception of James as parenesis, to clarify the proper use of comparative materials, and to appreciate the intertextual connections in James's moral instruction.

James 1:22-25 in Context

However complex at the metaphorical level, James's statement makes a simple point. Consistent with his letter as a whole, James contrasts two modes of human response. One person is content with the verbal profession of conviction. The other enacts convictions in behavior. The contrast is carried in this case by those who are "hearers of the word only" and those who are "doers of the word." In fact, the contrast is established by a carefully balanced parallelism:

I		II
Hearers		*Doers*
hearers only		
deceive themselves		
	like a man who	
sees		gazes
natural face		perfect law of freedom
	in a mirror	

goes away	remains
forgets	does not forget
	doer of the word
	happy in his doing

So much is clear and corresponds perfectly to James's consistent preoccupation with the disparity between the merely verbal and the active (cf. esp. 2:14-26).[4]

Several other features of the contrast also deserve attention. First, the human response is at least implicitly fitted to two divergent *measures*. The passage apparently contrasts a person's "natural appearance" (literally, the face of begetting), and "the perfect law of freedom." This, too, should not surprise us. Throughout James, there is the opposition between the "natural world" as a closed system of operations which rejects God's claim and the world as shaped by God's creative word and action. In 3:13-16, we learn that the first perception of the world is a "wisdom from below" which is opposed to the "wisdom from above."[5]

In the present case, the "natural person" is contrasted to the measure set by the "word of truth" (1:18), which is characterized as an "implanted word" in 1:21. This word, we see, "comes down" as does "every good and perfect gift." There is also a correspondence between the "perfect gift" of 1:17 and "the perfect law" of 1:25. In 1:22-25, therefore, there is a contrast not simply between two ways of looking but also between *what is looked at,* between the measure of nature and the measure of God's word, "the perfect law of freedom."

Second, we observe how 1:22-25 functions in its context. The phrase "deceiving themselves" in 1:22 clearly corresponds to the "do not be deceived" in 1:16 and links the statements into a single coherent passage, which is rounded off by the distinction between true and false religion in 1:26-27, again spelled out in terms of practical action. The passage as a whole, furthermore, anticipates the fuller development found in the essays of chaps. 2 and 3. In 2:14-26 the contrast between merely verbal profession and enacted faith is fully displayed. In chap. 3 we read of the difficulty of controlling the tongue (3:1-12), as here in 1:19 and 1:26. Then we see the contrast between friendship with the world and friendship with God

4. A constant motif in Hellenistic moral instruction, summarized by Seneca in *Epistulae Morales* XX.1 as *verba rebus proba*.

5. See my essays "James 3:13–4:10 and the Topos περὶ φθόνου," pp. 182-201, and "Friendship with the World and Friendship with God: A Study of Discipleship in James," pp. 202-220, both in this volume.

(3:13–4:10), which displays the opposition between the two measures and makes clearer the meaning in 1:27 of "keeping oneself unstained from the world."[6]

If that much is clear, we can address the third and most problematic aspect of the passage, which is the metaphor of the mirror itself. M. Dibelius complains that commentators overinterpret the passage, but his own explanation is curiously flat and unsatisfying, consisting more in denials than in clarifications.[7] This is at least partly due to the fact that Dibelius did not grasp the meaning of the metaphor as part of a Hellenistic *topos*.[8] He refers to the use of the metaphor in Hellenistic religious literature but, not surprisingly, finds no connection between it and James.[9] J. B. Mayor, in contrast, lists a rich collection of useful parallels — together with many references that are not so useful[10] — but makes no real use of the material in deciphering the passage.[11]

6. Johnson, "Friendship with the World," esp. pp. 216-220.

7. Dibelius, *James*, pp. 115-116.

8. For this, see Johnson, "James 3:13–4:10," p. 189, and the literature cited there.

9. He correctly denies the pertinence of the material gathered by R. Reitzenstein, *Historia Monachorum und Historia Lausiaca* (Göttingen: Vandenhoeck & Ruprecht, 1916), 242-255.

10. As always, Mayor is the indispensable starting place for comparative material, although — also as always — it is indiscriminately handled. In this case, Mayor's citations from Seneca, Plutarch, and Epictetus (the moralists) are helpful. Those from the apocryphal *Acts of John* 95:25 and passages in Philo are less useful; see J. B. Mayor, *The Epistle of St. James*, 3rd ed. (London: Macmillan, 1910), 71-72.

11. Commentaries are notorious for assembling parallels and failing to exploit their significance. In this article, I discuss the key passage from Plutarch, *Mor.* 42B. It is cited already by J. J. Wettstein (*Novum Testamentum Graecum* (Amsterdam: Dommerian, 1752], 2:664) and is included by Mayor. In Dibelius, it disappears. Of the passages directly cited by Dibelius, only Wis 7:26 and 1 Cor 13:12 offer any real parallel. His references to Sir 12:11; *1 Clem.* 36:2; Theophilus, *Ad Autolycum* 1.2; and *Odes Sol.* 13:1 are not *ad rem* for this passage. The same is true for the reference to *Acts of Thomas* 112 by H. Conzelmann, *A Commentary on the First Epistle to the Corinthians* (Hermeneia; Philadelphia: Fortress, 1975), 227 (to illustrate 1 Cor 13:12). The point of such citations often seems to be whether a word occurs elsewhere, but the real significance lies in similarity of usage or function: is the word or concept doing the same or a similar thing in parallel places? When we turn to S. Laws (*The Epistle of James* [HNTC; San Francisco: Harper & Row, 1980], 85-86), we find that the only extrabiblical citations are to the *Odes Sol.* 13:1 and to Philo, *Life of Moses* 2.11. In this last, the idea of the mirror does not occur at all, but only the notion that torah portrays paradigms of the soul. F. Vouga (*L'épître de Saint Jacques* [CNT 2/13a; Geneva: Labor et Fides, 1984], 65) correctly asserts that mirrors "ont fréquemment servi d'illustration à la littérature et à l'enseignement éthique," but he has not checked the sources. He refers to Seneca, *Natural Questions* 1.17.4 and Epictetus, *Discourses* II.14.21 and in n. 11 avers that he got these references from Dibelius. But Dibelius does not cite them! Learning in this matter has not progressed beyond Wettstein and Mayor.

The proper starting point is the text itself. We notice first how the metaphor of the mirror makes the text *more difficult*. It intersects the dominant contrast between hearing/doing with its verbs of seeing, gazing, departing, remaining. The reader is confronted with a bewildering combination of aural, visual, and spatial images with no instruction as to how to align them. Next, we observe the allusive quality of the metaphor. Everything is not spelled out. The first man gazes into the mirror at his natural face. The second gazes into the perfect law. It is true that the law is not explicitly *called* a mirror, as Dibelius insists.[12] But neither is the law explicitly called "the Word," yet virtually every reader of James makes that identification, and rightly so, for the force of the metaphor itself demands it. We have, then, at least by implication, two mirrors: that presented by "nature" and that by "the law of God."[13]

But we still do not know what to make of the comparison itself. What are the persons supposed to *see* in each mirror? And why does James characterize their responses here simply as (in one case) "going away and forgetting" and (in the other case) "remaining and not forgetting"? By implication, the first person sees something but does not act on it (or at least so we expect by the "hearing/doing" contrast). The second sees and acts. But why has James encoded this as "forgetting" and "not forgetting"? James can leave these loose ends untied because his Greek-reading readers would naturally have knotted them. They were familiar with the conventions associated with mirrors in a way that the contemporary reader is not. To place ourselves in the position of James's first readers, we must rediscover some of the ways in which the mirror was used as a metaphor for moral instruction.

The Mirror in Moral Instruction

The mirror — made of polished metal in those days (cf., e.g., Sir 12:11)[14] — was an artifact with few practical uses but many possibilities for theorizing.[15]

---

12. Dibelius, *James,* p. 115.

13. So Laws, *James,* pp. 82-87; Dibelius, *James,* p. 115.

14. See *"katoptron," Paulys Real-Encyclopädie der classischen Altertumswissenschaft* (1st series; ed. G. Wissowa; Stuttgart: Metzlerscher Verlag, 1921), 21:29-45.

15. For a survey of the use of the mirror in religious literature, see A. E. Crawley, "Mirror," in James Hastings, ed., *Encyclopedia of Religion and Ethics,* 14 vols. (Edinburgh: Clark, 1908), 8:695-97; and B. A. Litvinskii, "Mirrors," in M. Eliade, ed., *The Encyclopedia of Religion,* 16 vols. (New York: Macmillan, 1987), 9:556-559.

Some of these concerned the relationship of mirrors to the "natural order of things": were rainbows, e.g., substantial or were they due to a "mirror-effect" (Seneca, *Natural Questions* 1.15.7)? Was the soul simply the "mirror" of the body, receiving from the body's sensations its impressions and images (Plutarch, *Table Talk* V, *Mor.* 672E)? Was the face on the moon really due to its mirroring of the earth's surface (Plutarch, *Face of the Moon* 3, *Mor.* 920F-921A)? Images in mirrors could also be deceptive and lead to illusions (Plutarch, *Sign of Socrates* 22, *Mor.* 591E). And since images in mirrors were not permanent, they could be the metaphor for what is transitory, as when Dio bewails the fading of beauty when it is disregarded and ill-esteemed, as the fading away of reflections in a mirror (Dio, *Oration* 21:2).[16]

The mirror had some technical applications (Seneca, *Natural Questions* 1.17.2-3), but its most obvious use was for the contemplation of personal appearance. This is what enabled the mirror to become a moral metaphor. A mirror should not be used simply as an instrument of luxury but as a tool for self-improvement. Seneca declares, "Mirrors were invented in order that man may know himself," and spells this out not in terms of physical appearance but in terms of character. The handsome man is to avoid infamy, "the homely man to understand that what he lacks in physical appearance must be compensated for by virtue." The young man is reminded to learn and do brave deeds while the old man is to think thoughts of death (Seneca, *Natural Questions* 1.7.4). In his dialogue on anger, however, Seneca recognizes the limits of this method. Although an enraged person might see in the mirror the accurate reflection of his distorted face, this might not deflect him, for that is just what he would wish to see (Seneca, *On Anger* 36, 1-3)!

Plutarch recommends a similar use of the mirror for self-improvement. He advises the mistress of a household, when she holds a mirror in her hand, to talk to herself: ". . . for the ill-favored woman to say to herself, 'What if I am not virtuous?' and the beautiful one, 'What if I am not virtuous as well?'" concluding that it is better to be loved for character than for beauty (Plutarch, *Advice to Bride and Groom* 25, *Mor.* 141D).[17]

---

16. It is the *obscurity* of the mirror's reflection and the knowledge it grants which is emphasized in Paul's use of the metaphor in 1 Cor 13:12: *di' esoptrou en ainigmati,* rather than mystical or magical transformation. The metaphor there is also located in a thoroughly parenetic context. Note the use of *deiknymi* in 12:31 and *zēloute* in 14:1, as well as the contrast between the child and adult (13:11) and the partial and perfect (*teleios,* 13:10).

17. There is a similar turn in Philo's statement that the women in the wilderness donated their mirrors for the building of the tabernacle (LXX Exod 38:26) so that they "may be helped to see themselves reflected by recollecting the mirrors out of which the laver was

Plutarch also advises the wife to reflect her husband's character as a mirror which "shows a true likeness." She is to fit her life to her husband's and her character to his (*Advice to Bride and Bridegroom* 14, *Mor.* 139F). Because of its ability to reflect one's image, therefore, the mirror served as a metaphor for moral self-improvement. According to Bias, a man not only gazes at his face in a mirror but especially at his deeds (*praxeis*) in order that he might adorn the noble ones and cover over the shameful (Stobaeus, *Greek Anthology* iii. 21.11).[18]

By extension, the mirror can be regarded as an instrument for improvement in another way, which brings us closer to the use in James 1:22-25. In this case, the mirror does not give an accurate image, but an *ideal* one. In the mirror, one can see a *model* for proper behavior. To imitate the virtue of another, therefore, is to gaze in a mirror which reflects a better self.[19] A humorous example is provided by Plutarch, when he proposes the ant as a model for human social relations: "Nature has, in fact, nowhere else so small a mirror (*katoptron*) of greater and nobler enterprises . . . among ants there exists the delineation of every virtue" (Plutarch, *The Cleverness of Animals* 11, *Mor.* 967D).

So also can the moral teacher provide such a mirror. In a typically vigorous "testing" of a visitor to one of his lectures — a man he has shown to be in need of the "things most necessary and important for happiness" — Epictetus protests that he has done the man thereby no harm "unless the mirror also does harm to the ugly man by showing him what he looks like" (Epictetus, *Discourses* II.14.17-23). So also can the moral exhortation itself serve the function of the mirror. In his advice to Nicander on the proper way to listen to lectures, Plutarch stresses that he should "use all diligence to sound the deep meaning of the words and the intention of the speaker, drawing from it what is useful and profitable (*chrēsimon kai ōphelimon*). He is to "remember" (*memnēmenon*) that he has come "with the purpose of amending his life (*bios*) by what is said (*tō logō*). In order to do this, the young man is to examine the *effect* of the lecture on his attitudes, "whether he has acquired enthusiasm for virtue and goodness."

---

fashioned (*enoptrizōntai heautous kata mnēmēn tōn esoptrōn*) . . . not [to] overlook any ugly thing showing itself in the appearance of the soul . . ." (*On the Migration of Abraham* 98).

18. The saying is attributed to Socrates by Plutarch (*Advice to Bride and Groom* 25 [*Mor.* 141D]) and by Diogenes Laertius (*Lives* II.33).

19. The transformative effect of gazing at the mirror is emphasized in 2 Cor 3:18; but although in that case it is the image of the Messiah which is seen, that image is an *ideal* one which changes those who contemplate it; see V. P. Furnish, 2 Corinthians (AB 32A; Garden City, NY: Doubleday, 1984), 214-215.

Plutarch compares this process of self-examination to that of gazing in a mirror at the barber shop, when one checks to see "the difference made by the trimming." Likewise, on his way home from a lecture, "it would be a shame not to direct his gaze forthwith on himself" to see if there has been any improvement after listening to the lecture (Plutarch, *On Listening to Lectures* 8, *Mor.* 42A-B).

In his treatise *The Education of Children,* Plutarch places the image of the mirror within the context of moral instruction. He sketches certain "rules of conduct" for the young (14, *Mor.* 10B), which include, we notice, "control of the tongue" (as in Jas 1:26; 3:1-12) and "conquering anger" (as in Jas 1:19-20). These rules can be expressed by short maxims (17, *Mor.* 12D). But Plutarch precedes these rules with a series of examples *(paradeigmata)* which illustrate them by making the virtues "more intelligible" *(gnōrimōtera);* they are given life by being enacted by Socrates and other heroes from the past. The main example provided children for their imitation, however, is that of their father, who has the major responsibility for educating his children in virtue (13, *Mor.* 9D). This task involves first of all training the children's *memory,* "for the memory of past activities serves as a pattern *(paradeigma)* of good counsel for the future" (13, *Mor.* 9F). It is for the father, therefore, to provide the main example, as in a *mirror:* "Fathers ought, above all, by not misbehaving and by doing as they ought to do, to make themselves a manifest example *(paradeigma)* to their children, so that the latter, by looking at their fathers' lives *as at a mirror (hōsper katoptron apoblepontes),* may be deterred from disgraceful deeds and words" *(ergōn kai logōn,* 20, *Mor.* 14A).

Plutarch uses the image of the mirror in much the same way in *Progress in Virtue.* As in the case of James, the context is one in which the necessity of action and not merely speech is being addressed: "The translating of our judgment into deeds *(erga)* and not allowing our words to remain mere words *(logous)* but to make them into actions *(praxeis)* is, above all else, a specific mark of progress *(prokopē;* 14, *Mor.* 84B). Plutarch then turns to examples of such "translation" that can be emulated and imitated *(zēlōn kai mimoumenos, Mor.* 84C). Before taking any action, Plutarch advises his readers they should "set before their eyes" good men of the present or the past and ask what they would have done in similar circumstances (15, *Mor.* 85A). He continues: "Before such mirrors *(esoptra)* as these, figuratively speaking, they array themselves or readjust their habit, and either repress some of their more ignoble utterances or resist the onset of some emotion." He explicitly calls this an act of memory *(mnēmē)* which gives support to those making progress in virtue (15, *Mor.* 85B). In this passage as in James, therefore, we find together in one place the contrast between speech and action as the sign of moral progress, the mirror, the role of memory, and the use of models.

A final and impressive example of the mirror metaphor in moral exhortation is found in Seneca's *On Clemency*. He begins his treatise to Nero by saying that he intends it "to serve as a sort of mirror" by which "I can show yourself to you" (I.1.1). The image of the mirror is carried through the opening paragraph by the use of the verbs *inspicere* and *inmittere oculos*. As Seneca holds this (flattering) mirror of Nero's "true self" before him, so also Nero is to be a model for the Romans to imitate (*exemplar, imitari,* I.6.1). The note of memory is struck when Seneca says that the Romans need never fear Nero's "forgetfulness" of himself (I.1.7). Seneca proposes the gods to Nero as his best models for being king (*optime exemplum principi,* I.7.1), but also provides numerous terrestrial examples of clemency for Nero's imitation, concluding with the example of the fond father (I.15.3). Once again, we find the combination of elements: mirror, memory, models.

A reader schooled in such conventions would readily supply what is lacking in James's elliptical use of the metaphor of the mirror. The man who goes away and forgets what he looks like is immediately recognizable as the man who has not properly used a mirror for self-improvement by turning "hearing" into "deeds." James's readers would also in all likelihood have recognized the implied contrast between the "natural self" and "the perfect law of freedom" as sources of moral reflection. In this case, the law stands in place of the moral teacher (Epictetus), the father (Plutarch), or even moral lectures (Plutarch) in supplying, as in a mirror, the better image of what one should become.

The metaphor is not found frequently in the literature of Hellenistic Judaism, but the few instances show the use to be consistent. In the Wisdom of Solomon 7:26, we find Wisdom *(sophia)* called "a reflection of eternal light, a spotless mirror *(esoptron akēlidōton)* of the working of God, and an image of his goodness." This passage has often and appropriately been read for its value in deciphering NT christological statements.[20] In its original context, however, it closely resembles the use of the metaphor in James. The point of this encomium of Wisdom, after all,

---

20. So on Heb 1:3, see B. F. Westcott, *The Epistle to the Hebrews* (London: Macmillan, 1909), 10-11; O. Kuss, *Der Brief an die Hebräer* (RNT; Regensburg: Pustet, 1966), 30-31; on Col 1:15, see E. Lohse, *Colossians and Philemon* (Hermeneia; Philadelphia: Fortress, 1971), 45-52; on John, see R. E. Brown, *The Gospel According to John (i-xii)* (AB 29; Garden City, NY: Doubleday, 1966), lii-lxvi, cxxii-cxxv.

is her ability to teach Solomon not only about the shape of reality (7:17-22) but above all how to live (8:8-18). The importance of Sophia's reflecting the working of God and his goodness, therefore, is that by gazing into that mirror, right knowledge might be gained, superior to that granted by "nature": "I could not possess wisdom unless God gave her to me — and it was a gift of insight to know whose gift she was — so I appealed to the Lord and besought him" (8:19-21). As in James, therefore, a "wisdom from above" (Jas 3:17) comes by way of a gift from God (Jas 1:17), which makes of those who receive it and live by it "friends of God" (Wisdom 7:27; cf. Jas 4:4).[21]

The Wisdom of Solomon does not make the connection between the mirror and torah. That link is established by Philo.[22] In *The Contemplative Life*, Philo describes the practices of the Therapeutae with regard to torah, which he describes as "fostering and perfecting *(teleiountai,* cf. Jas 1:25) knowledge and piety" (25). By reading torah, they "keep the memory of God alive and never forget it" *(alēston echousi tēn tou theou mnēmēn,* 26). They interpret torah allegorically. In a difficult passage, Philo seems to suggest that the Therapeutae found the exemplar for so doing in torah itself: they imitated *(mimountai)* the examples *(archetypois)* that were left in Scripture as "memorials" *(mnēmeia,* 29). Discussing such allegorical interpretation at a later point in *The Contemplative Life*, he says this:

> For to these people the whole law book seems to resemble a living creature with the literal ordinances for its body and for its soul the invisible mind laid up in its wording. It is in this mind especially that the rational soul begins to contemplate *(theōrein)* the things akin to itself and looking through the words as through a mirror *(hōsper dia katoptrou)* beholds the marvelous beauties of the concepts, unfolds and removes the symbolic coverings and brings forth the thoughts and sets them bare to the light of day to those who need but a little reminding *(hypomnēseōs)* to enable them to discern the inward and hidden through the outward and visible. (78)

21. For the intricate connections between these images and their occurrence elsewhere, see D. Winston, *The Wisdom of Solomon* (AB 43; Garden City, NY: Doubleday, 1979), 184-190.

22. Philo uses the metaphor of the mirror in various ways. In addition to the passage from *On the Migration of Abraham* 98 (discussed in n. 17 above), see *Questions on Genesis* I.57 (the wisdom of the world is like a mirror of the powers of God — very close to Wisdom 7); *On the Decalogue* 105 (the number 7 mirrors God's acting in the world); and *On the Migration of Abraham* 190 (the mind converses with itself, "fixing its gaze on truth as on a mirror").

Philo apparently regards actions as well as concepts to be capable of such discerning; later in his text he applies the example of Moses and Miriam leading men's and women's choirs at the Red Sea to the contemplatives' practice of choral song and dance. The contemplatives' practice is a "copy of the choir set up of old beside the Red Sea" (85, 88).

Neither for Philo nor for James was there anything particularly mystical about imaging God's law as a mirror for moral instruction. It was literary convention of prosaic and predictable use. This survey of how the convention operates helps us see why the note of memory is so intimately connected to the mirror and also how "the perfect law of freedom" could so easily become a mirror of moral instruction. It remains to see how James uses that image to remind his readers of the models they are to imitate.

Models for Imitation

In another place I tried to show how seriously James reads torah and uses it to shape his moral exhortation. His close reading of Lev 19:11-18 enables him to use that segment of the law as a guide to explicating "love your neighbor as yourself" (2:8) in order truly to do it "according to the Scripture."[23] By proposing "the perfect law of freedom" (1:25) as a mirror, I suggest, James also prepares his readers to find in it models of moral behavior for imitation. He displays four such models: Abraham and Rahab, Job, and Elijah. Each shows how faith is "perfected" (or: "finished") by appropriate action.

Abraham and Rahab (2:20-26)

James's use of traditional interpretations associated with Abraham has been well demonstrated by R. B. Ward, who also argues convincingly that the plural "works" of Abraham (2:21) include his "works of mercy" such as hospitality, as well as his obedience in sacrificing his son Isaac.[24] Rahab's "work" was also that of hospitality, which is identified in the narrative of torah as an act of faith in the Lord (Josh 2:11). Abraham and Rahab together, furthermore, clearly function as *examples* for the moral lesson

---

23. See my essay "The Use of Leviticus 19 in the Letter of James," pp. 123-135 in this volume.

24. R. B. Ward, "The Works of Abraham: James 2:14-26," *HTR* 6 (1968) 283-290.

James is drawing in 2:14-17. As male and female they correspond to the "brother or sister" who are in need (2:15), but in contrast to those whose faith is merely verbal (or confessional), Abraham and Rahab both enacted their faith in "works of mercy" by showing hospitality to the needy.[25] And because they are counted among the righteous, they show how "mercy conquers even judgment" (2:13).

Other aspects of this passage connect it to the metaphor of the mirror. First, we notice that it is the "law of freedom" which will judge those who act with mercy or without it (2:12-13), just as it is the "perfect law of freedom" which is the mirror modeling merciful behavior. Second, James says that faith is "brought to perfection" by Abraham's works (2:22). The "perfect law" shows how faith is finished in deeds (1:25). The careful reader also cannot miss the allusion to 1:3-4: "The testing of your faith produces steadfastness, and let steadfastness have its full effect *(ergon teleion echetō)*." Third, and perhaps most intriguingly, James twice uses verbs of seeing when developing the example: *"You see* that faith co-works his deeds and out of his deeds faith is perfected" (2:22). Where do the readers "see"? In the mirror of torah. Likewise in 2:24, *"You see* that a person is justified out of deeds and not out of faith alone."

Job (5:10-11)

James's treatment of Job is much more succinct, yet makes the connection to the mirror metaphor even more clearly.[26] First, James explicitly tells his readers to "take as an example" *(hypodeigma)* the suffering and *makrothymia* of "the prophets who spoke in the name of the Lord." Second, he uses the verb "you have seen" in 5:11, even though it fits awkwardly with the immediately preceding *ēkousate;* the mixture of seeing/

25. Rahab is listed with Abraham as a model of faith in Heb 11:31 and her faith is explicated in terms of hospitality. Even more impressively, *1 Clement* 10 and 12 speaks of the "faith and hospitality" both of Abraham, "the friend of God" (*1 Clem.* 10:1, 7), and of Rahab (12:1-8). Clement begins his list of examples in this fashion: "Let us fix our gaze *(atenisōmen)* on those who have rendered perfect *(teleios)* service to his excellent glory" (11:2). Later, he uses the mirror metaphor of Jesus, again using the term "fixing the gaze" (36:2). Concerning the models from the past, Clement explicitly calls them the *archaia hypodeigmtia* (5:1), and he recites them for the purpose of "reminding" *(hypomimnēskontes,* 7:3) those who should become "imitators" *(mimētai,* 17:1). The connections of *1 Clement* with James are, of course, multiple: see Johnson, "James 3:13-4:10," passim.

26. For midrashic traditions concerning Job, see L. Ginsburg, *The Legends of the Jews* (Philadelphia: Jewish Publication Society of America, 1910), 2:225-242; 5:381-390.

hearing is, as in 1:22-25, created by the metaphor of the mirror, which demands the verb of seeing. Third, the readers have seen the *telos kyriou*. A difficult phrase, and much discussed.[27] As so often with *telos*, the senses of "end" and "goal" may both be intended. The readers can "see" in the story of Job both what God's purposes were and how they were accomplished. Fourth, the exemplary function of Job within the immediate context is obvious. James has just enjoined those undergoing persecution to have the same attitude of *makrothymia* by which he characterizes Job.[28] Fifth, when James says, "Behold, we count blessed *(makarizomen)* those who endure," he points the reader back to two earlier macarisms. James has said in 1:25 that the doer of the word will be *makarios en tę̄ poiēsei autou*. Even more impressively, in 1:12, James declares *makarios anēr hos hypomenei peirasmon*. Why? "Because he will receive the crown of life promised to those who love him" — for this Job provides the example. And who is the "him"? Clearly, the Lord, "who is compassionate and merciful" (5:11). Finally, we see again in this example how faith is "perfected" by deeds. The example of Job illustrates the opening exhortation, "Let endurance have a perfect work *(teleion ergon)*, so that you may be perfect *(teleios)* and whole, lacking in nothing" (1:4).

Elijah (5:16-18)

In the case of Elijah there are no verbal echoes of the mirror metaphor. That Elijah functions as an example to the readers is, however, made abundantly clear.[29] He is *homoiopathēs hēmin*, a characterization that is

---

27. See the discussion in Dibelius, *James,* pp. 246-247, and Mayor, *James,* pp. 164-165.

28. That *makrothymia* is a bit unexpected here (we would have anticipated *hypomonē*) was noticed already by John Chrysostom (PG 64: 1049). That Job had *makrothymia* is not at all obvious from the dialogues in the canonical book (despite the strange use of *makrothymēsō* in LXX Job 7:16) — although the framing of the story clearly indicates Job's reward for his fidelity (Job 42:7-17). In contrast, the *Testament of Job* shows a patriarch who corresponds to the popular image of "patient Job." His *hypomonē* remains constant (1:3). He tells his wife, "Let us be patient in everything *(makrothymēsomen)* until the Lord in compassion shows us mercy" (26:6-7), which is structurally very like Jas 5:10-11. Job also tells his children, "You must also be patient *(makrothymēsate)* in everything that happens to you, for patience is superior to everything" *(kreisson estin pantōn hē makrothymia,* 27:10). Placing this writing is itself difficult; see the bibliography in R. A. Kraft, *The Testament of Job* (SBLTT 5; Pseudepigraphical Series 4; Missoula, MT: Scholars, 1974), 17-20.

29. The midrashic traditions concerning Elijah are found in Ginsburg, *The Legends of the Jews,* 4:195-253; 6:316-342. Among the earliest materials, Sir 48:1-3 is particularly interest-

meaningless were it not for his exemplary role: it is because he is like them that his prayer can serve as a model for theirs.[30] So will their "prayer of faith" be effective in the community (5:15). The lesson precedes the example: "The prayer of a righteous man is powerful" (5:16). Again, the example picks up an earlier exhortation and gives it life. Elijah shows us the person who "asks in faith, not doubting anything" (1:6).

Such are the examples James wants his readers to see in the text of torah. They are models of how faith is "brought to perfection" by specific deeds. Abraham and Rahab exemplify the obedience and hospitality of faith; Job the endurance of faith; Elijah the prayer of faith. Because torah shows as in a mirror the "perfecting of faith" through such examples, it can justly be called "the perfect law of freedom" (1:25).

By examining the use of the mirror as metaphor within the context of Hellenistic moral exhortation, we discover not only how the verbs of "forgetting" in James 1:24-25 should be understood, but also how the metaphor helps pull together disparate parts of James's own composition. The examples of Abraham and Rahab, Job, and Elijah, are not random. They exemplify faith translated into deeds. The language used to present them alludes both to the mirror metaphor and to the maxims of chap. 1. James's use of the mirror of remembrance makes him an even more convincing sample of Hellenistic parenetic literature.

---

ing, since it says, "By the word of the Lord he shut up the heavens and also three times brought down fire," which corresponds to James's use of "in the name of the Lord" in 5:14. In 4 Ezra 7:39, the prayer of Elijah for rain is joined to the prayer of Abraham for the people. Dibelius (*James*, p. 256) thinks that James used such traditions rather than the biblical text itself, since the notion of prayer and of the specific time period is not found explicitly there. But James (like Sirach and 4 Ezra) could have understood the words from 1 Kgs 17:1, "except by the word of my mouth," as the first instance of prayer and the prostration of Elijah in 1 Kgs 18:42 as the second instance. That "the earth brought forth fruit" (Jas 5:18) is likewise lacking in the text of 1 Kings. But it fits nicely with James's parenetic intentions: as the dry land is to the fruitful, so is the sick man to the one raised to health. See also James's enjoining of patience (*makrothymia*) in 5:7: "Behold the farmer waits for the precious fruit of the earth, being patient over it until it receives the early and the late rain."

30. It is unlikely that James is concerned to deflect a perception of Elijah as superhuman; so, correctly, Dibelius, *James*, p. 257.

James 3:13–4:10 and the
Topos περὶ φθόνου

Few sections of the New Testament contain more infamous puzzles for interpreters than James 3:13–4:10. Otherwise confident commentators here become diffident. Not only are the problems many and difficult; they have also been dissected so many times that a quiet despair falls over any investigator sufficiently unwary to poke about in the area at all. Rather than rehearse all of these difficulties in detail, I will touch on only a sampling, and only long enough to suggest why it may be appropriate to begin approaching the text from another angle.

Exegetical Problems in James 3:13–4:10

The issues are both structural and thematic. Among the thematic, some are lexical. In 3:15, for example, a σοφία ἄνωθεν is contrasted to one which is ἐπίγειος, ψυχική and δαιμονιώδης. The "earthly" is a clear enough contrast to "from above." But what are we to make of ψυχική? The commentators review the appropriate Pauline distinctions between πνεῦμα and ψυχή (1 Cor 2:14; 15:46), and the characterization of opponents by Jude 19 as ψυχικοὶ πνεῦμα μὴ ἔχοντες; and all deny any real Gnostic engagement,[1] al-

---

1. A. Schlatter, *Der Brief des Jacobus* (Stuttgart: Calwer, 1932), 49; F. Mussner, *Der Jacobusbrief*, 3rd ed. (HTKNT 13; Freiburg: Herder, 1975), 171; J. Marty, *L'Epître de Jacques* (Paris: Felix Alcan, 1935), 144-145; J. H. Ropes, *A Critical and Exegetical Commentary on the Epistle of St. James* (ICC; Edinburgh: T & T Clark, 1916), 248; F. J. A. Hort, *The Epistle of St. James* (London: Macmillan and Co., 1909), 84; J. B. Mayor, *The Epistle of St. James*, 3rd ed. (London: Macmillan and Co., 1910), 129; S. Laws, *A Commentary on the Epistle of St. James* (Harper's NT Commentaries; New York: Harper and Row, 1980), 161-162. Cf. also B. Pearson, *The Pneumatikos-Psychikos Terminology in First Corinthians* (SBLDS 12; Missoula: Scholars Press, 1968), 14.

though Dibelius thinks to find illumination in the Mithras Liturgy.[2] All agree that a contrast with πνεῦμα is implied by the term, but no commentary has drawn attention to the πνεῦμα of James 4:5. Why? Because it is in "another section." The δαιμονιώδης of 3:15 is also difficult. It is a New Testament *hapax*. Without much cheer, some commentators look to 1 Tim 4:1 for help.[3] Others find a more useful reference in the Shepherd of Hermas, *Mand*. ix, 11: διψύχια ἐπίγειος πνεῦμα ἐστιν παρὰ τοῦ διαβόλου.[4] Although Hermas's use of διάβολος is helpful, no commentator has thought to look at James 4:7, where διάβολος is also found. Why? Because it is in "another section." A final lexical example: we find another *hapax* in 3:17, ἀδιάκριτος. What can it mean? Commentators naturally and properly look at the use of the cognate διακρίνομαι in 1:6 and 2:4, and suspect that might help determine the meaning here. And since in 1:6 the use stands as a characteristic of the ἀνὴρ δίψυχος they guess that here, too, the term has to do with "doubleness," or its opposite, "simplicity."[5] Once more, further aid is offered by the use of ἀδιακρίτως in the *Testament of Zebulon* vii,2, and in some passages of Ignatius of Antioch.[6] But here is a strange thing: in spite of the occurrence of δίψυχος in 4:8, no one has connected the meaning of ἀδιάκριτος to the usage there. For each of these words, the immediate context is ignored in the search for meaning.

One might attribute this to the chronically narrow focus of commentaries. But at least since the influential commentary of Dibelius, something else is at work. Dibelius raised a publishing vice to an exegetical virtue. Commenting on 3:17, he states, "Since the nature of this document, and, moreover, the nature of the enumerations such as the one in 3:17 *prohibit conclusions based on the context*, one may not conclude on the basis of 1:6 . . . nor on the basis of 2:4 . . ."[7] Dibelius, of course, was not only convinced that James was paraenetic, but also that parenesis was a genre[8] which lacked all structure.[9] Here, these general convictions dictate the

---

2. M. Dibelius, *A Commentary on the Epistle of James*, rev. H. Greeven, trans. M. Williams (Hermeneia; Philadelphia: Fortress, 1976), 211.

3. Ropes, p. 248; Marty, p. 144; Mayor, p. 128.

4. Marty, p. 145; Ropes, p. 248; Dibelius, p. 213; Laws, p. 161, who also cites *Mand* xi,5 and 17.

5. Marty, p. 150; Laws, p. 164; Hort, pp. 86-87; Mayor, p. 132.

6. Ignatius, *Magn* 15:2; *Trall* 1:1; *Eph* 3:2; Cf. Marty, p. 150; Dibelius, p. 214; H. Windisch, *Die Katholischen Briefe*, 2nd ed. (HNT 15; Tübingen: J. C. B. Mohr, 1951), 26.

7. Underscoring mine; Dibelius, p. 214.

8. Dibelius, pp. 5-6. He says, "large portions of James reveal no continuity in thought whatsoever" (p. 6).

9. It remains unfortunate that Dibelius remains the first and sometimes the only

method of interpretation, so that one may seek lexical help from Ignatius of Antioch, but not from eight verses away in James itself.

Dibelius sees 3:13–4:10 as a loose arrangement of independent units. 3:13-17 form a unit of thought joined only accidentally (perhaps by the linking word πικρός) to 3:1-12. The saying in 3:18 is completely independent in origin and function, and 4:1-6 begins a new inclusive whole. From 3:13 to 4:6, Dibelius can detect some "uniformity of tendency," but neither a train of thought nor a formal unity.[10] As for 4:7-10, this simply stands in contrast, formally and thematically, to the preceding verses. Finally, Dibelius rules out any connection to the section beginning in 3:1, dealing with διδάσκαλοι.[11] Although Dibelius is most decisive in his rejection of thematic or structural unity in this section of James, other commentators follow much the same path in practice, if with less clearly articulated principles.[12] Given such a view of parenesis and the composition of James, contextual interpretation is obviously out of the question. But is this view correct? Rather than prior convictions, the text itself should decide.

Before looking directly at the question of structural unity, it may be helpful to sharpen the issue by glancing at three further thematic difficulties in this section, which have bedeviled readers of James. The first is found in 4:2. The verse is notoriously hard to punctuate, and appears to contain an intolerable anticlimax in the movement from φονεύετε to ζηλοῦτε.[13] Of the various attempts at intelligible punctuation,[14] Mayor's is certainly the best, respecting as it does both the text and the thought:[15] ἐπιθυμεῖτε καὶ οὐκ ἔχετε· φονεύετε· καὶ ζηλοῦτε καὶ οὐ δύνασθε ἐπιτυχεῖν· μάχεσθε καὶ πολεμεῖτε. But so strange does the idea of murder appear in

point of reference for the meaning of parenesis among New Testament scholars. Not only do parenetic texts often have definite structure, but it is misleading to think of parenesis as a genre *(Gattung)* as Dibelius did (p. 1). All the more disastrous are attempts to fit this supposed genre to various social settings and social functions in a mechanical fashion, as is done by L. G. Perdue, "Paraenesis and the Epistle of James," *ZNW* 72 (1981) 241-256.

10. Dibelius, pp. 207-208.

11. Dibelius, pp. 208-209.

12. Cf. Laws, p. 158; Marty, p. 141; although Ropes, p. 5, takes 4:1–5:6 as a separate literary unit, he connects 3:13-18 to 3:2-12. And J. B. Adamson, *The Epistle of James* (NICNT; Grand Rapids: Eerdmans, 1976), 149, considers 3:13-18 to continue the section beginning in 3:1, as do Mussner, pp. 168-169, and Hort, p. 80.

13. Adamson, p. 168; T. Garcia, *Epistola Sancti Jacobi* (Roma: Lateranum, 1954), 170.

14. Cf., e.g., Marty, p. 155; Mussner, p. 178; and esp. Dibelius, p. 217.

15. Mayor, p. 136, says he saw it also in Hofmann. Mayor is followed by Ropes, p. 254, and Laws, p. 169. A very similar punctuation is arrived at by Hort, p. 89.

this phrase that those who do not interpret it spiritually,[16] find themselves attracted by the suggestion of Erasmus (despite a complete lack of Ms support) that φονεύετε be emended to φθονεύετε.[17] Even those who correctly reject this emendation,[18] and who argue in support of φονεύετε the tradition connecting envy and murder,[19] do not appear altogether convinced, especially since they cannot call upon the use of ζῆλος in 3:14 to help them.[20] The presence of "murder" here seems explicable because of associations with "envy," but one cannot argue confidently from the context for it being the right reading.

The difficulties presented by 4:5-6 are similar, if even more complex. This tangle involves questions of punctuation, the determination of grammatical subject and object, and the relation of the explicit scriptural citation in 4:6 to the ostensible citation (or allusion) in 4:5.[21] These verses have everything a *crux* could desire, including a long string of articles devoted to it,[22] the most recent, clearest, and best of which is that by Sophie Laws.[23] She argues convincingly that 4:5 should be punctuated so as to form two rhetorical questions: "Does the Scripture speak in vain?" and "Does the spirit he made to dwell in us long enviously?"[24] Her remarks on the use of the LXX by James and his possible use of the Psalter are perti-

---

16. Cf., e.g., Garcia, p. 170; C. L. Mitton, *The Epistle of James* (London: Marshall, Morgan and Scott, 1966), 147.

17. The Mss variation in 1 Pet 2:1 and Gal 5:21 between φόνος and φθόνος gives this some appeal; cf. Marty, p. 155; so Adamson, p. 168; Windisch, p. 27. Even Mayor is tempted: "certainly the process of thought is thus made easier" (p. 136). And Dibelius, p. 217, calls it "really a rather obvious solution."

18. Ropes, p. 254; Laws, p. 169; Hort, p. 89; Mussner, p. 171; J. Catinat, *Les Épitres de Saint Jacques et de Saint Jude* (SB; Paris: J. Gabalda, 1973), 199.

19. Frequent reference is made to T. Sim. ii,3; iii,1; iv,5; T. Gad iv,6; 1 Clem 3:2ff. Cf. Catinat, p. 198; Windisch, p. 27; Mussner, p. 178; Marty, p. 156; Ropes, p. 255; Mayor, pp. 134-137. So often do certain texts appear without comment, that one is tempted to think that there is something like a "lexical *topos*" employed by commentators.

20. Ropes states flatly, p. 256, that the meaning ζῆλος in 3:14 differs from that in 4:2, but does not really show why.

21. A short presentation of the options is given by Mitton, pp. 154-155; full and careful examination of the issues can be found in Marty, pp. 158-160; Ropes, pp. 262-264, and Mayor, pp. 140-145.

22. The bibliography in Dibelius, pp. 265-271, lists some fourteen studies devoted to this *crux*, a remarkable number given the relatively slender body of literature on James.

23. S. Laws, "Does Scripture Speak in Vain? A Reconsideration of James iv,5," *NTS* 20 (1973-74) 210-215. Cf. also the exemplary discussion in her commentary, pp. 174-179.

24. Laws, "Scripture," p. 212, and the translation of the passage in her commentary, p. 167.

nent,[25] and she correctly argues that φθόνος "would seem a quite unsuitable word to use in relation to God."[26] Laws does not adequately show, however, *why* φθόνος is inappropriate for designating "the divine zeal." Nor does she tell us why Prov. 3:34 could be regarded by the author as a pertinent citation in connection with φθόνος. And because she treats the verses in isolation, she fails to draw any support for her contentions from the context of 3:13–4:10, though she could have.

A final thematic difficulty has to do with the connection of 4:7-10 with anything which has gone before. The οὖν of 4:7 demands some sequence, but most observers think that, at best, only 4:6 forms the premise for this conclusion. Commentators are able to cite some precedents for "fleeing the devil,"[27] but do not see any reason to connect διάβολος here with the δαιμονιώδης character of ζῆλος in 3:15;[28] still less is 4:8-10 regarded as part of the same development.

The habitual perception of James as structurally fragmented, therefore, means that each of these problems is treated in isolation, which only reinforces the initial conviction that there is no unity of thought. The atomistic approach also obscures the issue of which materials from Hellenistic literature might prove helpful for understanding this part of James. In their consideration of James 4:1, for example, πόθεν πόλεμοι . . . οὐκ ἐντεῦθεν ἐκ τῶν ἡδόνων ὑμῶν . . . , commentators dutifully pass on standard references attributing war to untrammeled desires for pleasure.[29] But they seem unaware that an even more consistent connection is made among Hellenistic writers between φθόνος and wars.[30] The material cited gives lexical precedents, but little insight into the development of a

---

25. Laws, "Scripture," pp. 213-215.

26. Laws, "Scripture," p. 213. This is an important consideration, and it seems to have escaped Dibelius, usually attentive to matters of this sort, completely, p. 224.

27. Especially from the *Testaments of the Twelve Patriarchs* and *The Shepherd of Hermas*. Cf. Ropes, p. 268; Marty, p. 161; Laws, pp. 180-181; Mayor, p. 146; Dibelius, p. 226.

28. It is therefore possible for the most recent commentator to note, "the command to resist the devil does not fit," Laws, p. 167.

29. Most frequently, Plato, *Phaedo*, 66C; Epictetus I, 22, 14, and a smattering of passages from the *Testaments of the Twelve Patriarchs*. Cf. Catinat, p. 195; Mussner, p. 177; Marty, p. 154; Ropes, p. 253; Mayor, p. 133; Dibelius, p. 215. The comment made in note 19 applies here as well.

30. Windisch, p. 26, does make brief mention of envy in this connection. The view of Laws, p. 167, is more typical. She sees no link between 3:18 and 4:1, unless "the echo of ζῆλος, jealousy . . . is deliberate, but the transition from the subject of peace to the subject of war is an understandable one." But have these been the "subjects" at all?

theme. All of this is logical, of course, if one works with the conviction that there is no theme being developed.

Release from the unhappy task of picking over old exegetical bones will not come about unless the reader be willing to step back once more and see those bones as part of a living organism. We can begin by regarding James 3:13–4:10 as a single literary unit, namely, as a call to conversion which employs the Hellenistic *topos* on envy (περὶ φθόνου). To establish this perspective, it is necessary to show the structural coherence of the passage as a whole, and then indicate the ways in which the *topos* might make the passage more intelligible.

The Structure of James 3:13–4:10

For readers who have grown accustomed to seeing James as a pile of pieces, something of a leap of faith is here required, or perhaps only an adjustment in perspective. One must forget for a while the chapter and verse divisions, as well as the helpful but overdefining subject headings of the UBS New Testament. It is also helpful to remember the ways Hellenistic moralists go about their business, using traditional ethical materials in rhetorically effective ways.[31] In the end, however, some violence is required: we must simply pull out 3:13–4:10, call it a unit, and see what happens.

Taken as a whole, the passage appears as a call to conversion with two major parts: 3:13–4:6 sets up an indictment, to which 4:7-10 responds. The connective οὖν in 4:7 indicates that the series of imperatives (and assurances) is based on what preceded it. The exhortation itself is rounded off by the final command and promise: ταπεινώθητε ἐνώπιον κυρίου καὶ ὑψώσει ὑμᾶς (4:10), which returns to the ταπεινοί of 4:6 as well as the above/below pattern found there and in 3:13-17. As for the content of the exhortation, in addition to submission (4:7, 10), and the movement toward God rather than the devil (4:7-8), the commands demand ethical purification and mourning — in a word, conversion (4:8-9).

The indictment in 3:13–4:6 is more complex, and cannot be easily examined without going into tedious detail. Far from being disjointed, how-

---

31. When Ropes, pp. 10-18, discusses the "diatribal" character of James, it is not surprising to find a large number of illustrations drawn precisely from this section of the letter, for it is intensely sermonic, with a full battery of apostrophes, hyperbole, rhetorical questions, and the rest.

ever, it is a rhetorically polished presentation. We notice first how the discourse moves by means of rhetorical questions in 3:13, 4:1 (two), 4:4, and 4:5 (two). We also notice that the first and second of these are joined: 3:13 asks about the wise and understanding ἐν ὑμῖν and 4:1 asks about the source of wars ἐν ὑμῖν.

The rhetorical questions are each followed by exposition or accusation. In 3:13-14, an initial contrast between a wisdom from above and bitter jealousy is explained by a second set of antithetical statements in 3:15-16 (οὐκ ἔστιν . . . ἀλλά, and ὅπου γὰρ . . . ἐκεῖ), and 3:17-18 then resumes, with an emphasis on εἰρήνη, the thematic opposition established by 3:13: true wisdom is manifested in mild and peaceful behavior.

The second set of rhetorical questions forms a sharp antithesis to 3:17-18, and returns to the bitter jealousy of 3:14-15, now explicitly seen not only as a cause of ἀκαταστασία but of wars and battles. Rather than exposition, accusations follow these questions: ἐπιθυμεῖτε, φονεύετε, ζηλοῦτε, μάχεσθε, πολεμεῖτε (4:2). These are followed by a short explanation of why their requests do not get fulfilled (4:3), and another rhetorical question which reminds them of a traditional understanding of the irreconcilability of friendship with God and with the world (4:4). The climax of the indictment is reached in 4:5-6. However difficult it is to construe precisely, its rhetorical intent seems plain. The whole exposition comes down to the validity of the scriptural witness. Is all that the Scripture says in vain? Is envy really the proper sort of longing for the spirit God put in humans? The citation of Prov 3:34, in turn, sets up the exhortation of 4:7-10.

Looked at in this way, the thematic importance of envy appears obvious, for the climactic question concerns φθόνος. However apparent the contrast between war and peace, therefore, it is governed by the more fundamental theme of envy. I will show below why ζῆλος and φθόνος can be regarded as synonymous. For the moment, we can note the presence of ζῆλος πικρός in 3:14, ζῆλος καὶ ἐριθεία in 3:16, ζηλοῦτε in 4:2, and φθόνος in 4:5.

These are not the only thematic threads. The terms of the exhortation to conversion tend to correspond to the qualities described in the opening section. Thus, the purifying of hands and hearts by the δίψυχοι in 4:8 corresponds to ἁγνή and ἀδιάκριτος in 3:17. Fleeing the διάβολος in 4:7 matches the δαιμονιώδης in 3:15. The πνεῦμα God made to dwell in us in 4:5 contrasts with the ψυχική in 3:15. The lowliness and sorrow in 4:9-10 oppose the arrogance and boasting of 4:6 and 3:14, κατήφεια nicely balancing ὑπερηφανία.

It is possible, though much harder, to draw some connections between 3:13–4:10 and what goes before and after it in James.[32] But the very difficulty of establishing these makes the relative coherence of 3:13–4:10 the more impressive. If a plausible case can be made for regarding this passage as a call to conversion using the motif of envy, then we can turn to the sort of Hellenistic material in which that topic is treated.

The Character of Envy in Hellenistic Moral Philosophy

Envy (φθόνος) is treated with sufficient frequency and variety in Hellenistic moral philosophy to be regarded as a *topos*.[33] Typically, when ethicists are describing the nature of a particular vice or virtue, they tend to make distinctions which fall away when they are using the same categories in another context, in a less technical way. Thus ζῆλος (or ζηλοτυπία) can be distinguished from φθόνος, as in Aristotle's *Rhetoric* 1388A, ἐπιεικής ἐστιν ὁ ζῆλος καὶ ἐπιεικῶν, τὸ δὲ φθονεῖν φαῦλον καὶ φαύλων.[34] Aristotle calls ζῆλος

32. πικρός in 3:11 and 3:14 appears to be a word-linkage. We note as well "in your members," in both 3:6 and 4:1; a form of ἀκαταστασία in 3:8 and 3:16. Apart from these details, there is a fairly natural transition from the two sources of water and their fruits in 3:11-12 and the two sources of wisdom and their fruits in 3:13-18, and the cursing of one's brother (3:9) is not less antisocial than wars and battles (4:1). Above all, there is a natural and unmistakable link between the διδάσκαλοι of 3:1 and the τίς σοφός of 3:13; cf. especially Mussner, pp. 168-169. Connections on the other side are harder, since 4:11 is one of those passages in James which have a genuine air of independence. The note of judgment sounded in 3:1 is explicitly elaborated in 4:11-12, and it is possible to argue for a natural transition from arrogance to καταλαλιά, since it is found elsewhere in paraenetic materials (as in Hermas *Mand* ii,2, and especially 1 Clem 30:1-2). On 4:11, cf. my essay "The Use of Leviticus 19 in the Letter of James," pp. 123-135 in this volume.

33. It is found in the *Anthologium* of Stobaeus, III, 38 (Hense, pp. 708-721). The most thorough survey of this *topos* in Hellenistic philosophy has been done by E. Milobenski, *Der Neid in der griechischen Philosophie* (Klassisch-Philologische Studien 29; Wiesbaden: Otto Harrassowitz, 1964). That study provided some initial leads for the discussion here. On the subject of *topoi* and their use in New Testament exegesis, much work still remains. A start was made by D. Bradley, "The *Topos* as a Form in the Pauline Paraenesis," *JBL* 72 (1953) 238-246. The more recent article by T. Y. Mullins, "*Topos* as a New Testament Form," *JBL* 99 (1980) 541-547, is far too weighted on the formal side. *Topoi* in the Hellenistic writings resemble clusters of themes, and they can be fit to many forms and are found in many variations. An example of this sort of research applied to a particular text can be found in H. D. Betz, *Galatians* (Hermeneia; Philadelphia: Fortress, 1979), 220ff. See also R. C. Trench, *Synonyms of the N.T.* (London: Macmillan, 1880[9]), § xxvi.

34. So also James speaks of a ζῆλος πικρός in 3:14, which leads to πᾶν φαῦλον πρᾶγμα (3:16), whereas the wisdom from above is ἐπιεικής (3:17). For another saying joining φθόνος and φαῦλος, cf. Stobaeus III, 38, 36-37.

a sorrow caused by another possessing something because *we* do not have it. It can therefore be a positive incitement to achievement, so ζῆλος understood as "emulation." But φθόνος is a λύπη at possession by others simply because *they* have it (*Rhetoric* 1387B). It is possible, then, to speak of ζῆλος positively; it can be a vice or a virtue. But φθόνος is *always* a vice.[35] Another sort of distinction is made by Plutarch, between μῖσος and φθόνος: hatred always tends toward the harming of another, but envy need not.[36] So much for theoretical distinctions. In actual moral discourses, most authors use ζῆλος and φθόνος interchangeably.[37] This tendency is found especially in the Hellenistic-Jewish writings, but is widespread among the moralists when they are not dissecting the particular vices and virtues.[38]

Envy is always viewed as a particularly ignoble and disruptive vice. A saying attributed to Socrates runs, φθόνον ἕλκος εἶναι τῆς ψυχῆς.[39] If all vice is a "sickness," the image of an ulcer is especially graphic. Plutarch calls envy the only "unspeakable" sickness of the soul.[40] Envy is consistently associated with certain attitudes, among which are hatred (μῖσος), boorishness (ἀμαθία), faithlessness (ἀπιστία), tyranny (τυραννία), malice (βασκανία), hybris (ὕβρις), ill-will (δυσμένεια), ambition (φιλοτιμία), and *arrogance* (ὑπερηφανία).[41] The connection of φθόνος and ὑπερηφανία is particularly significant, because James brings them so close together in 4:5-6. We see in the Cynic Epistle of Heraclitus 2:7 that ὑπερηφανία is the cause of φθόνος directed at Heraclitus.[42]

The moralists regularly note the intensely antisocial character of envy, and its potential for violence.[43] Aristotle calls it a λύπη ταραχώδης (*Rhetoric* 1386B). Envy leads to ἔχθρα between people (cf. James 4:4). The association of φθόνος and ἔρις goes back as far as Hesiod (*Work and Days* 25-27) whose line "potter envies potter" became proverbial.[44] That envy leads to war is

35. Cf. Milobenski, pp. 69ff.

36. *De Invidia et Odio* 536F.

37. Cf., e.g., Plutarch, *De Fraterno Amore* 485D, E; *De Capienda ex Inimicis Utilitate* 86C, 91B; *De Tranquilitate* 470C, 471A; Plato, *Symposium* 213D; *Laws*, 679C; Epictetus, III, 22, 61.

38. Milobenski, *passim*.

39. Stobaeus III, 38, 48; cf. Milobenski, p. 117.

40. ὡς μόνον τοῦτο τῶν τῆς ψυχῆς νοσημάτων ἀπόρρητον, *De invidia et odio* 537E.

41. Cf. Milobenski, *passim*, and A. J. Malherbe, *The Cynic Epistles* (SBL Sources for Biblical Study 12; Missoula: Scholars Press, 1977), *passim*.

42. Malherbe, *Cynic Epistles*, p. 188. Milobenski, p. 100, n. 13, remarks, "Die Trias, 'Hass, Neid, Verachtung' ist topisch," and gives references.

43. Cf. Plato, *Lysis* 215D, and Plutarch, *De Capienda* 86C, 91B.

44. E.g., Plato, *Lysis* 215C, and Dio Chrysostom, *Oration* 77/78, 1.

frequently asserted.[45] Epictetus says that Caesar can free people from πόλεμοι καὶ μάχαι but not ἀπὸ φθόνου (III, 13, 9). In the *Laws* 862D, Plato shows how the passions (ἐπιθυμίαι) can lead to conflict and even murder. As such ἐπιθυμίαι, Plato lists θύμος, φόβος, ἡδονή, λύπη, and φθόνος (*Laws* 863E). These can lead to killing (*Laws* 870A, cf. James 4:1-2).[46] The violent and antisocial character of envy is reflected by its placement in the vice-lists of the New Testament.[47]

That φθόνος opposes friendship is obvious,[48] and since friendship involves a certain harmony (ὁμόνοια) between people, it follows that envy should destroy ὁμόνοια.[49] A good example is found in the *Sentences of Pseudo-Phocylides* 70-75. An initial command not to be envious (70) is supported by the model of the heavenly beings (οὐρανίδαι) who are all ἄφθονοι (71). The stars and moon do not envy each other, ἀεὶ δ᾽ ὁμόνοιαν ἔχουσιν. Harmony reigns in heaven. Line 75 concludes: εἰ γὰρ ἔρις μακάρεσσιν ἔην, οὐκ ἂν πόλος ἔστη. Envy leads to strife and discord. We are reminded of James 3:16, which tells us that where ζῆλος καὶ ἐριθεία are, there is ἀκαταστασία.

In his commentary on this part of *Pseudo-Phocylides*, P. W. van der Horst calls attention to two aspects of envy. The first is that of envy considered as a human vice (as in line 70). The second is ἀφθονία (lack of envy) as a divine attribute.[50] This last aspect has been thoroughly examined by W. C. van Unnik,[51] who notes that just as envy can be directed

45. Aristotle, *Nicomachean Ethics* 1131A, ἐντεῦθεν αἱ μάχαι (cf. James 4:1). Plutarch, *De Tranquilitate* 473B; *De Fraterno Amore* 487F; Epictetus III, 29, 26; III, 22, 61. Dio, *Oration* 77/78 17-29; for further references joining envy and war, cf. Milobenski, pp. 3, 15-16, 103.

46. Plato discusses the ambitious (φιλότιμος) man who through envy (φθόνος) or fear (φόβος) ends up committing murder (φόνος), *Laws*, 870C-D. In *Laws*, 934A, he calls for heavier punishments for robberies or murders which are due to pleasures, pains, desires, envies and rages.

47. ζῆλος is found next to ἔρις in Rom 13:13, 1 Cor 3:3, 2 Cor 12:20. φθόνος is beside φόνος and ἔρις in Rom 1:29, and next to ἔρις in Phil 1:15 and 1 Tim 6:4. In 1 Pet 2:1, it joins ὑπόκρισις and καταλαλιά (cf. James 3:17 and 4:11). Tit 3:3 attaches φθόνος to κακία, στυγητός and μῖσος. The extended vice-list of Gal 5:20-21 has, in order, ἔχθρα, ἔρις, ζῆλος, θύμος, ἐριθεία, διχοστασία, αἵρεσις, and φθόνος, a virtual summary of the *topos*.

48. Cf. Plato, *Philebus* 49D; Aristotle, *Politics*, 1295B; Plutarch, *De Fraterno Amore* 481A-485B; *De Invidia et odio*, 536F.

49. Milobenski, pp. 7-8.

50. P. W. van der Horst, *The Sentences of Pseudo-Phocylides* (SVTP IV: Leiden: Brill, 1978), 161-165.

51. W. C. van Unnik, ΑΦΘΟΝΩΣ ΜΕΤΑΔΙΔΩΜΙ (Brussels: Paleis der Academiën, 1971), and *De* ἀφθονία *van God in de Oudchristelijke Literatuur* (Amsterdam: Noord-Hollandschc Uitgevers Maatschapij, 1973).

from one who has not toward one who has, so the opposite can also happen: a person who has something (especially mystical knowledge or wisdom) can be "envious" or "grudging" in the sharing of it with others. ἀφθονία is therefore a quality of generosity, or liberality, and it becomes a significant divine attribute in the patristic literature. The possible pertinence of this nuance to James 4:6, μείζονα δὲ δίδωσιν χάριν, should not be overlooked.[52] Both van Unnik and van der Horst emphasize the continuing influence of two statements concerning envy by Plato, which provide a divine basis for human behaviour.[53]

In contrast to the bitterness which can be generated by the faults of others (including their φθόνος and ζηλοτυπία), Plutarch advocates a mild and gentle response. Instead of seeking to purge the evil of others by bitter medicine (harshness), Plutarch wants the person of good understanding to act like a physician, ἤπιος φαίνῃ καὶ μέτριος (De Tranq 468C).[54] Again, the contrast between bitterness and mildness reminds us of the opposition between ζῆλος πικρός and the wisdom from above which shows itself ἐν πραΰτητι (James 3:13-14). The same sort of contrast is also found in Dio Chrysostom's Oration 77/78, which is entitled περὶ φθόνου. Dio begins his discourse with Hesiod's proverb concerning strife caused by envy (1), and he sketches the sort of violence toward which envy can lead (17-30). But the discourse then shifts to a consideration of the ideal philosopher, one who is free from any sort of envy.[55] This positive ideal is drawn by means of contrasts. The philosopher οὐ στάσιν ἐγείρων οὐδὲ πλεονεξίαν οὐδὲ ἔριδας καὶ φθόνους καὶ αἰσχρὰ κέρδη, but he constantly reminds people of sobriety and righteousness καὶ ὁμόνιαν αὔξων (39). Instead of battling for *pleasure* (as do men moved by envy, 29), the wise man does battle for freedom from pleasure (ἡδοναί) and opinions (δόξαι), and struggles for liberty from the myriad ἐπιθυμίαι which afflict sick souls, among which is φθόνος

---

52. Van Unnik, ΑΦΘΟΝΩΣ, 39, and De ἀφθονία 24-29, connects ἀφθονία and ἁπλότης, but he does not think this idea is present in James 1:5, De ἀφθονίᾳ, 13. He does not discuss James 4:5-6.

53. In the *Phaedrus* 247A, when speaking of the divine assembly, Plato says, πράττων ἕκαστος αὐτῶν τὸ αὑτοῦ, ἕπεται δὲ ὁ ἀεὶ ἐθέλων τε καὶ δυνάμενος· φθόνος γὰρ ἔξω θείου χοροῦ ἵσταται. And in *Timaeus* 29E, Plato connects ἀφθονία as a divine quality to the demand imposed on those who would approach the divine: ἀγαθὸς ἦν ἀγαθῷ δὲ οὐδεὶς περὶ οὐδενὸς οὐδέποτε ἐγγίγνεται φθόνος.

54. For the mild and harsh response to vice on the part of Cynics, cf. A. J. Malherbe, "Medical Imagery in the Pastoral Epistles," *Texts and Testaments*, ed. W. E. March (San Antonio: Trinity University Press, 1980), 19-35.

55. Cicero says that the wise man is one who feels no envy *(invidia)*, *Tusculan Disputations* III, 21.

(40-45). In Dio, we see the *topos* περὶ φθόνου fitted to a protreptic discourse on the sage; will we find it totally inappropriate that in James it is fitted to teaching concerning διδάσκαλοι (3:1) and σοφοί (3:13)?[56]

Even this quick glance at Hellenistic materials has given us a good ground for considering James 3:13–4:10 to be dealing with envy. We have seen how ζῆλος and φθόνος can be used interchangeably; how ὑπερηφανία is associated with envy; how social upheaval and wars, as well as murder, are attributed to envy; and how the bitterness of envy is opposed by the gentleness of genuine wisdom. We are no further along, however, in understanding how this wisdom can be "from above," or what the devil might have to do with it, and how it comes by a "spirit" which is "indwelling." In short, much of the language here is specifically biblical. The question is, can we locate it more precisely with regard to envy?

Envy in Hellenistic-Jewish Writings

Φθόνος does not occur frequently in the LXX. In Sirach 14:10, the ὀφθαλμὸς πονηρὸς φθονερός characterizes a rich man who does not share what he has (cf. Sir 14:3-10). In Tobit 4:7, 16, an "envious eye" is again used of one who does not share with others by means of almsgiving. In 1 Maccabees 8:16, φθόνος and ζῆλος are used synonymously in the sense of "envy." This is not much.[57]

The most striking text in the Greek Bible on envy is in Wisdom 2:24, which states that although God created humans to be immortal, φθόνῳ δὲ διαβόλου θάνατος εἰσῆλθεν εἰς τὸν κόσμον. Here we find a direct link between envy, death, and the devil. But to what death is the text referring? The first possibility is the death fated for Adam and Eve (Gen 3:19) because Eve was seduced by the serpent (Gen 3:1-7).[58] It is also possible that

56. For Dio on the ideal philosopher, cf. A. J. Malherbe, "'Gentle as a Nurse': The Cynic Background to I Thess ii," *Novum Testamentum* 12 (1970) 203-217; on the antithetical structure, cf. L. T. Johnson, "II Timothy and the Polemic against False Teachers: A Reexamination," *Journal of Religious Studies* 6/7 (1978/79) 1-26.

57. It may be noteworthy, however, that in Tobit 4:13, the young man is told not to be arrogant, διότι ἐν τῇ ὑπερηφανίᾳ ἀπώλεια καὶ ἀκαταστασία πολλή (cf. James 3:16). As for ζῆλος, apart from Gen 37:11 (on which, see below), it is used in the sense of "zeal," as in Ps 69:9; Isa 9:7.

58. This is the view of D. Winston, *The Wisdom of Solomon* (Anchor Bible 43; Garden City: Doubleday, 1979), 121-122. Josephus, *Antiquities* I, 4, 42 attributes the Serpent's seduction of Eve to his being φθονερῶς. Winston cites apocryphal and Gnostic texts to the same effect. In addition to the studies mentioned earlier, van Unnik has pursued this aspect of

Wisdom is referring to the murder of Abel by Cain (Gen 4:1-9).[59] This is the first real death in Scripture, and it is by murder. In that text, neither envy nor the devil is mentioned. But we read that Cain ἐλύπησεν λίαν (4:5), and we remember that envy is described by the moralists as a kind of λύπη. We also notice that Cain did not offer his gifts ὀρθῶς (Gen 4:7), which reminds us somewhat of those who make requests κακῶς in James 4:3.

Neither Philo nor Josephus makes much of a connection between envy and murder when they discuss the Cain and Abel story. In his allegorical treatment, Philo moves into the contrast between true wisdom and sophistry, and in the *Post. Cain* 140, 150, he contrasts the ἀφθονία of wisdom to the grudging sharing of knowledge characteristic of sophistry.[60] Neither does Josephus explicitly call Cain envious, though he attributes vices to him which regularly accompanied the envious person.[61] The application of envy to Cain becomes explicit in Christian texts. Thus, 1 Clem iii,4 quotes Wisdom 2:24, and follows immediately with the example of Cain (λύπη being picked up from the text of Genesis), and he concludes: ὁρᾶτε ἀδελφοί, ζῆλος καὶ φθόνος ἀδελφοκτονίαν κατειργάσατο (1 Clem iv,7).[62]

Another place in the LXX where envy and (intended) murder come together is the Joseph story. Jacob's special love for Joseph caused dissension: ἰδόντες δὲ οἱ ἀδελφοὶ αὐτοῦ ὅτι αὐτὸν ὁ πατὴρ φίλει ἐκ πάντων τῶν υἱῶν αὐτοῦ, ἐμίσησαν αὐτὸν καὶ οὐκ ἠδύναντο λαλεῖν αὐτῷ οὐδὲν εἰρηνικόν (Gen 37:4). After Joseph's dream, ἐζήλωσαν δὲ αὐτὸν οἱ ἀδελφοὶ αὐτοῦ (Gen 37:11), and this led to their plan ἀποκτεῖναι αὐτόν (37:18). In his version of the story, Josephus emphasizes the role of envy.[63] Philo also makes the

---

envy in "Der Neid in den Paradiesgeschichte nach einigen gnostischen Texten," *Essays on the Nag-Hammadi Texts in Honor of Alexander Böhlig*, ed. M. Krause (Nag-Hammadi Studies III; Leiden: Brill, 1972), 120-132.

59. Winston, p. 121. Cf. J. A. F. Gregg, *The Wisdom of Solomon* (Cambridge Bible; Cambridge: Cambridge University Press, 1909), 22.

60. Elsewhere, Philo can speak of the "indwelling" of envy, *De Virtute* 223, and E. Goodenough, *Politics of Philo Judaeus* (New Haven: Yale University Press, 1938), 47 n. 15, says, "Philo uses φθόνος almost as an evil spirit."

61. Cain was driven by ἡδονή, ὕβρις, πλεονεξία, and these drives lead to all sorts of upheavals and battles: *Antiquities* I, 56-66.

62. The same attribution is made in Theophilus's *Ad Autolycum* II, 29. When Satan saw that Adam and Eve had not died, but had propagated children, he was moved with envy (φθόνῳ φερόμενος) and incited Cain ἀποκτεῖναι ἀδελφὸν αὐτοῦ Ἀβέλ (PG 6: 1097). Even more elaborate is Basil the Great in his sermon entitled περὶ φθόνου: he calls Cain ὁ πρῶτος μαθητὴς τοῦ διαβόλου, καὶ φθόνον καὶ φόνον παρ' αὐτοῦ διδαχθείς (Hom XI, 3; PG 21: 371-386).

63. Jacob φθόνον ἐκίνησεν καὶ μῖσος among the brethren, instilling in them a ζηλοτυπία

theme of envy explicit. In the *De Josepho,* he says φθόνος created division in the family, and since feelings unexpressed tend to grow more violent (5), the brothers' resentment bred disturbances (10), and finally led to the plotting of murder, φόνος (12). Here, φθόνος and φόνος are expressly joined.[64]

The role of envy in the betrayal of Joseph is recounted by Luke in the Stephen speech, καὶ οἱ πατριάρχαι ζηλώσαντες τὸν Ἰωσὴφ ἀπέδοντο εἰς Αἴγυπτον (Acts 7:9). Given Luke's love for prophetic typology,[65] it is not shocking to find him also attributing to the same vice the opposition of the Jewish leadership to the apostles (Acts 5:17; 13:45; 17:5). Even more strikingly, two of the Synoptics attribute to envy the resistance of Jewish leaders to Jesus: ἐγίνωσκεν γὰρ ὅτι διὰ φθόνον παραδεδώκεισαν αὐτόν (Mk 15:10; cf. Mt 27:18).[66]

Envy has been seen to play a role in the stories of Adam and Eve, Cain and Abel, Joseph and his brothers, Jesus and the Jewish leaders, and the apostles and Jewish leaders. The connection between envy and murder could not be more explicitly drawn in this Hellenistic-Jewish literature. The "devil," however, has been found explicitly in only one text, Wisdom 2:24. In order to get even closer to the language and outlook of James on envy, we must take a close look at the *Testaments of the Twelve Patriarchs.*

Envy, Death, and the Devil in the Testaments

The resemblance of parts of James to the Testaments of the Twelve Patriarchs has been noted often enough by commentators,[67] but it has been Mayor[68] and especially Ropes who have stressed the frequent points of contact in isolated verses of this section. Ropes considered the *Testaments* to have a "special affinity" to James in language, though not in structure or

---

(*Antiquities* II, 10). God countered their φθόνος by sending a second dream (II, 13), but when the brothers heard it, ἐλύπησαν (II, 17), so they planned to kill Joseph (II, 18).

64. It is not a surprise to find 1 Clem 4:9 include this example, ζῆλος ἐποίησεν Ἰωσὴφ μέχρι θανάτου, nor to see Basil state that the φθόνος τῶν ἀδελφῶν made Joseph a slave (Hom XI, 4).

65. Cf. L. T. Johnson, *The Literary Function of Possessions in Luke-Acts* (SBLDS 39; Missoula: Scholars Press, 1977), 41-76.

66. 1 Clem 5:2 picks up the envy of the apostles, but omits that directed at Jesus. Basil omits the apostles, but says that the death of Jesus was due to the envy of the Jews (Hom XI, 4, PG 21: 377).

67. So Catinat, p. 22; Laws, p. 11; Dibelius, p. 21.

68. Mayor, p. cxvii.

style.[69] Specifically, it has frequently been observed that the idea of "fleeing the devil" in James 4:7 is found often in these writings.[70] Among other incidental resemblances are the term δίψυχος (James 4:8),[71] the equivalent use of ζῆλος and φθόνος (James 3:14-15; 4:5),[72] and the theme of war (James 4:1).[73] Apart from Ropes, however, few have placed as much importance on the resemblance to the *Testaments* as to the *Shepherd of Hermas*.[74] And not even Ropes went beyond the collecting of lexical parallels.

The complex issues concerning the dating and integrity of the *Testaments* themselves cannot be treated here.[75] My purpose is simply to show how the treatment of φθόνος in them may throw some light on James 3:13–4:10. No direct literary dependence need be argued in order to show this. The disputes concerning the redaction of the *Testaments,* furthermore, center largely on the apocalyptic materials, whereas I am interested in the parenesis and the way it is illustrated by the character of the various patriarchs. A central event in the Genesis account is the betrayal of Joseph by his brothers. This event is retold from various points of view in the separate Testaments. The autobiographical accounts form the background and sometimes the basis for the ethical instructions. The distribution of these, in turn, is to some extent (there is much overlapping) indicated by the Greek titles, such as περὶ σωφροσύνης, etc.[76]

Much of the outlook and language of James 3:13–4:10 can be gathered from the Testaments as a whole, but the following points are of particular significance. A. There is a sharp contrast between the "two ways" of life (T. Asher i,3), governed by the "two spirits" of truth and falsehood (T. Jud. xx,1). Actually, there seem to be any number of πνεύματα (T. Reub. iii,5),

---

69. Ropes, pp. 20-21.

70. Ropes, p. 268; Mayor, p. 146; Dibelius, p. 226; Laws, pp. 180-181; Marty, p. 161; Catinat, p. 208.

71. Dibelius, pp. 226-227; Ropes, p. 270.

72. Marty, p. 156; Mussner, p. 183; Dibelius, p. 217.

73. Ropes, pp. 257-258, says, "This section of the *Testament of Benjamin* is full of parallels to James." Cf. also Mussner, p. 178; Windisch, p. 27; Catinat, p. 197; Marty, p. 154.

74. Cf. esp. Mussner, p. 37; Laws, p. 23; Dibelius, pp. 31-32.

75. Cf. the essays by M. de Jonge, "The Interpretation of the Testaments of the Twelve Patriarchs in Recent Years," and "Christian Influence in the Testaments of the Twelve Patriarchs," in *Studies on the Testaments of the Twelve Patriarchs,* ed. M. de Jonge (SVTP III; Leiden: Brill, 1975), 183-246, for an overview of these issues.

76. For this discussion, I am using the critical Greek text of M. de Jonge, *The Testaments of the Twelve Patriarchs* (PVTG 1.2; Leiden: Brill, 1978). The manuscript problems concerning the titles are discussed by R. H. Charles, *The Greek Versions of the Testaments of the Twelve Patriarchs* (Oxford: Oxford University Press, 1908), xliv-xlvi.

which go by a number of designations,[77] without a great deal of consistency. The particular "evil spirit" (T. Levi v,6) seems to be named more or less according to the vice being discussed.[78] These spirits empower humans toward certain actions (T. Naph. ii,2). Their resemblance to the *yetzerim* of Rabbinic texts is obvious, as is the same lack of precise psychology. The evil spirits are represented by Beliar,[79] whose words are "double" (T. Benj. vi,2). B. An evil spirit is given an opening in a person by an upset or disturbed mind (T. Dan iv,6-7). Besides being called Beliar, the evil spirit is known as the devil (διάβολος, T. Naph. viii,4) or Satan (σατανᾶς, T. Dan vi,1-2). He leads people to evil. In fact, he is said to "dwell" in a person (T. Naph. viii,6). In contrast, the person who does good has the Lord "dwelling" in him. The verb used consistently in these passages is that used by James 4:5 of the πνεῦμα "he made to dwell in us," κατοικέω.[80] C. Humans can choose between the domination of the Lord or the evil spirits. This is expressed in spatial terms as a "turning," as when Beliar is said to reward those who "turn" to evil (T. Benj. vii,1), or when one abandons God by "turning" to Beliar (T. Iss. vi,1). Likewise, one can "flee" Beliar (φεύγω, cf. James 4:7), and "approach" God (ἐγγίζω, cf. James 4:8).[81] D. This language about turning from one spiritual authority to another is an alternative way of speaking about a change of attitude and behavior in the world at the moral level. Next to the language about spirits, therefore, we find talk about "turning" from evil, envy and hatred of the brethren (as in T. Benj. viii, 1). It is here that the parenesis of the Testaments comes into play. The rule of spiritual forces is spelled out in vices and virtues. On the side of Beliar, we find among others, the attitude of boasting (cf. James 3:14),[82] arrogance (ὑπερηφανία, cf. James 4:6),[83] and hatred (μῖσος).[84] Associated closely with them is the vice of envy (ζῆλος and φθόνος being used interchangably as in James 3:14; 4:5).[85] Hatred and envy

---

77. So we find the πνεῦμα τοῦ μίσους (T. Gad iii,1; iv,6); πνεῦμα τοῦ θύμου (T. Dan i,8); πνεῦμα τῆς πλάνης (T. Reub. iii,5; T. Levi iii,3; T. Jud. xiv,8; T. Zeb. ix,7).

78. We therefore also find the πνεῦμα τῆς ὑπερηφανίας (T. Reub. iii,5) and the πνεῦμα τοῦ ζήλου (T. Jud. xiii,3; T. Dan i,6).

79. Cf. T. Levi iii,3; T. Dan i,7; T. Benj. iii,3.

80. T. Dan v,1-3; T. Jos. x,2-3; T. Benj. vi,4. Similarly, Joseph was comely, because no evil ἐνοίκησεν ἐν αὐτῷ (T. Sim v,1).

81. Cf. T. Iss. iii,17; T. Dan v,1-3; vi,1-2; T. Naph. viii,4; T. Benj. v,2; vii,1.

82. T. Levi xiv,7; T. Jud. xiii,2.

83. T. Reub. iii,5; T. Levi xvii,11; T. Jud. xiii,2; xviii,3; T. Dan v,6; T. Gad iii,3. The *Testament of Levi* is subtitled περὶ ἱεροσύνης καὶ ὑπερηφανίας.

84. T. Gad ii,1; iii,1; iv,6; T. Jos. i,4; T. Benj. viii,1.

85. T. Reub., iii,5; T. Dan i,6; T. Jud. xiii,3; T. Gad v,4; vii,3.

are almost synonymous in the Testaments (cf. T. Dan ii,5). The person who hates envies one who does good (T. Gad iii,3); μῖσος stirs up φθόνος and leads it to murder (T. Gad iv,5-6). There is a direct connection between hatred, envy, and wars (T. Gad v,1; T. Jos. i,4; cf. James 4:1). The Joseph story is obviously central to this perception, and we find Joseph himself stating that he has known both φθόνος καὶ θάνατος (T. Jos. i,3). E. If the way of life dominated by Beliar is "double,"[86] that guided by the Lord is characterized by "singleness" or simplicity (ἁπλότης),[87] which, as in James 4:8, can also be called a "purity" of heart (T. Benj. v,2). This singleness is opposed to all jealousy (ζῆλος) and envy (βασκανία) in T. Iss. iv,5. The person who is simple is able to show mercy ἀδιακρίτως (T. Zeb. vii,2; cf. James 3:17). And if the evil man shows arrogance (ὑπερηφανία), the single-minded person is characterized by lowliness (ταπείνωσις), as in James 4:6, 10).[88] The link between envy and death is found also in a reference to the Cain and Abel story. In the *Testament of Benjamin* vii,1-2, the readers are told φεύγετε τὴν κακίαν τοῦ Βελιάρ. The reason? He gives seven swords to those who trust in him. The first of these is envy (φθόνος). Then it says that διὰ τοῦτο, Cain received seven punishments from the Lord (vii,3). This text led Charles to emend φθόνος to φόνος, because "Cain's first sin was murder."[89] As in the suggested emendations of James 4:2 in the opposite direction, there is no manuscript support, and as little logic, for the text continues, οἱ ὁμοιούμενοι τῷ Κάϊν ἐν φθόνῳ εἰς τὴν μισαδελφίαν τῇ αὐτῇ κολάσει κριθήσονται (T. Benj. vii,5).

The motif of envy and murder is most extensively displayed in the *Testament of Simeon*, which is titled in Greek, περὶ φθόνου.[90] It is one of the shortest Testaments, and is dominated by the alternation of autobiography and exhortation. The resemblance to James 3:13-4:10 is found both in language and in structure, for in this Testament, the *topos* on envy is placed within an explicit framework of *conversion,* as in James. It therefore deserves close attention.

The Testament explicitly exploits the Genesis account (37:11), for Simeon says of himself, ἐζήλωσα τὸν Ἰωσὴφ ὅτι ἠγάπα αὐτὸν ὁ πατὴρ ἡμῶν (T. Sim. ii,6). To what does he attribute this envy? The ἄρχων τῆς πλάνης

---

86. Cf. the "two faces" in T. Asher ii,2 and "two tongues" in T. Benj. vi,5.

87. Cf. T. Reub. iv,1; T. Levi xiii,1; T. Iss. iii,2-8; vi,1.

88. Cf. T. Gad v,3; T. Jos. x,2-3.

89. R. H. Charles, *Apocrypha and Pseudepigrapha of the Old Testament* (Oxford: Clarendon, 1913), 2:357. Cf. also his *Greek Versions,* pp. 223-224.

90. Despite the variations elsewhere, the Ms evidence is remarkably strong for this title. Cf. Charles, *Greek Versions,* pp. xliv-xlvi.

(cf. James 3:14) sent the πνεῦμα τοῦ ζήλος (cf. James 4:5), and it blinded him (ii,7).[91] Simeon therefore sought to *kill* Joseph (cf. James 4:2), and was furious when he was thwarted (ii,7, 11). He says that every evil intention was aroused because of his envy of Joseph (ii,14; cf. James 3:16). In a later passage, he states that envy makes the soul savage, and destroys the body, leading to thoughts of ὀργὴ καὶ πόλεμος and the spilling of blood (iv,8; cf. James 4:1-2). Φθόνος, he says, disturbs (διαταράσσω) the soul (iv,9; cf. James 3:16), and *always* seeks to kill the one who is envied (iii,2-3). If people could straighten out their hearts and turn away from φθόνος, then καταπαύσει ἡ γῆ πᾶσα ἀπὸ ταραχῆς καὶ πᾶσα ἡ ὑπ' οὐρανοῦ ἀπὸ πολέμου (v. 1; cf. James 4:1).

That last point is the distinctive element in the *Testament of Simeon*. It holds out the possibility of repentance from envy. Simeon says that if someone flees to the Lord, the evil spirit will depart from him (iii,5; cf. James 4:7). A model for this conversion is given by Simeon's own life: καὶ μετανοήσας ἔκλαυσα καὶ ηὐξάμην κυρίῳ ἵνα ἀποκατασταθῶ καὶ ἀπόσχωμαι ἀπὸ παντὸς μολυσμοῦ καὶ φθόνου καὶ ἀπὸ πάσης ἀφροσύνης (T. Sim. ii,13; cf. James 4:8-9, 5). The exhortation of T. Sim. iv,4 is based on this model, and is strikingly similar to the call to conversion in James 4:7-10: φυλάξασθε οὖν τέκνα μου ἀπὸ παντὸς ζήλου καὶ φθόνου καὶ πορεύεσθε ἐν ἁπλότητι ψυχῆς καὶ ἐν ἀγαθῇ καρδίας ἵνα δῷη καὶ ὑμῖν ὁ θεὸς χάριν καὶ δόξαν καὶ εὐλογίαν. And in T. Sim. iv,7, the readers are told to love their brothers ἀγαθῇ καρδίᾳ καὶ ἀποστήσατε ἀφ' ὑμῶν τὸ πνεῦμα τοῦ φθόνου (cf. James 4:6).

In addition to the coherent thematic framework provided James 3:13–4:10 by the Testaments as a whole, then, the *Testament of Simeon* offers eight separate points of similarity: (1) the explicit call to conversion; (2) the synonymous use of ζῆλος and φθόνος; (3) the attribution of envy to a πνεῦμα which is a deceiver; (4) the tendency of envy toward murder; (5) the role of envy in generating societal unrest and war; (6) the turning from the evil spirit to God by prayer and mourning; (7) the giving of grace by God to those who turn from envy (or Beliar) and turn to the Lord; (8) the portrayal of envy's opposite as simplicity of soul and goodness of heart.

The emphasis I have placed on the *Testaments* is not intended to denigrate the similarities to James 3:13ff. in the *Shepherd of Hermas,* which have been frequently noted:[92] the contrast between διψυχία and

---

91. In T. Sim. iii,1, it is called the πνεῦμα τοῦ φθόνου, which is even closer to James 4:5.

92. Cf. esp. Marty, p. 144; Ropes, p. 248; Laws, pp. 161-162; Mayor, p. 128; Catinat, p. 31; Dibelius, p. 213.

ἁπλότης;[93] the indwelling spirit,[94] whether from above or from below;[95] the role of ὑπερηφανία;[96] the disruptive action of the demonic spirit,[97] and the image of fleeing the devil (*Mand.* xii, 4, 7, which we noted earlier). But these points are scattered throughout the larger work. What makes the *Testaments* a more appropriate source for understanding this part of James is the pervasiveness and density of this language. Above all, in the *Testaments,* this language is attached specifically to the theme of envy, which is entirely lacking in Hermas.[98]

Conclusions

Treating James 3:13–4:10 as a rhetorical unit which uses the *topos* on envy within the framework of a call to conversion throws light on a variety of smaller and larger issues. The study of Hellenistic moral literature and in particular the writings of Hellenistic Judaism supported the contention that the theme of envy runs throughout this section. Because of the characterizations which consistently attend φθόνος, we are able to identify words like πικρός, ἐπιεικής, ἀδιάκριτος and ἀκαταστασία as pertinent to that topic. We have been able to offer overwhelming support for the association of envy with murder, and therefore for the reading φονεύετε in 4:2. As for the citation of Prov. 3:34 in James 4:6, the choice of that verse with reference to φθόνος now becomes clear, for ὑπερηφανία has been so frequently associated with that vice.[99]

The precise meaning of 4:5 remains difficult, but in the light of the material from the *Testaments* both the provenance and intelligibility of the language seem clear. The πνεῦμα God made to dwell in us is certainly *not,* in this context, πρὸς φθόνον. The spirit is one God caused to dwell, and it does the longing, and the rhetorical question expects a negative answer.

93. *Mand.* ii,1; *Mand.* ix,7 and 11. In this last passage, and in *Mand.* xi,16, as we noted earlier, διψυχία is ἐπίγειος, παρὰ τοῦ διαβόλου.

94. *Mand.* v,4; ii,3; iii,1.

95. *Mand.* x,16; xi,8-16.

96. *Mand.* vi,2, 5; *Sim.* viii,95.

97. *Mand.* ii,3.

98. The closest thing is ὀξυχολία, which is called πικρός, and which is joined to anger and arrogance (*Mand.* v,2, 4-5) as well as double-mindedness (*Mand.* x,2, 5).

99. We might also note that the context of Prov 3:34 promises ζωή and εἰρήνη (Prov 3:2, 16, 22) to the man who has σοφία καὶ φρόνησις (3:13), and contains this warning only a few verses from the ones cited by James, μὴ κτήσῃ κακῶν ἀνδρῶν ὀνείδη, μηδὲ ζηλώσῃς τὰς ὁδοὺν αὐτῶν (3:31).

As for the odd phrase μείζονα δὲ δίδωσιν χάριν, in view of what is said else-where about the divine ἀφθονία, and in view of the hint of this notion ear-lier in James (1:5), a deliberate contrast to the attitude of evil human long-ing πρὸς φθόνον may be intended. God resists the proud who long enviously always to overcome others and assert themselves; but to the lowly who turn to him, he never "grudges," but gives more grace.[100]

Beyond these details, we have shown that it is possible to use Hellenis-tic materials in a more fruitful way than the simple search for lexical par-allels. It demands, however, an attention to the form and function of the New Testament passages as well as those of the Hellenistic writings. The examination must go beyond the occurrence of single words, to the con-sistent clusters and patterns which show the presence of a *topos*. In one sense, only at this point can the creative work of exegesis begin. For, once we know what sort of stereotypical rhetorical or ethical material the New Testament author was employing, we can begin to see what distinctive use he has made of it, if any.[101]

In this case, the reader will have observed that virtually everything in James 3:13–4:10 could find a comfortable home in Plutarch's *De Invidia et Odio,* and if not there, in the *Testament of Simeon.* But there have been two major exceptions: the first comes in 4:3, where James talks about asking κακῶς; the second follows immediately in 4:4, where the readers are re-minded (οὐκ οἴδατε) of an apparently traditional understanding that friendship with the world means enmity with God. But this understand-ing is precisely not found in the material dealing with envy, or indeed any-where else in the Hellenistic material which James so comfortably uses. Where does it come from, and what does it mean? It lies at the heart of this passage, it represents the distinctive touch of James, and it is the nec-essary next step in understanding James 3:13–4:10.

---

100. And this is the edge to the term ψυχικός — the human being who is envious does *not* have the divine spirit at work in him, but only natural drives, or worse, the inspiration of the devil (so the connection between διάβολος and δαιμονιώδης).

101. Cf., e.g., the way A. J. Malherbe places the Pauline treatment of "benevolence" and "the quiet life" in 1 Thess. against the contemporary discussions of those issues among phi-losophers, in *Social Aspects of Early Christianity* (Baton Rouge: Louisiana State University Press, 1977), 23-28, and the way R. Hock locates the discussion of Paul's self-support, in *The Social Context of Paul's Ministry* (Philadelphia: Fortress, 1980), 50-65.

Friendship with the World and Friendship with God:
A Study of Discipleship in James

A discussion of discipleship in the Letter of James must begin with some adjustments in perspective. We must first ask of James a different sort of question. To ask about discipleship in James is really to ask about the shape of Christian existence,[1] for in spite of the definite connections between James and the gospel tradition,[2] the distinctive synoptic way of defining Christian life is not found in James.[3] If our question, therefore, is, What does James tell us about the nature of Christian existence, we find ourselves looking not merely for specific observations or commands but for an overall sense of Christian identity.

The second adjustment required of us is to read James on its own terms. This adjustment demands three separate shifts from ways in which this often unread letter is too often read. When James is noticed at all, it is usually as a foil to Paul, even in those studies which seek to rehabilitate James from its stepchild status in the New Testament canon. The rather minor semantic differences between James and Paul on the matter of faith and works is treated obsessively as though it were all in James that is

---

1. That James is in fact a thoroughly Christian writing and not a lightly reworked Jewish document should no longer be doubted. Although Jesus is mentioned only twice (1:1; 2:1), the specifically Christian connections are pervasive. Some of them will emerge in this study.

2. Among others, see P. Minear, "Yes or No: The Demand for Honesty in the Early Church," *NovT* 13 (1971) 1-13; M. H. Shepherd, "The Epistle of James and the Gospel of Matthew," *JBL* 75 (1956) 40-51; and my essay "The Use of Leviticus 19 in the Letter of James," pp. 123-135 in this volume.

3. The terms characteristic of the Synoptics are either missing or used differently: "teacher" (διδάσκαλος) is used in 3:1 of community teachers; "to follow" (ἀκολουθέω) and "disciple" (μαθητής) are absent.

worth studying.[4] To treat James on its own terms means first, then, reading it neither as Pauline nor as anti-Pauline but simply as an extra-Pauline witness to Christian existence.

When a historical fixation is not operative, a literary one frequently is. I refer to the pervasive impact of Martin Dibelius's magisterial commentary on all subsequent study of James.[5] Building on the work of J. B. Mayor[6] and J. H. Ropes,[7] among others, and using his own extensive knowledge of Hellenistic literature, Dibelius stated that the key to understanding James was its genre *(Gattung)*, and that its genre was, simply, parenesis.[8] This was a great half-truth. Dibelius was correct in seeing James not as a systematic theology or innovative argument but, rather, as an exhortation which employs traditional ethical teaching, parallels to which can be found in many other Greek and Jewish writings.[9] Unfortunately, Dibelius's knowledge did have limits. He wrongly identified parenesis as a genre. It is better described as a mode of ethical teaching which can be fitted to many different literary genres. He was mistaken as well in his insistence that parenesis is totally without structure. Sometimes, parenetic materials do appear in loosely arranged aphorisms. But

4. For example, J. Jeremias, "Paul and James," *ExpTim* 66 (1965) 368-371; D. O. Via, "The Right Strawy Epistle Reconsidered: A Study in Biblical Ethics and Hermeneutics," *JR* 49 (1969) 253-267; J. G. Lodge, "James and Paul at Cross-purposes? James 2,22," *Bib* 62 (1981) 195-213.

5. First published in 1921 as part of the Meyer commentary series, its latest apparition is M. Dibelius, *James: A Commentary on the Epistle of James*, rev. H. Greeven, trans. M. Williams (Hermeneia; Philadelphia: Fortress Press, 1976). In subsequent commentaries which deal with the question of genre at all, the influence of Dibelius can be seen clearly in O. Bardenhewer, *Der Brief des Heiligen Jacobus* (Freiburg: Herder Verlag, 1928); T. Garcia, *Epistola Sancti Jacobi* (Rome: Lateranum, 1954); J. Catinat, *Les Épitres de Saint Jacques et de Saint Jude* (SB; Paris: J. Gabalda, 1973); H. Windisch, *Die Katholischen Briefe*, 2nd ed. (HNT 15; Tübingen: Mohr/Siebeck, 1951); F. Mussner, *Der Jacobusbrief*, 3rd ed. (HTKNT 13; Freiburg: Herder Verlag, 1975). The most explicit rejection of Dibelius is found in J. B. Adamson, *The Epistle of James* (NICNT; Grand Rapids: Eerdmans, 1976).

6. A great deal of comparative material had already been gathered by J. B. Mayor, *The Epistle of St. James*, 3rd ed. (London: Macmillan & Co., 1910), cf. esp. cx-cxxvii.

7. J. H. Ropes (*A Critical and Exegetical Commentary on the Epistle of St. James* [ICC; Edinburgh: T. & T. Clark, 1916]) saw the particular pertinence of the *Testaments of the Twelve Patriarchs* for understanding James (20-21) and emphasized the diatribal character of the writing (10-18).

8. Dibelius, *James*, 1-3.

9. In addition to the parallels collected by Mayor and Ropes, Dibelius made extensive use of lexical materials from the Greco-Roman moralists, Hellenistic Jewish writings such as *The Sentences of Pseudo-Phocylides*, and Christian parenetic writings like *The Shepherd of Hermas*.

other times, they are found in rather impressively articulated structures.[10] On the basis of this somewhat partial view of parenesis, Dibelius made rather sweeping judgments regarding James. He refused it any possibility of literary unity: James would be regarded only as a kind of storehouse of traditional lore. And if that was the case, then it was out of the question to find in James any theology, or even the basis for deriving a theology.[11] In both these assertions, Dibelius was wrong. It would be inappropriate to deny that part of Dibelius's great achievement which was correct, but it is important to recognize that wisdom writings, too, have their own inner coherence and that it is hazardous to move rapidly from general characterization to exegetical fiat.[12]

Finally, taking James on its own terms means not assuming ahead of time that we know what it means, whether because of its supposed genre, imputative historical setting, or its possible social functions.[13] This means being willing to expend the same exegetical patience on James that we do with Paul. This is all the more necessary because of the deceptive simplicity of wisdom writings. They often lack the punch of parables or the bite of argument, sometimes seducing us into a presumption that we grasp the message.[14] In the matter of trying to discover James's teaching on

10. See the observations of A. J. Malherbe, "Hellenistic Moralists and the New Testament," in *Aufstieg und Niedergang der Römischen Welt* (ed. H. Temporini; 3, 26 [forthcoming]), and the application of these to a particular personal parenetic letter in L. T. Johnson, "II Timothy and the Polemic Against False Teachers: A Reexamination," *JRelS* 6/7 (1978-79) 1-26.

11. Dibelius, *James,* 11. Dibelius's influence is seen in a recent attempt at describing the theological outlook of James in R. Hoppe, *Der theologische Hintergrund des Jacobusbriefe* (FzB; Würzburg: Echter-Seelsorge, 1977). As I do in this essay, Hoppe regards James 3:13-18 as part of James's own theology. But following Dibelius's literary norms (1), he separates 3:13-18 from 3:1-12 and 4:1-10 (9, 44), a procedure opposite the one followed here.

12. Dibelius does recognize some "treatises" in James (such as 2:1–3:12) but resists all further attempts at finding structure (*James,* 22). Certainly, overly clever schemes should be avoided. But one can note simply that statements of theme made by way of aphorism in chap. 1 have a rather consistent way of being developed by way of essay in the other chapters, so that the opening set of verses functions as a sort of "table of contents" of the book: see, e.g.. 1:2-4, 12-15 (trials), in 5:7-11; 1:9-11 (rich and poor), in 4:13-5:6; 1:19-21, 26 (speech), in 3:1-18; 1:22-26 (doing the word), in 2:14-26; 1:5-8, 16-18 (true wisdom), in 3:13–4:10.

13. See the unfortunate examples of M. T. Townsend, "James 4:1-14: A Warning Against Zealotry?" *ExpTim* 87 (1975) 211-13; and L. G. Perdue, "Paraenesis and the Letter of James," *ZNW* 72 (1981) 241-56.

14. Wisdom literature may be general in intention, but it is particular in expression. Even minimal arrangement of materials represents an interpretation and point of view. Furthermore, aphorisms may be worn to cliches, but they do claim to make statements

Christian existence (discipleship), this attitude implies a readiness to follow the contours of particular texts in their particularity, not seeking too quickly to fit them to molds, exercising instead the classical rules of our discipline. They insist we attend carefully both to the content and context of statements, both to their form and function. We allow them to become very strange before our eyes and ears, so that we can be sure it is the text and not our own presuppositions to which we hearken.

The Immediate Context

My proposal here is a simple one: to pay close attention to a single verse in James, to see where it will lead. The text is James 4:4: "Unfaithful creatures! Do you not know that friendship with the world is enmity with God? Therefore whoever wishes to be a friend of the world makes himself an enemy of God." At first glance, this does not appear to be either a pleasant or promising statement. But it may open for us some of the distinctive richness of James's understanding of Christian existence.

What first drew me to this verse was its appearance of sane clarity in an otherwise hopelessly confused section of James. This first impression quickly changed as the verse began to look stranger and increasingly difficult to swallow. But first, the reason for that first impression: the mess surrounding the verse on either side. James 3:13–4:10 is notorious for its exegetical problems. Questions concerning the proper text,[15] the meaning of words,[16] and the way to punctuate[17] abound. Some time spent hacking through this tangle, however, convinced me that the problems were con-

---

about reality — not only to say something well but to say something. Testing such statements may require very special tools, but they should be no less sharp than those laid to argument and narrative. The characterizations of James found in J. T. Sanders (*The Ethics of the New Testament* [Philadelphia: Fortress Press, 1975], 115-28) show no such acuity.

15. Should we read φονεύετε ("you murder") in 4:2, or φθονεύετε ("you are envious")? Erasmus thought the context demanded the latter, so he emended it to that. But the harder reading is "you murder," and it is supported by the connection between killing and envy in the moralists' discussions.

16. The δαιμονιώδης ("devilish") of 3:15 and the ἀδιάκριτος ("without uncertainty") of 3:17 are *hapax legomena* and difficult until they are linked to the διάβολος ("the devil") of 4:7 and the δίψυχος ("double-minded man") of 4:8, although commentators never make this linkage.

17. The punctuation of 4:2 and 4:5-6 is complex and much discussed by commentators. For 4:2, the best solution is that of Mayor (*Epistle of St. James,* 136); for 4:5-6, see S. Laws, "Does the Scripture Speak in Vain? A Reconsideration of James 4:5," *NTS* 20 (1973-74) 210-15.

nected to the habit Dibelius had instilled in us of reading James as a set of disconnected sayings. As an experiment, I pulled 3:13–4:10 out as a unit for closer inspection. What did I find? In broadest terms, I discovered a coherent literary structure: as a whole, it appears as a call to conversion from one way of life to another. James 3:13–4:6 sets up an indictment, to which 4:7-10 responds.[18] The connective "therefore" (οὖν) in 4:7 indicates that the series of imperatives following it is based on the indictment. The conclusion, "Humble yourselves before the Lord and he will exalt you" (4:10), clearly picks up from 4:6, "God . . . gives grace to the humble." The section containing the indictment (3:13–4:6) is even more refined in its rhetoric, moving forward by a series of antithetical contrasts and rhetorical questions. Far from a congeries of aphorisms, then, this part of James appears as a coherent rhetorical unit.

My next step was to read the passage against the broad background of Hellenistic moral philosophy. When I did this, I found that James was using a *topos* on envy to give substance to his conversion call.[19] To know how the vice of envy is typically discussed by moralists is to understand not only the repeated presence of "bitter jealousy" in 3:14, and "jealousy" in 4:2, and the climactic "envy" in 4:5, but also to see why many other terms denoting social unrest (ἀκαταστασία, 3:16), warfare (πόλεμοι, μάχαι, 4:1), and even murder (φόνος, 4:2) are found here, for they are commonplace associations in discussions of envy.[20] Greek moralists, however, would not have put quite the emphasis James has on murder, nor on those cosmic forces, the spirit (πνεῦμα, 4:5) and the devil (διάβολος, 4:7). These symbols are due to the development of the theme of envy in Hellenistic Jewish texts, beginning in the Septuagintal Book of Wisdom (2:24) and elaborated most extensively in the Greek *Testament of Simeon.*[21]

As a call to conversion employing the *topos* on envy, we see that James

18. The vocabulary of 4:8-10 recalls the threat/repentance language of the Prophets in the Septuagint: ταπεινόω ("to humble"), Hosea 5:5; 7:10; καθαρίζω ("to cleanse"), Ezek. 36:25; πένθος ("mourning"), Amos 8:10; Lam. 5:15; πενθέω ("to mourn"), Amos 9:5; Joel 1:9, 10; Isa. 24:4; 33:9; Jer. 4:28; 14:2; κλαίω ("to weep"), Joel 1:5; 2:17; Isa. 22:4; 30:19; 38:3; Jer. 9:1; 22:10.

19. See L. T. Johnson, "James 3:13–4:10 and the *Topos* περὶ φθόνου," pp. 182-201 in this volume.

20. For a thorough review of the *topos* in Greek writers, see E. Milobenski, *Der Neid in der griechischen Philosophie* (Klassisch-Philologische Studien 29; Wiesbaden: Otto Harrassowitz, 1964).

21. The *Testament of Simeon* is entitled in Greek περὶ φθόνου and places the *topos* within the context of "two spirits" language and a call to conversion, as in James. See esp. *Testament of Simeon* 2:13; 4:4; and Johnson, "James 3:13–4:10."

3:13-4:10 is organized according to sharp contrasts. The most obvious is that between the attack and the command, between the indictment and the exhortation. The reader is told to replace one way of life with another.[22] Corresponding to this contrast is another between two measures of reality, which derive from different sources and lead to different actions. The wisdom from above which leads to goodness and peace (3:17) derives, we gather, from the spirit which God made to dwell in humans (4:5). In contrast there is a wisdom from below, which is characterized by bitter envy and which comes from another force, the devil (4:7). It is demoniacal, psychic (that is, without spirit), and "earthly" (3:15-16). Those addressed by James are told to shift allegiance from one power to another and from one measure of reality to another. They do this by "turning," here expressed in terms of "resisting" the devil and "drawing near" to God (4:7-8). This means, in effect, submitting to the power of God (4:7, 10). What is most striking in all of this is that the only part of this section of James that cannot be paralleled in Hellenistic or Jewish texts is 4:3-4, to which we must now turn. What does it say, and how does it fit into the context I have described?

The Text: James 4:4

I will now examine this single text carefully in each of its parts, and from several points of view. Such a procedure seems particularly appropriate in this case. Despite a superficial air of clarity, James 4:4 makes a fairly outrageous and not-at-all-clear claim.

"Unfaithful Creatures!"

The Greek μοιχαλίδες is both more specific and harsher: "You adulteresses!" Now, it is characteristic of diatribal material to have sudden expostulations.[23] But what has motivated such an unprecedented outbreak in

---

22. The descriptive terms of the exhortation mirror the terms of the indictment: the "lowering" of 4:7 and 10 corresponds to the "from above" in 3:15; the "cleansing of heart" in 4:8 picks up the "selfish ambition in your heart" in 3:14; the κατήφεια ("dejection") of 4:9 opposes the ὑπερηφανία ("pride") of 4:6; the δίψυχοι ("double-minded men") of 4:8 matches the ἀδιάκριτος ("without uncertainty") of 3:17; the cleansing and purifying of 4:8 corresponds to the "pure" of 3:17.

23. See Ropes (*James,* 10-15) who isolates many dialogical-diatribal features in

James? And why adulteresses? He has not been accusing them of adultery in the literal sense but of envy and violence. Some early scribes apparently thought that it was a matter of sexual sin and wanted to be fair, so they made it "you adulterers and adulteresses!"[24] We can ask, further, whether it is self-aggrandizing attitudes and antisocial jealousies in general which have so exercised James, or whether it is, in particular, a way of praying.

He has just mentioned in 4:3 that they ask for what they desire (ask God we presume), but they do not receive because they ask "wrongly." They turn to prayer, we notice, only as a last expedient, and then they ask wrongly. But is the Greek word κακῶς adequately translated by "wrongly"? Better would be "wickedly." Why is this important? For one thing, the term "wrongly" could be taken to mean that they did not follow the right method of prayer, whereas it is really a question of praying wickedly, in a perverted way. How is this? They are trying to use God as one more means of gratifying their desires: "[You ask] to spend it on your passions." They see God as part of a closed system with themselves. This is, of course, the attitude characteristic of idolatry: to regard God solely as the fulfiller of our desires.[25] This reminds us, in turn, that the language of adultery is used frequently by the prophets in their accusations against Israel of covenantal infidelity, an infidelity which almost always was associated with idolatry.[26] The first part of this verse places us rather squarely, therefore, in the context of idolatry and covenant fidelity. But let us go further.

"Do You Not Know?"

οὐκ οἴδατε is a stock phrase in parenesis, in which the point is remembering traditional ethical standards, not learning new ones.[27] This is the only time it occurs in James,[28] though it is an expression familiar to us from

---

James. The best treatment of the diatribe is now S. K. Stowers, *The Diatribe and Paul's Letter to the Romans* (SBLDS 57; Chico, Calif.: Scholars Press, 1981) esp. 85-100.

24. μοιχοὶ καὶ μοιχαλίδες is found in ℵ², P, ψ and the mss of the *koine* tradition. The shorter and better reading is held by ℵ*, A, B, and others.

25. We are not surprised, then, that one of the few occurrences of "wicked prayer" in the Septuagint is in a characterization of idolators (Wis. 14:30).

26. Cf. e.g., Hosea 3:1; Ezek. 16:38; 23:45; Isa. 57:3; Jer. 3:9; 13:27.

27. See Malherbe, "Hellenistic Moralists," and idem, "Exhortation in First Thessalonians" (a paper delivered to the Society of Biblical Literature Seminar on the Thessalonian Correspondence, 1981) 2.

28. Similar expressions, indicating recollections of previous knowledge, are found at 1:3

Paul's letters, where it introduces elements of traditional Christian under-standing,[29] or even proverbial sayings.[30] The phrase not only reminds the readers of what they already know; its negative phrasing suggests a rebuke as well — they should not need reminding. It also serves to establish a ground of shared understanding: if they agree to this, then they can fol-low the conclusion built on it as well.

"Friendship with the World Is Enmity with God"

This is the content of what they know. No problem with the Greek: the genitive constructions are plainly objective; that is, the friendship is one directed toward, not received from, the world.[31] A bigger problem has to do with the supposedly traditional nature of this statement. Why should they know this? We know of no such proverb in all the Hellenistic litera-ture, nor is it found in Old Testament wisdom texts or in the Hellenistic Jewish literature.[32]

Critical editions and commentaries point us to another Christian text, 1 John 2:15-17, and it is, without question, the closest parallel to what we find in James 4:4:[33]

> Do not love the world or the things in the world. If any one loves the world, love for the Father is not in him. For all that is in the world, the lust of the flesh and the lust of the eyes and the pride of

---

(γινώσκοντες); 1:19 (ἴστε); the series of negative rhetorical questions following ἀκούσατε in 2:5-7; 3:1 (εἰδότες); 5:11 (ἠκούσατε, εἴδετε); and the alternative reading at 5:20 (γινώσκετε).

29. "Do you not know that you are God's Temple?" (1 Cor. 3:16); "Do you not know that the saints will judge the world?" (1 Cor. 6:2).

30. "Do you not know that a little yeast leavens the whole lump?" (1 Cor. 5:6). Cf. also Rom. 6:16; 11:2; 1 Cor. 9:24.

31. Dibelius, *James*, 220; Ropes, *James*, 260.

32. Mayor's suggestion — "The reference is to our Lord's words, Mt 6:24" — is surely wrong, for though the substance of the statement is similar, the phrasing, and even the sense, are different. The commentators are not able to adduce any parallels from the Helle-nistic or Jewish materials. In the *Testaments*, which otherwise parallel James on so many points, there is only the expression "from the desire of the world" (ἀπὸ τῆς πλάνης τοῦ κόσμου), *Testament of Issachar* 4:6. For many expressions in the Apocrypha of *hostility* to the world as an evil place, see Dibelius, *James*, 194. None of them really correspond to James's usage.

33. It is far closer than another New Testament text sometimes cited, 2 Tim. 3:4, which says of false teachers that they are "lovers of pleasure rather than lovers of God" (φιλήδονοι μᾶλλον ἢ φιλόθεοι).

life, is not of the Father but is of the world. And the world passes away, and the lust of it; but he who does the will of God abides for ever.

There are some obvious similarities between the two passages. They have a similar structure. 1 John 2:15-17 makes a statement on the division between the world and God and follows it with a conditional sentence — "whoever loves the world" — just as James does in 4:4. In addition, the notion of "desires" is in each case associated with the world. The language of 1 John, though, is one of love, not of friendship; it lacks the note of enmity toward God; and the essential contrast is between the permanence of God and the transitoriness of the world. Still, it is the most helpful analogy to the passage in James.[34] But what is the connection between them? Few would want to argue for a literary relationship between John and James, so it may be that both were independently working out of a shared tradition (whose origin we no longer know), each shaping it to his own perceptions. John does not much help us, then, except to make even clearer the distinctly Christian sentiment here being expressed,[35] and to suggest that the dualism here is less cosmological than religious or ethical. It is not, in either text, the "world," as the place of trees and cities, which is the problem, but "the world" as a system of untrammeled desire and arrogance. We have yet to discover the exact shape of James's perception, though, and will have to delay that until we look a bit at the last part of 4:4.

"Therefore, Whoever Wishes to Be a Friend of the World Makes Himself an Enemy of God"

The Greek here is, again, clear enough. It is a question of friendship toward the world and enmity toward God. But notice how the "therefore" (οὖν) creates a small argument. The truth of the first statement ("Do you not know?") permits a conclusion, "Therefore." We note in passing that the conclusion leads to one direction for life. Another "therefore" in 4:7 points out the other direction. Although the sentence seems almost tau-

---

34. For a discussion of 1 John 2:15-17, see R. E. Brown, *The Epistles of John* (AB 30; New York: Doubleday & Co., 1982), 306-28. The fact that the Johannine writings generally are comfortable with "friendship" language makes the differences here the more striking. In John 15:19, e.g., we find: "If you were of the world, the world would love its own" (εἰ ἐκ τοῦ κόσμου ἦτε, ὁ κόσμος ἂν τὸ ἴδιον ἐφίλει). See also John 15:13-15; 16:27; 20:2; 21:15-17; 3 John 15.

35. See the discussion by H. Sasse, "κοσμέω, κτλ.," *TDNT* 3 (1965) 894-95.

tologous, two small features deserve attention. First, the "wishing" (βούλομαι) indicates an effective choice, as it does also in James 1:8. Wanting to be a friend already has another consequence. That consequence is expressed in especially harsh terms: "makes himself" is too weak for the Greek verb καθίστημι, which in the New Testament and elsewhere has almost an official tone.[36] Better would be "is established as" — the desire itself has the effect of placing one in a state of enmity with God! Only in one other place do we find a similarly harsh characterization: in Rom. 8:7, Paul says, "The desire of the flesh is enmity toward God."

We have now disassembled the verse and have found it to be as threatening as we first suspected. The only parallel passage we could find was just as harsh. But we have not yet made much progress in understanding it, for we do not yet know how to evaluate the two key terms in the verse: "friendship" and "world." How is James using these terms? Is he establishing a metaphysical dualism, whereby material reality must be shed if one is to find God? Or is he presenting an ethical dualism? If so, how precisely are we to understand it? Where is this "world"? Is it outside us or also within us? Does James define it cosmologically or axiologically? We cannot affirm or reject this fundamental assertion by James — an assertion which clearly anchors this whole section — unless we grasp securely what he means by "world" and "friendship."

The Terms "World" and "Friendship"

"World" (κόσμος)

James uses the term "world" (κόσμος) three times outside this passage, and each time it means something more than the merely material world or even the structures of human society. It points to a kind of measure or system of meaning.

1. The occurrence in 3:6 is the most difficult and elusive. James calls the tongue a κόσμος τῆς ἀδικίας, a "world of wickedness," or if we take the genitive adjectivally, "a wicked world," among the members of the body. It is an ambiguous expression,[37] but it is clearly metaphorical, and it moves

---

36. Cf. LSJ, s.v., καθίστημι, and the use in (LXX) Exod. 2:14 and Ps. 8:7, picked up by Acts 7:10 and Heb. 2:7, respectively, as well as Matt. 24:47, Luke 12:42, Rom. 5:19.

37. We notice that καθίστημι appears here as well, so that the Dibelius-Greeven-Williams translation seem apt: "And the tongue is a member [the tongue presents itself

in the direction of understanding "world" as a category of value. Notice that James says it "stains the whole body" — we meet this idea of "staining" again shortly.

2. The use of "world" in 2:5 is somewhat clearer. There, James says that God chose τοὺς πτωχοὺς τῷ κόσμῳ) to be rich in faith and heirs of the kingdom promised to those who love God. The question is how to put together the words "world" and "poor." It could be read simply as "the poor," but then "the world" would be redundant. Or it could mean "poor people in the world," as one textual variant has it.[38] But the best text uses what we can loosely call a dative of reference,[39] which enables us to read "poor from the world's point of view," or "according to the world's measure, poor." That this is at least generally correct is shown by the way in which the expression is contrasted to the measure of God's kingdom, the measure of faith. In this passage, therefore, "world" is a measure distinguishable from God's.

3. The usage in 1:27 is decisive. James characterizes "pure and unstained religion before God and the Father" as one expressed by the visiting of orphans and widows in their distress and by "keeping oneself unstained from the world" (ἀπὸ τοῦ κόσμου). What exactly does this mean? First, there is absolutely no indication in James that Christians are to observe ritual separation from other people or from any class of objects which are regarded as "impure." Nor does James ever suggest that Christians flee the customary social structures and seek or establish alternative life styles. On the contrary, as we shall see, he envisages Christians taking full part in the affairs of the world: commerce, landowning, judging, owning and distributing possessions, having houses for hospitality.

Being "unstained from the world," then,[40] does not mean physical or ritual separation. Instead, "world" here stands as a measure or standard, which is distinguishable from that of "God and the Father." "World" and

---

among our members as the evil world] staining the whole body" (Dibelius, *James*, 181). See his discussion, 194-95, as well as that of Sasse, "κοσμέω," 883-84.

38. Both ἐν τῷ κόσμῳ and τοῦ κόσμου have poorer attestation, are longer, and are more easily explained as clarifications of τῷ κόσμῳ, which is shorter, harder, and better.

39. See the discussion of ambiguous datives by C. F. D. Moule, *An Idiom-Book of New Testament Greek* (2d ed.; Cambridge: Cambridge Univ. Press, 1959) 45-46, and his second thoughts concerning James 2:5 (204). See also J. H. Moulton, *A Grammar of New Testament Greek* (vol. III: N. Turner, *Syntax* [Edinburgh: T. & T. Clark, 1963]), 238.

40. We have seen how that "world of wickedness," the tongue, "stains" the whole body (3:6). "Pure religion" is here called ἀμίαντος. We notice as well that the call to conversion demands "cleansing" the hands and "purifying" the heart (4:8).

"God" are opposed as measures of valuation. We notice as well that meeting God's measure is done not just by control of speech (the subject of the context, 1:26) but, above all else, by "visiting orphans and widows in their affliction."[41] These actions show one to be unstained by the world's view of things. But as we can see everywhere in the Law and Prophets, effective care for orphans, widows, and sojourners is shorthand language for meeting covenantal obligations.[42] It is also a sign of conversion to the covenant after apostasy.[43]

These three uses of "world" confirm what we saw in James 4:4. In James, "the world" does not refer positively to God's creation. Nor is it used neutrally to mean the arena of human endeavor. Rather, it represents a measure of reality, or a system of meaning, which can be contrasted to that of God. Indeed, these passages virtually suggest that "the world" is a measure that does not take God's existence, and therefore his claims, into account. But this may be anticipating. We need now to look at the other key word, "friendship."

"Friendship" (φιλία)

What does James mean by this term? We shall not get far if we view friendship in contemporary terms, as a sort of affection, benevolence, or positive attitude toward another. In the Greek world, friendship was among the most discussed, analyzed, and highly esteemed relationships. Epicurus included it among the highest of goods available to humans.[44] The Pythagoreans founded a way of life on its basis.[45] For Plato, it was the ideal paradigm for the city-state.[46] Even the more pragmatic Aristotle considered friendship the prime metaphor and motive for society.[47]

---

41. The obvious salvific implications of ἐπισκέπτομαι ("to visit") as it is used in the Septuagint (cf. Gen. 21:1; Exod. 3:16; 4:31; and many more times) is picked up in the New Testament mainly by Luke-Acts (cf. Luke 1:68, 78; 7:16; Acts 7:23; 15:14).

42. Cf. Exod. 23:10-11; Lev. 19:9-10; 23:22; Deut. 14:28-29; 26:12-15; Amos 2:6-8; Hosea 12:7-9; Micah 3:1-3; Zeph. 1:9; 3:1-3; Mal. 3:5; Isa. 3:5, 14-15; 5:7-10; 30:12; 58:3; Jer. 5:25-29.

43. Cf. Zech. 7:8-10; Jer. 21:12; 22:3; Hosea 12:6; Isa. 33:15-16; 56:1-6; Jer. 7:5-7; Ezek. 18:7-9.

44. Among Epicurus's *Sovereign Maxims* is the following (number 27): "Of all the means which are given by wisdom to ensure happiness throughout the whole of life, by far the most important is the acquisition of friends." For other notes on friendship among the Epicureans, cf. Diogenes Laertius 10.10, 11, 120.

45. Cf. Diogenes Laertius 8.10; Iamblichus, *VP* 5.26-27, 18.81; Porphyry, *VP* 5.29, 6.30-32.

46. Plato, *Republic* 24A, 449C-D, 462A-C; cf. *Laws* 708D, 742E.

47. Aristotle, *Politics* 1287B, 1280B.

The word "friend" was not used lightly in these circles, nor was friendship considered simply a casual affection. On the contrary, it was regarded as a particularly intense and inclusive kind of intimacy, not only at the physical level but, above all, at the spiritual. Already in the *Orestes* friends are called "one soul" (μία ψυχή),[48] and Aristotle quotes this among other proverbial expressions of the sort by means of which the Greeks typically expressed their deepest perceptions.[49] To be "one soul" with another meant, at the least, to share the same attitudes and values and perceptions, to see things the same way. Indeed, the friend was, in another phrase frequently repeated, "another self."[50] Still another proverb had it that "friends hold all things in common." So seriously was this taken that communities of shared possessions were founded on that ideal.[51] The sharing of material possessions symbolized a sharing in spiritual values. Fellowship (κοινωνία) *was* friendship, because "friendship is equality."[52]

The ideal of friendship moved in the direction of equality, or even identity. And if James understands by "the world" a system of values distinct from God's, how would the phrase "friendship with the world" be heard by ears of that age? It would be heard not as a statement of positive regard for God's creation but, rather, as a statement of profound agreement with a measure opposed to God's. One would see things exactly the way "the world" does.[53]

48. Euripides, *Orestes* 1046.

49. Aristotle, *Nicomachean Ethics* 9.8.2, where he also quotes κοινὰ τὰ τῶν φίλων ("friends hold all things in common") and ἰσότης φιλότης ("friendship is equality"). For μία ψυχή, cf. also Plutarch, *Am. Mult.* 96F.

50. Aristotle, *Nicomachean Ethics* 9.4.5, 9.1, 9.10. Cf. Cicero, *De amicitia* 21.80; Plutarch, *Am. Mult.* 93E.

51. See L. T. Johnson, *Sharing Possessions: Mandate and Symbol of Faith* (OBT; Philadelphia: Fortress Press, 1981), 117-48.

52. Plato, *Laws* 757A, 744B; Aristotle, *Nicomachean Ethics* 8.5.5, 6.7, 8.5; Iamblichus, *VP* 29.162, 30.167; Plutarch, *Frat. Am.* 484B-C. For the role of "likeness" in friendship, cf. Plato, *Lysis* 214B; Cicero, *De amicitia* 14.50, 19.69; Plutarch, *Am. Mult.* 96D. For a general guide to the *topos,* see the references in G. Stählin, "φίλος, κτλ.," *TDNT* 9 (1974) 147-57; G. Bohnenblust, *Beiträge zum Topos περὶ φιλίας* (Berlin: Universitäts-buchdruckerei von Gustav Schade, 1905); and L. Dugas, *L'Amitié antique* (Paris: Felix Alcan, 1914).

53. That friendship involved such a sharing of values can be seen in Iamblichus, *VP* 17.75, 33.240; Cicero, *De amicitia* 4.15, 6.20; Plutarch, *Am. Mult.* 96F; Plato, *Laws* 693C, 694B, 697C. That both Luke and Paul use such friendship language in connection with the sharing of possessions has been noted often before; see L. T. Johnson, *The Literary Function of Possessions in Luke-Acts* (SBLDS 39; Missoula, Mont.: Scholars Press, 1977), 2-5, 32-36. Paul can also use the language effectively apart from considerations of monetary sharing: Phil. 2:1-2 stresses the sharing of outlook in spiritual fellowship.

Friend of God

This understanding is given further support by James's only other use of friendship language. James 2:23 states that Abraham was called "friend of God."[54] James says this was so because he "believed God" (Gen. 15:6) and because, when he was tested in the matter of sacrificing his son Isaac, he allowed faith to find its perfection in his faithful actions (2:22).[55] We should note exactly what is being said. Once more, the genitive is objective: Abraham shows himself to be "friend toward God." But why did faith make him so? For James, it is because Abraham accepted God's way of seeing the situation and acted on it. According to the measure of "the world," the sacrifice of his own beloved son would have been senseless, and doubly so since Isaac was a gift from God himself (Gen. 18:9-10; 21:1-2). If Abraham had seen things the way "the world" did — a measure of reality, we remember, which excludes God's claim — he would have rejected God's call to obedience. He would have striven "according to the flesh" to create a blessing for himself with this possibility of biological de-

---

54. The roots of James's expression here remain obscure and cannot be clarified satisfactorily in this paper. The following points are intended only as a guide. (1) The "friendship" language of the Septuagint is restrained. There are discussions of friendship in the wisdom writings (Cf., e.g., Sir. 6:1-17; 37:1-6), but without the distinctive Hellenistic coloration. In Wis. 1:16 we find people who are friends with death, and in Deut. 13:6 there is a warning against ὁ φίλος ὁ ἴσος τῆς ψυχῆς σου leading one astray into idolatry. (2) The possibility of friendship with God is found explicitly only in the Book of Wisdom: the gift of wisdom (7:7) enabled "friendship with God" (φιλία πρὸς θεόν, 7:14), and it is said that wisdom enters souls and makes "friends of God and prophets" (φίλους θεοῦ καὶ προφήτας, 7:27). (3) The only individual explicitly called a friend of God is Moses. God spoke to him face to face as if he had been speaking to his own friend, φίλον (Exod. 33:11) — translating the Hebrew r'hw. Abraham is not called "friend." In 2 Chr. 20:7 and Isa. 41:8, the Septuagint translates the Hebrew 'hb with forms of "to love" (ἀγαπάω). (4) The passage concerning Abraham that gave rise to calling him a friend of God seems, above all, to be Gen. 18:17: "Shall I hide from Abraham what I am about to do . . . ?" Philo rendered this: μὴ ἐπικαλύψω ἐγὼ ἀπὸ Ἀβραὰμ τοῦ φίλου μου, *Sobr.* 56. Note that friends share spiritual goods. (5) A full discussion of the usage in Jewish texts is found in M. Dibelius (*James*, 172-74). A more convenient listing of Philo's references to the patriarchs as friends can be found in Stählin, "φίλος," 158. (6) In contrast to the treatment of Dibelius, I am less concerned with the general understanding of the term in James's environment — a concern made critical, given his methodology — or with fitting it to a Pauline understanding of faith than I am with connecting it to James's own perceptions.

55. It is *faith* which is brought to completion: deeds (not works of the law) bring faith itself to expression (cf. 1:3-4). Faith co-works the works. The distinctive emphasis of James here should not be missed. For a fine treatment of Abraham in James, see R. Ward, "The Works of Abraham: James 2:14-26," *HTR* 61(1968) 283-90.

scent.[56] But he did not. He showed himself friend toward God. His faith made him act according to a measure that made the world not a closed system of meaning, but a system open to the meaning given by God's word.

Conclusions

By studying James 4:4 in the light of his other language about the world and friendship, therefore, we can reach the following conclusions:

1. The world can be regarded as a system of meaning and values which excludes God from consideration and is hostile to God's claim.

2. Friendship with the world means accepting that system as one's own, identifying oneself with it, measuring oneself by that measure.

3. Doing so makes one an enemy toward God. Indeed, simply *willing* to be friend to this closed system establishes one in a state of enmity, which means, of course, alienation and estrangement.[57]

4. This "friendship" language, therefore, makes a statement about human freedom, values, and ways of acting. One can choose the system of values by which one will live. One can lead one's life as though God had no claim on it — be a friend to the world — or one can acknowledge that claim in faith and action as did Abraham and be a friend toward God.

The question immediately arises: Am I over-reading this small verse? Is there evidence elsewhere in James that this interpretation accurately represents his view? Yes, it is everywhere.

Living by Opposing Measures

Living According to the Measure of the World

1. We find this in the immediate context of James 4:4. James is attacking actions that flow from envy: social unrest, divisiveness, hostility, murder. Why does envy lead to such behavior? The ancients defined envy as a kind of sorrow that is experienced simply because another has some-

---

56. I am aware of the Pauline tone of this characterization (Cf. Rom. 4:1-2). James would have referred to an "earthly wisdom" (3:15). I am suggesting, of course, that at a deep level Paul and James see the choice before humans in a remarkably similar fashion.

57. Cf. the use of ἐχθρός ("enemy") in Rom. 5:10 and 11:28; Gal. 4:16; Col. 1:21; and ἔχθρα in Eph. 2:14-16. Cf. also LSJ, s.v., ἐχθρός, III.

thing.[58] If I see the world as a closed system, if I forget that everything comes as a gift from God (1:17), then I identify what I have with who I am. And I can be more only if I have more. If another has more, then the other is a threat to me, makes me less. Envy, then, moves inexorably toward hostility and murder: I can be more only if I eliminate the other. Among the pious, this logic might work itself out in manipulating God in prayer, so that I can gain something and "spend it on my drives" (4:3). If the world is a closed system (one unmeasured by the transcendence of God), then self-aggrandizement has a certain implacable logic.[59]

2. In James 3:6-8 we hear of the vicious use of speech — the tongue as instrument of destruction. James points out the conflict between perspectives: we curse people with the same tongue with which we praise God. But the one we curse is made in God's image (3:9).

3. James 4:13-16 gives us another sharp vignette: this time, of people carrying out grand business projects as though the future were secured by the plans they make, as though the world were a closed and utterly predictable system. They forget their own utter contingency — they are like mist that passes away (4:14). They forget that only God's will determines all futures (4:15). They act as though God had no power over or claim on the world. They boast in their arrogance (4:16).

4. In 2:1-7 we find Christians discriminating between wealthy and poor in their assemblies — showing themselves to be corrupt judges by allowing themselves to be bribed by the powerful impression made by the wealthy.[60] They forget that God has chosen the poor for the kingdom (2:5), that the rich will pass away like the flower of the field (1:10), and that God will judge those who judge by the standard they have used (2:12-13).

5. In 5:1-6 wealthy landowners defraud workers of their wages and ignore their cries of suffering. They trust in their storehouses of gold and silver (5:3). They kill innocent people (5:6). They forget that the Lord is judge and that judgment is certain (5:7-8). So do people act who live according to the measure of the world, who are "friends of the world."[61] And

---

58. Aristotle, *Rhetoric* 1387B.

59. I have developed this line of thought in *Sharing Possessions*, 80-88.

60. For the setting here, cf. R. Ward, "Partiality in the Assembly," *HTR* 62 (1969) 87-97.

61. James puts a definite and sardonic twist on the "friendship" language. The Hellenistic *topos* constantly asserts that true friendship is possible only between the virtuous and is incompatible with envy. Here, "friendship with the world" is illustrated precisely by envy. Cf., e.g., Iamblichus, *VP* 17.75, 22.101-2, 31.198; Plato, *Lysis* 214D; Cicero, *De amicitia* 5.18, 7.23-24, 18.65, 22.83; Plutarch, *Frat. Am.* 484B, 485B; Aristotle, *Nicomachean Ethics* 8.12.6, 9.3.2, 12.3; Plato, *Laws* 837A-B; Pseudo-Phocylides, *Sentences* 71-75.

because they ignore God's claim, they establish themselves thereby as his enemies.

God's Measure

We are able to see the measure of the world as inadequate precisely because we have been given another measure by which to view it. For James, this measure is a gift which is given humans by God. The ultimate dependence of all on God is fundamental for James: "Every good endowment and every perfect gift is from above" (1:17). And James 1:18 adds, "Of his own will he brought us forth by the word of truth that we should be a kind of first fruits of his creatures." James is speaking not only of "creation" here but of the re-creation of humans by that faithful utterance which is God's Word, most specifically, the Gospel (as in Col. 1:5, Eph. 1:13).[62] This makes those who receive it a sign and promise of what all "creatures" can be.

In 1:21 we find this: "Receive with meekness the implanted word, which is able to save your souls." What is symbolized by the "implanted word" here is exactly what is signaled by the "wisdom from above" in 3:17, the "spirit God made to dwell in us" in 4:5, and "grace" in 4:6.[63] God has made available to humans another way of viewing and measuring reality: not as a closed system but as an open one. God's word has given us birth, has been implanted in us; we can receive it, and we can become "doers of the word" (1:22). What this means specifically is living out the demands of the law of the kingdom, "Love your neighbor as yourself" (2:8), as this is explicated by the words of Scripture and as understood in the light of Jesus the Messiah.[64]

---

62. 1:18 is undeniably difficult. Despite the dissenting voice of L. E. Elliott-Binns ("James 1:18: Creation or Redemption?" *NTS* 3 [1957] 148-61), I think the views of Ropes (*James,* 166), Dibelius (*James,* 105), and Mayor (*Epistle of St. James,* 63), to be correct. It should be noted, though, that it is still a measure from God in either case — the world is to be regarded as answerable to God. In this light, see how James calls the envious attitude one which "boasts and is false to the truth" (3:14, cf. also 4:16).

63. More work is still required on the sort of psychology presupposed by the language of James. As in the Rabbinic talk of the *yetzerim* or the loose characterizations of the spirits (πνεύματα) in the *Testaments of the Twelve Patriarchs,* there do not seem to be hard and fast distinctions drawn between "created" and "un-created" factors. For James, all comes from God, both the gift and the possibility of receiving it (cf. 1:21). The connection between spirit and wisdom in James 3:13 and 4:5 seems clear enough. See J. A. Kirk, "The Meaning of Wisdom in James: Examination of a Hypothesis," *NTS* 16 (1969) 24-38.

64. This positive side of James's teaching is developed in Johnson, "Use of Leviticus 19," 132-33.

But a "law of God's kingdom" which is a law of love — therefore, of self-disposing concern — makes sense only if the world is not closed in on itself, only if we dwell in a fundamentally open system (one in which God is judge), not a closed one which destroys those who give it their friendship.

The Double-Minded

It is, finally, in this connection that we meet the one James is specifically addressing with this call to conversion, the "double-minded" person (δίψυχος).[65] What makes someone double-minded is precisely the desire to live by both measures at once, to be friends with everyone. In James 1:8 we meet him as the man who wants to pray, but he does so without really being convinced that this is an open system. He doubts and therefore never breaks out of his idolatrous circle. And in this call to conversion, we read, "Cleanse your hands, you sinners, and purify your hearts, you men of double mind" (4:8). Purity of heart, of course, is simplicity: not that of compulsion but that of choice. For James, one must choose one's friends; one cannot have it both ways. Even to "wish" to live by the world's standard is already to live by its measure.

This whole call to conversion in James 3:13–4:10, then, reminds those Christians who would like to hedge their bets that the process of turning from one measure to another is never over, that it must continually be renewed. Although that word which shapes their Christian identity has been "implanted" in them, they must still "accept it with meekness," they must continually become "doers" of it; therefore, even for those already converted, the prophetic call to conversion is appropriate.[66] So soon as they even wish to compete enviously with one another (3:14–4:2); so often as they rely on a merely formal profession of God's existence (2:14-19)

---

65. For the term, see O. J. F. Seitz, "Antecedents and Significance of the Term 'Dipsychos,'" *JBL* 66 (1947) 211-19; idem, "Afterthoughts on the Term 'Dipsychos,'" *NTS* 4 (1957) 327-34; and W. Wolverton, "The Double-minded Man in the light of Essene Psychology," *ATR* 38 (1956) 166-75.

66. Is it by accident that 3:13 — "By his good life let him show his works in the meekness of wisdom" — is the last appearance of ἔργον in James? Up to this point, he has used it some fourteen times. The point is always the contrast between verbal or ideal assent to truth and the living out of it. This is a contrast typical of Hellenistic moralists. Among countless examples, cf. Lucian of Samosata, *Hermotimus* 79; *Timon* 54; *Runaways* 19; Epictetus, *Dissertations* 2.1.31, 2.9.21, 3.22.9; Julian the Apostate, *Oration* 7:225a; Dio Chrysostom, *Oration* 35.2, 3, 11.

without translating that into effective care for others and obedience as did Abraham (2:20-26); so much as they would wish to manipulate the divine power in prayer (4:3), not praying in the simplicity of faith as did Elijah, who also was only a man (5:15-18); so frequently as they would wheel and deal and cheat and hold violent grudges against each other (4:13-5:9), rather than wait patiently for the judgment of the Lord, as did the patient Job (5:10-11); then they are not really "doers" of God's word (1:22) but double-minded, and must be called back, as James now calls them, to that other measure, knowing that for those who do submit themselves to the measure of God's power even greater gifts will be given, and they will be raised up (4:6, 10; cf. 5:15).

Conclusion

This short analysis cannot pretend to exhaust the meaning of discipleship, or of Christian existence, in the Letter of James. I hope that it has shown something of the distinctive way James employs the language and perceptions of Hellenistic culture and of the Scripture and of faith in the Lord Jesus Christ, as well as the way theological warrants like that in James 4:4 function within his work as a whole. Most of all, by trying to respect the way in which James gives expression to his Christian witness, I hope I have shown he deserves such respect.

Gender in the Letter of James:
A Surprising Witness

The testimony of the Letter of James on the question of gender can be heard only by attending carefully to the voice of the composition itself. This may seem an obvious procedure, but it is one that has seldom been employed when studying thematic elements in this small writing. More often, theories about the putative author and his supposed place in the development of early Christian history have substituted for close analysis of the text itself. Thus, James has largely been read from the perspective of a "Jewish Christianity" that, connected to James of Jerusalem, is more or less antagonistic to Paul,[1] or a late "Paulinist" Christianity that seeks to rescue Paul from the hands of libertines who distort his teaching on righteousness by faith rather than works of law.[2] In either case, what is considered to be of interest in the composition amounts to a handful of verses that can be compared to Paul, and most of what is truly fascinating about the composition eludes comment.

A way out of such unhappy and uncreative reductions may be afforded by three quick (but well-supported) adjustments. The first is to sever the composition from the diverse hagiographical traditions concerning the Brother of Jesus in early Christianity, recognizing that even if that James is the author (as well he might be), we are unable to argue from his portrait to the meaning of his composition.[3] The second is to allow

1. The classic example is M. Hengel, "Der Jakobusbrief als antipaulinische Polemik," in *Tradition and Interpretation in the New Testament*, ed. G. F. Hawthorne and O. Betz (Grand Rapids: Eerdmans, 1987), 248-278.

2. See, for example, J. Jeremias, "Paul and James," *ExpTim* 66 (1955) 368-371; J. C. Lodge, "James and Paul at Cross-Purposes? James 2:22," *Bib* 62 (1981) 195-213.

3. The recent *James the Just and Christian Origins*, ed. B. Chilton and C. A. Evans (Leiden: Brill, 1999), continues to focus on the James of Josephus/Eusebius. A more complex ap-

the composition to locate itself in early Christianity. When we do this we discover that the Jewishness of the writing is pretty much the same as with most other writings in the NT canon — that is, it interprets reality within the symbolic world of Torah in the light of Jesus — and that internal evidence suggests that James may well be among our earliest Christian compositions.[4] Third, we allow the composition's own preoccupation provide the frame for our inquiry, recognizing that the question we put to the text may not be the one it is itself seeking to answer. In the present case, this means recognizing that James's concern is to sharply distinguish the moral patterns of "friendship with God" and those of "friendship with the world," and in particular to summon those he designates as "double-minded" to the realization that they cannot be friends with everyone but must make their practice conform to their profession.[5]

I approach James, then, with the two (not ungrounded) premises that it is the voice of the composition rather than that of its putative author that we seek, and that the voice is one from the first generation of the Christian movement that, in the broadest sense, speaks wisdom.[6] The validity of these premises is best tested by the quality of the reading of James they enable. I propose to read James for gender through three approaches, looking first at explicitly gendered language and roles, second at sexual imagery, and finally at the implications of James's contents in comparison to other wisdom writings. The convergence of these lines of evidence will support an overall characterization of James's testimony on gender.

---

proach to the "historical" James is required, starting with the recognition that the several sources each have interests in James as a hero that shape their respective accounts; see L. T. Johnson, *The Letter of James* (Anchor Bible 37A; Garden City: Doubleday, 1995), 94-106.

4. There are six basic reasons why James should be dated in the first generation: 1) it lacks *any* of the classic signs of development in doctrine or institution or delay of parousia; 2) it reflects the social realities and outlook of a counter-cultural sect in the early stages of its existence; 3) it uses sayings of Jesus in a stage closer to that of Q than to the Synoptic redaction; 4) it resembles our earliest datable writer, Paul, across a wide range of points; 5) it has many incidental details suggesting a Palestinian provenance; 6) it is almost certainly used by Clement of Rome; see Johnson, *Letter of James*, pp. 118-121.

5. See my essay "Friendship with the World and Friendship with God: A Study of Discipleship in James," pp. 202-220 in this volume.

6. Among many others, see B. R. Halston, "The Epistle of James: Christian Wisdom?" *SE* 4 (1968) 308-314; E. Baasland, "Der Jakobusbrief als neutestamentliche Weisheitsschrift," *ST* 36 (1982) 119-139; R. Wall, *The Community of the Wise: The Letter of James* (Valley Forge, PA: Trinity Press International, 1997).

Explicitly Gendered Language and Roles

At first glance, James shares the casual androcentrism typical of his time and of the symbolic world of Torah. He never uses the noun "woman" *(gynē)*. God is designated as *patēr* ["father"] (1:17, 27; 3:9), and Abraham as "our father" (*ho patēr hēmōn*, 2:21). Consistent with the use of fictive kinship language common among early Christians,[7] James addresses his readers with the vocative *adelphoi mou* ["my brothers," 1:2; 2:1, 14; 3:1, 10, 12; 4:11; 5:7, 9, 10, 12, 19] and *adelphoi mou agapētoi* ["my beloved brothers," 1:16, 19; 2:5]. Should such vocatives be taken as including women members of the community? The evidence is mixed. In 1:9, James refers to "the lowly brother" [*ho adelphos ho tapeinos*] but this is matched by 2:15, which speaks of "a brother or sister" [*adelphos ē adelphē*] going naked and hungry. These instances would suggest that James's language is androcentric but not in principle exclusive.

Against this, however, is the letter's frequent use of *anēr* in several of its aphorisms, a word impossible to take with reference to both genders (1:8, 12, 20, 23; 2:2; 3:2). Four of these occur in the first chapter, which is aphoristic in character. Perhaps James's language is influenced here (as in other ways) by the Septuagint, especially in the wisdom literature, in which *anēr* stands without apology as the subject of instruction.[8] The usage in 3:2 is equally sapiential. In 2:2, the use of *anēr* may be owed to the fact that James speaks of a specific male rather than people in general. But this is all quibbling, really. Basically, James's language is androcentric, and there's an end to it. We could scarcely expect otherwise.

James presents to his readers three male figures from Torah as moral exemplars. Abraham exemplifies the obedience of faith spelled out in works (2:21-23), Job personifies the patient endurance of faith (5:11), and Elijah represents the powerful prayer of faith (5:17).[9] James includes Rahab together with Abraham as an example of how faith is expressed in works: her hospitality to the scouts of Israel embodied her faith in the one God (2:25-26).[10] The designations James uses for the male heros indicate their

7. W. A. Meeks, *The First Urban Christians: The Social World of the Apostle Paul* (New Haven: Yale University Press, 1983), 87, 225.

8. *Anēr* is used some 144 times in Proverbs, 12 times in Ecclesiastes, and 85 times in Sirach. For the influence of the Septuagint on James, see Johnson, *Letter of James,* pp. 7-8.

9. For the way in which these examples function literarily in the composition, see my essay "The Mirror of Remembrance: James 1:22-25," pp. 168-181 in this volume.

10. When Rahab meets the scouts, she recounts what she has heard about the Lord's deeds, and confesses, "For the Lord your God is he who is God in heaven above and on

place of honor within the tradition of Torah. Abraham is "our father" (2:21) and "friend of God" (2:23). Job is connected to "the prophets who spoke in the name of the Lord" (5:10). Elijah, although "a person like us in nature" [*anthrōpos homoiopathēs hēmin*], is "a righteous man" [*dikaios*, 5:16]. In contrast, Rahab is identified solely as "the harlot" [*hē pornē*], a designation that is not exceptional within the midrashic tradition,[11] but is nevertheless hardly honorific. It has been argued with some justice that the combination of Abraham and Rahab, together with the otherwise odd use of the plural "deeds" *(erga)* in 2:22, might point toward midrashic traditions concerning the hospitality of these ancient characters.[12] In that case, Rahab's generosity corresponds to the "sister in need" just as Abraham's corresponds to the "brother in need" (2:15). There is an inclusiveness of sorts here, even if Rahab is given neither the attention nor the explicit honor paid to the male exemplars.[13]

Perhaps a more interesting and fruitful way to pursue the question of explicitly gendered language and roles is to turn from designations to characterization. Here we find something unexpected. The males who dominate the action within the composition do not necessarily act according to gender stereotypes.[14] Some males are indeed boastful (3:14; 4:16), are envious, competitive and cause social unrest (3:14-16), are among

---

earth beneath" (Josh 2:11). Her action of saving the scouts expresses this conviction. Her faith is also singled out for praise by Heb 11:31, and the examples of Abraham and Rahab are combined once more in *1 Clement* 10 and 12.

11. For the celebration of Rahab as a proselyte and as an example of hospitality, see *b.Meg.* 14b-15a; *Mekilta on Exodus* par. Jith. Amal. 18:1; *Exodus Rabbah* 27:4; *Numbers Rabbah* 3:2; 8:9; 16:1; *Deuteronomy Rabbah* 2:26-27; *Ruth Rabbah* 2:1; *Song of Songs Rabbah* I,3,3; I,15,2; IV,1,2; VI,2,3; *Ecclesiastes Rabbah* V,6,1; V,11,1; VIII,10,1; Josephus, *Antiquities* 5:5-30.

12. R. B. Ward, "The Works of Abraham: James 2:14-26," *HTR* 61 (1968) 283-290.

13. The figure of Rahab is the only aspect of gender in James touched on by S. Dowd, "James," in *The Women's Bible Commentary*, ed. C. A. Newsom and S. H. Ringe (Louisville: Westminster/John Knox Press, 1992), 368-369.

14. For a guide to such "gender stereotypes" in Hellenistic culture, see Xenophon, *Oecumenicus*, which praises women who are docile (VII, 10), discreet (VII, 14), work indoors (VII, 22), are trustworthy (VII, 41), fearful (VII, 25), temperate (IX, 10), loyal (IX, 12), affectionate (VII, 24). They are fitted to indoor work because they lack the physical strength of men (VII, 23); when they have a capacity to command, they are called "manly-minded" (X, 1). In contrast, men are outdoor types because of their naturally greater strength (VII, 23); they also have courage (VII, 26), ambition (XIV, 10), leadership qualities (XXI, 7-8). It is appropriate for them to train intensively for war (XI, 12 and 17), exercise rule (XIII, 10), and be able both to accuse and defend others in open forum (XI, 22). At least Xenophon pays attention to women. For an extreme androcentrism, see the discussion of "Greatness of Soul" in Aristotle, *Nicomachean Ethics* 1123B-1125B.

the rich oppressors (2:6-7; 5:1-6), are heedless in pursuit of financial gain (4:13-14), slander and curse their neighbors (3:9; 4:11), engage in war and murder (4:1-2). What unites all these behaviors is that they show such people to be "friends of the world and enemies of God" (James 4:4). Other males within the composition exhibit qualities not stereotypically associated with masculinity. These are the ones James considers "enemies of the world and friends of God." Thus Abraham's faith in God is demonstrated by his willingness to give up what was most precious to him rather than to seize or secure it (2:21). Thus Job is praised not because of his conquest of suffering but for his endurance of it with patience (5:11). Thus Elijah is characterized as one who turns to the power of God in prayer rather than as one who is self-reliant and self-sufficient (5:17). The only mention of Jesus outside the greeting (1:1) associates him with the (scarcely dominant) attitude of faith (*pistis*, 2:1).

Notice further that the poor man who is rebuffed by the community is declared the recipient of God's promise (2:5), just as God stands at the side of the righteous man to resist the arrogant oppressor (5:6),[15] just as God gifts with a harvest the farmer who waits patiently for the rain (5:7), and rewards with the crown of life the one who endures testing (1:12). These males who are "friends of God" are depicted in terms that are more often stereotypically female: they are faithful, they defer, they endure, they pray, they wait, they sacrifice what they have been given.

James has little to say about leaders in the community, but what he does say follows the same pattern. He designates himself in 1:1 as a *doulos*, and while in some contexts self-description as a slave can bear overtones of authority,[16] it is not an obviously self-aggrandizing title. James mentions teachers in 3:1, but only by way of warning: teachers do not dominate others but rather fall under a harder judgment; they should therefore exemplify that "wisdom from above" that is characterized by lowliness, meekness, reasonableness, and every sort of peace-seeking (3:13-17). Finally, James speaks of the elders in 5:14, not with reference to their administration of the community or their command over others, but strictly in terms of their service. They are at the call of the sick, responding when they are summoned by the weakest and most marginal in any community

---

15. This interpretation depends on reading *ouk antitassetai hymin* in 5:6 as a question, with *theos* as the implied subject, therefore rhetorically echoing the statement in 4:6, *ho theos hyperēphanois antitassetai*; see L. A. Schökel, "James 5,2 [sic] and 4,6," *Bib* 54 (1973) 73-76, and Johnson, *Letter of James*, p. 305.

16. See D. B. Martin, *Slavery as Salvation: The Metaphor of Slavery in Pauline Christianity* (New Haven: Yale University Press, 1990), 50-61.

to anoint their bodies with oil and pray over them and engage in mutual confession of sins (5:14-16). In sum, James presents a remarkable portrait of male leadership within the community, a portrait that shares with his depiction of males who are "friends with God" qualities not of arrogance and control but attitudes of meekness and service. This first approach to the composition leads to the conclusion that although James's language and focus are androcentric, his value system is one in which traits stereotypically associated with male patterns of aggressiveness and dominance are evil, while traits associated with stereotypical female patterns of passivity, patience, and self-donation are good, even when expressed by males.

Sexual Imagery

James uses explicit sexual imagery in two passages, with the interpretation of each uncertain and disputed. The first occurs after the macarism of 1:12 that assures those who endure testing that they will receive the promised crown of life:

> 13. Let no one when tested say, "I am being tempted by God." For God is not tempted by evils. Nor does he himself tempt anyone. 14. Instead, each person, by being drawn away and lured, is tempted by his own desire [*epithymia*]. 15. Then the desire [*epithymia*], once it has conceived [*syllabousa*], brings forth sin [*tiktei hamartian*]. And when sin is brought to term [*hē de hamartia apotelestheisa*], it gives birth to death [*apokyei thanaton*].

The use of female sexual imagery is obvious and powerful and negative, leading in a rhetorical climax from conception to full term of pregnancy to a birth that is, in shocking reversal, a death. Two cultural conventions support the imagery. The first is the feminine gender of the noun *epithymia,* which enables a female personification according to the conventions of the Wisdom tradition, in which the wise man is seduced by the "foreign woman."[17] The second is the strong connotations that attach themselves to the noun *epithymia* in Hellenistic moral discourse: although it can be used for any sort of "desire," whether positive or nega-

---

17. Above all, Proverbs 2:16-22; 5:15-23, and especially 7:5-27. See C. A. Newsom, "Wisdom and the Discourse of Patriarchal Wisdom: A Study of Proverbs 1-9," in *Gender and Difference in Ancient Israel,* ed. P. L. Day (Philadelphia: Fortress Press, 1989), 142-160.

tive, more frequently it is used negatively, and with a specifically sexual dimension.[18]

What should we make of this female personification? J. L. P. Wolmarans argues that it has direct gender implications.[19] Using passages in Philo and Paul that he says subordinate the lower (female) passions to the higher (male) reason, Wolmarans thinks that James has in mind the same sort of subordination of the sensual and unreliable feminine to the reasonable and steady masculine.[20] He says that desire is here cast in feminine terms as a deliberate contrast to (masculine) reason in 1:18.[21] He combines this text with James 4:4 (the second to use sexual imagery):

> You adulteresses [*moichalides*]![22] Do you not know that friendship with the world is enmity with God? Therefore, whoever chooses to be a friend of the world is established as an enemy of God.

Wolmarans thinks that characterizing sinners as female sexual offenders is consistent with the sexual personification of desire and sin in 1:15.[23] Assuming that James is a second-century composition, Wolmarans moves directly to the conclusion that such language functions in support of a developing patriarchal church and the suppression of women.[24]

I must delay until the next section the main reason why Wolmarans's overall conclusions about James are wrong. But his reading of the sexual imagery itself is faulty on several counts. First, his use of Philo and Paul is inadequate.[25] Second, even if he were correct in his estimation of James's

---

18. For extensive documentation, see Johnson, *Letter of James*, pp. 193-194.

19. Wolmarans, "Male and Female Sexual Imagery: James 1:14-15, 18," *Acta Patristica et Byzantina* 5 (1994) 134-141.

20. Wolmarans, p. 136.

21. Wolmarans, pp. 137-138.

22. Some MSS (the second hand of Sinaiticus, P, the Koine tradition) add *moichoi kai* to the beginning of the line, making "you adulterers and adulteresses!" While we might applaud the even-mindedness of this reading, it is probably an addition (lacking, e.g., in the original hand of Sinaiticus, Vaticanus, the Old Latin and the Peshitta, as well as other Greek witnesses), based on a literal rather than a metaphorical understanding of the passage.

23. Wolmarans, p. 139.

24. Wolmarans, pp. 139-141.

25. It is difficult to know what to make of Wolmarans's careless citation of texts. He cites Rom 7:5 to support his statement that "Paul speaks of sinful desires that bear fruit for death" (p. 136), but Paul there speaks of *pathēmata* rather than *epithymiai*, and nothing in the language of Romans 7 connects to Wolmarans's theme of the "immoral woman." For that matter, neither do his citations from Philo. He cites *On the Creation of the World* 152, but it

language, he would not be justified in moving directly from sexual characterization to social roles: the relation between cultural scripts — even clear ones — and real life is never so simple. Third, his appreciation for the language itself is too literal and limited.

The image of conception and birth in 1:15 is a powerful one, but it is, after all, one of many such metaphors in this remarkably compressed composition. Already before this verse, James has compared doubting people to waves of the sea driven and tossed by the wind (1:6), and the rich person to a flower of the field that withers and falls (1:11); later, James will speak of the tongue as a consuming fire and as a "world of wickedness" in the body (3:5-6). Some of his metaphors derive from Torah,[26] some from the commonplaces of Hellenistic rhetoric,[27] some may be his own crafting. But they are metaphors that resist literalization. Wolmarans succeeds in clumsily literalizing the metaphor when he argues that James is trying to reject "illicit" sexual relations (presumably initiated by females) and accept "licit" sexual relations (initiated by males) and thereby reinforces patriarchal values.

The use of female language for desire is also metaphorical, shaped, as I have suggested, by the grammatical gender of *epithymia*, its sexual associations in rhetoric, and the sapiential tradition of the seductive woman. Note that in his only other use of a cognate term, James speaks of desire in terms of a coveting *(epithymein)* after possessions which, failing to secure its desire, turns to war and murder (4:2). Once more, desire leads to death, but in this case with no literal sexual connotations at all.

Even more strikingly, in 1:18, James uses the same verb for "giving birth" *(apokyein)* with reference to God (named as "father," *patēr* in 1:17):

---

should be 151; he cites *On the Cherubim* 54ff in support of his interpretation that Philo considers man's sensory perception to act as an immoral woman that victimizes male reason. The pertinent passage is actually 57, which contains a striking parallel to the image used by James, but in no manner is it connected to a sexually "immoral woman." Philo's treatment of Eve in these passages is both more complex and (from our contemporary perspective) sadder than Wolmarans's perceives.

26. The metaphor of a rich person as a flower of the field echoes Isaiah 40:6-7, that of wealth being eaten by moths, Isaiah 51:8.

27. James's use of the metaphor of the bridle as a means of controlling the tongue (1:26; 3:3) is well-attested in Greek moral discourse for controlling the passions (see Plato, *Phaedrus* 246B-247C) or speech (Philo, *On Dreams* 2:165). Similarly, the metaphor of the tongue as a rudder (3:4) is found with reference to the control of moral behavior (Dio Chrysostom, *Oration* 12:34; Lucian, *Double Indictment* 2; Philo, *On the Cherubim* 36).

By his decision [*boulētheis*] he gave us birth [*apekyēsen*] through a word of truth, in order that we might be a kind of firstfruits of his creatures.

That a female image of maternity is attributed to a grammatically male *theos* shows just how provocative and paradoxical James can be in his use of metaphorical language. It reminds us as well of the dangers of literalizing. No more than "the father of lights" in 1:17 should be taken with reference to the physical appearance or limitation of *theos*, should his "giving birth" be taken as an indication of God's gender. Similarly, the female grammatical gender of *sophia* and the strong feminine associations with the personified figure of *sophia* in the Wisdom tradition should not lead us to conclude that James is making a point about God's gender (James 1:5; 3:13-17). The importance of finding James using birth language in both in 1:15 and in 1:18 is that we thereby gain some clue to his real point.

The first chapter of James — indeed the entire composition — is structured by the polar opposition between the way of life measured respectively by the world, and by God.[28] The contrast between 1:15 and 1:18 is not between modes of sexual activity, but what is "given birth" respectively by these measures. God is neither tempted by evils nor does God tempt others (1:13); instead, God is the source of every good and perfect gift (1:17). God's birthing through the word of truth — whether James means here the word of creation, torah, or the gospel[29] — brings forth humans who can represent (as "first-fruits") all God's creatures (1:18). In contrast, those who live apart from God's measure are seduced and lured by "their own desires" (the *idias epithymias* in v. 14 is emphatic) rather than by the "will of God" (1:18). These desires issue in the dreadful murder of other creatures through word and through deed. For James, it is a matter of which source of reality one recognizes, by which measure one lives. It is a matter of friendship, or in the terms of Torah, of covenantal loyalty.

It is for this reason that James uses the female *moichalides* ("you adulteresses") in 4:4 in his charge against those choosing to live by the "wisdom from below" rather than the "wisdom from above" (3:13-17). It is not, as Wolmarans says, that "he exhibits suspicion of the female; women are dangerous." The language has nothing to do with actual women, for clearly it is men who are doing the violence in 4:1-3. Rather, James is using

---

28. For James's use of polar oppositions throughout the composition, see T. C. Cargal, *Restoring the Diaspora* (SBLDS 144; Atlanta: Scholars Press, 1993); for the oppositions in James 1, see Johnson, *Letter of James*, pp. 174-176.

29. For discussion, see Johnson, *Letter of James*, pp. 197-198, 205.

the conventional language of the prophets to express infidelity to the covenant. If the Lord is bound by covenant to Israel as a husband is to a wife, then Israel's infidelity to the covenant is appropriately imaged as adultery.[30] And so here.

The first two ways of questioning the composition have had equivocal results. James's gender language is androcentric as is his choice of moral exemplars. The use of Rahab and of the "sister in need" breaks the pattern, but not decisively. We have seen, however, that James's perspective on gender roles is not stereotypically patriarchal. While his bad males are active and aggressive and boastful, his good males exhibit the traits of acceptance, gentleness, patience, self-sacrifice, and service. And while his use of sexual imagery may at first be seen as sexist, a closer examination of his metaphors shows that he is far from such an attitude. Indeed, his language about God giving birth and his association of *sophia* with God suggest that his sense of gender is both fair and flexible. These ambiguous conclusions prepare for the last and perhaps most helpful way of approaching James on the issue of gender.

The Egalitarian Perspective of James

A third way of inquiring into James's testimony on gender is to examine the overall voice of the composition in comparison to other writings in the wisdom tradition. Such a comparison is justified both by the sapiential character of the composition and by its explicit thematic attention to *sophia* (1:5; 3:13-17).[31] Noticing the absence in James of elements that are standard — even dominant — in other wisdom literature helps us locate its distinctive outlook. It is not surprising, for example, that James should use kinship language, for it is found everywhere in wisdom literature. But what does give pause is that James lacks any *generational* kinship language such as is found even in the Letters of Paul. In James, we find nothing of the transferred sense of "father/son" relations that dominate the genre from the *Instruction of Vizier Ptah-Hotep* to the *Testaments of the*

---

30. See, e.g., Isa 54:4-8; 57:3; LXX Ps 72:27; Jer 3:6-10; 13:27; Hos 3:1; 9:1; Ezek 16:38; 23:45.

31. Some of the basis for such a comparative approach is given by J. G. Gammie, "Paraenetic Literature: Toward the Morphology of a Secondary Genre," *Semeia* 50 (1990) 41-77, and L. G. Perdue, "The Social Character of Paraenesis and Paraenetic Literature," *Semeia* 50 (1990) 14-27, and some of the evidence given here appears also in my essay "The Social World of James: Literary Analysis and Historical Reconstruction," pp. 101-122 in this volume.

Twelve Patriarchs.[32] James does not claim to be the "father" of his readers in the way that Paul sometimes does (1 Cor 4:14-17; Gal 4:19; 1 Thess 2:11); he is simply the *doulos* of the God who is alone "father" of all creatures (1:17-18, 27). The absence of this register of language is of first importance, for when exhortation is framed as from "father to son," the very structure of the communication tends to privilege males over females.

Even more unusual, James has none of the conventional concern for generations even within the natural household. In fact, the *oikos* as a social institution does not come within the range of James's concern, which is entirely dedicated to the intentional community he calls the *ekklēsia* (5:14). As a consequence, James entirely lacks the attention given to marriage in virtually all wisdom literature, attention which serves to locate women within the household and in subordination to males.[33] Indeed, in contrast to most wisdom literature, which exhorts the individual to virtue,[34] James's concern is addressed to the community as such. Individual cases are cited only for illustration. Equally unusual, this composition is entirely devoted to moral behavior, and pays no attention to manners at all.[35]

The largest part of James's moral concern is with the use of possessions and the use of speech; both topics are well-represented in the wisdom genre. James is distinctive, however, in giving no attention at all — apart from citing the commandment, "do not commit adultery" (2:11) — to sexual behavior.[36] James does not take up the subject of the care or dis-

32. Note how Pseudo-Isocrates, *Demonicus* plays on the convention that advice is communicated from "father to son" (1-3, 9-10).

33. For discussions of marriage, see *Sentences of Syriac Menander* 45-51, 118-122; *Instruction of Prince Hor-Dedef*; Sir 7:25-26; 26:1-9, 13-18; 40:19; Prov 5:15-20; 31:10-31; *Instruction of Vizier Ptah-Hotep* 320-340; *Counsels of Wisdom* (Obverse 23); *Sentences of Pseudo-Phocylides* 3, 179-197, 201-206; *Sentences of Sextus* 235-239; *Instruction of Ani* 3,1; 8,4; 9,1; 1 Cor 7:1-24; Col 3:18-25; Eph 5:21-6:4; 1 Thess 4:4-5; 1 Tim 2:9-15; Tit 2:3-5; Heb 13:4; 1 Pet 3:1-7.

34. In the Bible, see Proverbs, Sirach, Qoheleth. In other literature, see *Instruction of the Vizier Ptah-Hotep* (ANET 412-414); *Instruction for King Meri-Ka-Re* (ANET 414-418); *Instruction of Amen-Em-Opet* (ANET 421-424); *Counsels of Wisdom* (ANET 426-427); *Words of Ahiqar* (ANET 427-430); *Sentences of Pseudo-Phocylides*; *To Demonicus*; *Sentences of Sextus*; *Sentences of Syriac Menander*. A partial exception is *The Testaments of the Twelve Patriarchs*.

35. Contrast Prov 23:1-9; Sir 4:27-31; 7:14; 9:18; 31:12-20; 32:1-9; *Words of Ahiqar* X, 142ff.; *Counsels of Wisdom* 20; *Sentences of Syriac Menander* 11-14, 57-62, 99-101, 148-153, 181-184; *To Demonicus* 15, 20, 27, 41; *Sentences of Sextus* 149, 157, 164, 252, 265; *Sentences of Pseudo-Phocylides* 81-82, 98, 123, 147-148, 156-158, 211-212; *Instructions of Vizier Ptah-Hotep* 139; *Instruction of Amen-Em-Het* I, 4-5; *Instruction of Ani* 6.1; 7.7; *Instruction of Amen-Em-Opet* 9, 23.

36. Compare *Sentences of Pseudo-Phocylides* 3, 198; Sir 7:24-25; 9:1-9; 25:21-26; 26:11-12; Prov 2:16-21; 6:24-32; 7:10-17; 9:13-18; *To Demonicus* 15, 21; *Sentences of Sextus* 60, 67, 70, 71, 73, 75, 102,

ciplining of children,[37] a topic taken up by at least some NT writings (see Col 3:20-21; Eph 6:1-4). In short, the topics that have to do with the establishing of the civic and domestic social order are absent from this writing, and since in antiquity this social order invariably subordinated women, such studied silence is not insignificant for our topic, and is the final reason why Wolmarans' construal of James's sexual imagery is more than improbable: nothing in the letter otherwise supports such a reading, and everything argues against it.

We can take the elements absent from James together with his specific emphases and combine them in an attempt to locate James's distinctive kind of wisdom, together with its implications for the question of gender.

1. James is concerned with morals rather than manners. Virtually all wisdom literature devotes substantial attention to getting along in the social world as it is traditionally defined. James has nothing about such "knowing and keeping one's place." He says nothing about obedience to rulers, gratitude to benefactors, reverence toward the elderly, reciprocal generosity to friends. He has no interest in table manners, courtesy, or conformity. In wisdom literature both Jewish and Greek, honor and shame function as powerful motivations for behavior in conformity with the established order.[38] Note that apart from one paradoxical usage (2:5), James utterly lacks such honor and shame language. He is concerned not with conformity to the customs of the world but with moral choices that conflict with many of those customs. His wisdom is subversive rather than supportive of the social structures and symbols of society.

The implications for gender are real. James is not concerned with the adornment and clothing of women; indeed, the only character dressed opulently and adorned with jewelry is a man (2:2). Women are simply not, for James, a "special problem" needing control by males. They may be in need, just like men (2:15). They may also be moral agents, just like men

---

139, 240, 346, 449; *Testament of Reuben* 4:1-6:5; *Sentences of Syriac Menander* 170-172, 240-249; *Instruction of Ani* 3.13.

37. See *Words of Ahiqar* 6.79; 7.106; 9.138; *To Demonicus* 14, 16; *Sentences of Pseudo-Phocylides* 207-217; Prov 13:1-2; 30:11-14; Sir 3:1-16; 7:28; 16:1-5; 30:1-6; *Sentences of Sextus* 254, 256-257; *Sentences of Syriac Menander* 5-6, 9-10, 20-24, 94-98, 194-212; *Instruction of Vizier Ptah-Hotep* 565-595; *Instruction of Meri-Ka-Re* 55-60; *Instruction of Ani* 7.17.

38. See B. J. Malina and J. H. Neyrey, "Honor and Shame in Luke-Acts: Pivotal Values in the Mediterranean World," in *The Social World of Luke-Acts* (Peabody, MA: Hendrickson, 1991), 25-66, and especially D. DeSilva, *The Hope of Glory: Honor Discourse and New Testament Interpretation* (Collegeville: Liturgical Press, 1999).

(2:25). By focusing on moral action challenging to "the world" James cuts the ground from under all the ways of thinking about women in terms of decency and conformity.

2. James addresses an intentional community rather than a household. This point follows naturally from the last: the reason why James lacks all attention to household duties and the conventional roles assigned within the *oikonomia* of antiquity is that he is concerned exclusively with the *ekklēsia*, a congregation of moral agents drawn together by shared values, summarized in the shorthand of "the faith of Jesus Christ" (2:1). The community has both male and female members, but James lacks any of the tension that we find in Paul between the (egalitarian) standards established by baptism *en christō* and the social expectations of the *oikos*. If women are therefore to be defined in terms of their moral agency rather than in terms of their biological or social roles, then generativity is a matter of moral choice for both males and females. Men can be self-seduced and be adulteresses, just as a woman who is a *pornē* can show faith through hospitality, just as *theos* can by his will give birth by a truthful word to truth-dealing humans.

3. James is egalitarian rather than authoritarian. The kinship language in this composition, as I have noted, is entirely egalitarian. The readers are "brothers and sisters" not only to each other but to the author as well. He does not assume any paternal authority nor does he recognize such authority in others. The teachers and elders within the community, as we have seen, may be male, but they are defined in terms of service. James does not single out any class of people within the community. All alike are called to covenantal loyalty, to "friendship with God" (4:4; 2:23). Each is responsible for the correction of others when they stray from the way of truth (5:20). The egalitarian outlook of James is shown also in his emphatic rejection of *prosōpolēmpsia*, or partiality in judging (2:1, 9), as well as all kinds of boasting (3:14-15; 4:16) and all forms of arrogance (4:6, 10). This composition is hostile toward the rich who use their wealth to oppress others (1:11; 2:6-7; 5:1-6). It condemns the slanderous speech and slighting judgments that assume the moral superiority of one member over another (4:11-12). It need scarcely be argued that social arrangements that place some in authority over others, whatever the overt basis, tend to favor the large, the strong, the mobile, the aggressive, the loud, the male. Women are more often than not among the oppressed, not only economically but also in terms of moral valuation. An outlook that refuses to establish a fixed structure of authority or a system of mediation in which some funnel authority and benefits to others, but which assigns equal

moral worth and responsibility to all, is profoundly liberating for both men and women.[39]

4. James is communitarian rather than individualistic. This composition does not teach an ethics of individual perfection that redounds to the honor of its practitioner. James calls on individuals only insofar as their single-mindedness is required to build and support the ethos of the community. James vigorously opposes any sort of individualism that seeks gain at the expense of another. He condemns that "friendship with the world" that is built on envy and leads to every sort of rivalry, competitiveness, social unrest, war, and murder. He seeks instead a community of solidarity, based not on the logic of envy but on the logic of gift-giving and mercy (1:5, 17; 2:13; 4:6). In 5:12-20 in particular, James sketches a community whose speech and action express such collaboration and solidarity, nowhere more powerfully than in the gathering of the church in response to the summons of its weakest members, to touch healingly, to pray, and mutually to confess sins. The pertinence of such a vision for the issue of gender is patent. By his rejection of the way of the world and his construction of an alternative community ethos, James points to the possibility of thinking and acting about gender in ways that are not based on power but on presence, that are not a matter of competition but of cooperation, that live life not as a battle between haves and have-nots in which the one who dies with the most toys wins, but as a festival of gift-giving, in which humans show themselves to be the "first-fruits of creation" by imitating the God who birthed them.

---

39. My points here are in fundamental agreement with those expressed succinctly by L. W. Countryman, *Dirt, Greed, and Sex: Sexual Ethics in the New Testament and Their Implications for Today* (Philadelphia: Fortress Press, 1988), 222-224.

EPILOGUE

The Importance of James for Theology

The historical-critical paradigm that has until recent decades dominated biblical studies provides many benefits. Few would argue, though, that the historical-critical paradigm has had a positive effect on a theological engagement with Scripture. The evidence — not least that connected to the travails of the subdiscipline called "biblical theology" — points too decisively the other way.[1] The overall effect of historical analysis has been to keep all the texts of the New Testament fixed in the past, so that the question of what they might signify must always pass first through the baffle of what they first meant.[2] And conclusions concerning the historical authorship or situation of the New Testament writings have had the additional effect of assigning theological worth.[3] The historical-critical method has often had more to do with theology than with genuine history, and the theology with which it had to do was specifically marked by Protestant presuppositions.[4]

---

1. For a succinct depiction of the rise and main forms of New Testament theology following the inaugural declaration by Johann Philipp Gabler in 1787, see H. Boers, *What Is New Testament Theology? The Rise of Criticism and the Problem of a Theology of the New Testament* (Philadelphia: Fortress Press, 1979).

2. See the influential article by K. Stendahl, "Contemporary Biblical Theology," in *The Interpreter's Dictionary of the Bible* (Nashville: Abingdon Press, 1962), 1:418-432.

3. Perhaps the most impressive example is the treatment of Paul's letters to Timothy and Titus: a decision for inauthenticity usually means a decision for theological irrelevance; see the discussion in L. T. Johnson, *The First and Second Letters to Timothy* (Anchor Bible 35A; New York: Doubleday, 2001), 42-90.

4. See J. Z. Smith, *Drudgery Divine: On the Comparison of Early Christianities and the Religions of Late Antiquity* (Jordan Lectures in Comparative Religion 14; Chicago: University of Chicago Press, 1990), 1-35; L. T. Johnson, *Religious Experience in Earliest Christianity: A Missing Dimension in New Testament Studies* (Minneapolis: Fortress Press, 1998); L. T. Johnson and W. S. Kurz, *The Future of Catholic Biblical Scholarship* (Grand Rapids: Eerdmans, 2002), 3-34.

Given the negative characterization of the Letter of James by Luther,[5] and given the fact that the Protestant presuppositions driving the historical-critical paradigm have been largely Lutheran, it is not surprising that James in particular finds itself on the margins. If James is late and pseudonymous, it is not part of that magic age of origins (read: Paul) which provides the measure for all authentic Christianity.[6] And if it is read primarily through 2:14-26, which is understood as a corrective to a "misunderstanding of Paul," then it has little importance as a theological resource beside Paul and John and 1 Peter, which, as Luther memorably put it, "show thee the Christ."[7] And if "theology," further, is defined in (mostly Protestant) terms as "Christology," then James appears quite rightly to be neglected. In Dibelius's famous characterization, "James has no theology."[8]

James in Classic New Testament Theology

To demonstrate the point, I will discuss the treatment of James in three classic expressions of the subdiscipline we call the theology of the New Testament. The first is the earliest, found in the second volume of Adolf Schlatter's *Theology of the New Testament*.[9] Schlatter's first volume was, in effect, a study of the theology of Jesus as found primarily in the Gospels of Matthew and John. Schlatter emphasizes the way in which Jesus' identity was expressed by his commitment to God's will.[10] His second

5. See Martin Luther's "Preface to the New Testament" of 1522 as well as his introductions to James and Jude in that same edition, found in *Luther's Works*, vol. 35: *Word and Sacrament I*, ed. E. T. Bachmann (Philadelphia: Fortress Press, 1960), 362, 395-397.

6. For representative statements on the historical-critic as the one who recovers the essence of Christianity, see, e.g., F. C. Baur, *Paul, the Apostle of Jesus Christ: His Life and Work, His Epistles and His Doctrine: A Contribution to the Critical History of Primitive Christianity*, 2nd ed., ed. E. Zeller, trans. A. Menzies, 2 vols. (London: Williams and Norgate, 1875), 1:2; P. Wernle, *The Beginnings of Christianity*, 2 vols., trans. G. A. Bienemann (London: Williams and Norgate, 1903), 1:ix-x; and for a great example of the enterprise, see A. Harnack, *What Is Christianity?* trans. T. B. Sanders (London: Isbister and Company, 1903).

7. Luther, "Preface to the New Testament" (1522) in *Luther's Works*, 35:396.

8. M. Dibelius, *James: A Commentary on the Epistle of James*, rev. H. Greeven, trans. M. A. Williams (Philadelphia: Fortress, 1976), 11.

9. A. Schlatter, *Theology of the New Testament*, vol. 1: *The History of the Christ: The Foundation for New Testament Theology*, trans. A. J. Köstenberger (1923; Grand Rapids: Baker Books, 1997), and *Theology of the New Testament*, vol. 2: *The Theology of the Apostles: The Development of New Testament Theology*, trans. A. J. Köstenberger (1922; Grand Rapids: Baker Books, 1999); page references to the second volume are given parenthetically in the text.

10. See Schlatter, *History of the Christ*, pp. 53-61, 265, 363-372.

volume begins with a short sketch of the beliefs and practices of the early church before turning to "The Convictions Held by Jesus' Followers." Schlatter emphasizes the way in which Peter, Matthew, James, Jude, and John all show unity of teaching among themselves and continuity with the teaching (and practice) of Jesus; then he turns to a lengthy consideration of Paul ("The Calling of the Nations through Paul") (pp. 187-322). After Paul, Schlatter takes up the writings of Mark and Luke, Hebrews and Second Peter ("The Share of the Apostolic Associates in Doctrinal Formation," pp. 323-360), and he concludes with a synthetic statement concerning the doctrine and practice of the early church (pp. 361-416).

Schlatter's treatment of James appears at first to be full and eminently fair. In "Traditions Received from Jesus," he discusses James's statements concerning God, especially God's unfailing goodness and human faith directed toward God (pp. 82-83), then statements concerning Christ (pp. 83-85) and the community's obligation (pp. 85-86). Next, Schlatter considers James's "New Material": his depiction of sin (pp. 86-87), instructions regarding faith (pp. 88-89), indictment of the rich (pp. 89-90), and the goal of the community's life (pp. 90-91). After this catalogue of themes, Schlatter considers "James' Relationship with the Jews," which involves both points of fellowship (pp. 91-93) and points of difference (pp. 93-95). Finally, Schlatter discusses "James' Place in the Apostolic Circle" by locating James with reference to Peter, Matthew, John, and Paul (pp. 95-103).

A closer analysis, however, reveals some of the limitations of Schlatter's treatment of James. First, he pays no attention at all to the prominent theme of speech in James (see Jas 1:26-27; 3:1-9; 5:9, 12). Second, Schlatter is aware of no hermeneutical difficulty presented by the letter; he thinks that he presents the New Testament teaching just as it presents itself. In Philipp Gabler's terms, Schlatter seeks a "true biblical theology."[11] He is blissfully unaware of any distinction between history and theology. Third, his presentation of James is therefore a flat recital of contents: there is no real exegetical engagement.[12] Schlatter does not expose

---

11. See H. Boers, *What Is New Testament Theology?* pp. 67-74.

12. Not even the notoriously knotty 4:5-6 is daunting. He makes it one of the texts demonstrating that "James arrives at the concept of the Spirit," clearly implying the Holy Spirit. Then Schlatter remarks in a note, "the difficult statement of 4:5 apparently refers to the spirit that has indwelt man since creation" (p. 84 n. 41). But since this is the only use of *pneuma* in the letter apart from the analogy in 2:26, it can scarcely govern those passages Schlatter lists as evidence for the Spirit (1:5; 3:15, 17) that do not use the term.

questions but only lists answers. Nowhere is the voice of James heard, only a list of his positions. Fourth, since his entire presentation is in service of showing continuity and communality among the first-generation teachers, Schlatter folds what is distinctive in James's teaching within the frame of Jesus (on one side) and other early writers (on the other). Fifth, it is clear that Schlatter's ultimate interests are historical rather than in the proper sense theological. His early dating of the letter and his concern to show the continuities among James and other early teachers serve to establish James's theological value by means of historical placement.

Rudolf Bultmann had great respect for Schlatter, but his own *New Testament Theology* could hardly be more different.[13] Rather than a "true biblical theology," Bultmann represents what Philipp Gabler called a "pure biblical theology": he sought less to report on the contents of the canonical writings than to enucleate and elucidate those elements within the canon that are of permanent pertinence.[14] Bultmann's approach to the New Testament was decisively shaped by the History of Religions School, by his Lutheran theological convictions, including the embrace of *sachkritik,* and by his Heideggerian hermeneutics.[15] In contrast to Schlatter, Bultmann does not consider Jesus as the beginning of New Testament theology but rather as its presupposition (in the section titled "The Message of Jesus," 1:3-32); despite this, no less than Schlatter does Bultmann find deep resonances between the proclamation of the word by Jesus and the kerygma that is the basis for New Testament theology.[16] Bultmann follows the historical progression of earliest Christianity traced by his History of Religions predecessors Heitmüller and Bousset: he considers first the Palestinian church ("The Earliest Church as the Eschatological Congregation," 1:33-62), then "The Kerygma of the Hellenistic Church aside from Paul" (1:63-184), in each discussion providing a historical description of the life and convictions that can be drawn from the extant sources.

Bultmann devotes most of his attention to the two New Testament

---

13. Rudolf Bultmann, *Theology of the New Testament,* 2 vols., trans. K. Grobel (New York: Scribner, 1951-55); subsequent citations will be given parenthetically in the text.

14. Boers, *What Is New Testament Theology?* pp. 75-80.

15. See the perceptive review by N. A. Dahl, "Rudolf Bultmann's *Theology of the New Testament,*" in *The Crucified Messiah and Other Essays* (Minneapolis: Augsburg, 1974), 90-128.

16. Bultmann says that Jesus' preaching "only directs man into the Now of his meeting with his neighbor . . . fulfillment of God's will is the condition for participation in the salvation of his Reign . . . these imperatives are clearly meant radically as absolute demand with a validity independent of the temporal situation" (1:19-20).

writers whom he considers to have been theologians in the proper sense of the word. Paul (1:187-352) and John (2:3-92) not only bear witness to the *kerygma;* they also provide interpretations of the human condition before God that reveal the basic drama of authentic or inauthentic existence. Just as Luther recommended Paul and John as the writers who "show thee the Christ," so does Bultmann focus on them as the theological voices that also show the true dimensions of the choice faced by all humans. Next to these giants, the other writings of the New Testament are relatively insignificant. Just as Bultmann mined them indiscriminately to depict the historical progression before Paul and John, so at the end he discusses all the other writings as a historical progression, "the Development Toward the Ancient Church" (2:95-236). Paul and John, then, loom above the historical flow with timeless grandeur. Before them, only history; after them, only history. Theology is what transcends history by addressing human existence before God. And consistent with his Lutheran presuppositions, the progression toward the early church is a story of development that is in reality a story of decline.[17]

Given Bultmann's presuppositions and the shape of his project, we would scarcely expect him to show much appreciation for the theology of James. In fact, it is difficult to find James at all. Bultmann refers to James of Jerusalem three times, twice concerning his leadership of the church in Jerusalem (1:52, 59), and once concerning his theological impact on Jewish Christianity: it was the influence of James the Brother of the Lord that was partly responsible for a "retrogression" from the sayings of Jesus, so that "the old scruples and fidelity to the law had gradually gained ground" (1:54). What about the Letter of James? Bultmann follows the lead of his predecessors in considering James pseudonymous, and therefore a source of information about Hellenistic Christianity apart from Paul together with "other sources of a later date" (1:64). As it turns out, though, Bultmann only notes that James agrees with Acts and Hebrews in its expectation of an imminent world judgment (1:74), and that James stands with Acts, Jude, 2 Peter, the Didache, 2 Clement, and Hermas among early Christian writings in not speaking of the sacrificial death of Christ (1:84). When he deals with the "development toward the ancient church," Bultmann mentions James twice. Speaking of the development of right teaching, he asks rhetorically, "And can the treatment of the

---

17. For a similar reading of early Christian history as decline, see H. von Campenhausen, *Ecclesiastical Authority and Church Order in the Church of the First Three Centuries,* trans. J. Baker (Stanford, CA: Stanford University Press, 1969), esp. 107-120.

theme of 'faith and works' in Jas. 2:14-26 be understood in any other way than that it is a debate against misunderstood ideas of Paul?" (2:131). In his (obligatory) summary of the contents of James, which consists of three short paragraphs, Bultmann touches only on the expectation of judgment, the keeping of the law (with no effort to discern what James means by law), and, once more, the way 2:14-26 is distinct from Paul (2:162-163). Bultmann says with respect to James on the law, "the Pauline idea of freedom is just as remote from the author's mind as is Paul's concept of Faith" (2:162). And he concludes his exposition with another evaluative comment: "Every shred of understanding for the Christian's situation as that of 'between-ness' is lacking here. The moralism of the synagogue has made its entry, and it is possible that James not merely stands in the general context of this tradition but that its author took over a Jewish document and only lightly retouched it" (2:163). Bultmann reads James entirely with reference to Paul and entirely to the disadvantage of James.

The *New Testament Theology* of G. B. Caird (completed and edited by L. D. Hurst) has as its first sentence, "New Testament theology is a historical discipline."[18] Caird-Hurst eschews the ambitious historical and hermeneutical engagement of Bultmann and seeks only to describe the contents of the canonical sources on a number of topics that can be called theological in nature. The book employs the conceit of a "round-table" (modeled on the "apostolic council" in Acts 15) at which every composition can have its say, without any obvious privilege accorded to any single author.[19] In fact, however, the soteriological framework used to organize the agenda for the discussion is clearly derived from Luke-Acts, so it can fairly be said that the privileged place Bultmann assigns to Paul and John is accorded to Luke-Acts by Caird-Hurst. For Caird-Hurst, furthermore, the "theology of Jesus" is part of New Testament theology: "the theology of the New Testament began with the ways in which Jesus thought and spoke about himself and his people" (p. 419). But unlike Schlatter, whose focus on Jesus was his perfect obedience to God's will, Caird-Hurst focuses on the political character of Jesus' ministry: *"for him, politics and theology were inseparable"* (p. 357, emphasis original).[20]

18. G. B. Caird, *New Testament Theology,* completed and edited by L. D. Hurst (Oxford: Clarendon Press, 1994), 1. Subsequent citations will be given parenthetically in the text.

19. Caird and Hurst, pp. 18-26.

20. The continuation of this basic approach can be seen (from quite different approaches) in the works of two of Caird's students, Marcus Borg, *Jesus, a New Vision: Spirit, Culture, and the Life of Discipleship* (San Francisco: Harper and Row, 1987), and N. T. Wright, *Jesus and the Victory of God* (Minneapolis: Fortress Press, 1996).

The round-table format would, it seem, provide the chance for James to speak in its own voice. But the soteriological agenda tends to suppress the letter's distinctive theological voice just as effectively as Bultmann's anthropological focus had. Superficially, James is mentioned more often in Caird-Hurst than in Bultmann. The index provides 33 references to 24 different verses. Closer analysis, however, shows that frequency of reference does not equal substantive attention. The only characterization of the letter provided by Caird-Hurst is less substantial than Bultmann's: "While the Epistle of James continues to be a source of much discussion, what remains clear is that it is addressed to the twelve tribes of the dispersion by an author who sees himself as standing in the unbroken Jewish tradition of James of Jerusalem and who looks back to Abraham, as 'our father' (2:21); yet it is marked out as a Christian document by two mentions of Jesus Christ and by the author's obvious familiarity with his teaching" (p. 54).

For the most part, James is cited along with other texts in clusters of evidence for some point or other: Christian teaching on the moral life (p. 125), baptism and rebirth (p. 182), judgment (p. 77 n. 1), enmity with God (p. 156), cleansing (p. 119). Remarkably, a number of these proof-texts seem to derive from a careless use of the concordance and distort James's actual meaning (see, e.g., pp. 53, 88, 119, 125, 156, 222). Only a few aspects of James's own voice manage to emerge. Under the topic, "abolition of discrimination," for example, Caird-Hurst notes (on p. 237) that "the Epistle of James furthermore castigates those who would show any form of discrimination within the worshiping church (2:1-7)." But this is stuck on at the end after a lengthy consideration of other authors, even though James is by far the most powerful and explicit witness on the subject.

The letter's strong position with regard to speech is ignored, and James's prohibition of oaths (5:12) is cited only as a corrective to the Matthean version of Jesus' logion (p. 389). The only sustained attention to James comes, once more, through comparison with Paul on the subject of "the sovereignty of grace." Caird-Hurst devotes a paragraph to the passages in James that pertain to the subject, culminating in 2:17-26. In contrast to Bultmann, Caird-Hurst considers that "on this point there is no disagreement between James and Paul, only a difference in emphasis" (p. 190). But this is to be expected, since the very structure of the book leads toward the harmonization rather than the differentiation of voices. And, despite its avoidance of any formal embrace of *sachkritik*, Caird-Hurst ends up by focusing on the same single aspect of the letter as did Bultmann.

These three theologies of the New Testament are representative. Even though they differ in perspective and method, they all keep the voice of James in the past and relatively submerged. James is read primarily with reference to other voices: Jesus, Paul, Matthew, and Peter. Or his letter is mined as a source for the history or practice or doctrine of early Christianity. New Testament theologies fail either to engage James's theological voice directly or to hear that voice as speaking to Christian existence in the present.

Engaging James in Theological Conversation

Throughout the history of interpretation, James has been most appreciated theologically when allowed to speak in its own voice, and when (as appropriate for a sapiential-prophetic composition) allowed to speak directly to the present.[21] A good contemporary example is Richard Bauckham's study of the letter of James,[22] which, after considering the composition in its historical, literary, and canonical contexts, turns to a consideration of "James in Modern and Contemporary Contexts."

For the modern context, Bauckham takes the great nineteenth-century thinker Kierkegaard as exemplary for a passionate engagement with James unmediated by scholarship, an engagement in which James itself becomes the "mirror of remembrance" (Jas 1:22-25) for the reader's self-examination.[23] Bauckham appreciates that Kierkegaard is not an exegete in the sense defined by historical critics; he does not try to determine

---

21. For examples in the last two centuries, see J. P. Lange and J. J. Osterzee, *The Epistle of James*, 2nd ed., trans. J. I. Momsert (New York: Charles Scribner's, 1867); R. W. Dale, *The Epistle of James and Other Discourses* (London: Hodder and Stoughton, 1859); C. F. Deems, *The Gospel of Common Sense as Contained in the Canonical Epistle of James* (New York: Ketcham, 1888); R. Johnstone, *Lectures Exegetical and Practical on the Epistle of James*, 2nd ed. (Edinburgh: Oliphant, Anderson and Ferrier, 1889); S. Zodhiates, *The Epistle of James and the Life of Faith*, vol. 1: *The Work of Faith: An Exposition of James 1:1–2:13*; vol. 2: *The Labor of Love: An Exposition of James 2:14–4:12*; vol. 3: *The Patience of Hope: An Exposition of James 4:13–5:20* (Grand Rapids: Eerdmans, 1959-60); A. T. Robertson, *Practical and Social Aspects of Christianity: The Wisdom of James* (New York: Doran, 1915); W. Stringfellow, *Count It All Joy: Reflections on Faith, Doubt and Temptation through the Letter of James* (Grand Rapids: Eerdmans, 1967).

22. R. Bauckham, *James* (New Testament Readings; London: Routledge, 1999).

23. Bauckham uses Kierkegaard in his prologue to set the frame for his book (pp. 1-10), and devotes pp. 158-174 to a fuller analysis of Kierkegaard's appropriation. Bauckham acknowledges the work done on Kierkegaard as reader of James by T. H. Polk, *The Biblical Kierkegaard: Reading by the Rule of Faith* (Macon, GA: Mercer University Press, 1997).

what the text meant to its first readers. Instead he reads James as Scripture, as a word directed to his own life; he was especially fond of the first chapter of James, and above all James 1:17-21, to which he returned time after time in his edifying discourses. Kierkegaard does not so much try to figure out what James meant as to consider what his own life means in light of James:

> It makes no sense to ask where his reading of James ends and his own creative thinking begins. But this is the way biblical texts have always had their creative effects both in the thought of the great Christian theologians, and also in the lives of the exemplary followers of Christ, known and unknown, who have lived creatively the texts they loved.[24]

Bauckham identifies four aspects of James that Kierkegaard makes thematic in his own work. The first, remarkably for a Danish Lutheran, was "faith and works" (pp. 162-165): Kierkegaard suggested that Luther himself would have used James to criticize the Lutherans of the nineteenth century who had turned "faith alone" into an excuse for a comfortable bourgeois life-style. The moralist in James appealed to the social and religious critic in Kierkegaard, and James's insistence on profession leading to practice is the constant theme of the theologian's masterpiece, *Works of Love*. The second dimension of James found obvious expression in the title of Kierkegaard's *Purity of Heart Is to Will One Thing*, which drew on James 4:8 as its text. For Kierkegaard as for James, "double-mindedness" was incompatible with authentic faith, and he called for a manner of life that was simple, transparent, and single-minded in its devotion to God. The third element of James that Kierkegaard, like the theological tradition before him celebrated, was God as the unchangeable giver of good (pp. 169-170).[25] Kierkegaard devoted four discourses to James 1:17, finding in its declaration that God is the giver of every good and perfect gift an inspiration for a grace-drenched view of reality, leading to attitudes of thanksgiving and hope. The fourth theme of James that Kierkegaard appropriated in his own thinking was that of equality in neighborly love (pp. 170-172): he draws from James's linking of the royal law of Love (2:8) to the forbidding of partiality in judgment (2:1-4, 9), and also from James's theme of the reversal of fortunes by God (1:9-11; 2:5).

---

24. Bauckham, *James*, p. 161. Subsequent citations will be given parenthetically in the text.

25. See L. T. Johnson, *The Letter of James* (Anchor Bible 37A; Garden City: Doubleday, 1995), pp. 138-139, 204.

Bauckham also notes two limitations in Kierkegaard's theological appropriation of James (pp. 173-174). The first is the complete neglect of the letter's eschatological dimension. Kierkegaard's thought plays within the gap between the eternal and the finite, rather than the already and not-yet. The second limitation is Kierkegaard's concentration on the individual rather than the community. Bauckham recognizes that James's exhortations frequently have the individual's behavior in view, but he also recognizes, quite rightly, that James's ethic is solidly communitarian; he is nowhere more like Paul than in his concern for shaping a community of character more than the perfection of individuals. Although he could not transcend his own very modern context in these respects, Kierkegaard nevertheless provides a stunning example of how James, when taken straight, can stimulate and shape theological reflection.

Bauckham calls his own effort at engaging James theologically "Reading James at the Turn of the Millennium" (pp. 174-208). He begins by proposing two complementary models for reading. In the first, the text creates a world into which readers can be drawn, with all they know of their own contemporary life, and so, "drawn into the text," can measure their own lives by what they find there. In the second, the text functions as a script, which readers seek to "perform" or enact in their lives: "We cannot sufficiently know what the biblical writings mean until they are appropriated and lived in the way they expect to be" (p. 176). James's text then is not simply "gazed into," as a mirror, but is put into practice by the patterns of Christian life.

Bauckham correspondingly develops four theological aspects of James that provide a script, which can be enacted by Christians. The first is wholeness and integrity (pp. 177-185). Bauckham shows how James calls for an integration of character, for the exclusion of what does not fit that character, for completion of character in performance, and for consistency, and shows also how all these moral demands are connected to James's language about the divine perfection (pp. 177-185). Next, Bauckham focuses on the theme of solidarity with the poor, associating himself with the goal of liberation theology to identify with the poor and oppressed of the world, in accordance with God's own choice of the poor, and developing a number of issues of contemporary relevance concerning such solidarity with the poor (pp. 185-203). More briefly, Bauckham takes up the issue of speech ethics, a theme that he rightly recognizes as central to the letter itself yet oddly neglected by theologians (pp. 203-205). More succinctly still, Bauckham concludes with remarks on prayer in James, noting that the letter is concerned to show both that God responds to prayer as the giver of all good gifts, and the way in which prayer is an articulation of faith, rather than "double-minded" (1:8) or even "wicked" (4:3).

It is very much to Bauckham's credit that in each of these discussions he does not remain content with listing the passages in which James elaborates one theme or another, nor with observing that the ideal presented ought to be practiced. Instead, he seeks to discover what it might mean to perform the script provided by James in the context of contemporary life: what does genuine character mean in today's world, who are the poor among us, why does morality in speech matter, and how can Christian prayer be distorted? By seeking what the text of James might mean in the practice of the Christian life, Bauckham in turn suggests dimensions of meaning inherent in the text itself. His is a genuinely theological engagement.

Enlarging the Conversation

Of the eight aspects of James singled out by Kierkegaard and Bauckham, only one (God as the unchangeable giver of gifts) clearly has God as subject; the rest pertain to the moral life of Christians. If we are to have a full appreciation of the theological voice of James, we must start by appreciating the richness of James's specifically theological language. Because scholars have sought "theology" in complex discussions of soteriological issues, and because Protestant scholars in particular have tended to identify theology and Christology, and because James speaks of Jesus explicitly only twice (1:1; 2:1) and of salvation without reference to Jesus (1:21; 2:14; 4:12; 5:15, 20), they can easily conclude that "James has no theology."

In fact, however, the Letter of James is one of the most properly theological compositions in the New Testament. Its explicit attention is given to *ho theos* ("God") rather than Jesus or the Holy Spirit. The term occurs fifteen times (1:1, 5, 13, 20, 27; 2:5, 19, 23 [2]; 3:9; 4:4 [2], 6, 7, 8). In apposition to *ho theos,* James speaks of *patēr* ("father") in 1:17, 27; 3:9. And at least some of the time, his use of *kyrios* ("Lord") certainly has *ho theos* as the implied referent (see 1:7; 3:9; 4:10, 15; 5:4, 11). In his 108 verses, James has some 24 explicit references to God.

What James says about *ho theos* reveals a perhaps surprisingly complex set of affirmations. Together with other Jews, James agrees that God is one (2:19), but his understanding of God goes far beyond an assertion of simple monotheism. His is the Living God, who makes "the demons tremble" (2:19) and is "the Lord of Hosts" (5:4). James describes God in negative terms as the one with whom there is no change or shadow of alteration (1:17), who does not tempt and is not tempted by evil (1:13), whose righteousness is not associated with human anger (1:20). James's positive assertions, however, move in the direction of God's powerful presence to creation and humanity. God is not only "light" but the "father of lights" (1:17), who expresses his will and by a "word of truth" has, paradoxically, "given birth" to humans as a kind of first-fruits of creatures (1:18), and has created them in his own image (3:9).

Most striking is God's continuing involvement with the world and specifically with humans. God has revealed his will in "the perfect law of liberty" (2:8-11) and will judge humans on the basis of that revelation (2:12; 4:12). James states emphatically, "There is one lawgiver *(nomothetēs)* and judge *(kritēs)* who is able to save *(sōsai)* and destroy *(apolesai,* 4:12). But humans are not left with only a verbal norm as their guide. The word of truth is also an "implanted word" that is able to save souls (1:21), and God has "made to dwell a spirit" within humans (4:5). God remains in charge of human affairs (4:15) and can declare as righteous and his friends those who have faith in him (2:23). The true human story, indeed, is told by those whom Scripture shows to have been such friends of God through their faith: Abraham (2:23), Rahab (2:25), Job (5:11), Elijah (5:17).

James defines God in terms of mercy and compassion (5:11). Thus, God promises the crown that is life to those who love him (1:12; 2:5); has chosen the poor in the world to be rich in faith and heirs of the kingdom (2:5); regards true religion as including the care of widows and orphans (1:27), even as God himself hears the cries of the oppressed (5:4), raises up the sick (5:15), hears the prayers of those who pray in faith (1:5-6) rather than wickedly (4:3), and forgives the sins of those who confess them (5:15). This is a God who approaches those who approach him (4:8), raises up the lowly (4:10), and enters into friendship with humans (2:23; 4:4). But this is a God who also resists those who arrogantly exalt themselves over others through oppression (4:6; 5:6).

Most distinctive in James's understanding of God (as patristic interpreters and Kierkegaard perceived) is that God is the giver of gifts. James makes the point three times. In 4:6, James takes from the text of Proverbs 3:34 ("God resists the proud but gives grace to the lowly") the lesson that "God gives more grace" *(meizona de didōsin charin)*. That this is neither a random nor a careless observation is shown by James's very first statement concerning God in 1:5, that God "gives to all simply *(haplōs)* and without grudging *(mē oneidizontos)*." Finally, there is the programmatic statement in 1:17, "every good and perfect gift comes down from above from the father of lights with whom there is no change nor shadow of alteration." Taken together, these three statements assert that God's giving is universal, abundant, without envy, and constant. Such a view of God is the basis for James's perception of reality as God's creation, open to his constant care but also answerable to God as the source of all that is good. This view of God is, in turn, the deep premise for James opposing an ethics of solidarity to the logic of envy, for in the first the world is construed as an open system in which cooperation makes sense, while in the second the world is considered a closed system in which competition is demanded.

Because God does not exist in isolation from the world but is in constant and active relationship with the world, human existence is defined in terms of a story in which both God and humans play roles. The story has as its past what God has already done: created the world and humans as representatives ("first-fruits") of that creation; revealed his will in the law and the prophets and "the faith of Jesus Christ"; implanted in humans the "word of truth" and "wisdom from above" and "spirit." The story has as its future what God will do in response to human behavior within God's creation: God will judge the world; will reward the innocent and faithful and persevering, who have spoken and acted according to "the royal law of liberty." And God will punish the arrogant and oppressive who blaspheme the noble name by their aggressive and hostile attitudes and actions against God's people. The present of the story-line is found in the moral decisions made by James's readers, above all their choice to live as friends of the world or as friends of God (4:4).

It is of first importance, then, to understand that James does not "do theology" in an abstract manner, as a form of speculation about or study of God. Rather, James uses his theological propositions precisely as warrants and premises for his moral exhortation. His statements about God and his commands do not sit side by side in accidental juxtaposition. The two kinds of statements are intimately related. In James's 108 verses, there are some 59 imperatives (46 in the second person, 13 in the third person). And these imperatives are almost always accompanied by explanations or warrants, for which James uses participial constructions (1:3, 14, 22; 2:9, 25; 3:1), *gar* clauses (1:6, 7, 11, 13, 20, 24; 2:11, 13, 26; 3:2, 16; 4:14), and *hoti* clauses (1:12, 23; 2:10; 3:1; 4:3; 5:8, 11). The commandments are also sometimes connected to purpose clauses (1:4; 5:9) or used in the context of an implied argument signified by the use of *oun* (4:4, 7; 5:7, 16), *dio* (1:21; 4:6), or *houtōs* (1:11; 2:12, 17; 2:26; 3:5). In these connections, it is always the theological statement that stands as the cause or the purpose or the motivation or the warrant for the moral action recommended. James's moral exhortation, in short, is *grounded* in James's understanding of how humans are related to God. Because of this, each of the moral exhortations in James invites reflection by readers not only about their own lives — how to translate and perform James's script in the texture of their actual existence — but also about the nature of the world and of the God who creates, shapes, and saves the world in which humans are invited to participate as a sort of "first-fruits."

James and the Contemporary World

Two aspects of James's distinctive theological voice are of special importance to a world that is increasingly pluralistic (both culturally and religiously) and morally embattled.

The first is the way that James grounds moral behavior in God rather than in the distinctive Christian set of experiences and convictions rooted in Jesus Christ. It is precisely James's *theological* rather than *christological* focus that enables it to be a precious resource for ecumenical conversation, not alone between Christians and Jews, but also among all those belonging to monotheistic faiths, and perhaps even all those who interpret reality religiously. A glad embrace of James by Christians enables them to open a conversation that tends to be closed by more exclusive Christian discourse. Here, within one of the defining canonical compositions of the Christian tradition, we find an understanding of God that is, to be sure, consonant with the "faith of Jesus Christ," yet is also in every other respect connected to the belief structure of both Judaism and Islam, not least in the respect shown to Abraham as the father of obedient faith. The element in James that in an era of Christendom seemed an embarrassment — its lack of explicit Christology — now in a post-Constantinian era becomes a special (and unique) gift within the Christian canon. Without in the least abandoning their own insider understanding of the triune God revealed through Jesus and the Holy Spirit, Christians can, with the help of James, enter into serious theological and moral conversation with those who worship the same God in different terms and within different traditions. At the very least, James can help Christians reach agreement with those in other Abrahamic traditions that we all are to be judged by the same God on the basis of our deeds, and that we should therefore "so speak and so act as people who are going to be judged by the law of freedom" (2:12).

The second aspect of James's theological voice that is of particular importance for Christianity's engagement with the contemporary world is the way in which theology is interconnected with moral instruction. One of the pressing issues facing religious people is how to live together despite different or even competing religious convictions and claims. Ours is a world that, because of a diminished space in which to live together with increased awareness of difference on fundamental points, faces a crisis of survival. James provides at least two resources for those seeking better mutual understanding and a form of social ethics that can enable cooperation among those of differing faiths.

Alone among the New Testament writings, James emphatically asserts the truth that humans are created in the image of God (3:9) — all other instances of "image of God" language in the New Testament are connected to Christ — and that any religious response to the one God must correspond coherently with moral behavior toward fellow humans created in the image of God. James uses the example of speech ("the tongue"): "With it, we bless the Lord and Father. And with it, we curse the people who have been made according to God's likeness. Blessing and curse come out of the same mouth! My brothers, things like this should not happen!" (3:9-10). The principle clearly does not apply only to speech. It can be extended to virtually all realms of human behavior. An appeal to this principle enables Christians to engage those of other faiths not on a christological but on a theological basis for a wide range of issues touching on human dignity and rights.

Likewise, James draws its moral exhortation from both Jewish and Greco-Roman traditions and shapes them into a single, coherent if dualistic, vision. By so doing, James embraces a wider world of moral discourse. And, by his use of Greco-Roman moral *topoi*, James invites readers to reflect more deeply on the philosophical and theological bases of his exhortations. Examples of this are almost as many as the topics James addresses. But one stands out as particularly pertinent. When James opposes the "wisdom from above" and the "wisdom from below" in 3:13–4:10, he employs the Greco-Roman (and Hellenistic Jewish) moral *topos* on envy. The philosophical discussion of vice that leads to every sort of acquisitiveness and competition is of first importance for at least two issues of tremendous importance in today's world. One is the question whether humans, as the "first-fruits of creatures," are to be stewards of the world through patterns of ecological respect, cooperation, and nurture, or are to ruthlessly exploit and dominate not only other humans but the earth itself, in a never-ending quest for competitive edge. James's use of this philosophical topic enables people of all faiths to examine and reflect on the *logic* embedded in these respective responses, and therefore on the deep grounding of the ethics that springs from "the wisdom from above." The other pressing issue today is war and peace. Peace is an ideal everywhere in the New Testament, and for the Letter of James as well (3:18). But James is alone among the New Testament witnesses in entering into the causes of war in the human heart. His linking of war to the impulses that are "battling within our members" because of the spirit of envy is profound and perceptive, whether the "wars" are between family members, neighbors, or nations, and deserves a far more extensive development than theologians have ever attempted.

James and the Contemporary Church

In any number of ways, James also provides a resource for theological reflection concerning the church in the contemporary world, and particularly how the church might live according to "the faith of Jesus Christ" and "the law of love" (2:1, 8) in a manner that bears authentic witness to God. I will here touch on only three.

Integrity in Speech

Richard Bauckham correctly notes that James's astonishing attention to speech-ethics (see Jas 1:19-20, 26; 3:1-12; 4:11-12; 5:9, 12) is often subordinated to the other value by which he defined "pure religion," namely through the helping of the poor (1:27). But although Bauckham points to the need to develop this dimension of the letter, his own brief discussion remains broadly programmatic.[26] Taking his lead, I would like here to suggest some of the ways in which James's focus on speech might be incorporated into thinking about the church's stance toward the world and, equally important, about its own practice.

Immediately intriguing is the way James's discourse on speech in 3:1-12 makes a connection between creation and speech. James echoes Gen

---

26. Bauckham recommends the monograph by W. R. Baker, *Personal Speech-Ethics in the Epistle of James* (WUNT 2/68; Tübingen: Mohr [Siebeck], 1995), which does indeed offer a good amount of exegetical and comparative material but does not develop theological implications.

1:26 when he insists that humans are created in the likeness of God (3:9), and his mention of "beast and bird, of reptile and sea-creature" that can be tamed by humans alludes to Gen 1:27-28. It is with respect to such creatures in Gen 2:19 that humans exercise the first power of speech in naming the animals. The first and most distinctive mark of humans is the power to name, to create language, and by creating language to continue God's own creative activity in the world. But when that power is distorted and misused, the tongue becomes a "world of wickedness within our members . . . [it] sets aflame the cycle of life" (3:6).

Language is a world-creating capacity, an awesome power by which humans can either structure life according to the "word of truth," so that humans are "a kind of first-fruits of his creatures" (1:18), or make a structure of meaning in which God is omitted, ignored, or denied. The greatest peril of speech is not the passing angry word or casual oath or even the malicious slander — though these are, as James has it, a "death-dealing poison" (3:6) — but the shaping of distorted worlds of meaning within which the word of truth is suppressed.

If the church is to be a community that "receives with meekness the implanted word that is able to save," then it is called on one side to resist and challenge the distortions of speech (and therefore distortions of the world) in the world, while at the same time cultivating that simplicity and transparency of speech — letting its yes be yes and its no be no (5:12) — which reveals purity of heart.

The church has the responsibility to challenge, rather than be co-opted by, the distortions of language in our culture, which is a virtual babel of linguistic confusion and misdirection. The entire advertising industry is based on the use of language to deceive and seduce. It seeks consciously to create, by means of words and images, multiple illusions in pursuit of which other humans can spend their energies and their fortunes. Advertising operates with a cunning awareness of how desire, avarice, and envy can "seduce the heart" (Jas 1:26). The slippery half-truths of advertising, in turn, have become the staple of politics as well. Messages to the public are crafted precisely in order to "sell" a candidate. Slandering opponents in "negative ads" is measured not by morality but by effectiveness. Political agendas are advanced by appeals to the electorate's most primitive fears and most unworthy prejudices. Such distortions of speech are by now so pervasive that the "hermeneutics of suspicion" is a necessary element in deciphering virtually all communication. No generation in history has been so self-consciously aware of the capacity of speech to shape perceptions of reality and thereby to shape human reality itself.

And no generation in history has deployed the awesome resources of communications technology in service of distorted speech and perverse desire. No generation in history, indeed, has so systematically set itself to shaping a perception of the world that excludes God's claim on humans and eliminates all notion of transcendence.

The church's ability to challenge such patterns of speech is lost when the language of the church itself is corrupted. When the church defines itself in terms of power, influence, and numbers of adherents, it is using the same language and the same criteria of success as the world. A church whose language is indistinguishable from the world of advertising has nothing to say to a world held captive by advertising. The church therefore has an obligation to tend its own language. The language of faith is not something that can be taken for granted. It is fragile and constantly threatened, for it insists on the truth of what the entire world colludes in insisting is an illusion: God's claim on the world. The language of faith must therefore be nurtured and preserved, not through artificial regulation, or through an obsessive concern for doctrinal formulations (important enough, to be sure), but through a use of language that remains open to the mystery of God's power and presence in creation. A theological language that is correct but does not connect to the real experience of God in human lives is, as James says, as dead as a faith without deeds (2:26).

James 3:1 insists that it is above all the teachers in the community who bear the greatest responsibility. Teachers generally are vulnerable to failures in speech, not only because their profession demands of them that they speak more than others in public and before captive audiences, but because such a setting provides temptations for virtually every form of evil speech: arrogance and domination over students, anger and pettiness directed to inattention or contradiction, slander and meanness toward absent competitors, flattery of students for the sake of vanity. No wonder James warns against many taking up the role of teachers, for "we will receive a more severe judgment!"

Teachers within the church — those who have the special task of shaping its theological language — likewise bear the greatest responsibility for preserving and enlivening the language of faith and, with it, the capacity to hear God's word in the world. If preachers corrupt the language of faith in order to sell the gospel like merchandise for profit, then they receive a more severe judgment. And if they deaden the language of faith by removing it from the experience of God in the world, then they receive a more severe judgment. And if, no matter how they speak, they show in their manner of life the "bitter jealousy and selfish ambition in [their] heart," then they also "lie against the truth" (James 3:14).

James says, "If anyone considers himself religious without bridling his tongue and while indulging his heart,"[27] this person's religion is worthless. This is pure and undefiled religion before the God who is also Father: "to assist orphans and widows in their trouble, and to keep oneself unstained from the world" (Jas 1:26-27). By this measure, the church fails its basic mission as often by its neglect of its own and the world's speech as it does by its neglect of the world's and its own needy.

Envy and Arrogance

In separate essays, I have argued that James 3:13–4:10 is a coherent rhetorical unit that forms a call to conversion addressed to the "double-minded" among James's readers to a "purity of heart" and a singleness of devotion to God. In this call to conversion, James uses the Hellenistic topic of envy as a way of sketching the manner of life that is opposed to God and the source of human conflict. And at the heart of his call to conversion James places the small argument that gives the most precise expression to his theological voice, the choice between "friendship with the world and friendship with God" (4:4). I further argue that to appreciate fully James's language, we need to place it in the context of Greco-Roman thought concerning friendship. For James, being a "friend of the world" means sharing the world's perceptions and values and acting accordingly, just as being a "friend of God" means measuring by God's own measure and acting according to that measure. In short, "friendship with God" is for James precisely the sort of hermeneutical and moral criterion that "the mind of Christ" is for Paul (see 1 Cor 2:16).[28] It can be used to evaluate all of the activities of life.

In fact, James himself provides in 4:11–5:6 three examples of human behavior that fall within "friendship with the world" because they demonstrate the envy and arrogance that James made thematic in 3:13–4:6: slander of the neighbor (4:11-12), boasting in business (4:13-17), and oppression of the poor (5:1-6). The section is held together by the statement "God op-

27. For this translation, see the discussion in Johnson, *James,* pp. 210-211.

28. See my essays "James 3:13–4:10 and the *Topos* περὶ φθόνου," pp. 182-201, and "Friendship with the World and Friendship with God: A Study of Discipleship in James," pp. 202-220, both in this volume.

poses the arrogant" in 4:6 and the concluding rhetorical question in 5:6, "Does not [God] oppose you?"[29] For each example, James provides as well the measure by which those who are friends of God ought to measure (4:12; 4:15; 5:4). These three examples of envy and arrogance are not arbitrary. They reveal the consistency of James's theological voice and invite not only individual believers but also the church as such to reflect on the measure by which it lives.

Envy, said Aristotle, is a certain sorrow that one experiences because someone else is in possession of something one does not have (*Rhetoric* 1387B-1388A). Paradoxically, this most "needy" of vices lies also at the heart of arrogance. The logic of envy is based on the perception of the world as a closed system of limited resources for which humans are in competition. Envy and arrogance are two sides of the same competitive struggle. Envy spurs the "have-nots" to violence against those who have what they want. Arrogance spurs the "haves" to boast over those from whom they have taken in order to "be more" by "having more."

The great value of James's examples is that they show how subtle and pervasive are the manifestations of arrogance, how sneaky and secretive are the mechanisms of its violence. It is not only in murder for hire or in wars between nations that envy and arrogance operate. They more frequently appear as the normalized "way of the world," even within the church. James calls us to a more rigorous self-examination than is accomplished by an easy condemnation of arrogance's most obvious forms.

His first example — slander against the neighbor (4:11) — makes the point beautifully. Not much thought is required to agree that this "evil speech done in secret," which specifically seeks to tear down another so that I can appear superior (as critic, as judge), is driven by envy. Whatever I consider my rival to possess that I do not (status, reputation), I seek to take away, at least in the perceptions of those whom I try to influence by my slander. A bit more reflection helps us see the appropriateness of James's including this also as a form of arrogance, not only against my neighbor, but also against the law of God, which forbids such slander (see Lev. 19:16). "Who are you," asks James, "to judge your neighbor?" (4:12). Slander arrogates to oneself the divine powers of knowing the hearts of others and of condemning them.

To this arrogance, James opposes the understanding that should guide the practice of those who are "friends of God," namely, that God alone is lawgiver and judge, who is able to save and to destroy (4:12). And, I

29. For a full discussion, see Johnson, *James*, pp. 299-310.

suggest, James invites us to recognize that slander is one of the most common and destructive forms of arrogance within the church as well as outside it. The willingness to use the "death-dealing poison" of secret speech against the neighbor has become so normalized that it is difficult for many of us to any longer recognize it as evil: from the whispered comment behind the hand in the pew during a sermon, through the screaming headlines of tabloid publications, to the rich stew of gossip in television talk-shows, slander works to destroy those created in the image of God.

James's second example of arrogance ("you boast in your arrogance," 4:16) is provided by the ancient entrepreneurs who planned their trips and anticipated their profits in the vain assumption that the world is predictable and controllable and that they can define their being in terms of their having ("we will get gain," 4:13). James reminds his readers that they can make no such arrogant assumption. They are fragile creatures who depend on God for every breath (4:14-15). James speaks powerfully and directly to the contemporary world of conglomerates and multinational corporations, where the bottom-line of profit and loss is the only value worth considering, where everything is reduced to a commodity and everything has its price. This pan-commercial outlook perfectly expresses the logic of envy — to have more is to be more — and the logic of arrogance: those who have the most rule over those who have less. Here is the perfect expression of the measure of the world as opposed to the measure of God. On one side is the view of reality as a closed universe of limited goods for which all are in competition. On the other side is faith in the God who gives to all generously and without reproach (1:5), and who calls for sharing what we possess (2:14-16).

The church ought always to be the strongest and most convincing critic of this "way of the world." The church, both in its speech and in its practice, ought to represent "friendship with God" in its rejection of consumerism and commodification. But it is a serious question whether the church today — at least in those places where capitalism reigns supreme — can exercise the prophetic voice to which James summons it. Is not the church itself so compromised by its own embrace of commercial language and practice — if not always in strictly monetary terms, certainly in terms of its zeal for program over presence, for success over fruitfulness, for influence over truthful witness — that the language of James needs first to be turned toward the church itself for self-examination?

James's final example of arrogance is the most overt and shocking (5:1-6). Being heedless of anything but making a profit is bad enough, but committing actual violence against others in order to live luxuriously oneself is, in James's view, literally to commit a crime that "cries out to heaven" (5:4). We see here again the way James connects the diseases of the human heart and the distortions of the social order. And it is clear that James's prophetic outrage applies not only to ancient absentee landlords who abused the laborers in their fields, but equally if not more to contemporary economic and political practices. Envy and arrogance take systemic form in economic and political structures that privilege the few and punish the many, that exploit the resources of the earth for the extravagant life-style of those who happen to live in the first world rather than in the third, that reduce the laborers in the field (and in sweatshops and factories and fast-food eateries) to slaves by patterns of income and taxation perpetuating inequality, that commit legal murder against the innocent by means of litigation and the corruption of the court.

Liberation theology — especially in the third world — has used this passage in James to challenge the obviously oppressive systems of government and finance (often sponsored by first-world corporations and governments) that marginalize and abuse the vast majority of the world's population that is desperately poor. It has appropriately identified the ways in which the church itself has in such lands too often identified with oppressors rather than the oppressed. But churches in the first world have been much slower to challenge the systems of meaning that perpetuate such abuses from within corporate headquarters down the street from suburban congregations. Perhaps this is once more because the church has accommodated itself all too easily to the logic of envy and arrogance in its own life. James tells us that we cannot close our eyes to such realities and still claim to live by the "faith of Jesus Christ" or the "royal law of love." A church that proclaims the good news of Jesus but does not prophesy (not only in its words but in its manner of life) against the evils of oppression is exactly like the man who says to the naked and starving brother and sister, "go in peace," without giving them the things needed for the body (James 2:16).

A Community of Solidarity

In contrast to his attack on those forms of speech and action that are governed by the logic of envy and arrogance, James presents two powerful examples of the way in which the church can exemplify the logic of cooperation or solidarity. James uses the term "assembly" in both examples (2:2

and 5:14), and shows how the community as such should live by the standard of "the faith of Jesus Christ" (2:1) and the "royal law" of love of neighbor (2:8).

The first example is the more familiar: in contrast to the behavior of the rich, who withhold wages (5:1-6) and oppress the poor by dragging them into court (2:6), the community is to act by God's standard, which is revealed by the choice of the poor to be rich in faith and heirs of the kingdom (2:5). The community, therefore, is not to dishonor the poor, but to show the same honor that God has shown. It is not to deny the help needed by the poor, but to respond with concrete and practical help (2:14-16). And, like Abraham and Rahab, it is to show its faith by welcoming others in hospitality.[30] The church can resist the oppressors through its own practices of economic solidarity.

The second example is equally powerful but less well appreciated: James sketches the response of the *ekklēsia* to those who are sick. The sick person is to summon the elders. They are to pray over the sick person and anoint the sick person with oil in the name of the Lord. And the community, in turn, is to confess their sins to each other and pray for each other, so that they may be healed (5:13-16). Sickness is not the same as sin, nor does James suggest that sickness derives from sin. Yet, sin and sickness are analogous in their social effects. Sickness is a profound threat to the identity and stability of any community. The healing of the sick person, therefore, like the restoration of the community after sin, must take into account both the physical and spiritual dimensions of this threat.

The challenge to the community of faith posed by physical or emotional or mental illness is to test whether the community will act as a friend of God or as a friend of the world (4:4).

According to worldly wisdom, the logical response to any threat is self-defense. Only the fittest should survive, and competition identifies the fittest. Envy seeks strength at the expense of others, and has as its ultimate goal the elimination of others (James 4:1-2). Has someone known to us fallen ill? Then that person is weak and should be left behind. The resources devoted to the ill sap our strength and diminish us. The sick leech at the healthy and deprive them of their full power; attention given to the sick distracts us from cultivating our own potential and weakens us in our own struggle for supremacy. The elimination of the sick will leave more resources available to those who remain.

The logic of friendship with the world is therefore to isolate the sick

---

30. See the discussion of the "works of faith" in Johnson, *James*, pp. 248-249.

and the weak from the healthy and the powerful. The healthy organism recoils from what is diseased in order to protect itself. Sickness, then, becomes the occasion for social isolation and alienation. This "natural reflex" of survival, however, also becomes a form of sin when it leads to the deliberate exclusion of the sick from the community's care and support, when the physical distance imposed by sickness is exacerbated by a spiritual distancing of the sick from the life of the community.

In James, it is precisely the sick who are empowered to summon the leaders of the community. This is as remarkable a reversal of the logic of envy as is the way the community is to honor rather than scorn the poor (2:5). Not those who are well, but those who are sick are to define the truth of the situation.

And in the speech of those gathered in the presence of the sick person, James explicitly calls for the mutual recognition and acknowledgment of the weakness and failure of all, so that not only the person manifestly ill but all those in the community might be "saved/healed" *(sōzein)* by the confession of sins and the prayer of faith.

The scenario sketched by James of an intentional community structured on the principles of solidarity and mutual gift-giving, in which the powerful and the leaders are to honor and respond to the poor and weak, not only provides the most direct challenge to contemporary culture's practices with regard to the poor and the sick but also encourages the church of today to engage in self-examination concerning all those who are weak and alienated from a full participation in life.

It is patent that the larger society is increasingly organized by the logic of envy: competition as a form of social Darwinism runs through our culture. The sick and the poor — who are most often the same — represent a threat to survival that must be repelled by, at best, official neglect, and at worst, fraud, oppression, and murder.

The harder question is whether the church operates by a different and countercultural logic or not. According to James, it is the "manner of life" (3:14) that demonstrates whether we live according to the wisdom from above. How does the church work with and for the care of children, the poor, the ill, the elderly, the dying? Does the church, like the world, seek to secure its own survival by defending itself against the threat of weakness? Or does the church seek friendship with God by embracing the logic of gift-giving revealed by the God who gives to all generously and without reproach (1:5), so that the strength of each one is gathered from the shared strength of all?

From its first words to its last, the Letter of James witnesses to a way of life that is genuinely radical in its implications. It challenges individual Christians to an integrity in thought, speech, and action. But more than that, it challenges the church to realize in its communal life a vision of the world that is the opposite of that offered by the logic of envy, and to live as a community of true solidarity within a world defined by the gift-giving God.

Index of Authors

Index of Scripture References

Index of Ancient Sources

Index of Ancient Sources

287

faith w/o works dead
works w/o faith is dead p. 79.

40049262R00181

Made in the USA
Lexington, KY
22 March 2015